New Institutional Economics as Situational Logic

Drawing on phenomenological and realist approaches, this book surveys the theoretical evolution of new institutional economics.

For all its popularity and explanatory power, new institutional economics is not a homogenous field but encompasses a range of different theoretical approaches starting from Coase and the introduction of transaction costs. In particular, the concept of rationality is a rich source of dispute leading to a bifurcation between 'insider' and 'outsider' perspectives. The insider view refers to studying conscious human beings – the economic actor – who seek their self-interest and find themselves in their mundane situation. The self-interest of the economic actor bestows him with logic. It makes the logic of the situation *the* method of economics, as Karl Popper establishes. Thus, the book argues for the positioning of new institutional economics as situational logic, that is, an economic theory that formulates and studies single-exit situations that face the economic actor. Ultimately, this book presents a critical appraisal of new institutional economics theories based on a substantiated methodological perspective that effectively navigates the theorist between realism and rigor.

This book will be of interest to readers of new institutional economics, economic theory, and the philosophy of economics and social sciences.

Piet de Vries is a former senior researcher and assistant professor at the University of Twente and a lecturer at the Twente School of Management, Enschede, the Netherlands.

Routledge Frontiers of Political Economy

Critical Theory and Economics
Philosophical Notes on Contemporary Inequality
Robin Maialeh

Corporate Financialization
An Economic Sociology Perspective
Marcelo José do Carmo, Mário Sacomano Neto and Julio Cesar Donadone

The Political Economy of Corruption
Edited by Chandan Jha, Ajit Mishra and Sudipta Sarangi

Post-Keynesian Theories of the Firm
Kalecki and Radical Uncertainty
Nobantu L. Mbeki

Socialist Economic Systems
21st Century Pathways
Steven Rosefield

COVID-19 and Economic Development in Latin America
Theoretical Debates, Financing Dilemmas and Post-Pandemic Scenarios
Monika Meireles, Bruno De Conti and Diego Guevara

Marxist Political Economy and Bourdieu
Economic and Cultural Capital, Classes and State
George Economakis and Theofanis Papageorgiou

New Institutional Economics as Situational Logic
A Phenomenological Perspective
Piet de Vries

For more information about this series, please visit: www.routledge.com/
Routledge-Frontiers-of-Political-Economy/book-series/SE0345

New Institutional Economics as Situational Logic
A Phenomenological Perspective

Piet de Vries

Routledge
Taylor & Francis Group

LONDON AND NEW YORK

First published 2024
by Routledge
4 Park Square, Milton Park, Abingdon, Oxon OX14 4RN

and by Routledge
605 Third Avenue, New York, NY 10158

*Routledge is an imprint of the Taylor & Francis Group,
an informa business*

British Library Cataloguing-in-Publication Data
A catalogue record for this book is available from the British Library

ISBN: 978-1-138-79038-4 (hbk)
ISBN: 978-1-032-54485-4 (pbk)
ISBN: 978-1-315-76422-1 (ebk)

DOI: 10.4324/9781315764221

Typeset in Times New Roman
by SPi Technologies India Pvt Ltd (Straive)

To Anneke Schoneveld

Contents

Preface

In the *Wealth of Nations*, Adam Smith studies a commercial society in which 'every man thus lives by exchanging, or becomes in some measure a merchant'. It denotes what Edmund Husserl would designate as *Lebenswelt*. In Husserl's phenomenology, the lifeworld of conscious human beings is the pregiven and unquestionable 'foundational nexus' of any scientific discipline. It traces back to the philosophical realist position that manifests itself in the notion that human consciousness bears an *a priori* concept of the essences and the structure of the world. In this respect, Alfred Marshall's economics as engaged in 'mankind in the ordinary business of life' refers to studying conscious human beings who seek their self-interest and find themselves in their mundane situation. Their self-interest bestows them with logic. It makes the logic of the situation *the* method of economics, as Karl Popper establishes. Obviously, institutions dimension the situational logic that occasions Ludwig von Mises to assert that institutional economics is an unnecessary term; that is, 'there is economics'. New institutional economics may merely denote an emphasis.

This book surveys some theoretical developments of NIE as initiated by Ronald Coase. The situational logic concept alludes to economics from within and of conscious human beings who experience the world as meaningful. It makes this NIE survey *par excellence* eligible for phenomenological interpretation as studying human consciousness. In this aspect, Alfred Schutz presents a meaningful construction of the social reality. He creates ideal types, homunculi, as exact constructs of the mundane constructs we use in our daily life interaction to arrive at terms with each other, for example, to exchange a commodity. This offers the opportunity to preserve NIE as an exact science notwithstanding its preoccupation with human beings who face information issues, that is, uncertainty. Schutz's analysis of the meaningful construction of social reality dovetails with Felix Kaufmann's methodology of analysis of meaning. This precedes the empirical research of the explanation of facts. Actually, economics is famous for its analysis of meaning that results in theoretical propositions, in theorems that invite further researching their assumptions if they conflict with empirical evidence.

Looking back on my writing this book, I increasingly experienced that I became acquainted with the mental legacy of Alfred Schutz and Felix

Kaufmann. It has truly given me a sense of insight. Furthermore, I have changed my mind regarding the relative significance of Coase and Knight for the development of NIE. It is probably the appealing suggestion of exactness of the transaction cost concept that has established Coase's name as a founder of NIE. However, it is Knight's uncertainty concept and his identification of property rights as economics' founding concept – prior to Coase – that make him the pioneer of NIE by exploring the important consequences of his Knightian uncertainty.

The latter conclusion is one of the many ideas I discussed with John Groenewegen, emeritus professor of economics of infrastructure at TU Delft. John has been my reader since I submitted my book proposal. After completing a chapter, we met each other at our homes, alternating between Delft and Amsterdam. I experienced these meetings as intellectual high points and his constructive criticism as encouragement to proceed. I am most grateful to John for his support.

Furthermore, I am very grateful to Jenny Hill of American Pen for checking my English, aware as I am that a foreign language remains a more or less poorly fitting suit. Thanks also to Sylvia Joostema, Library of the University of Twente, for her support in finding literature. Finally, I am also thankful for Manon Jannink and Annette van de Tuuk, University of Twente, Department of Public Administration, for their assistance with some graphics.

1   Economics as analysis of meaning

1.1 Introduction

It is originally Austrian philosopher Karl Popper (1945a, vol. II: 97) who advances that 'the analysis of the situation is, in fact, *the* method of economic analysis'. Known for his falsification doctrine, he deviates from it regarding the social sciences. In this aspect, Popper demonstrates an affinity with his fellow Austrian Friedrich von Hayek in their aversion to the idea of society as a grand design. It is the '"man on the spot"' who finds himself in a situation, and who acts accordingly that is the appropriate point of departure for the social scientist, they stress (Hayek 1945: 524). This man on the spot of Hayek's classical paper, 'The Use of Knowledge in Society', finds himself in a situation in which decisions concern a matter of *'how much more or less difficult* to procure' or 'how much more or less urgently wanted are the alternative things he produces or uses' (ibid.: 526). This deliberating economic actor is connected to a decentralized market system that communicates relevant information to everyone. This market is 'a kind of machinery for registering change', a paragon of an 'economy of knowledge' (ibid.: 526–527).

The situational logic of more or less also emerges in Ronald Coase's (1937) seminal paper, 'The Nature of the Firm'. Coase draws attention to the costs of Hayek's 'machinery'. The so-called marvelous decentralized market system brings about 'cost of discovering what the relevant prices are' and 'costs of negotiating and concluding a separate contract for each exchange transaction' (Coase 1937: 390–391). These costs of using the price mechanism, that is, transaction costs, may induce actors to replace a series of contracts of a firm owner with the factors that he is cooperating within the firm with one contract. At issue is the cost of an alternative contract type. Additionally, Coase discusses that owing to the risk attitude of contracting partners, they may opt for a long-term contract formulated in general terms and for leaving 'the exact details … until a later date' (ibid.: 292). The man on the spot, who is well informed about the details of the situation, uncertainties, and all else, constitutes the focus of the analysis. Coase's (1937) paper leads to the introduction of transaction cost as a founding concept of new institutional economics (NIE).

DOI: 10.4324/9781315764221-1

Douglass North and Oliver Williamson are important NIE exponents who elaborate on the theoretical consequences of positive transaction costs. According to North (1990: 17), 'traditional behavioral assumptions (i.e., economic rationality) have prevented economists from coming to grips with some very fundamental issues'. We need to take account of the notion that 'individuals make choices based on subjectively derived models that diverge among individuals', North continues (ibid.). Comparably, is the position of Williamson. In an overview paper of the NIE, Williamson associates '*Human Actors*' with one of the 'key good ideas' of the NIE. In this respect, he refers to Herbert Simon. 'Social scientists should be prepared to name the key attributes of human actors', that is, bounded rationality and self-interestedness (Williamson 2000: 600); according to Williamson (1991: 57), an awkward combination resulting in 'self-interest seeking with guile'. For Williamson, the bounded-rationality assumption is the complement of a positive transaction cost (ibid.: 56). Obviously, this cognitive attribute gives the human actor an appealing realisticness. At the same time, this sense of reality turns out to be a fundamental theoretical twist. Instead of transaction cost, it is an actor's cognitive limitations that now claim a theorist's attention, which is how Williamson enumerates a gamut of disciplines that may accomplish NIE. Williamson:

> Evolutionary economics of selectionist, population ecology, and ontogenetic kinds are in progress. ... How best to describe human actors is still unsettled, although evolutionary psychology holds promise.
>
> (2000: 611)

'The new institutional economics is a boiling cauldron of ideas', 'the little engine' that could afford 'more empirical testing, more fully formal theory', Williamson concludes (ibid.: 610–611).

Knowledge makes up a key issue in economics. Herein, these four Nobel Prize laureates agree with one another. In this aspect, they are at the basis of NIE.[1] At the same time, their approaches to the problem of knowledge feature a significant difference between Hayek and Coase, on one hand, versus North and Williamson, on the other. The former two take a purposive individual economic actor who is gifted with consciousness and practical knowledge as central to their analytical approach; an actor who applies the marginal calculus. North and Williamson, however, aim at an account of the theoretical consequences of the empirically diagnosed bounded rationality of the actor. It reflects a contrast between an economic analysis from the inside against an analysis from the outside. The theoretical heart of the former is a man's purview on the situation he finds himself in against the latter, which is a description of psychological and genetic variables explaining man's economic behavior and institutional context. An inside–outside contrast profiles what follows.

The chapter is organized as follows. The next three sections discuss the inside–outside contrast. Section 1.5 refers to the nineteenth-century *Methodenstreit*, of which the inside–outside contrast is reminiscent. Section 1.6 discusses the philosophical background of the two different perspectives, which traces back to the classic dichotomy in philosophical thought between realism and nominalism. Briefly, realism amounts to an analytical approach based on the perception that universal essences structure our world. Nominalism represents the notion that we, human beings, categorize the world we observe. The concept of meaning is the nucleus of the difference between the perspectives. In this dichotomy reemerges the inside–outside contrast. The nominalist camp prevails in modern economics. The meaning concept makes the new institutional economist opt for realism, as Section 1.7 explains. The subsequent sections elaborate the methodology that belongs to a realist perspective. Central in this elaboration is the distinction between analysis of meaning versus causal explanation of facts. At stake is initially formulating the concepts that constitute the subject matter as a theoretical exercise and then arriving at the empirical research part. The significant message of the methodology sections is not to confound analytical with empirical research.

1.2 From an inside versus an outside perspective

In an essay regarding his own 'Firm' and 'Social Cost' papers, Coase (1937, 1960) states his 'conception of the nature of our subject' (Coase 1988: 5).

> What differentiates the essays in this book is not that they reject existing economic theory, which, as I have said, embodies *the logic of choice* and is of wide applicability, but that they employ this economic theory to examine the role which the firm, the market, and the law play in the working of the economic system.
>
> (ibid.; emphasis added)

In accordance with this, Coase does not 'believe that economists will be able to make much headway until a great deal more work has been done by sociobiologists and other noneconomists' (ibid.).[2] An actor's logic of choice remains central to Coase's analysis. Remarkably, Coase's basic position cannot be traced back to Williamson's (2000) NIE overview.

Williamson, for his part, judges it as promising for delving into human actors' nature, for example, as done by evolutionary psychologists. He presents his 'little engine' NIE as an 'interdisciplinary tripod of economics, law and organization theory' (Williamson 1993: 44–50). However, it is rather a broad setup search for explanatory variables incited by observed regularities.

The inside–outside contrast in NIE is an excellent example while reading Joseph Schumpeter's (1954) treatment on 'The Technique of Economic Analysis', the first chapter in his *History of Economic Analysis*. According to Schumpeter, merely a twosome theory type suffices to cover the history of economic thought. 'The first and less important one makes theories synonymous with Explanatory Hypotheses' (ibid.: 14). Observations (from outside) frame the economic hypotheses. For instance, a theorist discovers a correlate between 'expectations of employment opportunities' and 'workman's expenditure on consumers' goods' (ibid.: 17). The hypotheses contain the final research results. The second type (Schumpeter: 'economic theory'), on the other hand, begins with abstraction and axioms, or hypotheses or principles, which may be '*suggested* by facts, but in strict logic they are arbitrary creations of the analyst' (ibid.: 15). A theorist's 'knowledge of *meanings* of economic actions' (from inside) enables the theorist to construct 'the logic of the situation' based on theoretical propositions, for example, concerning marginal analysis (ibid.: 16–17). The inside theorist is engaged in the logical essences of a class of phenomena in the search for ideal images or types. From this hypothetical fabric, he proceeds to empiricism.

Schumpeter established, *nota bene* in the 1950s, a tendency 'among economists and other social scientists to rule out economic theory from the realm of serious science' (ibid.: 20). Research based on empirical observation was receiving prevalence. In a footnote, he adds the consideration that our theoretical practice may simply be a matter of intellectual taste (ibid.: 20, n. 8). At the same time, Schumpeter denotes a more basic reason for this bias against (his own concept of) economic theory, namely, the awkward combination of science and metaphysics; empirical observation as a foundation seems to be the desired remedy against the latter (ibid.: 20). The tendency toward outside theory reflects the spirit of the times, as aptly worded by George Simmel (1990) in his *The Philosophy of Money*. Economic theory as an analytical construct originates from abstraction from the ephemeral, the contingency, in search for what is essential, steadfast substance. The stable core within the fleeting appearances finds its counterpart within ourselves as

> a being whose existence and character is centred in ourselves, a final authority which is independent of the outside world.
>
> (ibid.: 101)

The goal behind our thought is to grasp the reliable reality behind the ephemeral appearances. In sharp contrast with this aim stands the perspective of modern science in which a ceaseless development of relations between phenomena replaces the absolute stability of substances and forms 'centred in ourselves'. It results in a relativism that is oriented toward a search for outside relations between observed phenomena without a pre-reflected concept.

1.3 The outside purview dominates in modern economics

The bias toward empirical observation prevails in current social science research. New millennium economists see big data analysis as a promising challenge, announcing a definite turn in economics away from the economic principles with which they were once familiar. For instance, David Colander

(2000: 131) sketches how the 'dropped computational costs' open unprecedented opportunities for the new millennium economists. Colander:

> In 2050, economists no longer believe that a set of canonical principles will lead to a single model which is then tested in empirical work. Today, most of the simulation models that form the core of what students are taught deviate from the old-style canonical principles in some way or another. In 2050, the belief of economists in derived analytical models has given way to a belief that the underlying reality is too complex to be understood with these sorts of models. Economists in 2050 do empirical work in a wider variety of ways than they did at the turn of the millennium. They both create data and analyze it [*sic*]. Experimental economics is now an extremely important way of creating data; ... New Millennium economists do not believe that they are testing a particular model which was deduced from first principles; instead they are simply looking for possibly exploitable patterns in the data. The loose-fitting positivism of 50 years ago has changed to a loose-fitting pragmatism.
>
> (ibid.: 127–128)

John Davis could confirm Colander's prospect already during the first decade of the new millennium. '*All* the new research programs in economics have their origin in other sciences' (Davis 2007: 275). These programs create 'economics-within-science questions' that are addressed by 'science empirical practices such as experimentalism, neuro-imaging, subjective well-being analyses, cross-cultural surveys, etc.' (ibid.: 279). According to Davis, it is a structural change in economics that challenges economics as a separate science, that is, economics that studies human beings as deliberate economic agents. Central to modern research programs is the search for patterns. For instance, it is the mission of the Santa Fe Institute to understand patterns of order in the complexity that we find in all living nature.

> These patterns are found at all scales, from the molecular, through tissues, individuals, technology, the economy, and cultures.
>
> (Santa Fe Institute undated)

The Santa Fe research substantiates Davis's idea of 'economics-within science'. The modern social scientist has recourse to a variety of techniques and approaches ranging from 'non-linear dynamic, via information theory, and robust design, to formalisms coupling adaptive information with source of energy' (ibid.).

J. Doyne Farmer identifies 'traditional' economics as 'Cartesian' as it is based on 'feigned axioms'. It is a 'top down approach in which models come first and empirical confirmation come second'. Contrariwise, physics 'takes a bottom up approach in which data comes [*sic*] first'. The latter tradition traces back to Galileo and Newton (Farmer 2013: 378). It is experimental philosophy that counts. Farmer indicates that

> [i]n "experimental philosophy", propositions are inferred from the phenomena, and afterwards rendered general by induction. This approach is drilled into physicists.
>
> (ibid.: 380)

The quote aptly exhibits the basically naturalist disposition of the outside view. In the social science context, it implies omitting the inner condition, that is, the actor's meaning behind the phenomena. The experimental philosophy would continually compel economists to infer hypotheses about an actor's inner condition from observable phenomena. However, experimental behaviorist B.F. Skinner concludes that such hypotheses that result from 'empirical observation are "discarded as unnecessary and meaningless"' (Gunning 1986: 81). The ambition to define the inner condition through empirical observation is doomed to fail.

At the same time, human behavior obviously exhibits patterns that may be described statistically, offering data as rich sources for empirical hypotheses analysis. In particular, the increasing involvement of computers in economic transactions affords unprecedented econometric opportunities (Varian 2014). '"Big data" will change the landscape of economic policy and economic research', concludes a National Bureau of Economic Research (NBER) paper on big data use (Einav, Levin 2013: 26). However, the use of big data on human behavior is anything but an indifferent operation. These data 'produce a new organization of our experience of the external world', as Hayek (1952: 38) identifies. Databases pass over an actor's inner condition. Couched in observables, data facilitate a positivist version of economics, rendering it as yet a physical affair.

1.4 The inside purview marks institutional economics

Well known is the following methodological objection that can be leveled against merely positivist economics. Eventually, no theorist can merely lean on data as they will not substitute for 'common sense, economic theory, or the need for careful research designs. Rather, it will complement them', also concludes the NBER paper on big data (Einav, Levin 2013: 26). However, in an institutional-economics context, an additional objection makes itself particularly evident; that is, the outside view passes over the very nature of economics as a moral science in which the concepts present meaning. The economic world is one of the concepts that represent meaning; for example, institutions are such things.[3] The entire social reality is a manifestation of communally experienced mental structures. In this respect, I refer to a main point in Hayek's *The Counterrevolution of Science*. Hayek indicates:

The question is here not how far man's picture of the external world fits the facts, but how by his actions, determined by the views and concepts he possesses, man builds up another world of which the individual becomes a part. And by "the views and concepts people hold" we do not mean merely their knowledge of external nature. We mean all they know and believe about themselves, about other people, and about the external world.

(1952: 40)

Paraphrased, at issue is not to have recourse to such a thing as bounded rationality to explain (from outside) man's inept picture of the facts of the external world. What matters is man's moral sense, his knowledge of the world he lives in, and the manner in which he experiences the meaning of it, that is, his consciousness of the world. Knowledge and meaning generate and profile the world. In a broad sense, it is an institutional world that the economic actor lives in. Economics is a cultural and moral thing.

From economics as a moral science, it follows naturally that the analytic basic principle comprehends the inside purview of man as a consciously knowing creature. It constitutes the very reference point for reviewing new institutional economics. The inside purview, or "'egological'" approach, may offer insight into man's cognitive competencies in building his social reality, bestowing meaning to the world, and creating an institutional fabric (Prendergast 1986: 2). Therefore, an anthropocentric perspective features this monograph on NIE. It traces back to the awareness of the fact that the entire social-economic world we study initially and eventually concerns conscious human beings who act, and particularly interact, intentionally and with reason as enabled and accommodated by a meaningful reality, for example, of institutional systems, that originate from those very human beings. It is a perspective that accords with a tradition in economic thought from Adam Smith and beyond. (Smith 1776). For that matter, the anthropocentric view is by no means meant as a plea against approaches that originate from what I referred to as the 'outside', that is, from observables. The new institutional economist, however, cannot leave out man as a conscious human being.

1.5 An unremitting *Methodenstreit*

The two types of theory that are discussed are reminiscent of the *Methodenstreit*. Apparently, it remains a recurring issue to respect a balance between Austrian analytical principles and Prussian empirical significance. For instance, the Santa Fe exponents that are quoted clearly take the opposite direction of Hayek's Austrian position that bases an analysis on the individual actor's purview. *Mutatis mutandis*, the classic contrast, also resurfaces between the NIE exponents that are discussed. Hayek and Coase adhere to the logic of choice. Williamson (1975: 9), by contrast, abandons this analytical edge, enriching his framework with a 'set of *environmental factors* ... together with a related set of *human factors*'. Latent in these distinctions is the deduction-induction controversy. The contrasts reflect the dissension between social scientists about the subject matter and methods of their disciplines. In this respect, they contrast with natural scientists who do not bother about dichotomies such as theoretical versus realistic or objective versus subjective. At a cursory reading, Alfred Whitehead (1929: 180) states, physical science regards 'purely matter-of-fact'. The subject matter of physics is subjected to a few basic laws, a hierarchy of generalities, and particularities that are amenable to accurately calculated prediction.[4] In Newtonian natural science, subject matter (scope) and method coincide. The matter–method divergence in social sciences stems from the specific meaning dimension that human beings perform in the reality that the social scientist studies. The inside–outside distinction reflects whether the theorist takes account of it. Consequently, for instance, the objective–subjective dichotomy enters into the methodological debate. Therefore, the *Methodenstreit* witnesses that the subject-matter definition of economics highly depends on the method solution of economics. The methodological issue is, as Felix Kaufmann (1933: 381) puts forward, this: Which data may represent the subject matter of economics as an empirical science? Would the data merely concern observables, or should they refer to human meaning? The history of economic thought does not decisively answer this question; the logic of choice and hypotheses testing coexist. For instance, American original institutional economics is primarily a methodological critique of mainstream economics. Methodology appears to be a matter of taste. Basically, however, the ongoing debate originates from contrasting philosophical positions dating back to the scholastic dispute between nominalists and realists.

1.6 Nominalism versus realism

At issue is the idea of the basic structure of reality. It is, by definition, a metaphysical question as it concerns a 'meta' point of view on reality. Nominalists support the postulate that merely particulars exist. Accordingly, it is a human convention to categorize these particulars, as *nomina*, resulting in language as the instrument to perceive reality. Reality is perceptible in language and human thought. In our language, we create concepts that *have* meaning, that is, are attached to concepts (Kaufmann 1944: 17). Nominalism founds induction, that is, inferences from particular cases to the general case. Empirical observation founds our knowledge. Empiricism is the fruit of nominalism.

Against this stands realism. The realist postulates a reality that exists independent of human perception. At the same time, this reality is intelligible in universals. The latter regards *a priori* categories that logically precede particulars. It refers to the Aristotelian view that science must be based on necessity and immutability. Abstract concepts such as color, beauty, or art bear witness to the existence of universals, that is, concepts that *are* meaning (ibid.: 18). The scientist is searching for essences. The universals enable us to apply deductive analysis; the particular is deduced from the universal. Realism enables rationalism.

How to solve this dilemma between empiricism and rationalism? The realism postulate of universals concerns the philosophical cutting through of the Gordian knot of the endless search for self-evident truths as ultimate grounds for empirical science by claiming the possibility of an immediate knowledge of universals as essences, although 'not of facts' (Kaufmann 1944: 1). It is this radical act that resolves the controversy between empiricists and rationalists. Empiricists lean on sense perception, which results in naming (labeling) what they finally equate with knowledge. Rationalists argue that this 'copy theory' cannot forestall perception illusions as it fails to reconcile the variety in subjective perceptions. Therefore, sense perception requires reason, for instance, to explain the 'break' of the straight stick dipped in water (ibid.: 7). Consequently, an alternative theory of knowledge must encompass reason in order to address the 'discovering of universal invariants and principles of co-variation' (ibid.: 8). The solution is a compromise: '*critical rationalism* or *critical empiricism*'. Kaufmann:

> For, with rationalism, it is critical of sense unguided by reason; and, with empiricism, it is critical of reason unchecked by sense.
>
> (ibid.: 12)

Yet, sense experience requires reason as its guide. An important argument in favor of realism is that, in the concrete meaning of a word, an abstract meaning must be presupposed. For instance, an empirical proposition about an object presupposes abstract concepts of space, time, and physical qualities (e.g., colors). A linguistic term has meaning. Consequently, this meaning cannot be traced back to language. Therefore, besides 'terms' and 'sentences' that *have* meaning, there exist concepts and propositions that *are* meanings, that is, conceptual meaning (ibid.: 18). The latter features realist philosophy. For instance, 'scholastic realist' Charles Peirce denotes this conceptual meaning as '"Firstness"', that is, what is '"present and immediate"' in consciousness before man had drawn any distinction (Peirce, cited in Wennerberg 1962: 34).

Seemingly, the elegant critical-rationalism option decides the argument in favor of realism. Nevertheless, nominalism features the prevailing modern practice of economic research as sketched above. For instance, big data particularly constitute the material to construct a view of the world; man categorizes *a posteriori*. Conducive to this view have been the empirical feats of natural scientists since the seventeenth century. They have incited the transition from the Aristotelian to the Galilean mode of thought (Lewin 1931). According to the latter perspective, 'the ultimate constituents of the physical world are impenetrable particles which obey simple mechanical laws, governing their behavior in conjunction with a description of their relative position, masses, momenta, etc.' (Watkins 1957: 105). J.W.N. Watkins terms it 'half-way explanations', that is, (nominalist) descriptions that do not delve into the properties and the relations of the particles, as 'rock-bottom explanations' would arrive at (ibid.). The Galilean mode preaches a world of coincidentally uniform processes couched in formulas, replacing a given world in which universal essences may be discovered and classified.

The new millennium economics as discussed earlier accords with this nominalism. Instead of economic principles and 'feigned axioms', contemporary economists take, like physicians, 'a bottom up approach in which data come first' (Farmer 2013). It refers to Schumpeter's hypotheses-formulating statistical analysis, the route from big data to patterns. Seemingly different from this strictly empirical focus is Williamson's (1993: 44–50) 'interdisciplinary tripod of economics, law and organization'. Williamson (1975: 20) aspires to build a theoretical framework, however not a 'frictionless ideal'. In his *Markets and Hierarchies*, Williamson elaborates an 'organizational failures framework' in which human and environmental factors constitute an 'atmosphere' of five interrelated variables: 'bounded rationality, opportunism, uncertainty, small numbers, and information impactedness'. A figure illustrates the sophisticated relationships between these variables (ibid.: 40). The nature of this theoretical framework is nominalist; that is, empiricism has primacy. For instance, a key human factor 'bounded rationality involves neurophysiological limits on the one hand and language limits on the other' (ibid.: 21). Unmistakably, Williamson's approach is interdisciplinary as it is nominalist. Broadly seen, nominalism originates two versions of economics from an outside purview. On one hand, statistical analysis and hypotheses prevail. On the other, interdisciplinary approaches flourish that formulate alternatives to the inside purview of the logic of choice. This results in frameworks that, in fact, concern descriptions. Eventually, they are interrelated; interdisciplinarity will produce hypotheses to be tested statistically. What unites them is their origin from empirical observation.

Realism, however, also has a creditable track record in economics. It has founded the analytical tradition in economics since Adam Smith, and previous to that time. The realist position grants the economic actor his autonomy vis-à-vis a world that is knowable by means of *a priori* categories that logically precede the observation of phenomena. We observe colors and tones. It renders the economic reality amenable to deductive logic. It encourages the theorist to discover the essences of the phenomena that are being studied. Clearly, this position dovetails with the analytical nature of economics as the logic of choice. In this aspect, it is explicable that Schumpeter (1954: 107) considers the scholastic ideal of natural law as the origin of social science with corresponding analytical efforts. Social science's analytical nature refers to the natural-law concept that man is inherently a rational being who should behave accordingly. Schumpeter indicates, on natural law:

[T[he ideal of natural law embodies the discovery that the data of a social situation determine – in the most favorable case, uniquely – a certain sequence of events, a logically coherent process or state, or *would do so if they were allowed to work themselves without further disturbance*.

(ibid.: 112)

The quote is reminiscent of Coase's and Hayek's situational logic of choice. The same perspective returns in Alfred Marshall's description of the nature of economic laws. 'Every cause has a tendency to produce some definite result if nothing occurs that hinders it' (Marshall 1890: 31). The quotes phrase a concept of economic laws in which the scholastic normal price finds its counterpart in Coase's (1937: 387) adage: "'The normal economic system works itself'". The inside purview entails an analytical approach based on *a priori* concepts that reveal themselves in the working of the system. As a sequel of the scholastic natural law, this economic theory is based on realism; that is, universals do exist. Aristotelian realism profiles analytic economics, uncovering the essences and the nature of the economic reality. Analytical economics substantiate realism's necessity and immutability, in which its rationality principle is economics' equivalent of universal laws in physics, as Popper (1967: 359) states.

All the same, nominalist and realist exponents coexist in economics. For that matter, economic research with a bias towards empirical research increasingly outstrips pure economic theory. It reflects economists' methodological diversity as social scientists. However, the NIE theme forces taking sides.

1.7 Realism and meaning in NIE

In NIE, nominalism versus realism is anything but an arbitrary issue. The qualifying element in it is the indisputable fact that conscious human beings constitute the economic world, which they experience as meaningful. It entails the epistemologically significant consequence that man is not a *tabula rasa* but an autonomous human being gifted with reason and speech who commands *'paradigms'* (Armstrong 1983: 5). Nucleus is the concept of meaning. In the nominalist view, man attaches meaning to the phenomena; concepts *have* meaning. In a realist's world, meaning refers to universals; concepts *are* meaning. A realist's meaning refers to the essences of phenomena that are yet to be discovered. In this respect, I refer to Carl Menger, a declared advocate of realism in economics. Regarding economic phenomena, Menger discerns two mainstream types of research. He states:

> *die* individuelle *(die historische) und die* generelle *(die theoretische). Die erstere strebt nach der Erkenntniss des individuellen Wesens und des individuellen Zusammenhanges, die letztere nach jener des generellen Wesens und des Zusammenhanges der Erscheinungen.*
>
> (1883: 32)

The aim of the latter is to find the essences of the phenomena and to formulate exceptionless relationships between them, that is, exact laws, resulting in *'eine exacte ethische Wissenschaft'* (ibid.: 39, n. 18;). It is the realist view of a structured reality in which universal essences are knowable that enables Menger to aspire to economics as a nomological science. It renders the concept of meaning the analytical nucleus as it is the analysis of meaning that opens up the essentialia as building blocks of a scientific domain.

NIE basically accords with this Austrian tradition of realism in economics founded by Menger. Institutions are meaning since they constitute the essences of social reality. Accordingly, realism houses institutional economics. The structured social reality is an *institutionally* structured social reality. We create our social reality by means of institutions as defined by Searle.[5] *A prima vista*, this perception seems to support the nominalist case; the institution regards 'constitutive rules of the form *X counts as Y in C*' (Searle 2005: 10). This sounds rather nominalistic. The meaning that man attaches to a concept originates as an institution. However, Searle's realist counterargument is this:

> a socially constructed reality presupposes a reality independent of social constructions, because there has to be something for the construction to be constructed out of.
>
> (1995: 190–191)

Otherwise stated, apparently, the structure of reality is such that it originates institutions. For instance, the invisible-hand processes establish institutions that subsequently 'provide a structure within which one can create institutional facts' (Searle 2005: 10). Institutional facts found the economic reality and the other way around; without institutions, there is no economics. Therefore, as Austrian economist Ludwig von Mises (1949: 66) claims, actually, there is no such thing as 'a discipline of institutional economics. There is economics'.

Therefore, the institutional theme makes the economist opt for realism because of concepts that are meaning, *a priori* categories. They refer to universals that are, according to Aristotle, open to infallible intuition (Kaufmann 1944: 1). Obviously, this is a fundamental choice with a far-reaching methodological implication. The *a priori* nature of concepts determines the scientist to follow this logical order: the analysis of meaning concepts precedes the empirical research in which the concepts figure. The meanings of basic concepts are presupposed to describe a specific discipline: 'what facts can be described and explained', that is, what is the subject matter (scope) of a discipline? As discussed, in social science, the matter at issue entails another question: '[A]nd the second, which implies the first, what methods of investigation are most suited to such a task?' (Kaufmann 1933: 383). The latter question regards the empirical counterpart or, as stated by Kaufmann (1944: 16), 'the causal explanation of facts'. To bring these two questions in line with the realist view is at stake, that is, keeping them sharply distinguished and in that logical order. In this, I follow Kaufmann's (1944) *Methodology of the Social Sciences*. The two next sections present the questions in that order, with the analysis of meaning preceding the causal explanation of facts. The subsequent section shows that the analysis of meaning enters a domain that requires a philosophical compass. As a founding concept, meaning is beset by presuppositions as, for example, the nominalism–realism controversy shows. The compass of the analysis of meaning regards the phenomenological perspective that issues from reflection on human consciousness as engaged in meaning.

1.8 The analysis of meaning as the scope of a discipline

The meaning content of the theoretical statements originates from the analysis of meaning to be unified in a theory. In this aspect, the analysis comprehends two elements. First, it distinguishes essential from nonessential elements in a certain context of thought, that is, the proper analysis of meaning. Second, a meaning analysis eliminates inconsistencies of thought (Kaufmann 1944: 15). Together they enable the scientist to formulate his discipline as a nomological science that deals with ideal essences.

First, from a realist perspective, the *a priori* nature of the 'nexus of the categorial form of meanings' of concepts and truths is pivotal in the analysis. The scientist does not make objective validity of concepts but 'discovers them and has insight in them' (Farber 1962: 239). At the same time, such a type of discovery requires an intellectual tour. The departing point is the pre-reflective knowledge of 'what is actual in experience' (Whitehead 1929: 107). Even the actual experience of a mundane thing regards more than a simple presentation. Whitehead warns against the 'fallacy of misplaced concreteness', as stated by Alfred Schutz (1953: 1). Experience is a thought object, a highly complicated construct of, for example, 'space relations in order to constitute it as a sense-object of several senses, say of sight and touch' (Schutz 1953: 1). These constructs constitute our knowledge, a set of abstractions and formalizations 'specific to the level of thought organization' (ibid.: 2). This is not merely a matter of intuition. It results from the 'necessity in every act of thinking' in which isolation and abstraction constitute the heart of cognition. It refers 'to our capacity to distinguish red from green, … warnings from congratulations', Barry Smith (1990: 267) states. When interpreting reality, we merely grasp the aspect relevant to us both in common sense and in scientific knowledge. In science, at issue is to supersede the commonsense concepts with scientific thought objects, shedding the 'fluid vagueness of sense, replaced by [an] exact definition of thought' (Schutz 1953: 2). Here appears Alfred Schutz's phenomenological perspective to proceed. It affords the social scientist to grasp the very origin and nature of the concept of meaning that founds the essence of knowledge. Schutz gives a phenomenological sophistication of Max Weber's concept of *Verstehen* and the inherent interpretation of meaning. Interpretation requires a scheme of interpretation (*Deutungsschema*). It is, for instance, quite difficult to grasp the meaning of card players' observable actions without knowing which cards they are playing. The rules of a game constitute a law of interpretation that renders players' actions explainable. In the same manner, society consists of a diversity of circles of interrelated actors who perform a state of attitudes, a drama and action that involve reactions and attitudes of others to which apply a scheme of interpretation. This image substantiates the meaning analysis as stated by Kaufmann. In social science, and in economics in particular, a scheme of interpretation features the ideal types, that is, constructs of typical behavior and course of action, and stipulates their purposiveness that enables the social scientist to interpret the observed behavior as meaningful action. Chapter 2 further elaborates on this phenomenological analysis of meaning.

Second, the analysis of meaning is a deductive operation, removing inconsistencies. The concepts that result from it constitute the basis of analytic and synthetic propositions. The analytic makes a meaning explicit; the synthetic component is 'a *restriction of the frame of possibilities*; as a determination, it excludes other determinations' (Kaufmann 1944: 20). It is significant to note that the analysis of meaning does not refer to the truth or falsity of synthetic propositions. Kaufmann substantiates this as follows. A historic account, for instance, is intended to be subject to scientific verification; a novel is not, although it contains synthetic propositions (ibid.: 23). The intentionality behind the synthetic propositions determines whether their truth is relevant. However, the restrictive nature of the synthetic proposition determines the logical relations between two given propositions. Therefore, the truth tables of a textbook on logic are applicable to a set of propositions; for example, proposition p_1 may be deducible from p_2; they may be contrary to each other or called contradictory or subcontrary (ibid.). An example of contradictory propositions is that it is impossible for qualities 'blue and yellow to be at the same place at the same time' (Kaufmann 1941: 321). As engaged in their logical soundness, the analysis of meanings reveals such internal relations between elementary concepts. It is a privilege not granted to empiricism. However, meaning is not about truth. Truth refers to the empirical validity of the explanation of facts to discuss now, that is, Kaufmann's second question in the logical order.

1.9 The causal explanation of facts

The causal explanation of facts regards verification; in science – both the natural sciences and the social sciences – the logical supplement to the analysis of meanings. The empirical counterpart of science consists of a procedure of rules to decide whether a proposition changes the corpus of a discipline. Deductive inference regards deducing a proposition from other propositions and, therefore, does not change the body of a science. So, at issue is incorporating a new proposition, that is, a synthetic, restricting the frame of possibilities, for instance, a synthetic universal proposition stating, "'No *p* without *q*'" (ibid.: 80). Actually, such a proposition refers to a warranted *belief* in the truth of a proposition that it can withstand any empirical check. A single negative instance refutes the prediction of the synthetic universal proposition. However, refutation is by no means the end of a scientific procedure; rather, it is a point to proceed from. Kaufmann indicates:

Frequently, however, the non-fulfilment of a warranted prediction does not result in the elimination of any universal proposition.

(ibid.: 83)

Scientists aim to safeguard the warranted prediction derived from synthetic universal propositions by distinguishing between 'strict laws' and 'mere rules' or by adding to it the *ceteris paribus* condition. Obviously, these interferences leave the inconsistency of a universality claim versus a counterexample undisturbed; for example, an unspecified *ceteris paribus* clause emasculates the universal nature of a prediction. Apparently, science may proceed by formulating warranted predictions without being derived from synthetic universal propositions. Kaufmann refers to this alternative as 'a rule of procedure'. It declares, as an inductive inference, "'If p is known, acceptance of q is warranted'", referring to the 'state of knowledge in a given situation' (ibid.: 80). It regards propositions that cannot be falsified by a single counter instance and, therefore, no synthetic universal propositions. At the same time, it refers to a significant rule of procedure in the scientific business, searching for a better specification of the relevant *ceteris paribus* variables. From a given knowledge situation, science proceeds by replacing the rule of procedure, that is, the prediction, 'affected by the negative result of an empirical test' (ibid.: 85). A reinterpretation of the *ceteris paribus* conditions might safeguard the general 'law' that warrants a prediction. Nucleus, in this context, is the meaning of 'law'. In search for 'idealizations', the formulation of warranted predictions concerns 'prescriptions for scientific procedure' of preliminary nature, not yet fulfilled, that is, rules of procedure. Kaufmann states:

We shall call them *theoretical laws* as contrasted with *empirical laws*, which are synthetic universal propositions accepted in science.

(ibid.: 87)

The relation between these laws reflects the controversy between conventionalists and empiricists. The significance of theoretical laws makes clear that, without them, the observation of empiricists is directionless. However, the empirical laws instruct the conventionalists that an *a priori* synthetic universal proposition is nonexistent. Methodological settlement is reached by determining the relations between theoretical and empirical laws (ibid.: 88). Paraphrasing Kaufmann, the distinction of theoretical versus empirical law precludes a confounding analysis of meaning with a causal explanation of facts. The latter would result in presenting analytical propositions as synthetic universals. On the rebound, this deception might lead to the fallacious position that merely observed phenomena constitute the basis of the analysis.

The distinction between theoretical and empirical applies to both the natural and the social sciences. It negates ontological determinateness in both domains. Rigid determinateness implies that irrefutable predictions can be made, which is incompatible with the principle of permanent control and conflicts with the scientific procedure that apparently requires the preliminarily theoretical laws to proceed. Therefore, theoretical laws are required in natural science just as they are in social science. This is precisely lacking in the Humean perspective, which states that causal relations are merely external. The nominalist position reemerges in this view. '[B]ut he [Hume] did not perform a logical analysis of external relations', that is, the formulation of theoretical laws. (Kaufmann 1944: 233). However, considering the principle of permanent control, the principle of causality is not a law but rather a declaration not to renounce the search for causes and is valid in both natural and social sciences. The difference regards the empirical laws. Social science lacks the latter 'and even the tendency to establish such laws is not very strong' (ibid.: 174). The conclusion is that the distinction between theoretical versus empirical is instructively denoting that failed empirical evidence does not immediately render a theory invalid.

A crucial element in the decision situation concerning empirical evidence regards the protocol proposition, that is, a report of an observer regarding a synthetic proposition. At this point, the specific nature of social reality again makes itself evident in empirical research. Social science cannot suffice the identification of experience with sensory observation as it would exclude the meaning dimension of social reality (Schutz 1954: 262). There is a correlate of psychophysical phenomena with physical, providing an opportunity for three *beliefs* about it. At issue is the *validity* of such a belief (Kaufmann 1944: 125).

The first belief about the correlate delimits the objective knowledge of human behavior to knowledge of observable physical facts. Given the foregoing, such a reductionist belief is obviously invalid. Behaviorism is an exponent of it. A second interpretation of the correlate takes introspection as empirical ground. 'Self-observation' would justify the interpretation of the immediate experience of the observable behavior of other people. For that matter, this introspection is also the empirical ground of behaviorism as it presupposes that the teleological nature of the behavior is apprehended. Via the latter, behaviorism refutes itself (ibid.: 148–149). It is an additional argument against behaviorism as a sound empirical approach. In his discussion of behaviorism and marginal utility theory, Emil Kauder (1965: 124) suggests: 'It seems to me that introspection and behaviorism belong together'. At issue is, that 'a[n] (economic) theory cannot be constructed without figuring out how a rational person will act'. Both introspection and behaviorism labor under the idea of immediate knowledge that lacks intersubjectivity. A third interpretation, as discussed by Kaufmann, applies an analogy to give the correlate an empirical ground. The social scientist imaginary identifies himself with the actors in social reality, inferring the occurrence of analogously psychical processes in his fellow men from the overt physical facts, in particular from bodily movements, (ibid.: 125). This interpretation correctly acknowledges the indefeasibility of meaning in social phenomena. At the same time, it resorts to introspection to substantiate the correlate, overpassing the significance of the analysis of meanings for the correlate of psychophysical with physical facts. In other words, it disregards the analysis of constructs (of constructs), constituting the intersubjectivity of 'an objectively verifiable theory of subjective meaning-structures' (Schutz 1954: 270). The next section discusses the explicit relationship between scope and method, meaning and fact as argued by Kaufmann in finding empirical substantiation.

1.10 Meaning and fact in economics

The analysis of meaning renders '*die reine Nationalökonomie eine exacte ethische Wissenschaft*' (Menger 1883: 39, n. 18). It characterizes social science in that discussing the causal explanation of facts chiefly concerns a return to the analysis of meanings. It stems from the particular nature of the protocol proposition in social science. Empirical research of social reality concerns observable phenomena such as bodily movements and legislation. However, their causal explanation is initially possible within a scheme of interpretation, avoiding the fallacy of misplaced concreteness. In this respect, protocol propositions in social science differ from those in natural science. At the same time, their status as empirical verification is similar In both branches of science.

Based on an interpretation scheme, for example, economic rationality, it is the theoretical construct of a model of ideal types that are gifted with a specific consciousness that enables the social scientist 'to predict how such a puppet or system of puppets might behave under certain conditions', Schutz states. (Schutz 1954: 272). [6] He continues, quoting declared empiricist Ernest Nagel, 'and to discover certain "determinate relations between a set of variables, in terms of which ... empirically ascertainable regularities ... can be explained"' (ibid.). It literally concerns a causal explanation of facts. The scheme of interpretation finds its field of application in a particular type of societal circle at time *t* in place *p*. In this respect, Kaufmann uses an analogy. The laws of electrodynamics find their application in an electrical field. The analogy elucidates the classic holism debate: Do social collectivities exist independently from the human beings who form them? A social collectivity, for example, a company, 'exists' as a field of application of laws (of interpretation) and is inherently independent of the persons who happen to have their functions in it. It is to say that a field of application arises or disappears when a card game begins or ends. 'The same holds of states, legal orders, languages, and institutions of all kinds' (Kaufmann 1944: 162–163).

Kaufmann's electrical field analogy is reminiscent of Karl Popper's account of the concept of situational logic. Popper's basic methodological position is that, without postulating rationality as an interpretation scheme, there is no scientific discourse of social action. In this aspect, he compares the significance of the rationality principle in social sciences with the significance of universal laws in physics. Like 'Newton's universal laws of motion "animate" the model of the solar system', so does the rationality principle animate the model of a social situation (Popper 1967: 358). Popper adds that this animation does not refer to the human *anima* but to *replacing* 'concrete psychological elements by abstract and typical situational elements' (ibid.: 359). The only one animating law involved, he proceeds, regards 'the principle of acting appropriately to the situation'; 'we should pack or cram our whole theoretical effort, ... , into an analysis of the *situation*' (ibid.). Basically, Popper paraphrases Kaufmann's analysis of meaning.

At the same time, empirical relevance is the ultimate purpose of the theoretical construct. However, economics is not famous for its synthetic universal propositions, that is, for empirical laws that may be falsified by a single counter instance. Falsification in economics is problematic for several reasons. 'An empirical law does not make the assertion that something happens, but that it happens *under certain conditions*' (Kaufmann 1934: 105). Additionally, the complexity of economic phenomena requires a number of assumptions concerning initial conditions and idealizations, thwarting decisive test conclusions. Moreover, it is not very helpful in this respect that these conditions particularly concern dynamic processes.[7] Economists are more acquainted with theoretical laws, such as the law of demand. A counterexample will not prompt an economist to ignore the economic law that a rise in the price of a good results in a decline in the demand for that good. On the contrary, it will incite the economist to reformulate the theoretical law. For instance, the rise in the price of bread that caused a rise in demand for it during the nineteenth century, as noted by Sir Robert Giffen, prods defining the Giffen good as a commodity of which 'the positive substitution effect is swamped by the negative income effect', which results in a positive relationship between price and demand, that is, a positive price effect (Stonier and Hague 1953: 64–65). Therefore, Gresham's law does not exclude the madman who prefers to exchange his golden coins for inferior paper money (Croce 1913: 370). Deviating from these laws would be in contrast with the presupposed self-interest of the economic actor that is studied. This self-interest constitutes a scheme of interpretation of the economist by which he feels bound to his theoretical laws. It vitalizes the homunculus.

It is in particular social situations in which the economic subject matter prevails that are exceedingly amenable to a strict scheme of interpretation, resulting in 'a well circumscribed conceptual domain' (Kaufmann 1944: 168). It enables 'the economist [to] make[s] the economic logic of the situation appear with perfect clarity and consistency' (Swedberg 1998: 195). Since Adam Smith, a scheme of interpretation features economics and renders it a theoretical system of thought.

A scheme of interpretation and theoretical laws feature economics. It is the rent-seeking homunculus's behavior that explains the law of demand, Gresham's law, the tendency toward normal profits, and the Ricardian law of comparative cost differences in international trade. The caveat of the *ceteris paribus* clause renders these results of economic analyses non-falsifiable. At the same time, any empirical nonconformity with such a theoretical law demands further analysis, a search for disturbing variables that might explain the unfulfilled nature of the warranted prediction.[8] The theoretical laws determine the direction of the economic analysis.[9] The empirical nonconformity to the theoretical law exhorts formulating a new deductive logic addressing the incongruity. Determining whether the new answer is correct 'brings the procedural rules into play' (Kaufmann 1944: 232). Popper (1945b: 82, n. 8) calls this procedure the application of a '"null hypothesis"', that is, that agents comply with the rationality principle. In this aspect, he refers to Jacob Marschak who applies it when investigating the difference between an income tax versus a sales tax, of equal budgetary incidence in effect on the demand for consumers' goods. For this analysis, the null hypothesis reads:

> If an individual's income and all prices change in the same proportion, he continues to consume the same amount of various goods as before.
> (Marschak 1943: 40)

The *rationality principle* founds the hypothesis. However, if facts deviate from this hypothesis, the situational analysis proceeds by a search for new hypotheses. Marschak's null hypothesis corresponds to Hayek's pure logic of choice. Popper (1945b: 82) perceives it as 'a kind of zero co-ordinate' to compare actual versus model behavior. In this manner, Marschak proposes the concept of money illusion explaining the refutation of his null hypothesis. Clearly, this is what Alexander Rosenberg (1984: 378) refers to as 'the extremal strategy', that is, blaming the model and not the rationality principle.

Empirical nonconformity causes reformulating the *ceteris paribus* clause of the null hypothesis. Obviously, this extremal strategy is an immunizing stratagem, that is, bringing in *ad hoc ceteris paribus* clauses to safeguard an empirically refuted hypothesis, a strategy that Popper vehemently disputed elsewhere (Popper 1959). Popper's plea for the null hypothesis puzzles the positivist who seeks empirically tested propositions. It amounts to an unspecified *ceteris paribus* clause, which would relegate the proposition to the domain of tautologies. The apparent incompatibility between Popper's writings on falsificationism as applied in natural science versus his plea for situational logic for social science induces D.W. Hands to distinguish a Popper$_n$ and a Popper$_s$, respectively (Hands 1985: 90).

K. Klappholz and J. Agassi (1959) identify the incompatibility as an ostensible one. It stems from presenting testable hypotheses versus tautologies as an exhaustive dichotomy, they argue. However, not all untestable hypotheses are tautologies. For example, the law of demand is not a tautology. At the same time, it invites the theorist to expose the 'hypothesis to risk of falsification' (ibid.: 65). Klappholz and Agassi phrase it as 'being on the agenda for testing', that is, seeking for specification of the *ceteris paribus* conditions. It reflects their very 'generally applicable methodological rule: ... always ready to subject one's hypotheses to critical scrutiny' (ibid.: 60). Herein, they explicitly follow Popper's logic of scientific discovery. Bruce Caldwell (1991: 22) denotes it as '*critical rationalism*', denying that 'there is a foolproof method for the discovery of scientific theories'. It regards the critical attitude that requires both the falsification criterion and the theoretical search for hypotheses. Here reemerges

Kaufmann's methodological point of view discussed earlier, that is, '*critical rationalism*, or *critical empiricism*' (Kaufmann 1944: 12;). Additionally, however, Kaufmann emphasizes the logical sequence: the (theoretical) analysis of meaning precedes the (empirical) causal explanations of facts. The empirical test observes the demarcation line of science. It is the analysis of meaning in which the theorist may profile his proceeding critical attitude. Therefore, it is no sign of economists' narrowmindedness but contrariwise of their critical rationalism that they, since Adam Smith, are engaged in finding *ad hoc ceteris paribus* clauses that may warrant 'the normal working of the economic system'. It is the fruit of the analysis of meaning.

Finally, I discuss two instances that do not observe the strict distinction between analysis of meaning versus causal explanation of fact or the required sequence of them. First, the caveat of *ceteris paribus* may easily settle the idea that an analytical proposition, for example, concerning rational (market) action, actually regards a synthetic proposition. This idea may find further support in 'pseudo-philosophical' ultimate grounds for rational action which would be derivable from the very nature of man (ibid.: 216–217). Illustrative in this respect is von Mises's (1949) edifice of *a priori* synthetic propositions regarding rational action. In his theory, von Mises falls prey to a confounding analysis of meaning with matters of fact. The human motive that plays its role in explaining economic phenomena results from the analysis of meaning, that is, an item in the deductive logic of the scheme of interpretation, and is not to be conceived as indubitable a matter of fact.

Second, Mises's methodological sin is the very opposite of a more common practice of a confounding analysis of meaning with matters of fact, that is, formulating propositions based on statistics. The reason for passing over the analysis of meaning is understandable. Actually, the analysis of meaning and its search for *ceteris paribus* clauses of the null hypothesis hold a kind of intermediate position between deductive logic and empirical procedure. For instance, the perfect foresight of the ideal type enables the theorist, who applies his marginal analysis, to calculate the profit-maximizing output of the ideal-type producer considering the demand and cost function of the good produced. Thus far, it is an analytical procedure. However, a lack of foresight and a lack of insight into the functions at hand are actually the real problems faced by the economic actor. Clearly, the latter might serve as more than a mere indication that the economists' abstraction results in an unrealistic, useless project. It elicits strong reactions, for example, of institutionalist schools preferring 'knowledge in terms of opaque matter-of-fact' above 'knowledge in terms of some sort of a spiritual life imputed to the facts' (Veblen 1906: 605).[10] This critique disregards the logical sequence of analysis of meaning and causal explanation of facts. In the same manner, institutional economists such as North and Williamson confound the logical sequence when they drop the rationality postulate. Basically, the substituting bounded rationality is a reference to empirical reality and an instance of misplaced concreteness. It omits acknowledging the distinction between analytic and synthetic propositions.

The instance of a monopolist's market model might show the clarity of Kaufmann's distinction. In the model, the analytic component concerns the profit-optimizing price–output combination that is deduced from the presupposed information of the model, such as a demand function and a cost function. It arranges the script of a monopolist's situational logic. Subsequently, the functions concerned may be substantiated, replacing perfect knowledge. In this role, they figure as synthetic propositions whereby empirical status depends on their statistical reliability. In this respect, Kaufmann (1944: 220) distinguishes between '"logical rationality"' and '"empirical rationality"'. It is a theorist's engagement in the analytically determined variables of the situational logic that renders logical rationality. Subsequently, a detailed examination of these variables concerning preferences, production technique, and institutional configurations lends empirical significance to the situational logic, that is, empirical rationality. A final example in this respect concerns the empirical value of the marginal utility principle. This principle founds the theoretical law of consumer's rational behavior. The empirical supplement of the latter is to find to what extent the analytic construct may reveal information on economic reality. An important issue regards the measurability of marginal utility as an intensive (qualitative) variable in an extensive (quantitative) magnitude. A solution is an indirect measurement, for example, via coherence between demand and implicitly presupposed marginal utility. It enables the statistician to construct curves realizing that 'not only empirical data (which cannot do more than yield a *finite* number of points), but also general assumptions as to the simplicity of the curves' are utilized (Kaufmann 1933: 400).

In the latter discussion reemerges the compromise of '*critical rationalism* or *critical empiricism*'. The (rational) analysis of meaning cannot result in *a priori* synthetic propositions. However, the (empirical) explanation of facts cannot do without theoretical hypotheses. A sound scientific practice requires a permanent trade-off between reason and sensory perception. This sounds even more than patently obvious. Therefore, it is important to realize that the obviousness of this maxim is the direct fruit of philosophical realism concerning the ontological and epistemological assumptions about the structure of the world and the nature of knowledge, respectively. Basic in realism is the conception of the existence of the world as independent of human perception. At the same time, this postulate presupposes human beings who possess pre-reflexivity and autonomous beings who command paradigms. As shown earlier, this philosophy dovetails with the anthropocentric view that is selected. It is my departing point in discussing institutional approaches within economics: the existence of an intelligibly structured economic reality.

1.11 Recap

A difference in theoretical approach is prevalent within NIE. Its founding father, Ronald Coase, accords with the economic tradition of the logic of choice. Coase's transaction-cost concept does not obstruct this logic. However, Oliver

Williamson actually equates the recognition of positive transaction cost with failing rationality, rendering the logic that is meant to be unattainable and theoretically useless. Rather 'human factors' concern the variables that would explain economic behavior with more success, Williamson argues. At first glance, it regards a contrast between an inside versus an outside purview. The inside purview departs from a human actor who is armed with rationality. The outside version discovers the peculiarities of the actor and begins analyzing its economic consequences; for example, what is the effect of bounded rationality? Behind this inside–outside scheme, the philosophical nominalism–realism controversy is hidden. It is the nominalist position that allows the scientist to refuse to search behind the observable phenomena. Its fruit is empiricism. In contrast, the realist postulates to be aware of the universally structured nature of reality that prods him to find out the meaning of the phenomena and to discover the universals that carry this reality. Therefore, in a nominalist view, concepts *have* meaning; names are attached. In realism, concepts *are* meaning and constitute reality.

New institutional economists must take sides in this contrast. First, it is rather plausible to depart from the human being himself in investigating the reality of which this being is the center. It is inherently a form of realism to opt into economics for an anthropocentric perspective that takes account of conscious human beings who act intentionally. Second, this inside perspective urges the social scientist to view behind the observably physical phenomena that the actor performs, as the phenomena refer to concepts that are meaning, that is, universals. The concept of institution belongs to this category. Institutions are meaning; that is, they structure our social reality. The nominalist disregards the founding nature of meaning and, therefore, has no concern for the meaning nature of institutions.

Therefore, realism is the proper philosophical position for thinking about NIE. It entails an analytic approach in search of the essences of the economic reality, rendering it a nomological science. The latter originates from the analysis of meaning that determines the subject matter of a science in terms of theoretical statements. The meaning analysis requires an intellectual tour in order to avoid the fallacy of misplaced concreteness. The concepts that are aspired require delving into human consciousness in order to determine the origin of concepts and knowledge. In this aspect, it is phenomenology that reflects on consciousness and offers insight into meaning as a pivotal concept.

The empirical counterpart of this analysis is the causal explanation of facts. It regards the procedure of whether a theoretical statement changes the corpus of a discipline. Significant in this respect is to distinguish between theoretical laws versus empirical laws. It is the theoretical law that has a prominent role in economics and in social science in general. Whenever a theoretical law does not correspond to the empirical observations, its built-in *ceteris paribus* clauses offer opportunities to reformulate the theoretical statement. In contrast, the empirical law is not a device that offers social scientists much progress or justified amendment. Empirical statements are beset by a number of variables that might thwart the empirical test decision. Economics' empirical strength may be found in an unremitting endeavor to reformulate its theoretical statements if facts suggest they do not correspond with them. The important methodological virtue to observe the logical order of the counterparts remains: first, an analysis of meaning and, then, a causal explanation of the facts.

So, *pièce de résistance* in NIE is the analysis meaning as a procedure to create theoretical statements. It is the search for essences and the idealizations of the phenomena at hand. A scheme of interpretation is also required, *ein Deutungsschema*, such as knowledge of the rules of a game that enables the observer to interpret the actions of the players. Such a scheme originates concepts that are meaning, that is, ideal types, homunculi gifted with a consciousness although restricted 'so as to contain nothing but elements relevant to the performing of the course-of-action patterns observed' (Schutz 1954: 271). The ideal type originates from Weber's interpretive sociology, indeed. However, Schutz gives it a phenomenological sophistication that makes it suitable for the realist analysis of meaning.

Karl Popper (1945a, vol. II: 97) interprets the logic of the situation 'as *the* method of economic analysis'. It emphasizes the anthropocentric nature of economics, referring directly to the Hayekian '"man on the spot"' (Hayek 1945: 524). In this aspect, Popper's interpretation suggests a natural switchover from the man on the spot's logic to the 'pure logic of choice' performed by the homunculus. At the same time, it is particularly this changeover that requires the intellectual tour that is alluded to, otherwise, we would fall prey to the fallacy of misplaced concreteness. As announced, it is the phenomenological interpretation of the meaning analysis that offers insight into the origin of conceptual meanings and renders them suitable to theoretical laws. This phenomenological account aims to sophisticate Popper's 'logic of the situation as *the* economic method', making it suitable for a critical appraisal of NIE. This is elaborated in the next chapter. This and the next chapter together constitute the preparation for critically appraising the institutionally structured situational logic of conscious human beings, of the man on the spot.

Notes

1 Coase and Williamson were driving forces behind the foundation of the International Society for New Institutional Economics in 1997.
2 The quote is fairly ambiguous. Its rather ironic context removes the ambiguity. On the page preceding the quote, Coase writes:

> It may be, therefore, that ultimately the work of sociobiologists (and their critics) will enable us to construct of a picture of human nature in such detail that we can derive the set of preferences with which economists start. ... *In the meantime*, however, whatever makes men choose as they do, we must be content with the knowledge for groups of human beings, in almost all circumstances, a higher (relative) price for anything will lead to a reduction in the amount demanded.
>
> (1988: 4; emphasis added)

It is rather revealing that Oliver Williamson leaves out this context in the very same quote. On the contrary, Williamson replaces Coase's 'It may be, therefore,' for 'Instead he (Coase) observes that "ultimately the work of sociobiologists ... economists start"' (Coase, quoted in Williamson 1989: 230). Williamson's rephrasing is expedient in two respects. First, it renders Coase an ally in Williamson's search for 'aspects of human nature' that replaces 'the neoclassical conception of economic man' (ibid.). Second, the quote rephrased compares Williamson favorably to Coase. Coase's economic man stands out in stark contrast to Williamson's 'comprehensive model [that] include cognitive assumptions (such as bounded rationality) and self-interest seeking assumptions (such as opportunism).' (ibid.).

3 As a preliminary, John Searle's definition of the concept may be beneficial. 'An institution is any system of constitutive rules of the form *X counts as Y in C*. Once an institution becomes established, it then provides a structure within which one can create institutional facts' (Searle 2005: 10).

4 The mechanical principles render the scientist complete knowledge of the universe in terms of masses, positions, and velocities of all the particles at a certain point in time. Charles S. Peirce refers to it as 'necessitarianism', 'metaphysics inspired by classical mechanics' (Wennerberg 1962: 42). It puts physics' fame of its matter-of-fact nature into perspective. It is metaphysical as it omits what J.W.N. Watkins calls, a 'rock-bottom explanation' of such large-scale phenomena in terms of properties and relations of its constituent particles. Mechanism as a regulative principle merely renders an 'unfinished or half-way explanation' (Watkins 1957: 105).

This perspective may be supplemented with J.W.N. Watkins's perspective on the nature of physical laws. Watkins shows the specific relationship between subject matter and method in physics. The basic laws in physics originate from 'mechanism as a regulative principle according to which the ultimate constituents of the physical world are impenetrable particles which obey simple mechanical laws'. (Watkins 1957: 105). It is a metaphysical theory. In this

> [t]he existence of these particles cannot be explained -at any rate by science. On the other hand, every complex physical thing or event is the result of a particular configuration of particles and can be explained in terms of the laws governing their behavior in conjunction with a description of their relative positions, masses, momenta, etc., etc. There may be what might be described as unfinished or half-way explanations of large-scale phenomena (say pressure inside a gas-container) in terms of other large-scale factors (the volume and temperature of the gas); but we shall not have arrived at rock-bottom explanations of such large-scale phenomena until we have deduced their behaviour from statements about the properties and relations of particles.
>
> (ibid.)

Watkins discusses this methodology of physics to advocate an analogous principle in social science. The analogy is that methodological individualism enables the social scientist, in particular the economist, to achieve a rock-bottom explanation, replacing halfway explanations of large-scale phenomena, for example, of inflation and unemployment (ibid.: 106).

5 See note 3.

6 Carl Menger would certainly leave out the auxiliary verb *might*.

7 Douglas W. Hands enumerates a number of difficulties an economist faces applying Popperian falsification (Hands 1985: 88).

8 An instance of such an unfulfilled prediction, well known in international-trade theory, entails Wassily Leontief's statistical data of the United States' foreign trade that subverted the Heckscher-Ohlin account. The account reads that particular

goods need for economical production comparatively large amounts of specific factors. Therefore, differing factor endowments, by having influenced the pre-trade commodity price relationships, will determine the composition of exports and imports. However, Leontief's United States' figures show the opposite of what the Heckscher-Ohlin account predicts, inciting the formulation of alternative theories.

9 Coase:

> But a theory is not like an airline or a bus timetable. We are not interested simply in the accuracy of its predictions. A theory also serves as a base for thinking. It helps us to *understand* what is going on by enabling us to organise our thoughts. Faced with a choice between a theory which predicts well but gives us little insight into how the system works and one which gives us this insight but predicts badly, I would choose the latter.
>
> (1994: 16–17; emphasis added)

10 In this context, Thorstein Veblen contrasts pragmatic knowledge versus scientific knowledge. The former serves 'what had best be done', and the latter reflects 'what takes place' (Veblen 1906: 599). The following quote makes clear that Veblen would not be interested in such a thing as a scheme of interpretation, as discussed above. In Veblen's view, it is all matter-of-fact in which the scientist is engaged. Contrasting savage culture with science, Veblen shows his concept of science. He indicates:

> In this respect, it (the savage culture) falls in the same class with the civilized man's science; but it seeks knowledge not in terms of opaque matter-of-fact, but in terms of some sort of a spiritual life imputed to the facts. It is romantic and Hegelian rather than realistic and Darwinian. The logical necessities of its scheme of thought are necessities of spiritual consistency rather than of quantitative equivalence.
>
> (ibid.: 605)

In a corresponding manner, Veblen expresses his disdain for scholastic researchers engaged in pragmatic knowledge, 'aimed directly at rules of expedient conduct' (ibid.: 594). For that matter, he correctly presupposes 'a scheme of thought' or interpretation to deal with pragmatic knowledge.

References

Armstrong, D.M., 1983, *What Is a Law of Nature?*, Cambridge: Cambridge University Press.

Caldwell, B.J., 1991, Clarifying Popper, *Journal of Economic Literature, Vol. 29, No. 1*, 1–33.

Coase, R.H., 1937, The Nature of the Firm, *Economica, New Series, Vol. 4, No. 16*, 386–405.

Coase, R.H., 1960, The Problem of Social Cost, *The Journal of Law and Economics, Vol. 3*, 1–44.

Coase, R.H., 1988, *The Firm, the Market, and the Law*, Chicago, IL: The University of Chicago Press.

Colander, D., 2000, New Millennium Economics: How Did It Get This Way, and What Way Is It?, *The Journal of Economic Perspectives, Vol. 14, No. 1*, 121–132.

Croce, B, 1913, *Philosophy of the Practical; Economic and Ethic*, translated from the Italian by D. Ainslie, London: Macmillan.

Davis, J.B., 2007, The Turn in Economics and the Turn in Economic Methodology, *The Journal of Economic Methodology, Vol. 14, No. 3*, 275–290.

Einav, L., J.D. Levin, 2013, *The Data Revolution and Economic Analysis, Working Paper 19035*, Cambridge, MA: National Bureau of Economic Research, http://www.nber. org/papers/w19035/, accessed 20/01/2018.

Farber, M. 1962, (2009), *The Foundation of Phenomenology*, New Brunswick: Aldine Transaction.

Farmer, J.D., 2013, Hypotheses Non Fingo: Problems with the Scientific Method in Economics, *The Journal of Economic Methodology, Vol. 20, No. 4*, 377–385.

Furubotn, E.G., R. Richter, eds., 1991, *The New Institutional Economics*, Collage Station: Texas A&M University Press.

Gunning, J.P., 1986, The Methodology of Austrian Economics and Its Relevance to Institutionalism, *The American Journal of Economics and Sociology, Vol. 45, No. 1*, 79–91.

Hands, D.W., 1985, Karl Popper and Economic Methodology: A New Look, *Economics and Philosophy, Vol. 1, No. 01*, 83–99.

Hausman, D.M., ed., 1994, [1995], *The Philosophy of Economics*, 2nd ed., Cambridge: Cambridge University Press.

Hayek, F.A., 1945, The Use of Knowledge in Society, *The American Economic Review, Vol. 35, No. 4*, 519–530.

Hayek, F.A., 1952, [1979], *The Counterrevolution of Science*, Indianapolis, IN: Liberty Press.

Kauder, E., 1965, *A History of Marginal Utility Theory*, Princeton, NJ: Princeton University Press.

Kaufmann, F., 1933, On the Subject-Matter and Method of Economics Science, *Economica, No. 42*, 381–401.

Kaufmann, F., 1934, The Concept of Law in Economic Science, *The Review of Economic Studies, Vol. 1, No. 2*, 102–109.

Kaufmann, F., 1941, Strata of Experience, *Philosophy and Phenomenological Research, Vol. 1, No. 3*, 313–324.

Kaufmann, F., 1944, *Methodology of the Social Sciences*, Atlantic Highlands, New Jersey: Humanities Press.

Klappholz, K., J. Agassi, 1959, Methodological Prescriptions in Economics, *Economica, New Series, Vol. 26, No. 101*, 60–74.

Lewin, K., 1931, *Der Übergang von der aristotelischen zur galileïschen Denkweise in Biologie und Psychologie*. Quelle: Kurt Lewin, 1981, Werkausgabe. Bd. 1: Wissenschaftstheorie I., S. 233–278, Hrsg. von Carl-Friedrich Graumann, Bern and Stuttgart: Huber/Klett-Cotta.

Marschak, J., 1943, Money Illusion and Demand Analysis, *The Review of Economics and Statistics, Vol. 25, No. 1*, 40–48.

Marshall, A., 1890, [1920], *Principles of Economics*, London: Macmillan & Co.

Menger, C., 1883, [2005], *Untersuchungen über die Methode der Socialwissenschaften und der Politischen Oekonomie insbesodere*, Leipzig: Verlag von Duncker & Humblot; [Elibron Classics series].

von Mises, L., 1949, [2012], *Human Action*, New Haven, CT: Yale University Press [Martino Publishing]

North, D., 1990, [2005], *Institutions, Institutional Change and Economic Performance*, Cambridge: Cambridge University Press.

Popper, K.R., 1945a, [1962], *The Open Society and Its Enemies*, Vol. I, II, London: Routledge and Kegan Paul.

Popper, K.R., 1945b, The Poverty of Historicism, III, *Economica, New Series, Vol. 12, No. 46*, 69–89.

Popper, K.R., 1959, [1995], *The Logic of Scientific Discovery*, London: Routledge.

Popper, K.R., 1967, The Rationality Principle. In: D. Miller, ed., 1985, *Popper Selections*, 357–365, Princeton, NJ: Princeton University Press.

Prendergast, Chr, 1986, Alfred Schutz and the Austrian School of Economics, *American Journal of Sociology, Vol. 92, No. 1*, 1–26.

Rosenberg, A., 1984, [1983], If Economics Is Not a Science, What Is It? In: D.M. Hausman, ed., 1994, [1994], *The Philosophy of Economics*, 2nd ed., 376–394, Cambridge: Cambridge University Press.

Santa Fe Institute, undated, Mission Statement, http://www.santafe.edu/about/mission-and-vision/, accessed 3/5/2016.

Searle, J.R., 1995, *The Construction of Social Reality*. London: Penguin Books.

Searle, J.R., 2005, What Is an Institution? *Journal of Institutional Economics, Vol. 1*, 1–22.

Schumpeter, J.A., 1954, [1981], *History of Economic Analysis*, London: George Allen & Unwin.

Schutz, A., 1953, Common-Sense and Scientific Interpretation of Human Action, *Philosophy and Phenomenological Research, Vol. 14, No. 1*, 1–38.

Schutz, A., 1954, Concept and Theory Formation in the Social Sciences, *The Journal of Philosophy, Vol. 51, No. 9*, 257–273.

Simmel, G., 1990, [1907], *The Philosophy of Money*, Second enlarged edition, edited by D. Frisby, London: Routledge.

Smith, A., 1776, [2005], *The Inquiry into the Nature and Causes of the Wealth of Nations*, London: W. Strahan and T. Cadell; The Electronic Classics Series, Penn State: Pennsylvania State University.

Smith, B., 1990, Aristotle, Menger, Mises: An Essay in the Metaphysics of Economics, *History of Political Economy, Annual Supplement, vol. 22*, 263–288.

Stonier, A.W., D.C. Hague, 1953, [1964], *A Textbook of Economic Theory*, 3rd ed., London: Longmans, Green and Co Ltd.

Swedberg, R., 1998, *Max Weber and the Idea of Economic Sociology*, Princeton, NJ: Princeton University Press.

Varian, H.R., 2014, Big Data: New Tricks for Econometrics, *The Journal of Economic Perspectives, Vol. 28, No. 2*, 3–27.

Veblen, Th.B, 1906, The Place of Science in Modern Civilization, *American Journal of Sociology, Vol. 11, No. 5*, 585–609.

Watkins, J.W.N., 1957, Historical Explanation in the Social Sciences, *The British Journal for the Philosophy of Science, Vol. 8, No. 30*, 104–117.

Wennerberg, H., 1962, *The Pragmatism of C.S. Peirce*, Uppsala: Almqvist & Wiksells Boktryckeri AB.

Whitehead, A.N., 1929, [1967], *The Aims of Education & Other Essays*, New York: The Free Press.

Williamson, O.E., 1975, *Markets and Hierarchies*, New York: The Free Press.

Williamson, O.E., 1989, Reviewed Work(s): The Firm, the Market, and the Law, by R. H. Coase, *California Law Review, Vol. 77, No. 1*, 223–231.

Williamson, O.E., 1991, The Economics of Governance: Framework and Implications. In: E.G. Furubotn, R. Richter, eds., 1991. *The New Institutional Economics*, 54–82, Collage Station: Texas A&M University Press.

Williamson, O.E., 1993, The Evolving Science of Organization, *Journal of Institutional and Theoretical Economics, Vol. 149, No. 1*, 36–63.

Williamson, O.E., 2000, The New Institutional Economics: Taking Stock, Looking Ahead, *Journal of Economic Literature, Vol. 38, No. 3*, 595–613.

2 Phenomenology and the analysis of meaning

2.1 Introduction

Choice is a central concept in economics. It is central in Lionel Robbins's (1932: 16) definition. It is not uncommon to equate economics with rational choice theory, and in a specific manner, economics concerns the 'Pure Logic of Choice' (Hayek 1937: 35). Vilfredo Pareto (1900: 191) formulates it concisely as follow: 'Choices are the stones with which one builds the economic edifice'. It enables Pareto as a scientist to be engaged in 'choices which fall on things the quantities of which are variable and susceptible of measurement' (ibid.: 187–188). This viewpoint occasions for a polemic between Pareto and Benedetto Croce, whereby Pareto perceives choice as an external, natural thing. Croce (1901: 197) contends this indicating that economic reality refers to a 'series of representations which we have in our consciousness, and into which we can insert nothing except the light of our mental analysis'.

The contrast concisely illustrates the significance of the subject of this chapter: phenomenological philosophy and the analysis of meaning in economics. Pareto departs from the concreteness of choice, perceived from without. Croce, by contrast, postulates (economic) choice as a matter of conscious human beings. The latter entails profound questions. What is human consciousness? How does it bring such a thing as choice into being? It is precisely phenomenology that is engaged in these types of issues. It results from the reflection on the human experience of consciousness as attention directed upon objects, 'whether real or imagined, material or ideal; and all such objects are "intended"' (Wagner 1970: 5). Phenomenology delves into the 'immanent process of experience', into the manner in which those objects of attention and intentionality, such as choices, are constructed and 'actually seen or remembered later in *typified* fashion' (ibid.; emphasis added). In this chapter, I discuss 'the phenomenology of the social world' and, in particular, of the economic world (Schutz 1932).[1] In this I rely on Alfred Schutz, who confronts Max Weber's ambition to develop a value-free sociology with Edmund Husserl's aim to formulate presuppositionless concepts, that is, concepts as essences.

DOI: 10.4324/9781315764221-2

In phenomenology, the methodological lines of the situational-logic purview converge as discussed in the preceding chapter. Phenomenology provides the philosophical underpinnings of the primary features of situational logic, that is, its anthropocentric perspective, its analytical-theoretical bias, and realism as its philosophical base.

Regarding the first, the phenomenological starting point is genuinely anthropocentric. The lifeworld (*Lebenswelt*) of conscious human beings is the 'foundational nexus' (Schutz 1940: 166). The primary phenomenological reference concerns our daily pursuit, our just-living along. Obviously, this accords with the inside purview that has been discussed and refers to our natural attitude that perceives the world as pregiven and unquestioned. In our habitual way of thinking, we avail ourselves of objective concepts to organize our life. Herein, we experience the concreteness of the world. It gives us footing and obviousness to continue.

This leads to the second methodological point, that is, the analytical-theoretical bias. Positivist scientists borrow the obviousness referred to in founding their empirical evidence of objectivity from the natural attitude. Therefore, every person 'who sees "blue" in a place 'p' at time 't' may admit to the sentence "Blue is at the locus p, t," into science' (Kaufmann 1940: 133). Phenomenology disputes this type of objectivity and the positivist's 'naïve sensualism' with its '"hard" (unanalyzable) data of sensation' (ibid.: 132). The presumed objectivity is beset by presuppositions. In fact, objectivity originates from man's conscious experiences that refer to a highly complex structure of intentionality and anticipating perceptions. Therefore, 'phenomenological reduction' is of issue, that is, analysis of our conscious experience, explicating its implicit presuppositions. The phenomenologist suspends objectivity, that is, applies an *epoché* of 'belief in the "outer world"' (Wagner 1970: 6). He directs his attention to 'the processes of human consciousness and their "intended objects"' as transcendental objects that belong to the "inner world" of the conscious individual. This attention to the inner world of the individual accords closely with Max Weber's aim to understand human conduct as subjectively meaningful. In this aspect, Alfred Schutz (1932: 7) elaborates on the phenomenological foundation of Weber's *Verstehen* methodology 'that is based on a series of tacit presuppositions'. It renders a 'sociological baseline' of understanding interpretatively and explaining causally social action in its course and effects. At issue is to grasp the subjective meaning of social and economic conduct in order to formulate theoretical propositions. In this respect, the theorist avails himself of constructs of social conduct, of *Idealtypen*. These ideal types constitute the analytical concepts that profile the theoretical nature of the situational-logic purview. Theory precedes concreteness. In Kaufmann's (1944) vocabulary, the analysis of meaning precedes the causal explanation of facts.

Third, inextricably bound up with the analytical-theoretical approach is philosophical realism. In phenomenology, realism manifests itself in the perspective that human consciousness bears an *a priori* concept of the essences and structure of the world. It opposes the nominalist position that the concepts that man uses merely concern a matter of convention. The *a priori* notions referred to are logically 'prior to the assertion made in any judgment of experience' (Kaufmann 1940: 134). They concern concepts that *are* meaning, corresponding to Kaufmann's (1944: 16) 'conceptual or propositional meaning as essential elements for the context of thought' as discussed in the preceding chapter. This realist perspective is also central to Edmund Husserl's philosophy. In this aspect, Husserl distinguishes a deeper layer, that is, 'the "eidos" of the a priori forms of experience' (Wagner 1970: 6) that reflects Husserl's hope 'to come "face to face at last with the ultimate structure of consciousness"' (Husserl, quoted in ibid.). The latter strongly pervades with metaphysics. In any case, it is inconsistent with the nominalist proposition that every experience is the experience of a particular individual at a particular time, claiming that there are no *a priori* synthetic propositions. Apparently, the nominalist/ positivist assumes that the phenomenological procedure claims to produce those synthetic propositions *a priori*, irrefutable valid statements about the world. However, this misinterprets Husserl's concept of *a priori* in this context. Here, *a priori* refers rather to 'a set of presuppositions that "make experience possible"' (Kaufmann 1940: 135). Pivotal is that the presuppositions do not concern an arbitrary affair issued from conventions. Contrariwise, they must be revealed in a world that demonstrates being intelligible. In this aspect, they refer to '"necessary truth"', 'formulating the presuppositions contained in experience' (ibid.: 137). Schutz elucidates this as follows:

> But this is not the 'experience' of shallow empiricism. It is rather the immediate prepredicative encounter which we have with any direct object of intuition.
>
> (1932: 244)

The quote indicates the basic tenet of Schutz's phenomenology of the social world that ensues from the realist perspective.

These three integral methodological viewpoints substantiate phenomenology as an appropriate instrument for elaborating on the foundations of economics as situational logic. The phenomenological approach enables, in particular, specifying the analytical-theoretical bias of situational-logic economics.

The chapter is organized as follows: Section 2.2 discusses a number of preliminaries such as George Simmel's view on intersubjective engagement as featuring society. Simmel may be read as a precursor of Schutz's phenomenological approach to social phenomena. He emphasizes the subjective nature of our social reality. This poses a serious question to social scientists who aim at an objectively *wertfrei* scientific methodology. This question is the subject matter that occupies Max Weber in his interpretive sociology. Section 2.3 discusses Weber's basic sociological concepts. Central in his sociology is an actor's subjective meaning as the very cause of social action. At issue is how to grasp this pivotal, although subjective, cause. Weber fails in addressing it. Schutz concurs with Weber in identifying the very theme of an objective social science; however, he disagrees with Weber's elaboration. Schutz contends that interpretive social science, that is, the *Verstehen* methodology, requires a phenomenological sophistication. To grasp subjective meaning, we must study its origin: human consciousness. Section 2.4 discusses the social science significance of phenomenology by presenting two concepts, that is, time and intersubjectivity, concepts that feature consciousness. It preludes Section 2.5, which employs the phenomenological perspective to arrive at a system of objective knowledge concerning subjective meaning, that is, objectivity in social science. We daily become reconciled with our fellow men due to a commonsense objectivity. We avail ourselves of constructs that express our intersubjectivity. This is the departing point in reformulating subjective meaning in an objective system of knowledge. The primary theme in Section 2.5 is demonstrating the transformation of our daily constructs into scientific constructs that are stripped of the ambiguities and inconsistencies that are of no concern in daily life. Actually, it regards the phenomenological reformulation of Weber's ideal type, that is, the design of constructs of constructs as a route to a theoretical social science. Section 2.5 furthermore discusses the aspects of explanation, showing the significance of the realist position. Realism postulates the rationality of reality. Accordingly, explanation is perceived as a search for the essences that feature this rational world. The section demonstrates that the theoretical innovation of new institutional economics can be reformulated in the phenomenological approach. Section 2.6 provides concluding remarks.

2.2 Consciousness, intersubjectivity, and meaning

All phenomenological analyses of social reality begin with the lifeworld of the actor. This starting point accords with the methodological individualism that economists are familiar with. Eventually, social phenomena have their origin in the acts of individuals. In this context, the postulate by no means refers to an atomistic account à la Thomas Hobbes or Francis Bacon, who reduce sociology to a product of a scanty psychology. On the contrary, phenomenology is particularly engaged in social forms; it is true and recognized as products of modes of individual behavior. The phenomenological analysis of an individual's consciousness overcomes the classic dichotomy of individual versus society. In this respect, I refer to George Simmel's (1910) instructive analysis *How Is Society Possible?* It may be read as a finger exercise of Schutz's phenomenological analysis two decades later. Simmel's basic postulate is that we experience our *ego* as something independent of any representation, therefore, we believe that the *thou* is something that is 'just as really for itself (*genau so für sich ist*) as our own existence' (ibid.: 375). Therefore, Simmel continues:

within our own consciousness we distinguish very precisely between the fundamentality of the *ego* (the presupposition of all representation, which has no part in the never wholly suppressible problematics of its contents) and these contents themselves, which as an aggregate, with their coming and going, their dubitability and their fallibility, always present themselves as mere products of that absolute and final energy and existence of our psychic being.[2]

(ibid.: 376)

In the same manner, we recognize these conditions of independence in the soul of our fellow man. 'We are sure that the case stands the same way with the other soul and its contents'. Therefore, *a priori* conditions reside within individuals by which they combine themselves 'into the synthesis "society"' (ibid.). This analysis neutralizes the theoretical individual–society dichotomy. Simmel:

The book searches out the procedures, occurring in the last analysis in individuals, which condition the existence of the individuals as society.

(ibid.)

The consciousness of the *ego* and the *thou* as *a priori* conditions preclude the consideration of society from a nominalist perspective and as nothing but a (Kantian) representation. The nominalist perspective is a 'centerless perspective', as Thomas Nagel more recently phrased it. In a centerless perspective, the world contains all the people as contingent beings with their physical and mental features. It is 'a view from nowhere' (Nagel 1986). At the same time, this view from nowhere is unsuited for a perception of something that refers to the locus of my consciousness, my perspective of the world, and my acting in it. This centerless view cannot address the question, '"Which of these persons am I?"' because, by definition, it omits first-person facts (ibid.: 56). Against a centerless viewpoint, Simmel's analysis presents the universal essence of 'the individuals as society'.

Simmel's analysis reads as a prefiguration of Schutz's phenomenological analysis of the social reality. Like Simmel, Schutz postulates intersubjectivity as the foundation of the analysis of consciousness. This postulate enables him to elaborate on typifications 'which unite the individual consciousnesses' (Wagner 1970: 7). A '"common consciousness"' features a society of persons. A person's consciousness of other selves, Helmut Wagner continues by quoting Husserl,

offers us more than a reduplication of what we find in our self-consciousness, for it establishes the difference between 'own' and 'other' which we experience, and presents us with the characteristics of the 'social life'.

(Husserl, quoted in ibid.)

In this reflection on 'social life', Husserl substantiates it as the essence of intersubjectivity. It corresponds to the very analytical way in which Simmel arrives at society in terms of consciousness and intersubjectivity. In this perspective, the *Lebenswelt* renders a social world in which a human *ego* is aware of a t*hou* as an *alter ego* in whom he may be interested, with whom he, for instance, intends to deal with; concisely, a world that is structured meaningfully. Hence, subjectivity sways the lifeworld that the social scientist studies.

This perspective questions the unity of the sciences as the issue the scientist then faces, is this: How do I preserve my scientific objectivity? It is precisely this question that occupied Max Weber as it did contemporaries such as Wilhelm Dilthey and Heinrich Rickert during the *fin de siècle* of the 19th century. It induces Weber to develop his *Verstehen* methodology, a presumedly *wertfrei* device to attain objectivity. Weber aims at objectivity in social science, fully aware of the subjective nature of the domain that he studies. Social science remains a matter of thought that requires clear concepts to formulate distinctive propositions. The ideal type is such a thought concept.

Schutz states, in this context, that the very subjective nature of our social reality requires that the scientist determines a method that satisfies his standards of scientific objectivity. In this, Schutz concurs with Weber and recognizes his ideal type as a promising concept. However, their paths diverge in the elaboration of this concept. The qualifying difference concerns the role of intersubjectivity in understanding the concept of meaning as central to the typological approach. Weber (1947: 94) omits to deal explicitly with intersubjectivity and relies, for instance, on direct observation for understanding an actor's subjective meaning. Against this, Schutz (1932: 32) postulates meaning 'constituted as an intersubjective phenomenon' referring to *one* external, public world that 'is equally given to all of us'. The intersubjectivity postulate guides the transition from Weber's *Verstehen* methodology to a phenomenologically realist perspective that opens the route to

> law-constructing (or monothetic) social sciences, [which] are able to provide us with universally valid knowledge prior to all experience.
>
> (ibid.: 242)

Concerning the latter, Christopher Prendergast (1986: 2) remarks that 'to us, post-Kuhnians today it seems quaintly old-fashioned to speak of [the] basic concepts'. Be that as it may, it directly accords with Kaufmann's strict distinction between the analysis of meaning versus the causal explanation of facts as discussed in preceding chapter. The basic concepts constitute the building blocks of the theoretical laws based on the analysis of meaning. Clearly, in his phenomenological sophistication of Weber's ideal type, Schutz has a special ability for determining the underpinning that his analysis offers to theoretical economics, particularly to its Austrian version of marginal analysis. In the next section, I discuss a number of Weber's basic concepts of interpretive sociology that substantiate his ideal-type concept.

2.3 Weber's fundamental concepts of sociology

The most radically new element in Weber's methodology, Schutz (1932: 6) underlines, is that it is 'the action of the individual and its intended meaning alone [that] are subject to interpretive understanding'. Schutz:

> Never before had the project of reducing the 'world of objective mind' to the behavior of individuals been so radically carried out as it was in Max Weber's initial statement of the goal of interpretive sociology.
>
> (ibid.)

In interpretive sociology, it is only understanding an individual actor's subjective meaning that renders a causal explanation of social action, 'action in the sense of a subjectively understandable orientation of behaviour' (Weber 1947: 101). The object of cognition regards the subjective meaning-complex of action of '*individual* human beings', expressively not of individuals as, for example, 'a collection of cells, as a complex of bio-chemical reactions', rendering uniformities that, for that matter, may also yield valuable knowledge of causal relationships (ibid.). At issue is how to understand an actor's subjective meaning. Weber perceives two opportunities.

'Understanding may be of two kinds; the first is the direct observational understanding of the subjective meaning of a given act as such, including verbal utterances' (ibid.: 94). We understand directly the meaning of the calculation 2 × 2 = 4 when we hear it. We also understand the subjective meaning of an outbreak of anger in the physical manifestations of 'facial expression, exclamations or irrational movements'. And so, in direct observation we understand somebody who 'aims a gun at an animal. This is *rational* observational understanding of action' (ibid.: 95; emphasis added).

The second is explanatory understanding; its synonym is motivational understanding. Weber states:

> Thus we understand in terms of *motive* the meaning an actor attaches to the proposition twice two equals four, ... in that we understand what makes him do this at precisely this moment and in these circumstances.
>
> (ibid.: 95)

Therefore, explanatory understanding requires additional information about the circumstances of an act, that is, 'the context of meaning'. For instance, we understand the aiming of a gun if we know the person who is aiming it is hunting a deer for food. Injured pride also allows us to understand the motivation for an outbreak of anger. In this respect, Weber distinguishes these examples as rational motives versus irrational, affectually determined motives, respectively.

Weber's editors, A.M. Henderson and Talcott Parsons, add in a footnote that the context of meaning concerns 'a *Sinnzusammenhang*', referring to a coherent plurality of elements on the level of meaning, for example, 'the appropriateness of means to an end' (ibid., n. 13). It places an act in an understandable sequence of motivation, explaining the actual course of action. Apparently, in contrast to observational understanding, an explanatory understanding of subjective meaning requires a grasp of the context of meaning. The context renders the subjective meaning the 'intended meaning', *'gemeinter Sinn'*. Actually, the concept of intended meaning is a methodological device, a construct providing a logical framework within which observations can be made that meet the standards of scientific objectivity. In this aspect, it is irrelevant whether or not 'to the ordinary person such an intended meaning "really exists"', the editors explicate (ibid.: 96, n. 15). It alludes to Weber's ideal-type concept. In this respect, Weber distinguishes three contexts of meaning: (a) in a historical approach, an actually intended meaning for a concrete individual; (b) in cases of sociological mass phenomena, an average of the actually intended meaning; and (c) 'the meaning appropriate to a scientifically formulated pure type of a common phenomenon' (ibid.: 96). It is the latter category that enables the social scientist to arrive at an objective explanation of subjectively meaningful social action, *nota bene*, by means of the ideal type.

It is plausible that Weber considers the '"laws" of pure economics' as examples of category (c), the ideal type (ibid.). Pure economics of rational choice offers *Evidenz*, that is, 'the verifiable accuracy of insight and comprehension' (ibid.: 90). Rationality, be it logical, mathematical, or means–end rationality, constitutes the basis for the certainty in understanding. We find 'a lower degree of certainty' when we detect the context of meaning, for example, to understand our errors, 'by sympathetic self-analysis' (ibid.: 91).

Formally, Weber further qualifies the pure-type category (c) corresponding to four 'modes of orientation'. It results in four types of action: (1) *zweckrational*, (2) *wertrational*, (3) affectional, and (4) traditional (ibid.: 115). Actually, however, Weber is predominantly engaged in *zweckrational* contexts of meaning, offering the scientifically desirable *Evidenz*. Therefore,

> it is convenient to treat all irrational, affectually determined elements of behavior as factors of deviation from a conceptually pure type of rational action.
>
> (ibid.: 92)

At the same time, Weber comments that the promising *Evidenz* of a rational action context of meaning, for example, the maximization of economic advantage, is usually 'only an approximation to the ideal type' (ibid.: 96). Therefore, Weber infers that an adequate interpretation of the context of meaning such as a purely rational type cannot guarantee a causally adequate and valid interpretation. In Weber's opinion, ideal-type modeling is, on the level of causal adequacy, nothing but formulating 'peculiarly plausible hypotheses' (ibid.). In contrast to the clarity that a rational context of meaning suggests, the human reality of meaning and motives is rather unruly. Regarding this, Weber elaborates somewhat. He argues, for instance, that allegedly conscious motives may well conceal other motives and repressions that, in fact, form the driving force behind an action. Moreover, actors are often subject to conflicting motives and impulses (ibid.: 97).

A produced component of an ideal type as a hypothesis is verification. This amounts to verification of subjective interpretation by comparison with the concrete course of action. It is indispensable but difficult to achieve, Weber notes. He considers verification of motives as feasible merely 'in the few very special cases susceptible of psychological verification' (ibid.). The accuracy will be exceedingly various even in the case of statistically unambiguously interpreted mass phenomena, he continues. As an alternative, he points to the 'dangerous and uncertain procedure of the "imaginary experiment"' which consists in abstraction 'and working out the course of action, which would then probably ensue' (ibid.). Interesting is Weber's discussion of 'the *generalization* called Gresham's Law' as an example of such a 'dangerous procedure' (ibid.: 98; emphasis added). On one hand, Weber regards Gresham's Law as a rationally clear interpretation of human action that follows 'a purely rational course'. On the other, he writes that its statistical evidence, that is, 'the facts of experience were known *before* the generalization, which was formulated afterwards' (ibid.; emphasis added).

Thus far, Weber's interpretive-sociology concepts contain a number of ambiguities. For instance, it is vague in which respect the '"imaginary experiment"' of abstraction would be a 'dangerous and uncertain procedure'. It is particularly unclear in which respect this procedure differs from formulating the operational concept of 'intended meaning' and providing the social scientist 'a logical framework within which scientifically important observations can be made' (ibid.: 96, n. 15). A more general point is revealed in Weber's comment on Gresham's Law. Characterized as an afterward-formulated generalization, Gresham's Law apparently seems to be the fruit of induction. At the same time, it is presented as a clearly rational interpretation of human action and a result of a purely rational course of action, that is, of an adequate context on the level of meaning. This contrast manifests that Weber does not observe the logical sequence as identified by Felix Kaufmann as discussed in Chapter 1: the analysis of meaning precedes the causal explanation of facts. Notwithstanding his own ideal-type construct, Weber disregards the elaboration of purely theoretical concepts that precedes the causal explanation. As demonstrated, it is accordingly this logical order that preserves the theoretical strength of science and particularly of economics. Schutz's following comment on Weber may be read as an encouragement to a more profound analysis of meaning. Schutz:

> In essence, therefore, observational or direct understanding is simply the understanding we exercise in daily life in our direct relations with other people. Precisely for that reason, however, the inference from overt behavior to the intended meaning lying behind it is anything but a cut-and-dried matter.
>
> (1932: 30)

In his concept of direct understanding, Weber relies on concepts that have meaning in our daily life, that is, language. In this, he omits recognizing the fundamental significance of intersubjectivity in the constitution of our social reality. It originates an element of nominalism in Weber's *Verstehen* methodology. In particular, this nominalist bent provokes the phenomenological critique, which is discussed in the next section. At stake is the theoretical foundation of science and of economics.

2.4 Phenomenological sophistication of *Verstehen*

The methodological individualism that Weber adheres to determines the concept of subjective meaning as being central to a causal explanation of social action. In this, phenomenologist Schutz concurs with Weber. However, Schutz dismisses the straightforward manner in which Weber thinks to grasp this subjective meaning. In his approach, Weber falls prey to what Schutz (1953: 1) calls, in a reference to Alfred Whitehead, the 'fallacy of misplaced concreteness'. For instance, Schutz contends that Weber's conceptual pair of observational and motivational understanding labors under the metaphor that the actor *attaches* meaning to a behavior. Weber states:

> In 'action' is included all human behavior when and in so far as the acting individual attaches a subjective meaning to it.
>
> (1947: 88)

In the same manner, action becomes social action if the actor *attaches* a subjective meaning to it that takes account of others' behavior 'and is thereby oriented in its course' (ibid.). The metaphorical perspective presents meaning as an item to be separated from one's own or from another's behavior which, accordingly, is another discrete item. Therefore, an individual's behavior of taking the seven o'clock bus should be perceived as an item that may reflect meaning. As discussed, Weber adds a coherent 'context of meaning' as a requirement for understanding (ibid.: 95). Nevertheless, his 'item-approach' encounters serious conceptual problems. For instance, suppose that the context of meaning would be a commuter taking the bus at that time for many years. It is fairly certain that the individual does it mechanically. Apparently, the bus ride must be placed in a course of action as a context of meaning, for example, from waking up at six in the morning, eating breakfast, taking the bus, getting to the office in time, and so on. How do we value these different actions and arrive at an interpretive understanding of them, let alone arrive at a causal explanation in terms of their course and effects of social actions that take 'account of the behavior of others'? (ibid.: 88). The commuter example indicates that time as a sequential experience complicates being able to grasp a subjective meaning.

It is the concreteness of behavior, meaning, and action as distinguishable items that Weber must pay for in his search for subjective meaning. The concepts originate from man's inner consciousness which does not immediately warrant their tractability. They originate from thought. Therefore, at issue is 'The Organisation of Thought' (Whitehead 1929: 103). This organization of thought amounts to an anatomy of human consciousness. As previously alluded, two concepts are to be explicitly addressed: time and intersubjectivity, as Schutz's (1932: 12) embarkment on 'the laborious philosophical journey' makes clear. I discuss them respectively in two subsections. As Maurice Natanson (1968: 218) argues, 'Philosophy is inescapable for the social scientist who seeks clarity and rigor in his work'.

2.4.1 Time

Consciousness is an inner stream of duration, *durée*, a qualitative phenomenon that cannot be fixed or captured. Therefore, consciousness is an immediate datum. Schutz indicates:

> It is not: 'Feelings and thoughts exist' but, 'I think' and 'I feel.' Within each personal consciousness thought is sensibly continuous and changing, and as such, comparable to a river or a stream.
>
> (1970: 57)

The changing river of consciousness alludes to Henri Bergson's (1913), subtitled: 'Essay on the immediate data of consciousness'. Common sense teaches us, Bergson commences, 'that states of consciousness, sensations, feelings, passions, efforts, are capable of growth and diminution' (ibid.: 1). In this perspective, these states count as measurable items, in any case, well distinguishable. Bergson quotes John Stuart Mill as an example of this quantitative perception. Mill contends:

> I could have abstained from murder, if my aversion to the crime and my dread of its consequences had been weaker than the temptation which impelled me to commit it.
>
> (quoted in ibid.: 159)

However, this perception is obscure and untenable, Bergson argues. It disregards that our consciousness occurs in time as a qualitative phenomenon that cannot be represented in quantitative, that is, spatially homogeneous, magnitudes. States of consciousness, even successive, permeate one another. By nature, they lack extensiveness. Therefore, we do not have immediate access to these in-extensive sensations (ibid.: 94–95). To grasp them, they must be modeled. Bergson states:

> For their co-existence to give rise to space, there must be an act of the mind which takes them in all at the same time and sets them in juxtaposition.
>
> (ibid.: 94)

Space is an empty homogeneous medium that enables us to perceive under the form of extensive homogeneity what is given to the mind as qualitative hetero-geneity. We capture our conscious states by symbolically juxtaposing them in space much like we count sheep by setting them side by side in a homogeneous space. We constitute a type of multiplicity of states of consciousness in sym-bolic representations, coexisting beside the multiplicity of material objects that are spatial by nature (ibid.: 87). Language is the paragon of the symbolically spatial multiplicity. In language,

> speech dominates over thought, as external objects, which are common
> to us all, [and] are more important to us than the subjective states through
> which each of us passes, we have everything to gain by objectifying
> these states.
>
> (ibid.: 70)

The qualitatively heterogeneous nature of human consciousness should make us aware of the, by definition, artificial nature of any reflection on it, be it in daily life or in social science. Apparently, the opposite is normal as 'we gain by objectifying these states'. In the natural attitude, we avail ourselves of com-monsense concepts, unaware of the principally in-extensive nature of our con-sciousness as the very origin of our social reality. Bergson's philosophy may be read as a caveat against the positivist fallacy of objectivity as an immediate reality that results from sensory perception. The reverse is true; objectivity is a sophisticated matter. This idea is the fundament of Schutz's elaboration on the concepts of subjective and objective meaning. Bergson's perspective elucidates that Weber's metaphorical perspective on meaning as a concept that can be attached to behavior disregards its delicate nature.

The ambition to grasp subjective meaning faces a stream of 'a continuous coming-to-be and passing-away of heterogeneous qualities' (Schutz 1932: 45). Schutz, in an outline, follows Husserl:

> If we simply live immersed in the flow of duration, we encounter only
> undifferentiated experiences that melt into one another in a flowing con-
> tinuum. ... Then, as Husserl says, I live *in* my Acts, whose living intention-
> ality carries me over from one Now to the next. But this Now should not
> be constructed as a punctiform instant, as a break in the stream of dura-
> tion, as a cutting-in-two of the latter. For in order to effect such an artifi-
> cial division within duration, I should have to get outside the flow itself. ...
> Each phase of experience melts into the next without any sharp bounda-
> ries as it is being lived through; but each phase is distinct in its thusness, or
> quality, from the next insofar as it is held in the gaze of attention.
>
> (ibid.: 51)

Hence, the quote distinguishes two types of intentionality: one within the stream of duration as living intentionality and a second as reflective intentionality, a product of the gaze of attention. Husserl refers to these two types of intentionality, respectively, as '"longitudinal intentionality" (*Längs-intentionalität*) and "transverse intentionality" (*Quer-intentionalität*)' (ibid.: 46). The latter regards the living experience of the *ego* in the authentic time of duration. The former '"is constituted the quasi-temporal disposition of the phases of the flux"' set side by side (Husserl, quoted in ibid.). In the transverse-intentionality mode, I am unable to perceive any clearly differentiated experiences at all. My experiences wax and then wane. These inner-time experiences that are '"essentially actual"' comprise 'the closeness to that innermost core of the Ego' 'that must necessarily *be there* and that it remains *absolutely*' inaccessible to others' (ibid.: 52). Against this stands the longitudinal intentionality. 'The awareness of the experience in the pure stream of duration is changed at every moment into *remembered* having-just-been-thus' (ibid.: 47).

In remembering begins the process of an undifferentiated primal experience toward retention in spatial homogeneity, that is, language, as an 'after-consciousness of the primal impression' (ibid.: 48). Phenomenologist Marvin Farber provides, in accordance with 'Husserl's precise description', a descriptive analysis of animating the sense-complex as a gradually proceeding objectivating process (Schutz 1932: 47). The initial conception, the mere sign, appears as a given physical object, such as a word-sound. The first conception founds the second. Perception as an animated sense-complex originates signs that await the acts of signifying (Farber 1962: 236). This process follows the phenomenological order from 'matters of which one is in fact conscious as themselves given "in person,"', Dorion Cairns (1940: 5) notes, constituted as spatial objects to the act of meaning that genuinely founds the expression. Central in this transition from temporal to spatial is the appearance of meaning.

Thus far, the focus is on the anatomy of the consciousness of the solitary *ego*. This anatomy is comparably applicable to the We-relationship that, by nature, appears in the next subsection on intersubjectivity. In the We-relationship, the *ego* meets the *thou* who is 'a fellow man and not a shadow on a movie screen – in other words, he has duration and consciousness' (Schutz 1932: 108). Obviously, it is the We-relationship that is particularly relevant for social scientists in their search for meaning.

The impalpable stream of consciousness of lived experiences receives no meaning until '*a certain way of directing one's gaze at an item of one's own experience*' occurs (ibid.: 42). Therefore, meaning is not a feature attached to an experience but an 'attitude on the part of the Ego toward' the *durée* of the stream of consciousness, a lifted-out experience presented spatially; only then does a discrete experience render an 'item' (ibid.). Meaning regards an act of reflection, a looking back. Therefore, the natural attitude lacks meaning. The stream-of-consciousness perspective seriously questions Weber's (1947: 88, n. 8) *Verstehen* project, referred to as the 'interpretation of subjective states of mind and the meanings which can be imputed as intended by the actor'. It emphasizes the need for further (phenomenological) analysis.

2.4.2 Intersubjectivity

Seemingly, intersubjectivity is the privilege of scientists who may demonstrate truth as observably scientific evidence. It will convince a scientist's fellow man. Therefore, in the absence of such evidence, the philosopher cannot boast intersubjectivity. Philosophy is a private affair, one might infer. However, an individual who denies the fundamental intersubjectivity of philosophical truth finds himself in the impossible position of someone who is unable to agree with me as soon as I agree with his denial (Luijpen 1969: 21). This is one of the manners in which to substantiate the logical necessity of intersubjectivity as a truly philosophical base. Under this aspect, intersubjectivity justifies the phenomenological position that recognizes as genuine knowledge 'matters of which one is in fact conscious as themselves given "in person", matters that are "data" in the very sense that spatio-temporally individuated matters (including those sensuously perceived) are data' (Cairns 1940: 5). Cairns specifies:

> In short, the fundamental maxim of phenomenology requires that empiristic restrictions be rejected because they conflict with or lead one to ignore strictly self-given, observable, and ... intersubjectively verifiable 'matters themselves'.
>
> (ibid.: 6)

The maxim reflects the phenomenological principle delineated as the 'pre-reflexive consciousness' as the implicitly non-thematic consciousness of the person itself who constitutes one's inner self of being-in-the-world, that is, Husserl's natural attitude. Against this stands the reflexive consciousness of the *'experience vécue'*, of our un-reflected dealing with fellow man and things (Luijpen 1969: 90). Indeed, the latter requires the caveat as identified by Bergson.

In Schutz's phenomenological analysis, it is particularly in the We-relationship that the intersubjectivity postulate renders its foundational significance. Schutz's start in his approach to the We-relationship is similar to Simmel's to which I referred to earlier. Schutz states:

> Born into a social world, [man] comes upon his fellow men and takes their existence for granted without question. ... The Thou ... is conscious, and his stream of consciousness is temporal in character, exhibiting the same basic form as mine.
>
> (1932: 98)

> This [Thou-orientation] 'is a prepredicative experience in which I become aware of a fellow human being *as a person'*.
>
> (ibid.: 164)

In the intersubjective context, the awareness of the *thou* as a fellow man means the *ego's* awareness of its conscious, its living experiences, its remembering, and its meaning-endowing just like the *ego* himself. We may observe our fellow man and experience his very human nature. In a social science context, however, it is obviously relevant to think over the interaction between men as agents. It is from the reciprocity in the We-relationship that Schutz begins the quest for social science, that is, according to him, as 'an objective context of meaning constructed out of and referring to subjective contexts of meaning', George Walsh (1967: xxviii) notes in his introduction to Schutz's *The Phenomenology of the Social World*. Time and intersubjectivity are pivotal in this quest.

The phenomenological interpretation of time constitutes the analytical device to meet Schutz's social science definition, as previously quoted. The explicit attention to the role of intersubjectivity influences the phenomenologist to remain close to man 'in person', to the pre-givenness of his consciousness, and to analyze it in terms of *durée*. Briefly, the following contrast may be noted: the concept of time refers to analysis against intersubjectivity to a postulate. The concept of internal time consciousness Schutz (1932: 43) carries 'out within the "phenomenological reduction"'. It concerns a 'bracketing' of the natural world, that causes 'a complete change of attitude toward the thesis of the "world given-to-me-as-being there (*als daseiende gibt*)"' (ibid.). Against this, Schutz refrains from such phenomenological reduction regarding intersubjectivity. He explicitly states:

> The problem of how the intersubjectivity of all knowledge and thought can be transcendentally deduced is something beyond the scope of the present study, even though its analysis would completely clarify the concept of objective meaning.
>
> (ibid.: 32–33)

The quote implies that intersubjectivity is taken for granted. However, as Natanson (1968: 236) correctly argues, 'From a standpoint of the transcendental attitude, it is necessary to ask, How is it possible that there is such a structure?' Nevertheless, Schutz refrains from dealing with a philosophical deduction of intersubjectivity. What follows after the sentence quoted may explain this unevenness compared to his approach to the concept of time. In this Schutz establishes that Husserl stated the transcendental knowledge problem indeed, 'but by no means solved' it (ibid.: 233). It is probably therefore, that Schutz restricts himself to the role of social scientist, taking intersubjectivity as a fact of life.

The subsections merely offer a sketchy impression of Schutz's thorough 1932 treatise that was issued as *Der sinnhafte Aufbau der sozialen Welt*. The elements discussed thereof prelude the next section that outlines social science as objectively meaningful while taking into account the subjective contexts of the meaning of the *ego* and the *thou*. Actually, it amounts to an outline of an outline. I predominantly refer to some of Schutz's post–World War II papers.

2.5 Phenomenological analysis of meaning

Schutz (Schuetz 1953: 28) defines social science as 'a system of objective knowledge' to be constructed out 'subjective meaning structures'. The immediate question is, How to solve the objectivity–subjectivity paradox in it? *Nota bene*, this 'system of objective knowledge' regards the 'theoretical content of a science that consists of the meaning content of its theoretical statements which are independent of all accidents of a judger and the occasions of judgment' (Farber 1962: 239). Farber's formulation accords with Kaufmann's analysis of meaning as the scope of a science, as discussed earlier. It is the phenomenological perspective that reconciles the fluctuation of subjective, occasional meanings with the theoretical 'conception of meanings as ideal and hence fixed unities' (ibid.: 238). Actually, the fluctuation of meaning results from a

> fluctuation of the *acts* of meaning, i.e., there are changes in the subjective acts which invest the expressions with meaning; ... particularly with respect to the specific characters in which their meaning lies. *But the meanings themselves do not change.*
>
> (ibid.; emphasis added)

The latter clause gives away the realist position of the phenomenologist; meaning does not coincide with its expression. Meaning regards an ideal unity that itself does not fluctuate subjectively. Therefore, the analysis of meaning is tantamount to constituting theoretical propositions as ideal statement-meanings. The meaning analysis bases any empirical science, both the natural and the social sciences. It is the ideal unity, that is, the idealization that constitutes the bedrock of science as a 'system of objective knowledge' preceding the empirical counterpart of causal explanation of facts (Kaufmann 1944).

The phenomenological perspective makes clear that without idealization reality is literally meaningless. It founds the intersubjectivity that we experience in daily life and in our natural attitude of commonsense thought. At the same time, in mundane life, our acts of meaning are pragmatically driven, fashioned by occasion. Interpreting reality, we merely grasp the aspect relevant to us both in common sense and in scientific knowledge. However, in science, at issue is superseding these commonsense concepts with scientific thought objects, shedding the 'fluid vagueness of sense, [replaced by] exact definition of thought' (Schuetz 1953: 2). It is the procedure that originates electrons, atoms, and molecules. The scientist determines the observational field and the relevance of the conceptual constructs within a theoretical framework, for example, of classical mechanics. Outside the observational field of the natural scientist, the concepts do not have any meaning, and they definitely do not perform acts of meaning.

Contrariwise, the reality that the social scientist studies is itself structured as a field of conceptual meanings as pre-reflective knowledge of the human beings that people it. This commonsense knowledge is, at the same time, fragmentary, frequently a matter of familiarity, and taken for granted though 'sufficient for coming to terms with fellow-men, cultural objects, social institutions' (Schutz 1954: 263). Hence, the fellow man's overt behavior is not merely experienced as a physical spatial-temporal phenomenon but as a meaningful action, couched in commonsense thought constructs, that is, 'inter-woven in a specific manner with elements of inner consciousness and experience of one's own physiological processes' (Kaufmann 1934: 102, n. 1).

Therefore, the social scientist must reformulate the unquestioned conceptual constructs, transforming them 'by a process of inquiry into warranted assertibility' based on a theoretical framework (Schutz 1954: 265). In this way, the theorist is engaged in grasping the essences of his subject matter. Carl Menger advances this relationship between common sense and science in the *Methodenstreit* by distinguishing the difference with the German Historical school. The aim of scientific research, Menger (1883: 14) argues, is the transformation of the concreteness of a phenomenon into an exemplification of a law-conforming structured reality.[3] It is a transformation of aspects of man's *Lebenswelt* in terms of commonsense constructs into 'second-level constructs', that is, *Idealtypen*. Schutz:

> Exactly this layer of the *Lebenswelt*, however, from which the natural sciences have to abstract, is the social reality which the social sciences have to investigate.
>
> (1954: 266)

In natural science, the analysis of the meaning of the essential elements is a theorist's autonomy. Exact thought constructs derived from, for example, classical mechanics, straightforwardly delimit the observational field. In social science, it is the unquestioned common-sense-meaning constructs that direct the theorist's analysis of meanings. The social scientist must take a detour of 'constructs of constructs'. I discuss this detour in two respective subsections. They juxtapose the idealization of typifying in commonsense thought versus the construction of ideal types arriving at a genuine social science in a Weberian sense.

2.5.1 *Typifying in commonsense thought*

The inner-time nature of consciousness and the intersubjectivity of meaning feature commonsense thought. The meaning concepts of which we avail ourselves stem from a reflective intentionality regarding lived experiences. The meaning concepts are constructs of lifted-out lived experiences that we pay attention to as acts of meaning *in retrospect*. From this originates language and common sense as a natural attitude of reciprocal understanding, that is, intersubjectivity. It is the world within we act as human beings amidst fellow men using a stock of knowledge handed down by our predecessors as an organized world. 'The unquestioned pre-experiences are, however, from the outset, at hand as *typical* ones, that is, as carrying along open horizons of similar experiences' (Schuetz 1953: 5). Typifying refers to the very nature of meaning. Farber formulates it as follows. The meaning of a thought or an expression refers to an object. In the latter,

> we are referring to something unreal or 'ideal' as we may express it. Thought and experience in general have the peculiarity of such ideal identifications.
>
> (Farber 1962: 222–223)

'The world is ... from the outset experienced in the pre-scientific thinking of everyday life in the mode of typicality' (Schutz 1954: 267). It is a '"whole apparatus of commonsense thought"' of which we may dispose (Whitehead 1929: 124). However, in our biographically determined situation, it is the '"purpose at hand"' that defines which elements of this generalizing typification are relevant (Schuetz 1953: 6). It is the subjective act of meaning of the solitary *ego* that selects particular features of an object as individual and which are typical.

At the same time, it is in intersubjectivity that meaning manifests itself; without intersubjectivity, meaning as idealization is senseless. Knowledge is socialized from the outset. Schutz discusses the aspects of the intersubjectively socialized nature of common-sense knowledge.

1. It is socialized in the reciprocity of perspectives; two basic idealizations render typifying constructs of objects that supersede the thought objects of my and my fellow man's private experience. The first idealization is the interchangeability of the standpoints; if I change places with my fellow man I take for granted that his 'here' becomes mine, and vice versa. Second, I and my fellow man, 'We', share a congruency of the system of relevances; we interpret common objects in an '"empirically identical"' manner (Schuetz 1953: 7–8). Together, the idealizations constitute 'the *general thesis of reciprocal perspectives*', superseding 'the thought objects of my and my fellowman's private experience' (ibid.: 8).
2. The greater part of our knowledge is socially derived, handed down to me by my fellow men, and this in socially approved terms, that is, 'the vocabulary and the syntax of everyday language' (ibid.: 10).
3. It is socialized in its social distribution of knowledge, each individual knowing merely a sector of the world (Schutz 1954: 269).[4]
4. Moreover, 'the knowledge of these individual differences is itself an element of common-sense experience' (Schuetz 1953: 10).

Obviously, the inherently socialized knowledge of intersubjectivity features the structure of the social world. The commonsense typifications structure social reality. In this structured social reality, I, the human being, armed with the apparatus of commonsense thought, find myself in my biographically determined situation that is open to my attention, interpretation, and action. Open to me is a manifold of potential forms of social relations that vary in intimacy and anonymity, familiarity and strangeness, intensity, and extensity. This perspective is conspicuously egocentric in a literal sense. So, it is the *ego's* horizon, spatial or temporal, that determines the nature of his social relations. The nature of a face-to-face interaction differs from a social relation in a telephone call. These examples regard contemporaries. In addition to them, there are predecessors and successors with whom the relations have limitations. These social-relation variables generate a manifold of more or less structured layers of social relations that vary in anonymity.

The We-relationship is at the top of a gliding scale of waning familiarity. With the word 'We', only with reference to 'Us' whose center I am, I denote that I am aware of 'Us' by my biographically determined situation, in which I share with you an inner-time consciousness. We are growing older together, sharing traverse intentionality, for example, in a face-to-face talk or an à-quatre-main-piano music. Within the contemporaries category, the We-participants are "'consociates'" (Schuetz 1953: 12). It is significant that the We-relationship is not allowing typification. It regards unique biographical situations in which We are merely superficially aware of one another's stream of consciousness. The We-relationship is inaccessible to the social scientist.

Next in familiarity is the relationship in which others stand out as "'You" and in reference to "You," who refer back to me'. Lowest on the scale, but growing in anonymity, appear third parties who stand out as "'They'", a 'One' (ibid.: 11). It is in these relationships that we typify in our daily life in which 'the fellowman's self can merely be grasped by … forming a construct of a typical way of behavior, a typical pattern of underlying motives, of typical attitudes of a personality type' (ibid.: 12). It is in these relations, amenable to typification, that society expresses its structure. Schutz substantiates it with the mailbox example that he presents in different places.[5]

> Putting a letter in the mailbox, I expect that unknown people, called postmen, will act in a typical way, not quite intelligible to me, to the effect that my letter will reach the addressee within typically reasonable time.
>
> (ibid.: 13)

The scale of familiarity reflects the degree of anonymity. The 'They' may refer to whomsoever, everyone, lacking any form of individuality. In these anonymous relationships, we are merely fragmentarily interested in someone else, merely regarding his role in the social fabric as a postman, taxi driver, or cashier who are supposedly interchangeable. The societal patterns comprise personal types and course-of-action types, for example, etiquette and rules of thumb or making the idealization of "'I-can-do-it-again'" (ibid.: 16).

Action and interaction underlie the course-of-action and the personal type. Action, as identified earlier, is a concept that is difficult to comprehend. It refers to our inner-time consciousness and expresses our traverse intentionality. Therefore, Weber's metaphor of attaching subjective meaning to action is inadequate. Action is merely an inner-time-conscious moment. It merely acquires meaning in retrospection, fitting within a prefigured project, and recapped as an act. This perspective is the fruit of Bergson's temporal-versus-spatial contrast, indeed. In this respect, there is a correspondence with the social relation types. Essentially, the type amounts to spatially representing a fragment of someone's presence.

A motive underlies the project. As anticipated in the 'Future Perfect Tense', it is an in-order-to motive (ibid.: 15). In order to earn money, I go to the office. However, Schutz distinguishes the because-motive that refers to past experiences that determined the act as someone did; for example, social deprivation made him a criminal. This motive distinction is very fruitful in the analysis of social interaction as will now be discussed.

Social interaction is founded on intersubjective understanding. In projecting a social action, I anticipate that others will understand my action, for example, that my question will induce him to answer appropriately. Here appears the motive distinction. Asking a question is based on the in-order-to motive to gain information. The answer I receive is based on the because-motive of my partner in this interaction; he answers because … There is a reciprocity in this that raises series of commonsense constructs of the other's anticipated behavior. Clearly, the element of anticipation lubricates our social interactions. For that matter, within such an interaction, some inequality between the partners occurs. It is the initial actor who oversees his actions; on one hand, he 'knows "when his action starts and where it ends"' since it fits within the span of his project (ibid.: 18). His partner, on the other hand, might be rather unaware of what the initial actor is doing. This may put the reciprocity under pressure. Under this aspect, it would be helpful when the addressee would 'start from the observed act and to construct from there my underlying in-order-to motive' (ibid.). Obviously, a common set of relevances and purposes will augment the chance of reciprocity, resulting in fruitful interaction, as it happens for instance on the market. In this context, Schutz refers to Weber's principle of the "subjective interpretation of meaning" (ibid.: 19). Finally, this is a principle that bases course-of-action types that subsequently depend on the revealed motives.

The motives behind the course-of-action type concern personal types, of course. In the We-relationship, we may immediately experience and grasp the motives of our consociates. In the other, more anonymous relationships between contemporaries, it is anticipated that, to a certain extent, the course-of-action type corresponds to definite personal types. The train conductor anticipates typical behaviors from his passengers and vice versa. Additionally, the restauranteur expects a typical-guest attitude. The social world is beset with 'complicated mirror-reflexes' that are supported by common systems of relevances (ibid.: 20). An increasing standardization of the course-of-action augments the chance of adequately grasping the subjective meaning of an actor's act.

In accordance with Weber's bias toward analysis of rational action, Schutz also pays specific attention to rational action, that is, rational action within the commonsense experience. This attention is for good reasons. *Zweckrationalität* prevails in the human system of relevances and plays, as such, a major role in the *Verstehen* methodology. Also, rationality bears economics as a social science. Rationality is the very postulate that founds theoretical social science. Later, I will return to the latter.

In an *Economica* paper, Schutz (Schuetz 1943: 130) quotes Talcott Parsons's definition of rationality. Parsons:

> Action is rational in so far as it pursues ends possible within the conditions of the situation, and by the means which, among those available to the actor, are intrinsically best adapted to the end for reasons understandable and verifiable by positive empirical science.
>
> (Parsons 1937: 58)

It seems plausible to equate the rationality that human beings presumably apply with scientifically founded rationality as defined, for instance, by Parsons. However, Schutz enumerates a number of conditions demanded by this type of rationality, which are obviously unattainable for human beings in their mundane life. For instance, taking account of mutual expectations leads to an infinite regress of rational reactions. Moreover, the opposite is expedient. It is the 'unorganized knowledge ... of the particular circumstances of time and place' that is relevant in social cooperation and rational action, as Hayek (1945: 521) argues. '"Rational action" on the common-sense level', Schutz contends,

> is always action within an unquestioned and undetermined frame of constructs of typicalities of the setting, the motives, the means and ends, the course of action and personalities involved and taken for granted.
>
> (Schuetz 1953: 25–26)

Otherwise stated, rationality on a commonsense level amounts to a typically rational human being who aims to determine the logic of his situation and to act accordingly. It may concern a man on the spot who, in the marketplace, takes advantage of his unscientific knowledge of circumstances of time and place, a typical market vendor.

Thus far, typifying in the *Lebenswelt* constitutes the basis of a social scientist's subject matter. Humans' unremitting typifying originates a whole apparatus of commonsense thought that organizes social life. In it, a dichotomy of social domains becomes apparent. On one hand, there is a domain of consociates in which the

> We-relationship, which is the very form of every encounter with another person, is not itself grasped *reflectively* within the face-to-face situation. Instead of being observed, it is lived through. The many different mirror images of Self within Self ... are experienced as a continuum within a single experience'.
>
> (Schutz 1932: 170)

It is a domain that is difficult to access as it alludes to the inner-time conscious-ness of shared experiences. On the other hand, there is the domain of contem-poraries who vary in anonymity that is amenable to typification. This is the domain of constructs that people apply in their social life. This aspect expresses social life itself in structures. It is this domain to which the social scientist has access. It constitutes the lead in the next subsection.

2.5.2 *The construction of ideal types*

It is the social reality as experienced by human beings that constitutes the foun-dation of the ideal-type project. Its very aim is to interpret human action in terms of subjective meaning. Economics as engaged in the statistics of prices and of volumes of trade regards actually 'nothing else than a kind of an intel-lectual shorthand' (Schuetz 1953: 27). Behind the figures is a hidden human subjectivity that originates this world of statistics. In this context, Schutz refers to Hayek's essay *The Problem and Method of the Natural Sciences*, in which one can read the following. Hayek:

> the facts of our mind must remain not only data to be explained but also data on which the explanation of human action guided by those mental phenomena must be based.
>
> (1952: 39–40)

Then, at issue is solving the paradox as stated at the beginning of this section that poses two questions. The first is how to grasp subjective meaning scientif-ically. Second, how is it, then, possible to grasp by a system of objective knowl-edge subjective meaning structures? These questions refer to every level of social science. At the same time, the latter question alludes to an analysis of meaning, resulting in a *theoretical* corpus, as described by Kaufmann. A theo-retical social science, such as pure economic theory, amounts to 'the interpre-tation of the social world in terms of a system of determinate logical structure'. This requires 'a next step', which I discuss later (Schuetz 1943: 147). First at issue is the system of objective social science in general.

The social scientist places himself outside the theatre of social life, render-ing it an 'object of his contemplation on which he looks with detached equa-nimity' (ibid.: 143). In this shift in the point of view the social scientist

> replaces the human beings he observes as actors on the social stage by puppets created by himself and manipulated by himself.
>
> (ibid.)

The 'puppets' correspond to Weber's '"ideal types"', that is, homunculi. This creation corresponds to our typification in our daily life insofar as both regard the typification of human activities bringing about an intended effect and *per se* not of 'emanations of the personality of our fellow men' (ibid.). Schutz's procedure to arrive at ideal types is as follows.

First, the social scientist accepts a *system of relevances*; that is, he enters the corpus of his science within which he chooses his particular scientific problem, for example, scarcity, or exchange. This creates a '"being in a scientific situation"' within which the scientist determines what is relevant for investigation and what the level of research will be (Schuetz 1953: 29). Second, 'he (the social scientist) begins to construct typical course-of-action patterns corresponding to the observed events' (ibid.: 31). It regards the *postulate of subjective interpretation* expressing the ontological concept that

> we cannot understand the social phenomena otherwise than within the scheme of human motives, human means and ends, human planning -in short- within the categories of human action.
>
> (Schuetz 1943: 146)

Actually, he rearranges the patterns handed over by the apparatus of common-sense thought. 'Thereupon he co-ordinates to these typical course-of-action patterns a personal type', that is, the homunculus, a fictitious being gifted with consciousness (Schuetz 1953: 31). The scientist is the creator of this consciousness to which he attaches a set of typical in-order-to motives that fit in with the course-of-action under investigation. In the same way, he develops homunculi with because-motives as being reciprocal of the former. Interaction with other homunculi also follows a script determined by the scientist. The homunculus acts as a puppet of which the fictitious consciousness purely expresses the subjective meaning according to the scientific problem that is selected. Third, the theorist observes the *postulate of adequacy*; that is, the ideal type construct should be an adequate interpretation of the meaning of the actor, that is, referring to Max Weber, '"the typical construction would be reasonable and understandable for the actor himself, as well as for his fellow men"' (Weber, quoted in Schuetz 1943: 147).

Deference to these postulates may warrant the social scientist that his construction of ideal types results in an interpretive social science account of the subjective meaning context that is interpreted in an objective meaning context.

However, it requires 'a next step' to arrive at a *theoretical* social science such as economics (bid.). This next step concerns an additional postulate: the *postulate of rationality*, guiding the analysis of the meaning of formulating theoretical propositions. This is reminiscent of Karl Popper (1967: 359), who argues referring to economics, that the rationality principle is the scientific *sine qua non*. The commonsense thought comprises logical structures such as means–ends relationships. In economics, they emerge as the paradigmatic course-of-action type. This paradigm considers economics' rational man as a homunculus. In the theoretical realm, this homunculus acquires a maximum of anonymity; it is an 'every-man', a 'one'. This ideal type enables the theorist to construct a logically interrelated system of means–ends relations and constant motives; logical course-of-action types animated by rationally driven ideal types. Schutz states on it:

> The ideal type of social action must be constructed in such a way that the actor in the living world would perform the typified act if he had a clear and distinct scientific knowledge of all the elements relevant to his choice and the constant tendency to choose the most appropriate means for the realisation of the most appropriate end.
>
> (Schuetz 1943: 147–148)

It is the theorist who determines the type of rationality of the ideal type and the knowledge required to act accordingly. It emphasizes that the concept of rationality in social science is governed by the system of relevances and the stock of knowledge that is attributed to the homunculus. Therefore, in this context, the rationality concept that is applied definitely differs from the rationality concept of positive empirical science, as quoted earlier, which Parsons would suggest as the norm (Parsons 1937: 58).

Obviously, Schutz alludes to theoretical economics in the latter quote. Economics offers the fundamental hypothesis, for example, '"subjective value theory"', and the regulative motives for a system of ideal types, who apply the marginal principle of modern economics (Kaufmann 1933: 389; Schuetz 1943: 148). It renders economics 'a pure logic of choice' as a nomological science. It is the fruit of an intellectual tour ending in a typical construction of theoretical propositions. However, a disturbing question might come across. This is nothing but an intellectual game, is it not? What is its correspondence to reality? This world of social science, Schutz admits, 'is not the world within which we act and within which we are born and die'. However, science does not deal with reality 'if we consider as the pattern of reality the world of daily life', and 'one who asks for greater reality, I want to say that I am afraid I do not exactly know what reality is' (Schuetz 1943: 149). The latter quote expresses Schutz's phenomenological position, taking Whitehead's warning very seriously: beware of the 'fallacy of misplaced concreteness' (Schuetz 1953: 1). Above all, a purely theoretical social science is a paragon and inherently a device for demonstrating the deviations from it in commonsense thought. It enables the scientist to formulate a prediction as another 'device for ascertaining deviating behavior in the real social world', uncovering 'non-typified elements' (ibid.: 36). Finally, the very fruit of Schutz' phenomenology of the social world is that his sophistication of Weber's *Verstehen* methodology arrives at a methodology for formulating theoretical laws for which, for instance, economics is famous.

Finally, what is the resemblance between common sense versus scientific typification? The correspondence refers to Bergson's diagnosis of thought expression as an artificial affair. Merely thanks to increasing anonymity, we are able to grasp fragments of subjective meaning both in commonsense thought and in social science while observing the postulates of subjective interpretation and of adequacy. Distinguishing differences between the domains makes the respective systems of relevances, a biographically determined commonsense thought versus a detached orientation governed by the scientific problem. Yet, the domains contain another type of correspondence. In both precedes the typified course-of-action, the ideal type. Murray Rothbard, in his *Economic Thought Before Adam Smith*, substantiates this as the following quotes may demonstrate. Rothbard states:

> The essence of philosophic thought is that it penetrates the *ad hoc* vagaries of day-to-day life in order to arrive at truths that transcend the daily accidents of time and place. ... It arrives, in short, at a system of natural laws.
>
> (1995: 19)

He continues:

> But economic analysis is a subset of such investigation, because genuine economic theory can only advance beyond shifting day-to-day events by penetrating truths about human action which are absolute, unchanging and eternal.
>
> (ibid.)

The formulation of the ideal type follows after the typified course-of-action. Concisely, the quotes state the origin and purpose of the scientific construct. The course-of-action type originates from common sense while the ideal type arrives at nomological science, natural law.

This subsection concludes with a finger exercise, presenting the paradigmatic figures in Adam Smith's most famous sentence as homunculi. Smith:

> It is not from the benevolence of the butcher, the brewer, or the baker that we expect our dinner, but from their regard to their own interest.
>
> (1776: 17)

Exchange accomplishes the *postulate of relevances*. Self-interest expresses the *rationality postulate*. Furthermore, self-interest, and *per se* not benevolence, corresponds to the *postulate of adequacy* in relationships between these contemporaries and accords with the *postulate of subjective interpretation*. Voilà, the butcher, the brewer, and the baker who figure in economics as homunculi.

2.6 Conclusion

The *Lebenswelt* is the point of departure in phenomenology. This accords with economics as an anthropocentric affair. The mundane reality of conscious human beings makes the social scientist aware of subjective meaning as a concept of which to take account. It is Weber who accepts the challenge to match the subjective origin of the social reality with a *wertfrei* sociology. His *Verstehen* methodology is a rather straightforward approach to grasp subjective meaning as a central concept. Actually, Weber falls prey to the fallacy of misplaced concreteness. Schutz succeeds in a phenomenological sophistication of Weber's *wertfrei* interpretive sociology. Instead of an ostensibly direct observation of someone's subjective meaning, Schutz directs his analysis to the origin of meaning, that is, human consciousness. It is via Bergson's distinction between the qualitative inner-time consciousness versus the quantitative spatial dimension of objectivity that Schutz knows to bridge the subjective–objective dichotomy. Pivotal in what follows then is the concept of typification. Typification and idealization structure our world.

Human consciousness commands an apparatus of common sense thought partly handed over by fellow men, partly determined by a man's own system of relevances, that is, his interests. This apparatus represents meaning, and its concepts are meaning as they profile the social reality. Consequently, from this insight, the social scientist reformulates the concepts, and the commonsense constructs of the actors that he studies and formulates constructs of constructs. It constitutes the basis of the analysis of meaning, of formulating the theoretical propositions, that is, null hypotheses as points of departure of the causal explanation of facts.

Notes

1 The original German title of Schutz's (1932) book reads *Der sinnhaften Afbau der sozialen Welt*, which, I think, approaches the meaning of the book more closely.
2 Regarding Simmel's concept of contents as used in this context, it might be instructive to add Simmel's own description as quoted by Schutz. 'Everything present in the individuals (who are the immediate concrete data of all historical reality) in the form of drive, interest, purpose, inclination, psychic state, movement – everything that is present in them in such a way as to engender or mediate effects upon others or to receive such effects, I designate as the *content*, as the material, as it were, of sociation (*Vergesellschaftung*). … Sociation is thus the form (realized in innumerable different ways) in which the individuals grow together into units that satisfy their interests' (Simmel 1922, quoted in Schutz 1932: 4, n. 3). Against the contents concept, Simmel distinguishes 'reciprocal effects such as competition, domination, cooperation, and solidarity' which are the '*actualizing forms*' of social life (Schutz 1932: 4, n. 2). Schutz considers these concepts of Simmel as a lasting contribution to sociology (ibid.: 4).
3 ‚Das Ziel der wissenschaftlichen Forschung ist nicht nur die *Erkenntniss*, sondern auch das *Verständniss* der Erscheinungen. Wir haben eine Erscheinung erkannt, wenn das geistige Abbild derselben zu unseren Bewusstsein gelangt ist, wir verstehen dieselbe, wenn wir den Grund ihrer Existenz und ihrer eigenthümlichen Beschaffenheit (den Grund ihres *Seins* und ihres *So-Seins*) erkannt haben' (Menger 1883: 14).
4 In this respect, Schutz (Schuetz 1953: 11, n. 29a) refers to Friedrich von Hayek's *Economics and Knowledge* (Hayek 1937). Chapter 4, 'On Knight', refers also to the economic significance of dispersed knowledge.
5 For instance, in Schutz (1932: 184; 1954: 263).

References

Bergson, H., 1913, [2001], *Time and Free Will*, London, edited by G. Allen, New York: Dover Publications Inc.

Cairns, D., 1940, [1968], An Approach to Phenomenology. In: M. Farber, ed., 1940, (1968), *Philosophical Essays*, 3–18, New York: Greenwood Press.

Croce, B., 1901, On the Economic Principle; A Reply to V. Pareto, translated by C.M. Meredith, 1953, *International Papers, Vol. 3*, 197–202; (Replica all'articolo del Professore Pareto, *Giornale degli Economisti, Vol. I*, 1901, 121–130).

Farber, M., ed., 1940, [1968], *Philosophical Essays*, New York: Greenwood Press, Publishers.

Farber, M., 1962, [2009], *The Foundation of Phenomenology*, New Brunswick: Aldine Transaction.

Hayek, F.A., 1937, Economics and Knowledge, *Economica, New Series, Vol. 4*, 33–54.

Hayek, F.A., 1945, The Use of Knowledge in Society, *The American Economic Review, Vol. 35, No. 4*, 519–530.

Hayek, F.A., 1952, [1979], *The Counter-Revolution of Science*, Indianapolis, IN: Liberty Press.

Kaufmann, F., 1933, On the Subject-Matter and Method of Economic Science, *Economica, No. 42*, 381–401.

Kaufmann, F., 1934, The Concept of Law in Economic Science, *The Review of Economic Studies, Vol. 1, No. 2*, 102–109.

Kaufmann, F., 1940, Phenomenology and Logical Empiricism. In: M. Farber, ed., 1940, [1968], *Philosophical Essays*, 124–142, New York: Greenwood Press.

Kaufmann, F., 1944, *Methodology of the Social Sciences*, Atlantic Highlands, New Jersey: Humanities Press.

Luijpen, W., 1969, *Inleiding in de existentiële fenomenologie*, Utrecht: Uitgeverij Het Spectrum.

Menger, C., 1883, [2005], *Untersuchungen über die Methode der Socialwissenschaften und der Politischen Oekonomie insbesodere*, Leipzig: Verlag von Duncker & Humblot; [Elibron Classics series].

Nagel, T., 1986, *The View from Nowhere*, Oxford: Oxford University Press.

Natanson, M., 1968, Alfred Schutz on Social Reality and Social Science, *Social Research: An International Quarterly of Political and Social Science, Vol. 35*, 217–244.

Pareto, V., 1900, On the Economic Phenomenon; A Reply to Benedetto Croce, translated by F. Priuli, 1953, *International Papers, Vol. 3*, 180–196; (Sul Fenomeno Economico, *Giornale degli Economisti, Vol. II*, 1900, 139–162).

Parsons, T., 1937, [1968], *The Structure of Social Action*, Vol. I, New York: The Free Press.

Popper, K.R., 1967, The Rationality Principle. In: D. Miller, ed., 1985, *Popper Selections*, 357–365, Princeton, NJ: Princeton University Press.

Prendergast, Chr, 1986, Alfred Schutz and the Austrian School of Economics, *American Journal of Sociology, Vol. 92, No. 1*, 1–26.

Robbins, L., 1932, [1952], *An Essay on the Nature and Significance of Economic Science*, London: Macmillan.

Rothbard, M.N., 1995, [2006], *Economic Thought before Adam Smith*, Auburn, AL: Ludwig von Mises Institute.

Schuetz, A., 1943, The Problem of Rationality in the Social World, *Economica, New Series, Vol. 10, No. 38*, 130–149.

Schuetz, A., 1953, Common-Sense and Scientific Interpretation of Human Action, *Philosophy and Phenomenological Research, Vol. 14*, 1–38.

Schutz, A., 1932, [1967], *The Phenomenology of the Social World*, New York: Northwestern University Press; [*Der sinnhafte Aufbau der sozialen Welt*, Wien: Julius Springer].

Schutz, A., 1940, Phenomenology and the Social Sciences. In: M. Farber, ed., 1940, [1968], *Philosophical Essays*, 166–186, New York: Greenwood Press.

Schutz, A., 1954, Concept and Theory Formation in the Social Sciences, *The Journal of Philosophy, Vol. 51, No. 9*, 257–273.

Schutz, A., 1970, Phenomenological Baseline. In: H.R. Wagner, ed., 1970, *Alfred Schutz, on Phenomenology and Social Relations*, 53–71, Chicago, IL: The University of Chicago Press.

Simmel, G., 1910, How Is Society Possible? *American Journal of Sociology, Vol. 16, No. 3*, 372–391.

Simmel, G., 1922, [1950], *The Sociology of George Simmel*, translated by K.H. Wolff, New York: The Free Press.

Wagner, H.R., ed., 1970, *Alfred Schutz, on Phenomenology and Social Relations*, Chicago, IL: The University of Chicago Press.

Walsh, G., ed., 1967, Introduction. In: A. Schutz, 1932, [1967], *The Phenomenology of the Social World*, xv–xxix, New York: Northwestern University Press; [*Der sinnhafte Aufbau der sozialen Welt*, Wien: Julius Springer].

Weber, M., 1947, [1968], *The Theory of Social and Economic Organization*, translated by A.M. Henderson and T. Parsons, New York: The Free Press.

Whitehead, A.N., 1929, (1967), *The Aims of Education*, New York: The Free Press.

3   Scope and method of economics

3.1 Introduction

New institutional economics (NIE) originates from Ronald Coase's introduction of the concept of transaction cost into economics. Coase himself is prepared to admit this. Coase:

> It is commonly said, and it may be true, that the new institutional economics started with my article, "The Nature of the Firm" (1937) with its explicit introduction of transaction costs into economic analysis.
>
> (1998: 72)

The theoretically innovative dimension of the transaction cost introduction regards Coase's explicit adherence to the marginal analysis. On the first page of Coase's seminal 'Firm' paper, he emphasizes that concepts such as the firm must be

> tractable by two of the most powerful instruments of economic analysis developed by Marshall, the idea of the margin and that of substitution, together giving the idea of substitution at the margin.
>
> (1937: 386)

The firm as an institution proves to be the fruit of a marginal analysis of transaction cost, that is, to refer to "'formal relations which are capable of being *conceived* exactly'" (L. Robbins, quoted in ibid.: 387). The marginal analysis remains a constant of Coase's (1946, 1960) theoretical work, witness, for example, his seminal papers 'Marginal Cost Controversy' and 'The Problem of Social Cost'.

It is the featuring marginal analysis that marks NIE and distinguishes it from the preceding American original institutional economics (OIE) of exponents such as Thorsten Veblen and John Commons. NIE is a Post-Marginal Revolution economics that passed the transition from classical economics as engaged in the objectivity of national wealth toward neoclassical economics as engaged in the subjectivity of utility. This subjectivity entails the prominence

DOI: 10.4324/9781315764221-3

of the individual in the economic analysis, of people who consider an exchange as based on substitution at the margin. In his Nobel Prize lecture, Coase (1992: 718) refers to a scene of 'two individuals exchanging nuts for berries on the edge of the forest'. Something like that elementary bartering of individuals is the paradigmatic subject matter of (neoclassical) economics, Coase seems to argue.

The shifted emphasis from objectivity to subjectivity simultaneously uncovered by the Marginal Revolution triumvirate of Léon Walras, John Stanley Jevons, and Carl Menger during the 1870s raises the very question: How to accommodate this prevailing subjectivity with economics' scientific objectivity aspiration? On one hand, the infinitesimal calculus of the Marginal Revolution offers the economist an unprecedented analytical apparatus thereby opening a route for a rigor that resembles natural science.[1] In this aspect, Mark Blaug (1973: 10) establishes that 'in the end, what proved important about marginal utility was "the adjective rather than the noun"'. It affords the theorist to evade subjectivity, presenting human choices as stones, as Pareto (1900: 191) does: 'The stones with which one builds the economic edifice are the choices'. The Marginal Revolution initiates an age of axiomatization in economics and the flourishing of neoclassical general equilibrium theory. On the other hand, it is the subjectivity of utility that features the Marginal Revolution, threatening the theorist's scientific objectivity. This two-sidedness has institutional significance. The infinitesimal calculus of marginal utility can be without subjectivity and is not in need of an institutional setting. However, the noun is equally important, and utility *is* subjectivity; its subjects cannot live without institutions.

It is the issue of scope and method that lies at the bottom of this seemingly slight difference in emphasis. As discussed in Chapter 1, Felix Kaufmann (1933: 383) recognizes that in social sciences, the subject matter, that is, the scope, entails another question: '[A]nd the second, which implies the first, what methods of investigation are most suited to such a task?' This chapter substantiates this insight. The first Section 3.2 shows the effect of the Marginal Revolution on the scope of economics and defines it. The second Section 3.3 dehomogenizes the Marginal Revolution triumvirate. The emphasis on marginal calculus versus subjectivity adumbrates the theoretical and especially the methodological differences between Walras and Jevons, on one hand, against Menger, on the other. In this aspect, reemerges the contrast of nominalism versus realism. Section 3.4 elaborates on the preceding as related to methodological individualism. It shows again the relevance of the phenomenological perspective on situational logic as the method of economics. The final section presents some concluding remarks.

3.2 The scope of economics

As noted, scope and method, Kaufmann (1933: 382) identifies, do not coincide in economics as a social science. The definition of the scope as subject matter should be in accord with what it is '*as actually used*'. The prevailing interpretation is that exchange is the very subject matter of economics as it has been since Adam Smith. At the same time, the Marginal Revolution has brought in the concept of choice as a plausible alternative candidate. The infinitesimal calculus narrows, by nature, an economic subject's attention and concentrates it on a clearly quantified decision issue. Furthermore, a perennial tension exists between limited means and a broader gamut of ends. It results in Lionel Robbins's famous definition of economics. Robbins states:

> Economics is the science which studies human behavior as a relationship between ends and scarce means which have alternative uses.
>
> (1932: 16)

Therefore, Robbins's definition of choice as a matter of subject seems plausible. However, in his methodological essay, *What Should Economists Do?* James Buchanan takes on Lord Robbins as an adversary, stating, 'categorically, that his all too persuasive delineation of our subject field has served to retard, rather than to advance, scientific progress' (Buchanan 1979: 20). Since Robbins' economics definition emerged, it seems to be conventional wisdom that the economic problem involves the allocation of scarce means among alternative ends. Scarcity necessitates choosing, allocating means to an end. So, the economic problem is an allocation problem and a choice issue due to scarcity. Buchanan disputes this view. First, it renders economics a technical affair for which a single optimal solution exists. Robbins considers the problem of technique and the problem of economy as fundamentally different problems. 'The problem of technique arises when there is one end and a multiplicity of means, the problem of economy when both the ends and the means are multiple' (Robbins 1932: 35). Frank Knight features economics as engaged in definitely nontechnical problems when mutually excluding ends are present. Knight: 'The economic problem which is left is that of *allocating* (*given*, limited) means or resources among different modes or channels of utilization' (1934: 228). However, Buchanan rightly claims that further specification of the end, or 'channels of utilization', renders the so-called economic problem as technical. In this manner, the allocation problem changes economics in 'contributions to applied mathematics, to managerial science if you will' (Buchanan 1979: 24). Moreover, economics as a theory of choice presents a paradox. The fully defined utility function deprives the chooser of any genuine choice whereas a deficient function renders a choice real and unpredictable (ibid.: 25–26). A second, related objection to Robbins's definition refers to the anonymous nature of the problem. A close reading of the definition suggests that Robbins perceives scarcity as a universal issue, not *per se* related to someone in particular, a technical relationship between means and end, indeed. 'Robbins's definition errs in accepting any and all "given ends"', Howard S. Ellis (1950: 3) establishes. However, an end is, first of all, a matter of 'freedom of the individual to make the best of his situation as a producer or consumer' (ibid.). Moreover, the scarcity of resources reveals itself in costs, that is, 'costs to individual beings' (ibid.: 4). However, the original version of scarcity allows a non-individualistic interpretation. In particular, welfare economists have taken advantage of the impersonal given-ends approach that Robbins's definition does not exclude. For instance, a government commanding the means formulates an end, and the welfare economist recognizes this as an allocation problem. The fundamental objection is that economics is not engaged in solving artificially projected allocation issues but is involved in the economic actions of individuals. Buchanan (1979: 23) establishes that the produced part of an impersonal scarcity perception is that 'the definition of our subject (i.e., Robbins's definition) makes it all too easy to slip across the bridge between personal or individual units of decision and "social" aggregates'. For that matter, it is Robbins himself who warns against crossing this bridge. For instance, the ordinal nature of the valuations prohibits aggregation. 'Value is a relation, ... so, it follows that the addition of prices or individual incomes to form aggregates is an operation with a very limited meaning' (Robbins 1932: 56–57).[2] What is at issue is that Robbins's definition facilitates an ethical approach to welfare as a kind of social engineering and circumvents the individual by value judgments. Consequently, 'economists explicitly state their own value judgments in the form of "social welfare functions"' as a kind of invocation to 'feel free to maximize to their own hearts' content' (Buchanan 1979: 23). In the following quote, Robbins confirms Buchanan's claim:

> The generalizations of the theory of value (conditioned by the limitations of means in relation to ends) are as applicable to the behavior of the isolated man (Crusoe) or the executive authority of a communist society, as to the behavior of man in the exchange economy. ... The exchange is a *technical* incident, ... , but still, for all that, subsidiary to the main fact of scarcity'.
>
> (1932: 19–20)

It is against this background that Buchanan (1979: 26) proposes to remove the theory of choice 'from its position of eminence in the economist's thought processes'. The alternative that deserves prominence in the economist's thought is exchange. The reason for this is not as Robbins (1932: 19) claims 'one of *most interest and utility*'. It is, as Ellis (1950: 5) insisted on earlier than Buchanan, 'only to the degree that these costs and utilities to individuals can express themselves in the market can economic analysis exist'. In Ellis's quote surfaces the anthropocentric nature of economics. It ascertains that choice as a technical, and, in particular, impersonal, allocation problem is not of (human) nature. However, of more importance is that, without exchange, we go without prices. In this aspect, the Ellis quote corresponds to the challenge of von Mises (1935) presented to the advocates of the 'Socialist Common Wealth'. For this reason, Buchanan stresses the mutually beneficial nature of exchange that renders it the preferred candidate for defining economics. Therefore, Buchanan (1979: 26–27) would recommend terms 'such as *catallactics* or *symbiotics*', expressing mutual benefit, instead of talking about '*economics* or *political economy*'. It would restore Adam Smith's 'principle that gives occasion to the division of labor':

> It (division of labor) is the necessary, though very slow and gradual, consequence of a certain propensity in human nature, which has, in view, no such extensive utility; the propensity to truck, barter, and exchange one thing for another.
>
> (1776: 15)

Exchange should replace choice is Buchanan's position. For instance, Kenneth J. Arrow concurs with Buchanan as Robbins's definition lacks the social dimension, Arrow argues. The lonesome Robinson Crusoe merely faces problems of technique that is a 'choice-problem' indeed. 'But what we are interested in here is the role of interpersonal relations in the organization of society' as part of our mutual improvement (Arrow 1974: 18). We need this organization for at least two reasons. First, it may resolve the competition between the alternative uses that the scarcity of resources entails. It can accrue gains from cooperation. Second, it is an economy based on the involvement of the individual as a participant that may secure relatively efficient allocative solutions. It requires a limited need for knowledge and gives the individual 'a sense of freedom', although 'to a large number of people, very limited in scope' (ibid.: 21). The knowledge efficiency argument brings to mind the intersubjectively socialized nature of commonsense knowledge put forward by Schutz, as discussed in the preceding chapter (Schutz 1953: 10). The individual's economic decisions are 'marginal, that is, they conform to "the little more, the little less"' (Ellis 1950: 2). These references to Arrow and Ellis show that Buchanan's contrast between choice and exchanges is too strong. Obviously, it is the indispensable marketplace that enables the economic agent to take his quantified, marginal decisions. The Robbins definition omits that which has serious consequences for the significance of the institutional theme and renders, for example, economic order a neutral affair, as identified earlier. However, in exchange, as the very object of economic analysis, the actor is eventually engaged in solving his scarcity problem. Between the lines, Buchanan admits this aspect in his plea for the exchange definition: 'efficiency considerations are not wholly eliminated in the conception I am proposing'. 'The motivation for individuals to engage in trade, … , is surely that of "efficiency", defined in the personal sense of moving from less preferred to more preferred position'. Here, 'personal sense of moving' is a synonym of choice (Buchanan 1979: 31).

Finally, the definition requires awareness of the implicit individualistic nature of it, which needs market exchange to reveal these representations of cost and utility as rightly stressed by Ellis and Buchanan. Scarcity incites choices that profile exchange, that is, exchange by individuals who need institutional support. This conclusion is an honest compromise in which choice is subservient to exchange. The next sections elaborate on the close relationship between of scope description and 'methods of investigation' (Kaufmann 1933: 383). Unfolded the methods regard

(a) What kind of data can be regarded as suitable material? (b) On what general principles may one make inductive generalisations from the available data?

(ibid.: 384)

The next section shows the diversity of the Marginal Revolution exponents in addressing these questions.

3.3 The dehomogenizing methods of the Marginal Revolution triumvirate

All three contributors to the Marginal Revolution, Walras, Jevons, and Menger, adhere, in some respect, to general principles as meant under point (b). They all presume economic rationality and share a bias toward analysis and theory building. The main point that distinguishes them from each other regards the choice of the data that found their respective approaches, that is, referring to question (a). On the one hand, Walras and Jevons are engaged in data that are suitable for mathematical calculation. Opposite them stands Menger (1883: 5), who is engaged in '*die Erforschung der Typen und typischen Relationen der Erscheinungen*'. Walras's and Jevons's analyses feature, what William Jaffé calls, a '*logical* causality', resulting in neutral interdependence based on mathematical equations. Menger, in contrast, elaborates on an interdependence resulting from a '*generative* causality' (Jaffé 1976: 521). In the latter, it is *man* who constitutes the genesis of the causal processes in economic life. In accordance with this distinction applies the outside–inside contrast as presented in Chapter 1. These qualifying contrasts between Walras and Jevons versus Menger have fundamental bearings on the elaborations of the theoretical mission of each of them. They dehomogenize the Marginal Revolution. I discuss some, starting with Walras.

3.3.1 Walras

Walras opens his *Elements of Pure Economics* by discussing the definition of political economy. In reference to Adam Smith, Walras (1954: 54) perceives economics as both a science and an art. It is engaged in 'three generic phenomena' 'or groups of specific facts which result from … the scarcity of things': '*value in exchange, industry*, and *property*' (ibid.: 68). These fact groups govern three different domains of studying social wealth. 'Their respective *criteria* are the *true*, the *useful*, meaning material well-being, and the *good*, meaning justice' (ibid.: 64). They are related to Walras's remarkable conception of appropriability. Appropriation is an option for useful things limited in quantity, not *per se* a *sine qua non* of a competitive system as the domain of *'value in exchange'*. Basically, Walras argues that

> [i]f there were only one man in the world, he would be master of all things. Since this is not the case, ... all these ends and aims have to be mutually *coordinated*.
>
> (ibid.: 62–63)

Therefore, there is *value in exchange* generating a measurable magnitude engendering the pure theory of economics, 'a science which resembles the physico-mathematical sciences in every respect' (ibid.: 71). It is competition that solves the economic problem of allocation and engenders general equilibrium, as the theoretical feat Walras is famous for. Out of question remains the nature of appropriation of the scarce means. The domain of *industry* regards the technical efficiency of scarce means; neither for this domain seems the appropriation issue to be relevant. Walras relegates the appropriation option to the domain of *property*. It may ensue *'ownership of property'* which Walras presents as an optional form of appropriation, that is, 'appropriation in conformity with justice' (ibid.: 67).

A climate of competition is the logical prerequisite that causes a general-economic equilibrium. Walras is engaged in logical causality. He does not give a definite answer concerning the appropriation issue and disregards the incentivizing force of private property that governs the individual economic subjects (ibid.: 67). The functionality of competition suffices in explicating the general-equilibrium model. For instance, the institutional device of the Paris Stock Exchange facilitates competition to clear the market and leave aside the appropriation issue (Kregel 1992: 536). Walras bears an 'outside' perspective, here described as not engaged in what motivates the individual actor. The individual conforms to the prerequisites of the general-equilibrium model. Thomas Eberle points at a difference between Weber and Schutz regarding ideal types that may help to identify Walras's analytical approach. Eberle states (2010: 133): 'Ideal types in Weber's sense are constructions within a neo-Kantian framework', 'formal aprioris', designed to meet the requirements of the scientific method. Schutz's types, in contrast, 'are constructions within a phenomenological framework', 'material aprioris', which are based on 'concrete experiences of actors in their everyday world' (Eberle 2010: 133). In his scientific preoccupation with the general equilibrium, Walras has recourse to a perfect competition that conforms the individual as such, a Kantian *a priori* ideal type, that is, a formal construction that accords with the logical causality of his pure economics. Perceived from this perspective, it is plausible that Walras does not delve into the analytical consequences of vagueness regarding appropriation. From a phenomenological point of view, as engaged in human consciousness, such neglect is pernicious. Unspecified property rights leave men inconvenienced. In pure economics, Walras is not engaged in such day-to-day worries. At the same time, Walras expands on institutional issues as a matter of justice and ethics, showing an awareness of the non-mechanic nature of economics. All the same, his pure economics remains a domain strictly separated from the domain of justice and ethics. So, there is ambiguity in Walras's theoretical edifice, that is, the sacrifice to be paid for the logical causality of a general-equilibrium model.

3.3.2 Jevons

The discovery of marginal utility occasions Jevons to interpret the observed facts of Political Economy in mechanistic terms, that is, as a Calculus of Pleasure and Pain (Jevons 1871: vii). It is particularly Bentham's utilitarianism and its corresponding portrayal of man that govern Jevons's marginal utility theory. Value features the Marginal Revolution. Its change is the recognition of human need as the very origin of value. We cannot measure gravity or feelings in their own nature, Jevons (Jevons 1871: 14) argues, but 'we may estimate the equality or inequality of feelings by the varying decisions of the mind' as 'we measure gravity by its effects in the motion of a pendulum'. In Jevons's (1871: 82) elaboration, the primary concept of value 'merely expresses *the circumstances of its exchanging in a certain ratio for some other substance*'. And so, Jevons finds data that are suitable for the mathematical calculation. Logical causality preoccupies Jevons like Walras in his pure economics. At the same time, Jevons considers issues that may hinder the mechanic exchange process. For instance, conspiracy and speculation may thwart an unambiguous pricing process that may be remedied by, for example, publishing statistics to inform the market (ibid.: 87). It regards conditions and variables that determine the functionality of the mechanic process in which Jevons is engaged. It is not so much an attention to the valuing and economizing human beings that profiles his analytical discourse. Under this aspect, Jevons's *Theory of Political Economy* is an approach from 'outside' and deals with the general climate that optimizes the Calculus of Pleasure and Pain.

3.3.3 Menger

Against Walras and Jevons, Menger is an apologist of anthropocentric economics. It is his search for essentials in economics that results in his contribution to the Marginal Revolution. Generative causality features in which causes and effects stem from '*one's own person*, and any of its states are links in this great structure of relationships' (Menger 1976: 51; emphasis added). Several times in his *Principles*, Menger substantiates this basic postulate. I list some:

- In defining the concept of good, Menger specifies as a prerequisite 'human knowledge of the causal connection' between a thing's properties and its need-satisfying capacities (ibid.: 52).
- It is a practical man's purview that recognizes monopolies, goodwill, and other human intangibles as potential objects of exchange.

- The notion of causality in the *Principles* shows its generative nature also in the satisfaction of needs as 'a beginning and becoming' (ibid.: 67). Generative causality is inseparably connected with time and, therefore, with uncertainty that man exhorts to foresight and forethought that exposes him to error and misfortune.
- Foresight and forethought reemerge in Menger's concept of 'marketability' (ibid.: 241). In essence, it is the level of economic sacrifice of exchange that determines the marketability of a good. Mutually beneficial exchange directs economizing individuals to trade. However, sacrifices such as 'cost of correspondence, commissions, brokerage charges' precede the transaction or may otherwise hinder concluding it (ibid.: 189). It reflects the purview of the individual who applies the economic principle, that is, 'not to give up more commodities than is necessary to acquire a given set of commodities' (Kaufmann 1933: 391). Obviously, Menger's 'economic sacrifice of exchange' may be interpreted as a precursor of Coase's transaction-cost concept.
- Menger's marketability theory reads as a prelude to his theory of money. It is a matter of degree in marketability that renders a good as a money thing. In essence, money is a good that may be transacted without the economic sacrifice of exchange, that is, without a transaction cost. It features extreme marketability: the normal economic (market) system works itself, as another reference to Coase (1937).

It is a practical man's situational logic that frames the generative causality in Menger's *Principles*. It finds its philosophical counterpart in the phenomenological concept of lifeworld as the immediate and 'unquestioned ground of science' (Eberle 2010: 125). In this context, Menger's search for essentials requires a reinterpretation of common-sense constructs that figure in lifeworld in terms of scientific second-order constructs. Such a reinterpretation is certainly required as, after the turn of the century, Menger's methodological legacy faced a violent attack from particularly positivist sides regarding epistemological credibility. First, introspection is an unreliable knowledge base to found the concept of subjective meaning. Second, logical positivists point to the impossibility of a synthetic *a priori* Menger's universal essentialia presumed. Against this, Menger adheres to the realist position that 'we can know what this world is like', a world that is independent of human perception, although intelligible. Paragon, in this respect, is the derivation of the economic principle that is discussed resulting from the concept of marginal utility. The economic principle substantiates the notion of subjective meaning as a basis of explanation in economics. It founds the essence of pivotal concepts such as exchange and money. In Schutz's vocabulary, the economic principle becomes the device that governs a homunculus's conduct. The homunculus as an ideal type features in 'the analysis of meaning' and formulates theoretical propositions. It precedes the empirical counterpart of 'causal explanation of facts' (Kaufmann 1944). Ideal types rather than mathematical terms constitute the basic data in Menger's analysis.

3.3.4 Some dehomogenizing conclusions

It is the subjective-meaning interpretation that separates Menger from Walras and Jevons. Menger's *economizing* individual is an ideal type that engenders exchange and money as essentialia of the economic system. Walras's and Jevons's ideal types are instrumental in their mathematical approach. This results from an abstraction à la physico-mathematical sciences to construct '*a priori* the whole framework of their theorems and proofs' (Walras 1954: 71). In Jevons's (1871: vii) theory, it is a hedonist who is subservient to the Marginal 'Calculus of Pleasure and Pain'. According to Menger, the applicability of the natural-scientific methodology to economics is an 'idle play with external analogies between phenomena of economics and those of nature' (Menger 1976: 47). It is the notion of economics as engaged in purposively human activity that supports Menger's methodology. Human consciousness experiences the world as meaningful as reflected in subjective meanings.

The Marginal Revolution grants economics headway in two respects. First, it sets human subjectivity as the very foundation of economic life and renders the utility, and the inherent subjectivity, the origin of economic value. Second, the elaboration on the concept of utility leads to its eligibility for infinitesimal calculus. The former appeals to Menger, the latter to Walras and Jevons. Furthermore, Menger's notions of uncertainty and time exhibit affinity between him and Frank Knight (1921), as pioneering institutional economists, to whom I return hereafter. Together with Knight and Coase, Menger shares the basic position that economics concerns a nomological science that is engaged in the normal working of the economic system.

The next section extends the economic subject, that is, the individual who features the post–Marginal Revolution economics. At the same time, the differences between its exponents bear upon the perception of the individual. Obviously, the individual presented as a mathematical datum differs radically from a presentation of the individual as causes and effects stem from '*one's own person*, and any of its states are links in this great structure of relationships' (Menger 1976: 51; emphasis added). The data regarding the individual feature the method, as Kaufmann argues. The next section elaborates on it.

3.4 Methodological individualism

In his *The Common Sense of Political Economy*, Philip Wicksteed (1910a, b) takes stock of the results of the Marginal Revolution *and* interprets these instructively. In this aspect, Wicksteed qualifies the conventional perception of the economic motive as 'the desire to possess wealth'. He introduces the concept of 'non-tuïsm'.[3] It means this: 'the significance *to us* of what we are doing is measured not by its importance to the man for whom it is done, but by the degree to which it furthers our own ends' (1910b: 782). It silences discussions about the putative hedonistic nature or otherwise psychological foundations of economics. It is the genuine economic force in the exchange relationship that drives the two negotiating parties. Each is interested in his own, not *per se* selfish, purposes and not in those of others. The non-tuïsm concept accords with exchange as the scope of economics since Adam Smith that has passed through the Marginal Revolution. It refers to a pure theory in which the method is individualistic and open to formulating theorems. Furthermore, the societal dimension of reciprocity features in it. This economics of exchange results from 'a *modus procedenti*' of modern writers such as Walras, Jevons, and others that starts with wants and their satisfaction of 'individuals as independent units or agents' (Schumpeter 1909: 214).

> Marginal utilities determine prices and the demand and the supply of each commodity; and prices, finally, tell us much else, and above all, how the social process of distribution will turn out. ... This, *in nuce*, is the whole of pure theory in its narrowest sense.
>
> (ibid.: 215)

'Pure', in this context, may be interpreted as silent about the institutional setting that surrounds those 'individuals as independent units or agents'. Pure theory appears to focus on the individual chooser deliberating marginal quantities. In pure theory, the actor seems to behave like an atom reacting in line with its specifications. This is just one view of the individual's role. Apparently, the presumed purview of the individual has much to do with the nature of the theory that analyses his acting; broadening the concept of the individual will broaden the theoretical perspective. Who is this individual with his non-tuïsm, and what is his role in theories? Is it a psychological entity following his hedonistic calculations, a human being of flesh and blood, a social being that cannot live without a social fabric, or a methodologically required device in formulating social-scientific theory? In all cases, the individual is the leading figure whose institutional makeup and intellectual substance may vary. The perspective of the individual is a decisive variable in the profile of economics. The spectrum is individualism-holism that has significance for the theorist's methodology and refers to the ontological and epistemological issues that social sciences generally entail. In economics, the individual has occupied this role from the outset. Schumpeter (1908: 88) coins this base '*der methodologische Individualismus*'. He is credited with baptizing individuals' leading positions in economics as '"methodological individualism"', in English-speaking regions, in the 1909 *Quarterly Journal of Economics* (Schumpeter 1909: 231). In this paper, Schumpeter emphasizes that the market equilibrium 'is brought about only by the joint action of marginal and intra-marginal sellers and buyers' (ibid.). Apparently, Schumpeter's attention is on the process of marginal calculation rather than on the individual's conduct. This emphasis may explain his remarkable perspective regarding economic order.

   Obviously, Schumpeter assures, modern pure economics à la Walras and Jevons is individualistic in its method, but this has 'nothing whatever to do with the great problems of individualism and collectivism' (ibid.: 213). The built-in methodological individualism of the whole of pure theory is a matter of 'individualistic assumptions' and 'individualistic reasoning' (ibid.: 215). A communist society would not adhere to these assumptions, and therefore, methodological individualism would not be useful nor would the individual perform in such a society. Schumpeter:

> The means of satisfying such [social] wants are valued not by individuals who merely interact, but by all individuals acting as a community consciously and jointly. This case is realized in a communistic society. There, indeed, want and utility are not as simple as they are in the case of individuals. Altho it would have to be determined somewhat artificially what the wants of such a society were, it is clear that we could speak of social utility curves.
>
> (ibid.: 216)

Obviously, a marginal analysis is presumed to be applicable to these social-utility functions. Therefore, 'the fundamental theorems concerning value can be applied, whatever may be the organization of society', Schumpeter concludes (ibid.: 224). This is a remarkable proposition for an economist of Austrian origin. It concurs with Walras's neutral position regarding appropriation rather than with Menger's, which is reasoned from an individual's need situation. Schumpeter labors under the same fault as Robbins in his definition as discussed in the preceding section. Like Robbins, Schumpeter disregards that the individual requires cost and utility data as expressed in the market processes (Ellis 1950: 5). Economic theory cannot suffice with Schumpeter's 'individualistic assumption'. It must delve into the reality of the meaning of a practical man's conduct, as Ellis explains. Under this aspect, Weber projects the individual's meaning in a general sense.

3.4.1 Method and meaning

Weber refers to the 'inside' of the individual in his interpretation of the concept of methodological individualism which is closely connected to his interpretive (*verstehende*) sociology. Weber:

> Social collectives, such as states, associations, business corporations, foundations, ... in sociological work these collectivities must be treated as solely the resultants and modes of organization of the particular acts of individual persons, since these alone can be treated as agents in a course of *subjectively understandable* action.
>
> (1922: 13; emphasis added)

The core of interpretive sociology is its reciprocity. Understanding is an understanding of the meaning of others. In this manner, subjectivity of meaning renders objectivity, that is, common meaning. It opens the opportunity to a *wertfrei* social science. Before Weber, it is Georg Simmel who recognized that mutuality features society, that is, the material object of sociology. Simmel:

> I start then from the broadest conception of society, the conception which so far as possible disregards the conflicts about definitions; that is, I think of society as existing wherever several individuals are in [a] reciprocal relationship. This reciprocity arises always from specific impulses, or by virtue of specific purposes.
>
> (1909: 296)

This perspective makes the social scientist interpret the intended meaning stemming from, for example, specific purposes that bear a relationship. Weber's version of methodological individualism amounts to a typification of the intended meanings, that is, the ideal type founded on interpretation, not as statistical averages. Here reemerges Schutz, who departs from Weber, criticizes him, and further elaborates on the ideal-type concept. It was the main theme of Chapter 2. At issue here is that Schutz's phenomenology of the social world silences the debate concerning the questions mentioned above that always come up in this context: the individual as an atom and the individualism-versus-holism dichotomy.

Regarding atomism, I refer to Simmel (1910: 376) as Schutz's precursor who demonstrates that the perception of a conscious human being as an independent a-social someone is unthinkable. An *ego*'s consciousness as something independent of any representation exists merely by the grace of the belief that the *thou* is something that is 'just for itself'. 'We are sure that the case stands the same way with the other soul and its contents'. Such *a priori* conditions reside within individuals by which they combine themselves 'into the synthesis "society"' (ibid.). What the relevance of such a profoundly philosophical thought might be shows the adverse Pareto as an exponent of atomism in economics. Pareto states, speaking for Walras:

> All human conduct is psychological … and the facts of all such branches [of human activity] are psychological facts. The principles of an economic psychology … can be *deduced* only from facts, as are the principles of physics and chemistry. … A very general view of common well-known facts gave English writers the concept of a 'final degree of utility,' and Walras the concept of 'rarity'.
>
> (1916: 1442–1443)

Facts as perceived in this quote concern a manifest instance of 'misplaced concreteness' (Schutz 1953: 1). The very problem of such a perception of the individual as 'a degree of utility' is that it passes over the intersubjectivity of the economic relation. Therefore, Pareto, Walras, and Jevons are unable to think through the nature and significance of the institutional aspect of life. Therefore, Walras disregards the appropriation issue and uses the recourse to competition as a device to render a general equilibrium. Actually, this disregard concerns the general reciprocity of social relations and particularly the manifest reciprocity of the market. However, Walras's key concept competition cannot go without a market. Therefore, an atomistic economic theory is a fallacy.

The concept of societal reciprocity may settle the holism–individualism dichotomy like it disrupts the atomism fallacy. In the holism–individualism puzzle, the holist claims that society is more than its parts. Obviously, society affects individuals, and institutional settings constrain an individual's behavior. Therefore, for example, Geoff Hodgson (1994: 61) dismisses methodological individualism and adopts the concept of 'organicism'; that is, 'individuals both constitute, and are constituted, by society'.[4] However, the defender of individualism contends that only individuals have aims and behave in accordance with them. Finally, an individual's rational action may induce institutional reform.

Apparently, both positions have their valid reasons. It is the phenomenological perspective on intersubjectivity as reciprocal awareness between the *ego* and the *thou* as an *alter ego* that cancels out the primacy issue between an individual and society. Therefore, the individuality notion in methodological individualism can only exist in the societal context. For instance, language as an 'after-consciousness of the primal expression' is an inextricable process of intersubjectivity that, all the same, gives a founding institutional thing, that is, language (Schutz 1932: 48). It is the very same process of unintended consequences of individual conduct resulting in an institutional edifice that Menger (1976: 257) discusses in his 'Theory of Money'. For that matter, this spontaneous creation of such a thing as money results from a reciprocity of relationships that always arise 'from specific impulses, or by virtue of specific purposes' (Simmel 1909: 296). It is regarding this purposiveness that Hayek underlines that

> [e]conomic theory has nothing to say about the little round disks of metal as which an objective or materialist view might try to define money.
>
> (1979: 53)

It is our individual purposiveness that fuels our societal reciprocity in language, societal conduct, money, and exchange. In this reciprocity, the Schutzian homunculus construct finds his field of activity. Schutz arrives at a Weberian methodological individualism with a remake of the ideal type. As discussed in Chapter 2, the social scientist meets the condition of specific postulates, for example, of relevance and adequacy, in order to grasp the subjective meaning of an individual's action in an objective meaning context. The additional postulate of rationality enables the economist to arrive at theoretical laws, laws regarding choice and exchange. It is the latter postulate that features in methodological individualism, so far, the phenomenological account of it.

3.4.2 *Situational logic*

Schutz's phenomenological approach to the social sciences also offers insight
into Karl Popper's struggle with the unusual combination of 'institutional individualism', which bases his concept of the logic of the situation as *the* methodology of the social sciences.

On one hand, Popper (1994: 167) proposes the term '"social institution" for
all things which set limits or create obstacles to our movements and actions as
if they were physical bodies or obstacles'. On the other, Popper considers
methodological individualism as the

> unassailable doctrine that we must try to understand all collective phe-
> nomena as due to the actions, interactions, aims, hopes, and thoughts of
> individual men, and as due to traditions created and preserved by indi-
> vidual men.
>
> (1957: 157–158)

The primacy of the individual features social science, in general, and economics, in particular. Armed with the rationality principle, this individual is engaged in situational logic.

> The analysis of the situation, the situational logic, plays a very important
> part in social life as well as in the social sciences. It is, in fact, *the* method
> of economic analysis.[5]
>
> (Popper 1945, vol. II: 97)

This quote is an extract from a chapter on 'The Autonomy of Sociology' in
which Popper (1945, vol. II) disputes both Mill's psychologism and Marx's
anti-psychologism. Popper (1945, vol. I: 57) identifies these opposite positions
as the ancient nature-versus-convention issue concerning the origin of social
laws that 'has been questioned ever since the time of Protagoras'. The anti-psy-
chologists will defend the institutionalist view that any psychologist or behaviorist category, such as motives and psychological states, 'must be supplemented
by a reference to the general situation' and, in particular, to the environment.

> In the case of human action, this environment is very largely of a social
> nature; thus our actions cannot be explained without reference to our
> social environment, to social institutions and to their manner of
> functioning.
>
> (Popper 1945, vol. II: 90)

Against this argument, the psychologist camp may bring forward that social
institutions such as the market are inexplicable without human motives. Therefore, the typical economic institutions can be derived from the psychological
'phenomena of the pursuit of wealth', Popper continues with a reference to

Mill (ibid.: 91). Ostensibly, social institutions merely concern epiphenomena of human nature and its psychological categories. On one hand, this view deserves support as it protects us against the collectivism and holism of romanticists such as Hegel and Rousseau. It is the crux of methodological individualism that there is no such thing as a general will or a group mind. On the other hand, the psychological individualism view gets mixed up as it *'is forced to adopt historicist methods'* (ibid.: 92). It means that psychologicism is forced to attempt to explain the social institution by giving a historical account of human action and reaction that eventually results in traditions, conventions, and institutions. However, the very beginning of society remains unsolved. Without language and other forms of social environment, human nature cannot perform.

> Men – i.e., human minds, the needs, the hopes, fears, and expectations, the motives and aspirations of human individuals – are, if anything, the product of life in society rather than its creators.
>
> (ibid.: 93)

'Social institutions, and with them, typical regularities or sociological laws must have existed prior to what some people are pleased to call "human nature"' (ibid.: 93). This presumption is required to stop the built-in infinite regress of the historicist account of psychologism. Institutions do exist and are indispensable to human life. Here, Schutz (1932: 138) may put forward: 'It is deeply rooted in the human mind to look for a subjective meaning' behind all there is. How the 'objective' existence of an institution to subjective meaning be traced back? It refers to the perennial tension between subjective and objective meaning that, for instance, philologists face as interpretive scientists regarding the origin of language.[6] Obviously, this what-is-first issue also refers to the situational logic concept.

Popper's search for an infinite regress stopper may be found in Schutz's (1953: 10) analysis of intersubjectivity as discussed in Chapter 2. It is a realist position that enables the social scientist to be in charge of studying an individual who is exhibiting prominence and, at the same time, avails himself of a presumably prior existence of institutions, the latter in a broad sense, indeed. It is the reciprocity in relationships between the *ego* and the *thou* as discussed in a preceding subsection that emasculates the institution-individual contrast. Schutz, together with Simmel, offers a phenomenological account of Popper's aspiration to offer a piecemeal logic of agents who find themselves in a situation against the grand designs of social utopists. For that matter, Popper argues, the majority of institutions are concerned with the unintended results of human action. In other words, the intentions that drive our actions most of the time carry unintended or even intention-contrary consequences. Popper:

> It is the (main) task (of the social sciences) of analysing the unintended social repercussions of intentional human actions.
>
> (1945, vol. II: 95)

It is Schutz who addresses this task in his phenomenological account of the institution. The same reciprocity by means of typification that constitutes society renders, for example, money, the unintended fruit of intentional human actions.

Joseph Agassi (1960, 1975), in his turn, offers a remedy for Popper's institutional-individualism contrast, which may also be interpreted in Schutz's perspective. The impasse between the poles may be overcome by a proposition that accentuates the impasse regarding the contrast, Agassi argues:

> *If* 'wholes' exist *then* they have distinct aims and interests of their own.
>
> (1960: 245)

This proposition sharpens the opposing positions. The holist claim implies that the interest of the individual is subordinated to the existing social interest. Individualism only recognizes individuals and their interests. The latter is known as '*psychologistic* individualism', for example, atomism à la Hobbes. The exact opposite is 'institutionalism-cum holism', that is, mainstream holism (ibid.: 245–246). The two options reflect the *prima facie* either–or solution in accordance with the quoted proposition. In this aspect, Popper's approach emerges as he rejects this proposition.

'Wholes' do exist, Agassi continues. These concern 'social groups as well as social institutions, in the widest sense of the word', varying from customs to constitutions and from counties to states. At the same time, these 'wholes' may only comprise interests and aims as far as people attribute interests and aims to them. 'A society or an institution cannot have aims and interests of its own' (ibid.: 247). Nevertheless, an institution may be considered as acting accordingly with the interest ascribed to it. This refining results in the 'institutionalist-individualist' solution to the puzzle and actually offers several solutions.

- Although institutions do not have aims, their existence affects an individual's behavior.
- Similarly, the existence of institutions ('as well as people's adoption of definite attitude toward them') constrain the individual's behavior (i.e., institutional analysis).
- People may 'alter an institutional situation so as to abolish or enforce social constraints and alter other people's attitudes' (i.e., institutional reform).

(ibid.: 247)

This 'institutional individualism' corresponds to Schutz's methodological individualism. The first and the second solution 'relate to an important aspect of human behaviour – the unintended social consequences of individual action' (ibid.). Actually, Agassi's proposition, 'a society or an institution cannot have aims and interests of its own', amounts to a paraphrase of methodological individualism (ibid.). The first solution point introduces the institutional dimension that the individualist-psychologistic methodology merely knows as an endogenous variable. The institutionalist-individualist methodology, as elaborated on by Agassi, remedies the individual–holism dichotomy and alters the psychologistic rationality principle into 'what Popper calls "situational logic"' by taking into account institutions as an endogenous *or* exogenous variable.[7] For that matter, Schutz's perspective renders Popper's contrasting term superfluous. Agassi's interpretation makes Popper's situational logic eligible for phenomenological interpretation, referring to both a practical man's situation and a homunculus's situation.

Noretta Koertge specifies Popper's situational logic and confronts it with Popper's own methodological positions. Koertge (1972: 199–200) distinguishes in 'situational logic – *the* only methodology the social scientist may command – two 'super-laws': the Rationality Principle (RP) and the doctrine of unintended consequences.

In the situational-logic methodology, the theorist avails himself of the RP as a 'super-law'. The theorists describe an actor's situation, that is, his beliefs, motives, and goals, and determine what an actor's perception of the situation is 'and with the addition of the Rationality Principle, deduce what the agent will (or did) do' (ibid.: 201). Obviously, the RP differs from the inductive rationality that would fuel psychologistic individualism that aims at natural science rationality. The distinguishing feature of RP is suggestive of Hayek's (1952: 24) critique on 'the slavish imitation of the method and language of Science, speak of *scientism* or the *scientific* prejudice'. The RP of Popper rather concurs with Kaufmann's economic rationality: 'not to give up more commodities than is necessary to acquire a given set of commodities' (Kaufmann 1933: 391).

Well then, 'if a given action or belief appears to be irrational, always blame your model of the agent's situation, *not* the Rationality Principle' (Koertge 1975: 457). This dovetails with Kaufmann's methodological account as discussed in Chapter 1. Popper's RP concurs with Kaufmann's concept of theoretical law. It is remarkable that Popper calls in Weber's *Verstehen*-methodology to discern 'rational behavior' from 'irrational behavior', which is or is not in accordance with the logic of the situation. This solution reappears, for instance, in his *Objective Knowledge* that discusses the historian's methodology; 'he (the historian) *understands* the historical situation' (Popper 1979: 188). Apparently, Popper does not benefit from Schutz's phenomenological foundation of Weber.

The second 'super-law' is the doctrine of unintended consequences in the social theorist's explanation scheme, as quoted earlier. The very subject of this theorist is social life within the framework of institutions. It is the same societal reciprocity that accounts for the 'super-law', that is, the phenomenon extensively dealt with by Austrian economists. By definition, the psychologism version of individualism would be unable to deal with this unintendedness – which abounds in social life – as it considers social realities as epiphenomena of psychological states. In the same manner, disrupt the unintended consequences of any conspiracy theory. Volitional action generally carries a dynamic in social life that the individual is unable to control. This features the sociological (institutional) aspect of methodological individualism that the social theorist studies instead of the triviality of a straightforward link between intention and action. Therefore, the methodology of a decision-maker results in piecemeal engineering and takes into account of the repercussions of his actions as much as possible.

For that matter, both 'super-laws' apparently run counter to the situational logic approach and its inherent piecemeal engineering that Popper is advocating. The RP seems to have an universal application, and the unintended-consequences feature of action elicits the universal proposition: '"You cannot construct foolproof institutions"' (Popper, quoted in Koertge 1972: 200). Koertge identifies other inconsistencies in this context. For instance, the doctrine of unintended consequences should never be tested in reality, Popper claims. It gives way to his aversion to social experiments such as the Soviet Revolution. For that matter, this aversion also explains Popper's preference for piecemeal engineering. Concerning the RP, Popper emphasizes that, regardless of how irrational an action may appear to be, we should never infer that the RP is false. Given Popper's own demarcation between scientific and pseudoscientific propositions, Koertge concludes with Popper:

> then some of the most fundamental explanations of human behavior according to Popper, *viz.* those relying on the Rationality Principle, are not *bona fide* scientific explanations!
>
> (ibid.: 201)

In parentheses, Koertge adds:

> (It would also appear that even if we were to reformulate the RP so that it were falsifiable, it still might not support scientific explanations – if one believes in free will, then one can hardly ascribe *nomological* force even to a true universal generalization about human decisions.)
>
> (ibid.: 201)

This afterthought is significant. Human nature and man's free will render an inductive rationality inappropriate. Therefore, it is illustrative that Popper alludes to Weber and his methodology of *Verstehen* discussing his situational logic. It is the same Popper, frightening many a social scientist by his demanding demarcation test, who proposes a different methodology for the social sciences. Therefore, it is beneficial to distinguish a Popper$_S$ and a Popper$_N$, as employed by Douglas Hands following Imre Lakatos (Hands 1985: 90). Popper$_S$ refers to the Popper who writes on methodological issues faced by the social scientist and advocates situational logic and the formulation of theoretical laws à la Kaufmann. Popper$_N$ refers to the well-known falsificationist writer regarding the natural sciences, the standard Popper advocating scientific monism and manifestly paradoxical in more than one instance, indeed.

The phenomenological interpretation of Popper's concept of situational logic enables the theorist to comply with NIE in which the institution figures either as an exogenous or an endogenous variable. From the phenomenological perspective, it is a practical man's typification of his mundane situational logic that requires a theorist's reformulation as a homunculus's situational logic governed by the rationality principle. It may be further qualified as follows. In economics, a ring of four data complexes describes an actor's situation:

- Scheme of preferences;
- Quantities and qualities of resources;
- State of the technological art;
- Institutional environment.

It is the fourth data complex that is of specific significance to economics as, in contrast to the others, the institutional environment is immediately related to an economic actor's conduct. For instance, attenuated property rights entail repercussions on an actor's economic conduct. Therefore, the situational logic methodology regards, in particular, the data complex of an institutional environment. In the analysis of the situation, the institution and the individual take turns as endogenous versus exogenous variables, that is, NIE.

3.4.3 *Situational logic against inductive rationality, an afterthought*

Lawrence Boland (1982: 3) recognizes an 'uncommon distinction' between the methodology of the theorist embodied in neoclassical analysis versus the methodology of the decision-maker. Not uncommon is this distinction in a phenomenological perspective. The phenomenologist deliberately departs from the commonsense knowledge and reflexive perspective of the individual in the lifeworld. However, it is the detached perspective of the theorist who builds his constructs of the commonsense constructs as used in mundane life. Similarly, Popper's (1945, vol. II: 97) situational logic refers to 'a very important part in social life *as well as* in the social sciences' (emphasis added). The phenomenological approach and the situational logic methodology depart from the mundane reality and actor's commonsense situational logic as the foundation of the reformulation of the commonsense concepts that constitute the basis of the situational logic methodology as a deductive analysis in the search for theoretical laws. In the Marginal Revolution, it is Menger who gives examples of this methodology. As a philosophical realist, he departs from a practical man's deliberations to find the universal essences in them. It is the postulate of the rationality principle that founds this methodology.

Against the postulated rationality of the situational-logic methodology stands the inductive rationality of the social scientist who adheres to the philosophically nominalist position. The nominalist merely observes particulars in which he may perceive regularities to constitute generally synthetic-empirical propositions. Terence Hutchison is a marked exponent of this position in economics. The analytical part or pure theory creates a "'language for discussing of the facts'", Terence W. Hutchison (1938: 40) repeats after Frank P. Ramsey. This 'language' accounts for the very beginning of the inductive analysis. However, in the nominalist perspective, the 'pure theory' does not refer to universals about the world as it is. Contrariwise, it is the origin and status of the synthetic proposition that seems to be unambiguously clear, that is, induction by which particulars constitute a general synthetic-empirical proposition.

Eventually, it is the synthetic-empirical propositions that form economics' scientific nature, Hutchison argues. 'Scientific knowledge, explanation, and prognosis can only be based ultimately on empirical regularities' (Hutchison 1938: 163). Hutchison recaps his position as follows.

> Advance in economic knowledge depends ultimately on discovering, however limited, provisional, and tentative they may be, such regularities, and if such discoveries cannot be made – and we reject such a pessimistic view – economics as an empirical science can go no further.
>
> (ibid.: 164)

In this respect, Hutchison alludes to Popper's falsification test as the passably methodological route with factualness as the ultimate authority of scientific knowledge. It is plausible that Hutchison does not distinguish between an actor's and a theorist's rationality. In this context, it is merely inductive rationality that counts as scientifically valid. Moreover, it is the theorist who avails himself of it.

Brian Arthur is a more recent advocate of inductive rationality as it may address the extremely complex issues that the economist faces. Arthur:

> Economists have long been uneasy with the assumption of perfect, deductive rationality in decision contexts that are complicated and potentially ill-defined. The level at which humans can apply perfect rationality is surprisingly modest. Yet it has not been clear how to deal with imperfect or bounded rationality. From the reasoning given above, I believe that as humans in these contexts we use inductive reasoning: we induce a variety of working hypotheses, act upon the most credible, and replace hypotheses with new ones if they cease to work. Such reasoning can be modeled in a variety of ways. Usually this leads to a rich psychological world in which agents' ideas or mental models compete for survival against other agents' ideas or mental models – a world that is both evolutionary and complex.
>
> (1994: 411)

Seemingly, Arthur applies Boland's 'uncommon distinction'. He explicitly focuses on humans and their predicament of ill-defined decision contexts.

Arthur's quote reads that it is initially the actor who is modeled with inductive rationality. Unmarked, Arthur applies his *own* inductive rationality in modeling a situation, for example, the Bar Problem. A bar offers entertainment on a certain night. $N = 100$ persons is the maximum number that may attend the function at the bar. However, it is enjoyable if it is not too crowded. Actually, if there are fewer than 60 people present, there is a reason to return next week. The only information regards the number of visitors last week. Supplemented with some other assumptions, Arthur's computer modeling finds a diversity of possible results.

> The inductive-reasoning system I have described above consists of a multitude of "elements" in the form of belief-models or hypotheses that adapt to the aggregate environment they jointly create.
>
> (ibid.: 410)

This is a system in which learning takes place. What is at issue is how this ecology of hypotheses (e.g., regarding the number of bar visitors) evolves over time, Arthur (ibid.: 409) notes.

Obviously, this is merely a fragmentary presentation of Arthur's paper. It is relevant here that it is engaged in possible outcomes of an actor's inductive rationality and that an agent and a theorist coincide in this respect. Arthur's approach is an example of Colander's (2000) prospect of New Millennium Economics. As referred to in Chapter 1, Colander expects that the future of economics amounts to a 'simply looking for possibly exploitable patterns in data' (ibid.: 128). Definitely, Arthur is engaged in an actor's situation that is precarious in terms of information. As an exponent of the Santa Fe Institute, he belongs to the tradition of Hebert A. Simon and elaborates on the idea of bounded rationality. The complexity that the actors face urges them to have recourse to procedural rationality such as the complexity theory that the Santa Fe Institute is famous for. Simon:

> The theory of heuristic search, cultivated in artificial intelligence and information processing psychology, is concerned with devising or identifying search procedures that will permit systems of limited computational capacity to make complex decisions and solve difficult problems.
>
> (1978: 12)

Basically, these forms of procedural rationality regard inductive rationality as it is founded on statistical research of databases. Another Santa-Fe-Institute exponent, J. Doyne Farmer, words it rather explicitly:

> In "experimental philosophy", propositions are inferred from the phenomena, and afterwards rendered general by induction. This approach is drilled into physicists.
>
> (2013: 380)

As discussed in Chapter 1, Farmer presents it as an enlightened contrast against traditional economics based on 'feigned axioms' (ibid.). It is a strong reaction to the neoclassical tradition of rationality of maximization.

> The (neoclassical) promise of 'rationality' is that once the assumptions are explicitly stated, *anyone* can see that the conclusions reached are true whenever the assumptions are true. ... It is this universality of rational arguments that forms the basis of our understanding of behavior or phenomena.
>
> (Boland 1992: 93–94)

The consequent issue is how the decision-maker *knows* his objective function and the constraints; that is, how he is acquainted with the relevant information of the data ring? It is in line with the notion of inductive rationality that the decision-maker acquires knowledge with 'a logic which uses singular observations as assumptions and reaches general, universally true conclusions' (Boland 1992: 94).

It is their perspective on the knowledge issue that renders the neoclassical economists confrères of the theorists who are engaged in procedural-rationality devices. The neoclassical theorist ascribes inductive rationality to the actor he studies. The economic agent, reasons the neoclassical economist, may observe the quantity and quality of his resources, and naturally knows his preferences. Briefly, the actor is a positivist whose inductive rationality enables him, in principle, to know the relevant data of his situation. In this respect, the actor who figures in neoclassical economics corresponds with the actor in the sophisticated models of theorists who, as behaviorists from the outset, have no high opinion of the knowledge capacities of their actors as they have seen the ill-defined situation in which the latter may find themselves. The common ground of neoclassical economists and procedural-rationality theorists is the nominalist position that they share regarding the epistemological makeup of the actors they study. The positivist makeup of the actor who may observe the data that are required unites these schools. The difference concerns the degree to which the actor may succeed in acquiring the knowledge that is needed.

Boland's uncommon distinction helps to identify the fundamental contrast between the situational logic methodology versus inductive rationality that both have applications in economics. It is the rationality ascribed to the individual actor that turns out to be the shibboleth. Against the positivist makeup of the actor that gives away the nominalist position of his creator-theorist stands the individual actor as a second-order construct of the phenomenological theorist who, as a realist, endeavors to grasp the meaning of an individual's situational logic. It is as von Mises words it:

> economics is not about things and tangible material objects; it is about men, their meaning and action. Goods, commodities, and wealth and all

the other notions of conduct are not elements of nature; they are elements of *human meaning* and conduct.

(1949: 92; emphasis added)

In this afterthought recurs the contrast as distinguished in Chapter 1 between 'inside versus outside' theories. It is a leitmotif that has acquired its evidence and relevance due to the prominence of human subjectivity since the Marginal Revolution. This leitmotif may also be found in the distinction 'half-way explanations' versus 'rock-bottom explanations' (Watkins 1957: 106). What is at issue is whether it is merely nice to know which intentions of human beings fuel their actions or that these intentions are indispensable in explaining human action. A halfway explanation does not delve into the meaning of the individual. They may be divided into (1) statistical analysis and (2) sub-intentional explanations (Heath 2015: 6.1, 6.2). The rock-bottom version regards the specification of the meaning behind an individual's conduct. According to Schutz (Schutz 1953: 27), the halfway explanation that leaves out human subjectivity is an 'intellectual shorthand'. Finally, however, Schutz argues,

the postulate of subjective interpretation as applied to economics as well as to all the other social sciences means merely that we always can -and for certain purposes must- refer to the activities of the subjects within the social world and their interpretation by the actors in terms of systems of projects, available means, motives, relevances and so on.

(ibid.)

'The activities of the subjects' *are* meaning is the distinguishing postulate that bears the situational logic methodology in its phenomenological interpretation. Therefore, I consider this situational logic 'is, in fact, *the* method of economic analysis' (Popper 1945, vol. II: 97).

3.5 Conclusion

Under the heading 'Scope and Method of Economics', I discussed some of the vicissitudes of economic thought. The primary idea in this account is, first, to denote elements in the theory that are discussed that allude to or unambiguously raise the institutional matter. The second leitmotif in the excursion is a further exploration of moments in the economic thought that is discussed that may be enriched by the phenomenological perspective.

Scope and method, Kaufmann identifies, do not coincide in economics. The definition of the scope as subject matter should be in accord with what it is '*as actually used*' (Kaufmann 1933: 382). The prevailing interpretation is that exchange is the very subject matter of economics as it has been since Adam Smith. At the same time, the Marginal Revolution has brought in the concept of choice as a plausible alternative candidate. The infinitesimal calculus narrows, by nature, an economic subject's attention and concentrates it on a clearly quantified decision issue. Furthermore, a perennial tension exists between limited means and a broader gamut of ends. Therefore, Robbins's definition of choice as a matter of subject seems plausible. Buchanan, however, argues that this definition passes over the individual who requires market prices to found his decisions. Robbins opens the route to an institutionless economics that is engaged in calculating the pros and cons of a decision as a kind of welfare economics. However, economics exists in reciprocal interaction that features exchange. It is a social affair, in need of an institutional fabric. This is the scope of economics.

As defined in Chapter 1, the method question refers to (a) 'the kind of data can be regarded as suitable material' and (b) On what general principles may one make inductive generalisations from the available data?' (ibid.: 384). The Marginal Revolution determines the response to these questions. It introduces methodological individualism, that is, the data that represent the subject matter refer directly to the individual economic subject who, as a practical man, finds himself in a situation that urges him to take small steps of a more or less decision format. Regarding part (b) of the method question, it is Menger's analysis, as rephrased by Kaufmann, that gives the general maxim: 'not to give up more commodities than is necessary to acquire a given set of commodities' (ibid.: 391).[8]

This interpretation does not merely allude to but immediately raises the institutional matter as the general principles (b) refer to the exchange relation. In the phenomenological perspective, the reciprocity that features the exchange renders that it is, from the outset, an institutional phenomenon. More generally, it is an instance of misplaced concreteness to leave out the institutional dimension.

This brings in the relevance of phenomenology; the second leitmotif of this chapter. Schutz's phenomenology of the social world offers profound insights into the nature of the institutional dimension that have immediate significance for a further elaboration of the general economic principle as formulated by Kaufmann. In phenomenology, human consciousness is featured of man in his daily pursuit. Schutz's approach reconstructs the commonsense principle of a practical man's, more or less, considerations in second-order constructs of ideal types. Central in this is the process of typification of subjective phenomena that acquire objectivity. From this phenomenological perspective, I perceive Popper's situational logic methodology as *the* method of economic analysis.

This methodological position features the discussion of the Marginal Revolution triumvirate, separating Walras and Jevons from Menger. Walras and Jevons basically adhere to a nominalist perspective against Menger, who, as an exponent of Aristotelian realism, is in search of the essentialia that govern the domain of economics. A product of this difference is, for instance, that Walras and Jevons consider utility presented in mathematical terms as 'suitable material' (ibid.: 384) However, a unifying thought bears Menger's *Principles*; that is, a practical man's subjective value regards the genuine datum meant under question (a) earlier. This difference entails another one between

Walras and Menger. Walras is definitely engaged in the institutional dimension as, for example, his excursion on the Paris Exchange Bourse shows. However, in his pure economics, he applies competition as an assumption to arrive at a general equilibrium and disregards the appropriation issue as the essential institutional dimension without which the idea of subjective utility hangs in the air and lacks the footing to incentivize. The contrast of logical versus generative causality recaps the differences between Walras and Jevons, on one hand, and against Menger, on the other. The former reflect an endeavor to arrive at a formal system of interdependent variables. The latter urges the theorist to find evidence of human subjectivity as the origin of the working of the system. In this difference reemerges the basic opposition between nominalists and realists, respectively.

The fundamental origin of the dividing line that features in this chapter concerns the concept of meaning. This is the shibboleth. The phenomenological perspective delves into human consciousness and construes an analytical apparatus to grasp the meaning of human activity, for example, in economic life. Its witness to activity *is* meaning. It is the very opposite of economics that represents the nominalist position, doing economics as based on observables, revealed preferences, and choices as established facts.

Notes

1 According to William Jaffé (1976: 511), it is in Schumpeter's (1954) *History of Economic Analysis* that the term Marginal Revolution started as a tag for the lumped-together contributions to the economic analysis of Walras, Jevons, and Menger.
2 For that matter, Abram Bergson (1938) shows in his classic paper on welfare economics that value judgments appear to be indispensable in formulating welfare conditions in spite of the (individual) utility calculus as introduced by the Cambridge economists and, for example, Enrico Barone (1905), Vilfredo Pareto (1916), and Abba P. Lerner (1944).
3 See Kirzner (1960: Ch. 3, n. 34).
4 Hodgson realizes that adopting his 'organicism' results in an infinite-regress issue of mutual influences of an individual and society which might only be eliminated by the either–or choice, Hodgson argues. It is either "all reducible to individuals" or "it is all social and institutional" (Hodgson 1994: 62). Hodgson ascertains that methodological individualism 'takes the individuals as given'; it implies 'a rigid and dogmatic compartmentalization of analysis' (ibid.).
5 In several of Popper's publications reemerges the concept of situational logic (e.g., Popper 1967: 147; 1979: 70).
6 Schutz (1932: 133) discusses in extenso the relationship between the objective and the subjective meaning of products of action, which 'are *ipso facto* evidence of what went on in the minds of the actors who made them'. The tension between the objective and the subjective meaning of this evidence constitutes the key to *understanding* the structure of the social reality. What remains is the requirement of a decision, a radical step to stop the infinite regress between object and subject.
7 John Groenewegen et al. (1995: 473) point out that this 'institutional individualism' bridges OIE and NEI as shown in Douglass North's theoretical development.
8 Wicksteed's (1910b: 775) concept of non-tuïsm constitutes a variation on Kaufmann's (1933: 391) rationality principle, that is, 'not to give up more commodities than is necessary to acquire a given set of commodities'.

References

Agassi, J., 1960, Methodological Individualism, *The British Journal of Sociology, Vol. 11*, 244–270.

Agassi, J., 1975, Institutional Individualism, *The British Journal of Sociology, Vol. 26*, 144–155.

Arrow, K.J., 1974, *The Limits of Organization*, New York: W.W. Norton & Company.

Arthur, W.B., 1994, Inductive Reasoning and Bounded Rationality, *The American Economic Review, Vol. 84, No. 2, Papers and Proceedings*, 406–411.

Barone, E., 1905, The Ministry of Production in the Collectivist State. In: Hayek, F.A., ed., 1935, *Collectivist Economic Planning*, 245–290. London: Routledge & Kegan Paul.

Bergson, A., 1938, A Reformulation of Certain Aspects of Welfare Economics, *The Quarterly Journal of Economics, Vol. 52*, 310–334.

Blaug, M., 1973, Was There a Marginal Revolution? In: R.D. Collison Black, A.W. Coats, C.D.W. Goodwin, eds., 1973, *The Marginal Revolution in Economics*, 3–14, Durham, NC: Duke University Press.

Boland, L.A., 1982, *The Foundation of Economic Method*, London: George Allen & Unwin.

Boland, L.A., 1992, *The Principles of Economics*, London: Routledge.

Buchanan, J.M., 1979, *What Should Economists Do?* Indianapolis, IN: Liberty Fund.

Coase, R.H., 1937, The Nature of the Firm, *Economica, Vol. 4, (n.s.)*, 386–405.

Coase, R.H., 1946, Marginal Cost Controversy, *Economica, New Series, Vol. 13, No. 51*, 169–182.

Coase, R.H., 1960, The Problem of Social Cost, *The Journal of Law and Economics, Vol. 3*, 1–44.

Coase, R.H., 1992, The Institutional Structure of Production, *The American Economic Review, Vol. 82, No. 4*, 713–719.

Coase, R.H., 1998, The New Institutional Economics, *The American Economic Review, Vol. 88, No. 2, Papers and Proceedings*, 72–74.

Colander, D., 2000, New Millennium Economics: How Did It Get This Way, and What Way Is It? *The Journal of Economic Perspectives, Vol. 14*, 121–132.

Collison Black, R.D., A.W. Coats, C.D.W. Goodwin, eds., 1973, *The Marginal Revolution in Economics*, Durham, NC: Duke University Press.

Eberle, T.S., 2010, The Phenomenological Life-World Analysis and the Methodology of the Social Sciences, *Humanistic Studies 33*, 123–139.

Ellis, H.S., 1950, The Economic Way of Thinking, *The American Economic Review, Vol. 40*, 1–12.

Farmer, J.D., 2013, Hypotheses Non Fingo: Problems with the Scientific Method in Economics, *The Journal of Economic Methodology, Vol. 20, No. 4*, 377–385.

Groenewegen, J., F. Kerstholt, A. Nagelkerke, 1995, On Integrating New and Old Institutionalism: Douglass North Building Bridges, *Journal of Economic Issues, Vol. XXIX, No. 2*, 467–475.

Hands, D.W., 1985, Karl Popper and Economic Methodology, *Economics and Philosophy, Vol. 1*, 83–99.

von Hayek, F.A., ed., 1935, *Collectivist Economic Planning*, London: Routledge & Kegan Paul Ltd.

von Hayek, F.A., 1952, [1979], *The Counter-Revolution of Science*, Indianapolis, IN: Liberty Press.

Heath, J., 2015, Methodological Individualism. In: E.N. Zalta, ed., *The Stanford Encyclopedia of Philosophy*, Spring 2015 Edition, URL = http://plato.stanford.edu/archives/spr2015/entries/methodological-individualism/, accessed 09/2022.

Hodgson, G.N., 1994, The Return of Institutional Economics. In: N.J. Smelser, R. Swedberg, eds., 1994, *The Handbook of Economic Sociology*, 58–76, Princeton, NJ: Princeton University Press.

Hutchison, T.W., 1938, [1960], *The Significance and Basic Postulates of Economic Theory*, New York: Augustus M. Kelley [Reprint 1965].

Jaffé, W., 1976, Menger, Jevons and Walras De-homogenized, *Economic Inquiry, Vol. XIV*, 511–524.

Jevons, W.S., 1871, *The Theory of Political Economy*, London: Macmillan and Co.

Kaufmann, F., 1933, On the Subject-Matter and Method of Economic Science, *Economica, No. 42*, 381–401.

Kaufmann, F., 1944, *Methodology of the Social Sciences*, Atlantic Highlands, New Jersey: Humanities Press.

Kirzner, I.M., 1960, [1976], *The Economic Point of View*, Kansas City, MO: Sheed and Ward, Inc.

Knight, F.H., 1921, [1971], *Risk, Uncertainty and Profit*, Chicago, IL: Chicago University Press.

Knight, F.H., 1934, The Nature of Economic Science in Some Recent Discussion, *The American Economic Review, Vol. 24*, 225–238.

Koertge, N., 1972, On Popper's Philosophy of Social Science, *The Philosophy of Science Association (PSA): Proceedings of the Biennial Meeting of the Philosophy of Science Association, Vol. 1972*, 195–207.

Koertge, N., 1975, Popper's Metaphysical Research Program for the Human Sciences, *Inquiry, 18*, 437–462.

Kregel, J.A., 1992, Walras' Auctioneer and Marshall's Well-informed Dealers: Time, Market Prices and Normal Supply Prices, *Quaderni di Storia dell'Economia Politica, Vol. XII*, 531–551.

Lerner, A.P., 1944, *The Economics of Control*, New York: The Macmillan Company.

Menger, C., 1883, [2005], *Untersuchungen über die Methoden der Socialwissenschaften und der Politischen Oekonomie*, Leipzig: Verlag von Duncker & Humblot; [Elibron Classics series].

Menger, C., 1976, [2007], *Principles of Economics*, translated by J. Dingwall, B.F. Hoselitz, Auburn, AL: Ludwig von Mises Institute; original title: *Grundsätze der Volkswirtschaftslehre*, 1871.

Mises, L., 1935, Economic Calculation in the Socialist Common Wealth. In: F.A. von Hayek, ed., 1935, *Collectivist Economic Planning*, 87–130, London: Routledge & Kegan Paul Ltd.

von Mises, L., 1949, [2012], *Human Action*, New Haven, CT: Yale University Press [Martino Publishing].

Pareto, V., 1900, On the Economic Phenomenon; a Reply to Benedetto Croce, 1953, *International Papers, 3*, translated by F. Priuli, 180–196; (Sul Fenomeno Economico, *Giornale degli Economisti, II*, 1900, 139–162)

Pareto, V., 1916, [1963], *The Mind and Society*, Vol. I–IV, New York: Dover Publications, Inc.

Popper, K.R., 1945 [1962], *The Open Society and Its Enemies*, London: Routledge and Kegan Paul.

Popper, K.R., 1957, [1961], *The Poverty of Historicism*, London: Routledge and Kegan Paul.

Popper, K.R., 1967, La Rationalité et le Statut du Principe de Rationalité. In: E.M. Claassen, ed., *Les Fondements Philosophiques des Systèmes Économiques*, 142–150, Paris: Payo.

Popper, K.R., 1979, *Objective Knowledge*, rev. ed., London: At the Clarendon Press.

Popper, K.R., 1994, *The Myth of the Framework: In Defence of Science and Rationality*, London: Routledge.

Robbins, L., 1932, [1962], *An Essay on the Nature and Significance of Economic Science*, 2nd ed., London: MacMillan & Co, Ltd.

Schumpeter, J.A., 1908, *Das Wesen und der Hauptinhalt der theoretischen Nationalökonomie*, Leipzig: Verlag von Duncker & Humblot.

Schumpeter, J.A., 1909, On the Concept of Social Value, *The Quarterly Journal of Economics, Vol. 23*, 213–232.

Schumpeter, J.A., 1954, [1981], *History of Economic Analysis*, London: George Allen & Unwin.

Schutz, A., 1932, [1967], *The Phenomenology of the Social World*, New York: Northwestern University Press; [*Der sinnhafte Aufbau der sozialen Welt*, Wien: Julius Springer].

Schutz, A., 1953, Common-Sense and Scientific Interpretation of Human Action, *Philosophy and Phenomenological Research, Vol. 14, No. 1*, 1–38.

Simmel, G., 1909, The Problem of Sociology, *American Journal of Sociology, Vol. 15, No. 3*, 289–320.

Simmel, G., 1910, How Is Society Possible? *American Journal of Sociology, Vol. 16, No. 3*, 372–391.

Simon, H.A., 1978, Rationality as Process and as Product of Thought, *The American Economic Review, Vol. 68, No. 2*, 1–16.

Smelser, N.J., R. Swedberg, eds., 1994, *The Handbook of Economic Sociology*, Princeton, NJ: Princeton University Press.

Smith, A., 1776, [2005], *The Inquiry into the Nature and Causes of the Wealth of Nations*, London: W. Strahan and T. Cadell; The Electronic Classics Series, Penn State: Pennsylvania State University.

Walras, L., 1954, [1977], *Elements of Pure Economics*, translated by W. Jaffé, Fairfield: Augustus M. Kelley Publishers.

Watkins, J.W.N., 1957, Historical Explanation in the Social Sciences, *The British Journal for the Philosophy of Science, Vol. 8*, 104–117.

Weber, M., 1922, [1968], *Economy and Society*, edited by G. Roth, C. Wittich, Berkeley: University of California Press.

Wicksteed, P.H., 1910a, *The Common Sense of Political Economy*, 1933, edited by L. Robbins, Vol. I, London: Routledge & Kegan Paul Limited.

Wicksteed, P.H., 1910b, *The Common Sense of Political Economy*, 1933, edited by L. Robbins, Vol. II, London: Routledge & Kegan Paul Limited.

4   Frank H. Knight, pioneer in NIE

4.1 Introduction

Frank H. Knight is famous for his idea of uncertainty; Knightian uncertainty. Against risk as a statistically measurable concept, uncertainty is, in Knight's definition, unmeasurable and refers to unpredictable future events, our ignorance, and our limited knowledge. With this notion of uncertainty, central to his *Risk, Uncertainty, and Profit*, Knight is the precursor of new institutional economics (NIE). Before him the history of economic thought contains several notions that allow an NIE interpretation, for example, the instance of information asymmetry between the board of a regulated company and the administration members, as discussed by Adam Smith (1776: 627). Comparable instances also offer Carl Menger and Léon Walras, as discussed in the preceding chapter. However, it is Knight, whose thought as developed in his classic unfolds the theoretical foundations of NIE. His concept of uncertainty encompasses Ronald Coase's concept of transaction cost. Furthermore, it is Knight who identifies before Coase the concept of property rights as the very foundation of economics.

In some respects, Knight and Coase are kindred spirits. For instance, that Knight's (1924) criticism of Arthur Pigou concurs with Coase's decline of Pigou's ideas underlines their analytical affinity. The opening sentence of Coase's seminal 'Firm' paper reads:

> Economic theory has suffered in the past from a failure to state clearly its assumptions.
>
> (1937: 386)

In this aspect, at the same time Coase passes by his predecessor whose 1921 'essay' is a detailed analysis of the presuppositions of the economic system as a model of perfect competition. It is Knight who initiates investigating the *ceteris paribus* clauses that warrant Coase's adage '"The normal economic system works itself"' (Arnold Plant, quoted in Coase 1991: 38). Knight endeavors

DOI: 10.4324/9781315764221-4

to search out and placard the unrealities of the postulates of theoretical economics, not for the purpose of discrediting the doctrine, but with a view to making clear its theoretical limitations.

(ibid.: 11)

Since Adam Smith, the *general principles* of free competition feature this theoretical economics. Knight's criticism does not regard the simplicity of this competitive ideal 'but for not following it in a sufficiently self-conscious, critical, and explicit way' (ibid.: 10). Knight's project is to clarify the presuppositions of the automatic working of the economic system, that is, economists' null hypothesis. Accordingly, he states:

Economics is the study of a particular form of organization of human want-satisfying activity ... called free enterprise or the competitive system.

(Knight 1921: 9)

Basically, Knight is engaged in the methodological procedure as proposed by Felix Kaufmann as discussed in Chapter 1, that is, the search for new *ceteris paribus* clauses that yet may warrant the null hypothesis. He systematically unfolds the theoretical changes in the models of the economic system proceeding from static certainty toward dynamic uncertainty and progressive economic development.

Knight (1921: ix) starts his project with implications of certainty, that is, part two: 'perfect competition'. The economics of exchange is engaged in two basic problems that division of labor entails: first, assignment of tasks and, second, apportionment of rewards (ibid.: 55). Voluntary exchange between individuals solves these two basic problems *'together, as one'* (ibid.: 56). The foundation of this process is private *ownership* of productive resources. Paraphrasing the feats of the Marginal Revolution, Knight restates the 'fundamental law of conduct' in which alternative uses of resources yield equal amounts of resource *'equivalent returns in all fields'* (ibid.: 65). It rules Knight's 'imaginary society' that is peopled by a '"random sample" of the population of the industrial nations of to-day'; members of society who 'act with complete "rationality" who are supposed to "know what they want" and to seek it "intelligently"' (ibid.: 76–77). Shortly, Knight implicitly constructs (Schutzian) homunculi who abide by the law of conduct and demonstrate the automatic working of the economic system. The basic idea behind this working out of effects is the mechanistic idea of equilibrium. Like water that seeks its equilibrium level, so it is in economic phenomena.

Goods move from the point of lower to one of higher demand or *price*, and every such movement obliterates the price difference which causes it.

(ibid.)

The working of perfect competition renders the 'costs in the large identical with the distributive shares' of land, capital, and labor (ibid.: 18–19).

However, in reality, cost and value merely '"tend" to equality'. 'They are usually separated by a margin of "profit," positive or negative' (ibid.: 19) which, in Knight's analysis, is the shibboleth that betrays that the actual economic system fails to meet the conditions of normal working. The origin of this failure is uncertainty which Knight identifies as the most 'important underlying difference between the conditions which theory is compelled to assume and those which exist in fact' (ibid.: 51). Knight's project is to uncover the premises of perfect competition theory.[1] In this, he notes, the argument will differ 'very little from Marshall's "Principles"' (ibid.; Marshall 1890). Marshall develops his 'Copernican system' of a whole of simultaneous mutuality of demand and supply (Keynes 1933: 183). He goes on to confront his 'system' with reality; that is, he deals with a variety of instances when this mutuality (reciprocity) does not occur or a subsidiary requires additional provision, for example, in the case of external economies or lack of market transparency, respectively. Knight captures all the instances of deviation from perfect competition under the heading of uncertainty. It is the subject of part three: 'imperfect competition through risk and uncertainty' (Knight 1921: vi). This subject I elaborate, further leaving aside the certainty implications, as it is under risk and uncertainty that the new institutional economic insights acquire their very significance.

The greatness of Knight is that he lards his analyses with philosophical thought. Epistemological issues precede his economics, and a theory of knowledge accompanies the introduction of uncertainty. Intriguing is that particularly the latter accords with the phenomenological perspective as discussed in Chapter 2. Furthermore, Knight proves to adhere to philosophical realism. In this aspect, Felix Kaufmann's methodological insights as presented in Chapter 1 are straightforwardly applicable to interpret Knight. It concerns preliminaries that particularly gain relevance when uncertainty appears.

This chapter is divided into three sections. The first regards Knight's methodological and philosophical preliminaries. The second discusses his *pièce de résistance*, that is, the theoretical elaboration of the economic system under the sway of risk and uncertainty. It elaborates on the entrepreneur and the individual's enterprise as the very organization that is expedient to address the uncertainties men meet in the economy as a system that produces wants-satisfying goods for the general market. The final section, subdivided into a philosophical and an NIE afterthought, provides a review and concluding thoughts.

4.2 Knight's methodological and philosophical preliminaries

Knight's *Risk, Uncertainty, and Profit* is a fruit of the aftermath of the *Methodenstreit*, that is, a well-elaborated reflection on its concluding compromise. 'In the present writer's view, the correct "middle way"', Knight puts forward, is between deductive abstraction versus 'a purely objective, descriptive science' (ibid.: 6). At the same time, his methodological message aspires to be more challenging than merely steering the middle course. Knight aims to buttress economics as an exact science originating from deductive rationalism by scrutinizing its very limitations in empiricism. It is a methodological stand that is reminiscent of Kaufmann's elegant formulation, as referred to in Chapter 1. Kaufmann:

> For, with rationalism, it is critical of sense unguided by reason; and, with empiricism, it is critical of reason unchecked by sense.
>
> (1944: 12)

This critical rationalism, or critical empiricism, is an economist's methodologically appropriate attitude. 'There is abundant need for the use of both deduction and induction in economics as in other sciences' (Knight 1921: 6). At the same time, we require abstraction, '"pure theory"', as 'the *first step*' toward understanding our reality. Knight in a footnote:

> The importance of generalization arises from the fact that as our minds are built, it is nearly fruitless to attempt to observe phenomena unless we approach them with questions to be answered. *This is what a hypothesis really is, a question.*
>
> (ibid.: 7–8, n. 1; emphasis added)

In what follows in the footnote, Knight associates this questioning with our common-sense generalizations as the basis of human conduct. From this, he notes, 'Our knowledge of ourselves is based on introspective observation', albeit intuitive. What is significant is the extension of this 'introspective observation' regarding 'our fellow human beings [which] is also based upon interpretation of the communicative signs of speech, gesture, facial expression, etc.' (ibid.).

Knight explicitly adds that these 'statements must not be thought of as dealing with philosophical problems' (ibid.). In this respect, he mobilizes Mill's authority as an empiricist 'holding that all general truths or axioms are ultimately inductions from experience' (ibid.). Nevertheless, however, these statements exactly invite some further thought. The concept of 'introspective observation' may be interpreted as self-consciousness. Furthermore, Knight associates this concept with the human mind's basic attitude to construct hypotheses and generalizations to answer the questions posed by the observation. Knight: 'Superficial observation suggests questions [i.e., hypotheses, Knight notes] which study answers' (ibid.). Here reemerges the quest for generalization, leaving behind his adherence to Mill's empiricism.

Knight's footnote considerations reflect the puzzle of observation versus hypothesis in which each of them fights to gain the upper hand. From a phenomenological point of view, Knight's concept of introspective observation may be interpreted as common sense constructs that men command in their interrelationships, rendering their conduct founded on general principles. It is exactly this philosophical perspective that may explain that it is rightly in the field of economic phenomena 'where analysis is in any degree applicable and anything more than mere description possible' (ibid.: 8). Economic conduct is founded on mental constructs, commonsense hypotheses regarding one's fellow human being. This explains Knight's opening sentence:

> Economics, or more properly theoretical economics, is the only one of the social sciences which has aspired to the distinction of an exact science.
>
> (ibid.: 3)

As stated, it is Knight's methodologically inspired project to safeguard the exact nature of economics by scrutinizing its empirical limitations. Rephrased, in case of imperfect competition through risk and uncertainty, it regards a search for those *ceteris paribus* clauses that repair the working of the economic system.

At the same time, the introduction of risk and uncertainty renders it implausible to hold on to economics as an exact science. Risk and uncertainty bring along time, the very notion of human life, expressed in intensities and qualitative phenomena that exhibit their Bergsonian *durée*. Par excellence, human wants concern a matter of intensity referring to 'states of consciousness, sensations, feelings, passions, efforts, [are] capable of growth and diminution' (Bergson 1913: 1). They constitute the *'common starting-point of economic reasoning'*, Knight notes, and, at the same time,

> the most obstinately unknown of all the unknowns in the whole system of variables with which economic science deals.
>
> (Knight 1922: 455–456; emphasis added)

Humanity enters the analysis, leaving behind the mechanistic equilibrium of perfect competition. The unpredictability of human wants is the immediate issue that the dropping of the certainty assumption raises. The entrepreneurs base their productive services on anticipations of prospective human wants that will be upset, without doubt, 'producing a divergence between costs and selling price, which otherwise would be equalized by competition'; voilà, the rise of profits or losses (Knight 1921: 198). Pendant as a source of uncertainty is the contingencies that beset the productive services themselves.

No longer is knowledge a self-evident item or a non-issue for the omniscient actor. What is at issue is to denote the nature of knowledge, its function, and particularly the meaning of partial knowledge, that is, to denote a theory of knowledge. Knight's concept of knowledge offers things in common with Schutz's phenomenological approach as discussed in Chapter 2, albeit for a part. The very common thing in it regards the idea of human consciousness' authority as an analytical departing point. Knight words it as follows:

We *perceive* the world before we react to it, and we react not to what we perceive, but always to what we *infer*.

(1921: 201)

This quote reflects a philosophically realist position, postulating reality as existing independent of human perception. At the same time, it assumes that reality is intelligible in universals that logically *a priori* precede our particular knowledge of the world. In Kaufmann's vocabulary, universals regard 'concepts that *are* meaning' (Kaufmann 1944: 18). They cannot be further rephrased, for example, colors or man's identity. Knight paraphrases this stance as follows.

We have, then, our dogma which is the presupposition of knowledge, in this form; that the world is made up of *things*, which, *under the same circumstances*, always *behave in the same way*.

(1921: 204)

Knight's *things* refer to what Kaufmann calls 'a set of presuppositions that "make experience possible"' (Kaufmann 1940: 135). They refer to '"necessary truth"', 'formulating the presuppositions contained in experience' (ibid.: 137). Schutz elucidates this as follows:

But this is not the "experience" of shallow empiricism. It is rather the immediate prepredicative encounter which we have with any direct object of intuition.

(1932: 244)

'"Ultimate" things', designates Knight (1921: 205) that what may be grasped from the immediate pre-predicative encounter with reality. At the same time, it is obvious that our daily objects of experience do not meet such a fundamental description. The everyday '"things"' 'are complexes of things which really are unchanging' (ibid.).

It is science that unravels and analyzes 'the variable complexes into unvarying constituents, until now we have with us the electron' (ibid.). It corresponds to Schutz's concept of science. It replaces commonsense concepts with scientific thought objects, shedding the 'fluid vagueness of sense, [replaced by an] exact definition of thought' (Schuetz 1953: 2). In physics, it results in constructs such as the electron, Knight argues. However, the question is, What is the significance of this idea of scientific thought objects for the economist as a social scientist? The economic actor in his predicament of uncertainty requires '*workable* knowledge' instead of a dogma that the world is made up of ultimate things or universals (Knight 1921: 205).

Apparently, humans take things for granted that are sufficient for coming to terms with fellow humans and the world around them. Humans classify the world around them in 'a manageable number of *kinds* of things' (ibid.). Our limited intelligence makes us classify and infer similarities 'in respects not open to immediate observation' (ibid.: 205–206). It founds human thought. The properties of things, that is, universal concepts, 'are not shuffled and combined at random in nature', … This is the dogma of the "reality of classes" familiar to students of logic' (ibid.: 206). Again, the dogma expresses Knight's realist position.

Man's classifying operations are reminiscent of Schutz's commonsense constructs that humans employ. At the same time, Knight's analysis differs from Schutz's as he does not apply Schutz's distinction between first- and second-order constructs.[2] Knight elaborates on the manner in which we organize our knowledge in a 'workable number of properties or *modes of resemblance* between things' (ibid.). In this manner, we organize the facts of our lives that are basic for our conduct. In this aspect, Knight enumerates a number of propositions that make our conduct plausible in a world where, otherwise, only an infinite intelligence could grasp all the combinations of things.

Recapped, Knight postulates a limited number of 'distinguishable properties and modes of behavior', on one hand, and furthermore that 'the properties of things remain fairly constant' (ibid.: 207). In this aspect, Knight will allude to postulating rationality. On the other hand, it is 'the quantitative aspect of things and the power of intelligence to deal with quantity [that] is a fundamental element in the situation' (ibid.). The two postulates cover the situation in which uncertainty is absent, rendering an exact determination of conduct theoretically possible, that is, of the working of the economic system. However, these knowledge postulates disregard that it is rightly the indeterminateness of uncertainty that occasions the embarkment on knowledge theory. Therefore, Knight proceeds and argues that the postulates of intelligent behavior would be very incomplete without a formal insistence on the role played by the 'fact of consciousness in "objects" outside ourselves, in human beings and animals' (ibid.: 208).[3] This addition words the basic role of intersubjectivity, '"sympathetic introspection"', grasping that what is going on in someone else's '"mind"' is a mysterious interpretation capacity. For instance, we draw inferences from 'the configurations of the lines about the mouth, the gleam or "twinkle" of an eye' (ibid.). We avail ourselves of not-reasoned knowledge, intuition, and common sense; without measuring instruments that are not at hand, we estimate distances and weights. It is particularly this extension to Knight's perspective of knowledge that he requires to address the presence of uncertainty. It is reminiscent of Michael Polanyi's (1966: xviii) notion 'that it is impossible to account for the nature and justification of knowledge by a series of strictly explicit operations'. Knowledge is the fruit of intentionality which invokes 'deeper forms of commitment', Polanyi adds.

In the following quote, Knight gives an impression of a man engaged in his decisions, and it may be read as an explication of Bergson's concept of *durée*. Knight:

So when we try to decide what to expect in a certain situation, and how to behave ourselves accordingly, we are likely to do a lot of irrelevant mental rambling, and the first thing we know we find that we have made up our minds, that our course of action is settled. There seems to be very little meaning in what has gone on in our minds, and certainly little kinship with the formal process of logic which the scientist uses in an investigation.

(ibid.: 211)

'In so far as there is "real change" in the Bergsonian (i.e., Heracleitian) sense it seems clear that reasoning is impossible', Knight concludes (ibid.: 209).

Recapped, Knight distinguishes, on one hand, cases eligible for 'reasoning related to ideal or complete inference based on uniformity of association of predicates and which can be formulated in universal propositions' (ibid.: 211–212). On the other, he discerns large classes of cases in which this universality is unattainable and asserts that 'two predicates *sometimes* belong to the same subject' or overlap one another. We employ forms that belong to these classes quite commonly in our 'rough operations of everyday unscientific thinking' (ibid.: 212).

Finally, it seems that in Knight's knowledge theory, intersubjectivity plays a merely additional role; '"sympathetic introspection"' complements the classification postulates of the 'finite intelligence' (ibid.: 207–208). However, intersubjectivity is not that final piece; on the contrary, it is the very foundation of any 'working number of properties or *modes of resemblance* between things', as Knight also notes (ibid.: 205). Intersubjectivity enables us to recognize observably scientific evidence. We intersubjectively share its evidence, and so this holds for universal propositions. As conscious human beings, we experience our *ego* as something independent of any representation; therefore, we believe that the *thou* is something that is, as Georg Simmel (1910: 375) phrases, 'just as really for itself (*genau so für sich ist*) as our own existence'. This belief founds all our knowledge.[4]

In this respect, Knight falls short vis-à-vis Schutz who distinguishes two types of classification: commonsense versus second-order constructs. The latter type enables Schutz to reformulate vague commonsense concepts as being well-structured and scientifically unambiguous. Against this 'unification', Knight's theory of knowledge exhibits the ambiguity of two types of knowledge that Schutz manages to eliminate, as discussed in Chapter 2. At the same time, Knight's analysis, in effect, amounts to the application of a kind of second-order construct; witness his use of actors conditioned by presuppositions that render them (Schutzian) homunculi. This accords with the intersubjectivity postulate that also founds Knight's two classes of knowledge: reasoned, formal knowledge versus non-reasoned common sense. Uncertainty leads us away from the former to the latter. As shown, he adheres to a philosophically realist position; '"ultimate"' things structure the world that exhibits constancy. Against this determinateness, he poses '"real change" in the Bergsonian (i.e., Heracleitian) sense', resulting in indeterminateness (Knight 1921: 209).

In the elaboration of this dichotomy, Knight applies a rather straightforward taxonomy of knowledge, that is, a tripartite distinction to qualify 'reasoning that relates ideal or complete inference based on uniformity of association' of predicates rendering universal propositions (ibid.: 211). Against the scientific ambition of formulating universal propositions abound occasional propositions 'in the form of *"some X is Y"'* (ibid.: 212). This particular proposition occasions formulating the three kinds of knowledge to qualify:

1. *A priori* probability as applicable to games of chance;
2. Statistical probability based on induction;
3. Estimate of probability.

The rigor of the first and the second depends on the degree of homogeneous grouping. For that matter, the *a priori* probability 'is practically never met in business' (ibid.: 215).[5] It is the second, statistical probability that is extremely relevant in business as it enables the economic actor to design expedients that address uncertainty and transform it into risk, for example, by insurance or hedging. However, some events occur once in a while that are unfit for statistical treatment due to a lack of a homogeneous grouping. At the same time, in reality, absolutely unique events are improbable, so there will be some base of comparison as a basis for the third kind, that is, estimating a probability.

Uncertainty makes the actor rely on estimating the probabilities of the events of a course of action. The impossibility of dependable knowledge drives the actor to formulate opinions based particularly on intuition. This sharply contrasts the unambiguous proposition that features the scientist. At the same time, it is surmise and intuition that will initially guide both the deliberating scientist and the actor, for example, as a business manager, who makes up his mind about an investment. They share that their enigmatic intuition anticipates the future, the unknown, and renders a prediction that rests, Knight adds, 'upon the uniformity of nature' (ibid.: 230). The striking difference between the businessman vis-à-vis the scientist regards the liability of the estimating actor who finds himself in an uncertain situation to err. In contrast to a scientist's basic ambition to the rigor of exact knowledge, the former cannot exclude error. Knight:

> The fact of liability to error is painfully familiar and is all that concerns us here.
>
> (ibid.: 202)

The concept of error is in contrast with a mechanic worldview in which there is no room for intuitive consciousness. Apparently, mechanistic science falls short in explaining in terms of a past cause and is unable to cope with such a phenomenon as '"see things coming"', that is, anticipating a future situation (ibid.: 200). For that matter, in the significant role in which Knight adheres to intuition and consciousness, resting 'upon the uniformity of nature', reemerges

Knight's realist position (ibid.: 230). It is intuition that renders the world intelligible in a pre-predicative manner. As noted, he associates consciousness particularly with man's estimating faculty.

It is the estimate type of knowledge, Knight notes, 'which has been neglected in economic theory, and which we propose to put in its rightful place' (ibid.: 231). This theoretical disregard sharply contrasts with its relevance. Business decisions of investors, for instance, require anticipating a future situation that is featured by variables that are as yet unknowable. Moreover, they generally regard unique situations that lack statistically useful information. '*True uncertainty*' features these situations. 'Organization expedients' address measurable uncertainties, that is, risks (ibid.: 232). True uncertainty makes entrepreneurs who, having recourse to intuitive estimation, err. Significant to note is that, herein, Knight gives an endogenous explanation of the institutional devices. The economic system of competition develops 'organization expedients' that set off the effects of uncertainties, and the entrepreneur engages in the vicissitudes of true uncertainty, reaping the profit or dealing with the loss of it. Economics explains institutions.

4.3 Imperfect competition through risk and uncertainty

Grouping of instances, that is, the second kind of knowledge that is distinguished, for example, consolidation of activities, may turn uncertainty into risk. The uncertain outcomes may cancel out one another. Apparently, the risk-uncertainty distinction is amenable to human intervention. Moreover, it is not as strict as it seems to be, as empirical sorting based on homogeneity to render truly measured probability merely applies, to some extent, within narrow limits. Therefore, in the normal economic situation, 'the adventurer has an opinion as to the outcome, within more or less narrow limits' (ibid.: 237). He is exposed to more or less uncertainty, partly depending on his individual attributes and capacities to reduce it, rendering uncertainty a subjective concept, that is, estimated knowledge. The first subsection expands on this adventurer, that is, the entrepreneur. The second subsection discusses some broader aspects of the entrepreneurial system, such as its orientation on progressive change and growth. This subsection introduces uncertainty due to dynamic change.

4.3.1 Uncertainty and an organization expedient, the enterprise

The prominent source of uncertainty in economics is '*production for a general market*', which necessitates 'anticipation of wants and control of production with reference to the future' (ibid.: 241, 244). Knight refers to the two types of social-economic organization in the economic history of capitalism that address the uncertainties of the market: the handicraft economy and the free enterprise system. In the handicraft economy, it is the wholesale dealer who protects the single producer from market uncertainties. The Industrial Revolution introduced the entrepreneur who organizes mass production, coordinating the productive resources of land, labor, and capital. Knight describes the enterprise system as follows.

> The bulk of the producing population cease [*sic*] to exercise responsible control over the production and take [*sic*] up the subsidiary rôle of furnishing productive resources (labor, land, and capital) to the entrepreneur, placing them under his sole direction for a fixed contract price.
>
> (ibid.: 244–245)

The entrepreneur assumes the uncertainties of

a. the commonly substantial time length of the production process, increased since the Industrial Revolution;
b. coordination and control of the production process of 'large groups working together in a single establishment or productive enterprise' (ibid.: 245).

The very nature of the entrepreneur is that he unites consolidation and managerial coordination, as I also refer to hereafter.

In general terms, what is at issue is that rational conduct in adapting means to ends requires minimizing uncertainty. Knight distinguishes two basic points for doing so:

1. The possibility of consolidating instances;
2. Specialization in uncertainty bearing based on individual differences in preferences and possibilities regarding bearing uncertainty.

Re 1. Insurance represents an obvious device of consolidation of uncertainties. It replaces the uncertainty of a loss into the certainty of a risk premium. At the same time, it raises a new issue, that is, moral hazard. Insurance changes the incentive structure whenever the one who decides is not the same one who bears the consequences of the decision. Conduct becomes a moral fortuity in case the decisive factors making the decision 'are not amenable to objective description and external control' (ibid.: 251). Insurance may elicit hazardous behavior of the insured; indeed, at the expense of the insurer. The efficiency-enhancing-incentive structure may be restored as consolidation can be effected by one and the same individual or by an organization that can adequately arrange 'centralized responsibility and unity of interests' (ibid.: 252). Growth in the average size of the corporate organizations renders consolidation of uncertainties without harmful change in the incentive structure as the divergence between decision and consequence is left out. This reflects the basic trade-off in reducing uncertainty by consolidation that, in many cases, results in the institutional choice for the corporate organization as expedient.

Re 2. Speculation is the standard instance of specialization in assuming uncertainty (ibid.: 255). Apparently, some people are more uncertainty-averse than others. The instrument of the specialist in uncertainty bearing is again consolidation, converting uncertainty into a measured risk. The single producer shifts his uncertainty regarding, for example, the price of his raw material, to the speculator who enters a number of times in the market, canceling out his errors, leaving 'him a constant and predictable return' (ibid.: 256). Another instance of uncertainty specialization regards separating the uncertain aspects of an industry, for example, research and development, from the more predictable production placed under a separate corporation. Corporate finance arguments may support such a specialization. Investors in search for speculative profits give 'their exclusive attention to the launching of new enterprises', withdrawing as soon as prospects become determinate (ibid.: 257). This business practice amounts to a consolidation of the uncertainties, transforming them into measured risk by grouping. In the meantime, the uncertainty-bearing specialist builds up an information lead that enables him to exploit this in his transaction negotiation. It refers to another instance of moral hazard.

For both consolidation and specialization holds that the transfer of uncertainties to an external party raises managerial issues as it breaks the tie between a decision and its consequences. It changes the incentive structure and opens up opportunities to exploit the contract partner. New uncertainties announce themselves as morally hazardous conduct. Under this aspect, Knight infers a significant conclusion.

> Thus it is fundamental to the entrepreneur system that it tends to promote better management in addition to consolidating risks and throwing them into the hands of those most disposed to assume them.
>
> (ibid.: 260)

In uniting the consolidation of uncertainties with the management of the factors that potentially may mitigate the uncertainties, the enterprise renders the powerful institutional instrument the ability to restore the normal working of the competitive economic system.

In the curious world of uncertainty absent 'man's energies are devoted altogether to doing things' (ibid.: 268). The introduction of uncertainty renders economics a matter of thought and of conscious human beings who become aware of their predicament. In this context, Knight refers to 'a process of "cephalization"' (ibid.: 268). Theoretically, it regards the transition from mechanical conduct causing an equilibrium into deliberate decisions based on imperfect knowledge that nevertheless presuppose reasoned responsibility. In reality, economics is a mental affair; Knight underlines it by identifying the role of the entrepreneur in it. As yet, he assumes limited uncertainty with actors who are no longer omniscient by leaving out dynamic progress. Readjustments in this imaginary free-enterprise society are carried out by trial-and-error methods and motivated by 'the effort of each individual to better himself' (ibid.: 272). The setting regards a competitive situation in which some manifest as entrepreneurs and others offer productive services, that is, employees.

The entrepreneurs act and compete 'on the basis of what they *think* of the *future*' (ibid.: 273). The theoretical focus is on the entrepreneur who organizes industrial production at one's own expense.

In the industrial economy, as the length of production processes extends, the general level of economic life goes up with a growing diversity and the unpredictability of human wants, making production for the market highly unforeseeable. It is the modern enterprise that constitutes the very 'organization expedient' to address this true uncertainty.

What to produce and how are the two questions that the system of production for the general market poses. It is the producer's responsibility to forecast consumers' wants. In discussing the nature and the function of the entrepreneur, the focus is on the second question; that is, how does the new economic functionary, the entrepreneur, direct and control the production under the presence of uncertainty?

'Responsible direction' features the entrepreneur that splits up in two elements of responsibility and control, substantiating the "double contract" between that person and the employees, that is, of right to control in exchange for a guaranty (ibid.: 270). The entrepreneur is a specialist in uncertainty bearing, assuming to address the future-oriented questions of what and how to produce. Actually, it is the introduction of time that brings about uncertainty. An entrepreneur's conduct issues from estimated probability and conjectures about the future of the market and about the 'technological uncertainties' that beset the prospective production. It confronts the theorist with the question of how to safeguard my scientific ambition to formulate reasoned knowledge when investigating the conduct of individuals who 'are acting, competing, on the basis of what they *think* of the *future*'? (ibid.: 273).

What is at issue is this: How does one range imagination under a rational discourse? As discussed earlier, it is the recognition of human consciousness and its inherent intersubjectivity as the fundament of both our thought and imagination. Both are central in Knight's theory of the entrepreneur, showing that imagination and rationality are one another's pendant.

The setup of the analysis consists in 'random grouping' of employees and things under the control of other men as entrepreneurs (Knight 1921: 273). It constitutes a society in which entrepreneurs and employees are in competition.

> The laborer asks what he thinks the entrepreneur will be able to pay, and in any case will not accept less than he can get from some other entrepreneur, or by turning into [an] entrepreneur himself.
>
> (ibid.)

In the same manner, the entrepreneur will participate in the competitive process, and this whole calculation refers to the future. Past and present conditions are merely bases for employees' and entrepreneurs' anticipations. Basically, the competitive process is a social process of interchanging and comparing these anticipations, conjectures, and opinions. 'The meaning of the term "social" or "competitive" anticipation will now be clear', Knight notes (ibid.: 275). It is intersubjectivity that founds the socially competitive process towards 'an established uniform rate, which is kept constantly at the point which equates supply and demand' (ibid.: 274). Seemingly, this outcome corresponds with uncertainty absent. However, the uncertainty of future values remains present. The uniform and constant rate is the effect of the uncertainty-bearing specialization of the entrepreneur and merely removes employees' uncertainty. On one hand, the entrepreneur guarantees fixed remuneration for the productive services that are contracted. On the other hand, he *estimates* the data regarding the 'facts upon which the working-out of the organization depends' (ibid.: 276). The latter implies *liability to error* against *responsibility* for the correctness of the estimates considering the guarantees that are given. When this combination comes together in the managerial function, 'the nature of the function is revolutionized; the manager becomes an entrepreneur' (ibid.). The routine managerial functions may be remunerated as other productive services with fixed wages. In addition to the remuneration, there is a differential element, that is, profit. Knight defines it as follows:

> Profit is simply the difference between [the] market price of the productive agencies he employs, the amount which the competition of other entrepreneurs forces him to guarantee to them as a condition of securing their services, and the amount which he finally realizes from the disposition of the product which under his direction they turn out.
>
> (ibid.: 277)

Against the remuneration imputed to the productive agencies stands profit as a residue that accrues to the entrepreneur or a loss as a deficit that must be made good.

In the free-enterprise economy, the entrepreneur finds that the right figure to address the uncertainty inherent to production for the market is the entrepreneur. The basis for the decision to become an entrepreneur is *believing* that a superior profit can be yielded compared to others engaged in entrepreneurial activities. A dependable basis for such a belief in one's entrepreneurial ability would be a considerable number of trials. However, uniqueness features in most entrepreneurial cases. The comparison with pure gambling obtrudes itself. In spite of lacking reliable knowledge, we are unmistakably able to form estimates that generate entrepreneurial conduct. It occasions a 'sweeping reservation' in which intersubjectivity and consciousness found the argument. Knight argues:

> If men, ignorant of other men's powers, know that these other men themselves know their own powers, the results of general knowledge of all men's powers may be secured; and this is true even if such knowledge is (as it is in fact) very imperfectly or not at all communicable.
>
> (ibid.: 286)

Actually, this is a description of the working of the human mind engaged in '"social" or "competitive" anticipation' (ibid.: 275).[6] Continuing, Knight substantiates his proposition:

> If those who furnish productive services for a contractual remuneration know that those who bid for the services know what they are worth to themselves, the bidders, or each bidder knows this to be true of the others, the latter will be forced to pay all that they are willing to pay, which is to say they all can pay.
>
> (ibid.)

Knight's description of the socially competitive process is reminiscent of the Austrian perspective on spontaneous order as an unintended consequence of individual conduct, indeed. However, Knight emphasizes that, in the social process of coming to terms with our fellow man, we particularly have recourse to other men's opinions. The estimates we make for our individual decisions predominantly concern the worth attached to other men's opinions and capabilities. 'It is the importance of indirect knowledge of fact through knowledge of others' knowledge', Knight posits (ibid.: 288). 'Knowledge of others is one of the most important factors in our efforts to live together intelligently in organized society' (ibid.: 287).[7] In this quote reemerges the idea of reciprocal intersubjectivity as the foundation of society, as discussed earlier. Obviously, this reciprocal attitude initially refers to our mundane life. Knowledge in this context is particularly practical knowledge that is useful for Hayek's (1945: 524) '"man on the spot"'.[8]

The idea of the knowledge of others' knowledge is central to Knight's further analysis of an entrepreneur's uncertainty bearing. First, based on this idea, Knight (1921: 288–289) distinguishes between 'pure and undivided entrepreneurship' versus 'partly specialized and more or less distributed entrepreneurship'. The former follows from the assumed 'impossibility of knowledge by one person of another's capabilities' (ibid.: 288). Referring to the pivotal role of discussed indirect knowledge, this is a rather peculiar assumption. Knight infers from it that entrepreneurship will be unattainable without a credible guarantee of the contracted remuneration in terms of one's own property, pledging one's own earning power, or indemnity insurance (ibid.: 289, n. 1). Apparently, the assumption precludes estimating a probability on the part of the employee who is promised the prospect of a fixed remuneration. It furthermore hinders any arrangement to share with others the uncertainty bearing of entrepreneurship. The assumption might be made to show the theoretically extreme case, that is, undivided entrepreneurship, implying 'responsibility and control completely associated' (ibid.: 289).

Against the former, Knight distinguishes the distributed version, that is, the distribution of control and responsibility, resting on the assumption that 'men have knowledge, or opinions on which they are willing to act, of other men's capacities for the entrepreneur function' (ibid.). This reflects the reality case of entrepreneurship in which a range of constructions of partnership as well as distribution of responsibility and control appears and is enabled by the knowledge of other's knowledge to reach mutually profitable divisions of functions. At the same time, they will complicate the entrepreneurship and potentially generate efficiency harm. A prominent instance of the distributed version is the corporation.

The corporation combines 'diffused ownership with concentrated control' (ibid.: 291). It is particularly suitable for large-scale production. The corporation represents the very opposite of the undivided entrepreneurship hindered by the impossibility of the knowledge of others' capabilities. Against the latter, the corporation cannot exist without the indirect knowledge as staffed by a hierarchy of directors and layers of executive officials who organize its control and responsibility. Thoroughgoing division of tasks features the corporation. What is at issue is the organization of means as, upon a corporation's end, it is already decided, that is, to make money. The organizational structure distinguishes layers of tasks and inherent decision situations that are determined by a form of grouping activities that increase in complexity from the 'bottom'.

In line with the concept of indirect knowledge, business judgment chiefly amounts to the judgment of men. 'We know things by knowledge of men who know them', and '"control" consists mainly of selecting someone else to do the "controlling"' (ibid.: 290). Therefore, the knowledge required to accomplish responsible control of a specific function in the organization does not concern intrinsic knowledge of the situation or of problems of means for effecting changes that the function ensues, but the knowledge required is 'the knowledge of other men's knowledge of these things' (ibid.: 292). Knight adds:

> So fundamental to our problem is the fact that human judgment of things has in an effective sense a "true value" which can be estimated more or less correctly by men possessing it and by others -so fundamental is it for understanding the control of organized activity, that the problem of judging men's powers of judgment overshadows the problem of judging the facts of the situation to be dealt with.
>
> (ibid.)

Consequently, he continues, 'attention and interest shift from the errors in men's opinions of things to the errors in their opinions of men' (ibid.).

A reduction of uncertainty directs the formulation of functions and inherent activities and generates a grouping of them. However, this grouping cannot be done without a margin of tolerance. Any function, merely operative or exactly tactical, will be accompanied by peculiar circumstances that demand some inventiveness. This makes clear that the appropriate way to staff the organization is precisely the search for the right individuals who have knowledge of the situation. Central is finding people who may cope with 'new situations', who have or may become specialists in addressing this uncertainty, and who render their responsible control as a routine job. Therefore, it is crucial for the superior in the scale of the organization who assigns a task to a subordinate to have knowledge of the latter's quality of judgment that enables the individual to deal with uncertainty as a matter of routine. So, the functional division of tasks procures uncertainty reduction both by consolidation, that is, grouping activities, and by specialization rendering tasks a matter of routine. Apart from that, the latter reflects the universal tendency to economize on consciousness, Knight notes, addressing contingencies subconsciously like car drivers do (ibid.: 294).

From the bottom to the top of the organization, there is a successive judgment of, and selection of, the abilities of people to take responsibility in accordance with the job assigned to them. 'On up the scale the same relations [between superintendents and foremen] hold good until we come to the supreme head of the business' (ibid.: 297). A hired manager's job is also a 'routine' task. That individual is judged and selected to be able to cope with the uncertainties to which the task is exposed. There is no separation between control and risk, as in the selection of the manager or any other employee, 'the *crucial* decision is the selection of men to make decisions, that any other sort of decision-making or exercise of judgment is automatically reduced to a routine function' (ibid.: 297). The replacement of the knowledge of things with the knowledge of people generates a staff that absorbs uncertainties.

The fundamental difference between the hired manager at the top of the organization against the entrepreneur is that the task of the former is 'cut out for him by others and set to perform it' whereas the entrepreneur sets out his own task, measures his own capacities, and associates control *and* responsibility. The hired manager, however, is essentially engaged in routine activities selected *for* that person *by* the independent entrepreneur (ibid.: 298). The latter, as the owner of the productive services used in the business, ultimately bears the responsibility of the business in the hands of the hired manager. However, the scale of the undertaking usually prevents such an independent entrepreneurship. So, it naturally happens that the entrepreneur is, for a *part*, owner of the assets of the business and is required to guarantee the contractual remunerations. As noted, the corporation is a paragon of distributed control and responsibility as well as diffused entrepreneurship. Apparently, the specialization (regarding uncertainty bearing) is usually incomplete (ibid.: 298). 'It is seldom true that the guarantees given can be regarded as absolute', Knight notes (ibid.: 300). Under this aspect, he establishes that 'the distinction between stocks and bonds tends to fade out' (ibid.: 301). Furthermore, banks keep in touch with the management of the corporation in which they invest. Last but not least, it is labor that is exposed to the effects of the incompleteness of uncertainty bearing. Laborers engage themselves 'in hazardous enterprises at their own risk for an increase in wages which is a fraction of an adequate compensation for the chances they take' (ibid.). Social interest may explain legal devices such as 'prior claim laws [and] mechanics' liens' (ibid.).

4.3.2 Entrepreneurial system and progressive change

Without change, the future world would be foreknown since it would duplicate the past. However, 'whatever we find it pleasant to assume for philosophical purposes, the logic of our *conduct* assumes real indeterminateness, real change, discontinuity', Knight asserts (ibid.: 314). What is at issue is the irretrievable uncertainty of progressive change causing an increase in knowledge, for example, improved technology. In such an instance, the change and the uncertainty of change are inseparable. 'Though we cannot describe an invention in advance without making it, ... , yet, Knight puts forward, it is possible in a large degree to offset ignorance with knowledge and behave intelligently with regard to the future' (ibid.: 318). What may explain this paradox of ignorance versus intelligent conduct caused by a progressive change?

Progressive changes that raise real uncertainty stem from the 'improvement of technological processes, forms of business organization and the discovery of new natural resources' (ibid.). The most important phase of progressive change in the industrial economy regards the accumulation of capital of the modern industrial economy. It joins additional investment and technological development. Under this aspect, Knight notes basic differences between the modern economy and a premodern one. First, routine features the production processes of the latter. The immediate consequence of it is that there is no acute control question. Uncertainty is more or less absent, explaining the existence of common ownership.

A second difference between the premodern and the modern economy regards that, in the latter, people work '"to get rich"' (ibid.: 319). As Knight's definition of economics suggests, the economy is engaged in the satisfaction of wants and production for the purpose of human needs (ibid.: 9). This view requires some correction. First, the modern economy is not just engaged in the satisfaction of given preferences but is also intensively busy with the creation of preferences. Second, and most relevant here, is that production as a means of satisfying wants is 'by no means altogether directed to the ultimate satisfaction of wants in any direct sense' (ibid.: 319). In the modern industrial economy, it is the accrual of wealth that has become an end in itself. Knight:

> We must face the fact that men *do* "raise more corn to feed more hogs, to buy more land to raise more corn to feed more hogs to buy more land".
>
> (ibid.)

The modern economy moves in a circle of producing more wealth to be used to produce more wealth. So, a *net* increase of wealth issues from a surplus production for which the owners never plan to consume it.

The third difference with the premodern economy is that the modern economy raises surpluses that enable the latter to invest and engage 'in the making of equipment goods' that render it a progressive society. The first requisite of the creation of capital goods is 'the creation of a surplus', that is, saving (ibid.:

322). This course of events that feature the modern economy, Knight continues, 'is further complicated by the intervention of money' (ibid.: 323). Obviously, this regards rather basic economic ideas. However, few students of economics 'think back of the exchange function of money to the transfer of real things mediated by it', Knight adds (ibid.).

This modern economy of progressive change is intimately connected with private property (ibid.: 320–321). Private property fuels to note progressive changes, for example, in production technology. A lead in technology promises profitable investment, developing the awareness that the accrual of wealth is a beneficial affair. The concatenate phenomena structure the modern progressive economy. The entrepreneur renders it a free enterprise economy based on profit, assuming the inbuilt uncertainty of progress.

The creation of a surplus, that is, saving, is the prerequisite of 'the *diversion* of productive resources from the creation of consumption goods to ... producers' goods' (ibid.: 323). The transfer of savings by a loan to another person raises interest. Loaning renders *fluid capital* that enables a division of functions. One set of people accrues capital by saving against another that specializes in converting capital into capital goods, that is, investment. The latter set of people regards entrepreneurs who assume to address this 'burning question in practice': 'what form of new capital goods shall be created, where, by what methods, etc.' (ibid.: 325). This is the very entrepreneurial question requiring 'an exercise in *judgment* of far the highest type called for in the business world' (ibid.). Consequently, the division of functions regarding control and responsibility is organized along the lines as discussed earlier, selecting staff to exercise control based on the knowledge of its knowledge and capacities.

The 'machinery' of the capital market that furnishes an entrepreneur capital does not differ from markets that trade other productive services except that the prices established for the former are unusually uniform. In this respect, it is relevant to distinguish interest, rent, and yield. Interest is the payment for a loan. Rent is the payment for the use of a capital good, that is, a competitive market value. '*Yield of property* ... is the actual return realized from the exploitation of the material things' (ibid.: 329). The distinction issues two forms of profit. First, profit regards the difference between the yield of the property minus the competitive rent imputed to it. Second, the rent, in turn, includes competitive interest on the investment. The difference between rent and imputed interest is the second form of profit.

Another phenomenon that emerges in the progressive free enterprise economy regards the capitalization of property value. The 'modern' desire to accrue wealth also generates the anticipation of future income by capitalization, embarking on new ventures. Anticipating capital value change motivates the businessman. In this respect, Knight points at the information asymmetry between these businessmen hoping to profit from changes in capital values against those who control the targeted business. 'Matters become this worse' when this information asymmetry is used by the managers of the productive property to cause capital value changes by manipulating their industrial and financial policies (ibid.: 334). Obviously, the uncertainty that is present in the progressive economy occasions instances of deceit and fraud. At the same time, the search for profit by capitalization brings about a reduction of uncertainty through grouping and specialization by people who are fitted for and enjoy making new ventures (ibid.: 333).

The progressive change discussion shows that the combination of private property and technological invention embodied in capital goods constitute both the origin and the nature of the modern progressive free-enterprise economy. The upshot of this free-enterprise system is that the owner of the property occupies a crucial position in it. It is the owner of the material property who is in a position to make an effective guarantee against a loss 'and not the owners of the human services, the workers' (ibid.: 355). Therefore, Knight concludes as follows:

> We assume, then, that the entrepreneur system of organization, with production for the market impersonally, and concentration of direction, arise because it is superior to, or more satisfactory all around than any other *free contract* system.
>
> (ibid.: 351)

At the same time, Knight is well aware of the heroic assumptions that beset a pure free contract system. *Pure* freedom of contract means that control and ownership are interchangeable concepts; 'there is no other form of control' (ibid.: 352). It is in accord with the high idea of mutually voluntary human relations. However, the instance of external effects makes clear that this assumption renders an untenable view on reality. The attenuation of property rights abounds. Moreover, it is a fallacy that the concluded contracts would be carried out intelligently. Furthermore, pure freedom of contract would exclude state interference, for example, raising taxes to cover the cost of its enforcement of private property rights. 'And this modifying influence on private property, Knight notes, extends rapidly in scope as the *laissez-faire* theory of the State loses ground in the modern world' (ibid.: 354).

Finally, against the background of his plea for the entrepreneur system of markets, Knight alludes to the Planning Debate that was held in the first decades of the twentieth century. Basically, Knight declines to perceive the freedom of contract as a matter of deliberate design. 'However, he continues, the continuation of the system is a question which has been much discussed on its merits and which may ultimately be decided on the basis of discussion' (ibid.: 357).

How to address the two basic questions of the economic system as defined: What to produce, and how to produce it if the property were socialized? First, business would be transformed into public enterprises managed by 'hired functionaries'. Second, the position of the hired manager who controls a public enterprise changes vis-à-vis the private-corporation manager. The latter is subordinated to a small group of insiders who own and manage the company and 'generally know each other's personalities, motives, and policies tolerably well' (ibid.: 359). The salaried manager, who, under socialism, would eventually be accountable to society at large, escapes such direct accountability. The individual lacks the *feeling* that the result depends on his own activity (ibid.). Another point regarding the responsible officials of the public enterprise is that 'they universally show a tendency to "play safe" and become hopelessly conservative' (ibid.: 361).

Concluding, Knight gathers some points in favor of private property, actually the very basis of his uncertainty theory. First, as compared with socialized property, private property has good credentials to serve '"society" [as] a husbandman or "wirtschaftender Mensch"*, interested in getting its work done as well and as cheap as possible' (ibid.: 368). Second, is it really good for the individual that he assumes the risks of industry on which the entrepreneur system is based? Against this question, Knight brings in that

> [c]hange, novelty, and surprise must be given large consideration as values *per se*. ... Hence each individual must be given responsibility, freedom of choice, a wider sphere of self-expression than he can have in a system of organization where control is specialized and concentrated to the last degree.
>
> (ibid.: 369)

Referring to the latter, the dynamics of a progressive modern economy cannot be sustained without a private person's incentive to accrue wealth. Private property founds the stimulus to accrue wealth that enables others to invest this capital wealth in new technologies embedded in capital goods with an uncertain profit. It is this mechanism that fuels the entrepreneur system of inciting men to run progressively changing businesses and meanwhile reduce uncertainty by exercising control and taking responsibility. Exercising restraint, Knight concludes that

> the existing order, with the institutions of the private family and private property (in self as well as goods), inheritance and bequest and parental responsibility, affords one way for securing more or less tolerable results ... in carrying forward to new individuals born, ... besides the torch of life itself, the material wealth of the world, a technological system of vast and increasing intricacy and the habituations which fit men for social life.
>
> (ibid.: 375)

In this conclusion recur Knight's philosophical leanings. For that matter, they feature his analysis affording an economics that aspires to the distinction of an exact science and, at the same time, observes the subjective nature of the subject, that is, of conscious human beings.

4.4 Review and conclusions

Part two of *Risk, Uncertainty, and Profit* sets out the conditions of perfect competition under stationary conditions. It presents 'a clear, succinct statement of neoclassical price theory', George Stigler (1987: 56) notes in his New Palgrave entry on Knight. The subsequent turn from a certain, mechanistically determined economic system toward an uncertain economic reality manifests, first of all, as an epistemological issue. It prompts Knight to pad his theoretical account with philosophical excursions that grant a profound dimension to the mundane matter of economic activity and entrepreneurial initiative. The interwovenness of philosophical and economic thought grants Knight's entrepreneurial economics its strength. I recap them separately.

4.4.1 *A philosophical afterthought*

It is in an implicit way that Knight exhibits his realist position. We require abstraction, '"pure theory"' as 'the *first step*' toward understanding our reality, he argues (Knight 1921: 6). In this, he alludes to pre-predicative concepts that exist independently of an observer's perception. Concepts that *are* meaning may be grasped intelligently. In his theory of knowledge, with which Knight starts addressing the uncertainty issue, the realist position explicitly reemerges.

His philosophical thoughts lead him to the phenomenological basic postulate of human consciousness as an analytical starting point. It accords with the methodological individualism of the economics on which Knight reflects. He may reap the fruits of his philosophical excursions as it is particularly the presence of uncertainty that poses the theorist pressing questions regarding knowledge and human consciousness. Uncertainty renders economics a matter of thought, 'a process of "cephalization"' follows (ibid.: 268). Uncertainty regards preeminently the uncertainty of conscious human beings who find themselves in a situation in which logic cannot be definitely grasped. This is the basic issue in which Knight is engaged. Consequently, it is his concept of intersubjectively based knowledge that enables him to formulate his entrepreneurial theory. Intersubjectivity rephrased as 'knowledge of others' knowledge' enables the uncertainty-bearing entrepreneur to structure the production process, reducing the uncertainty by selecting functionaries who may routinely cope with contingencies (ibid.: 288). The presence of uncertainty changes the omniscient homunculus acting under perfect-competition conditions into a homunculus who knows what others' knowledge and capacities are worth. The latter selects subordinates who act routinely, like true homunculi.

It is the very intersubjectivity that reappears in the reciprocity of exchange. Reciprocity may also be found in Knight's 'sweeping reservation' that 'general knowledge of all men's powers may be secured', if men, ignorant of other men's power, 'know that these other men themselves know their own powers' (ibid.: 286). Further elaborated, the statement bases the description of social processes, such as price making and all other forms of spontaneous order, as unintended consequences of individual conduct.

Knight's philosophical notes constitute an underpinning of his claim in the opening sentence of his book, reading: 'economics as the ... social science which has aspired to the distinction of an exact science' (ibid.: 3). This aspiration holds particularly true for NIE, which is oriented toward the analysis and the explanation of the situational logic of conscious human beings who have recourse to institutional devices. Finally, Knight's philosophical digression on the knowledge concept constitutes a confirmation of the significance of the phenomenological interpretation of economics.

4.4.2 An NIE afterthought

The perfect competition model serves as the null hypothesis. What is at issue is, What hinders its normal working? Herein Knight corresponds with Coase. Knight diagnoses that uncertainty refutes economists' null hypothesis. Obviously, Coase's concept of transaction cost may be interpreted as stemming from the uncertainty that arises when perfect competition is absent. For instance, under failing competition, prices are no longer given and raise the cost of information. Uncertainty generates constraints, though calculable in a marginal analysis to compare institutional alternatives. This is the basic paradigm of NIE originating from Coase's 'Firm' paper. Coase has introduced in NIE the reciprocity of the transaction as the basic unit of analysis. It throws light on the problem of social cost.

Knight exploits this reciprocity as intersubjectivity between conscious human beings who, for instance, take advance of their differences in risk aversion, prompting progressive changes in the economic system. In this aspect, it is remarkable that Knight's introduction of the concept of moral hazard precedes decades before it features in NIE's principal-agent theory.

Both Knight and Coase are engaged in the *economic* analysis of institutional devices, be it market, entrepreneur or, more generally, the firm. Like Coase, Knight is fully engaged in the internal organization of the enterprise and exercises a real micro-micro analysis of the organizational expedient. The title of Coase's (1992) Nobel Prize lecture, *Institutional Structure of Production*, also covers the overtones of Knight's economics.

Finally, Knight's digression on knowledge affords him to give a more profound analysis of the working of the economic system than Coase. The initial position of Coase is that transaction cost hinders the market, prompting to look for other institutional devices. Knight, in comparison, shows humans' faculties, such as intuition and judgment, that enable the economic agents to address the uncertainty and turn it into a challenging encounter with competitors. It is rightly the same economic system of competitive markets that addresses the Knightian uncertainty. Knight's analysis gives a dynamic turn to the economic analysis of the institution of entrepreneurial capitalism. Briefly, Frank H. Knight is a pioneer in NIE who broadened its scope.

Notes

1 George Stigler distinguishes two competition concepts: on one hand, a Smithian concept of competition that refers to a '*behavioral process* of competing' between bargaining market partners (McNulty 1967: 398) and, on the other, competition regarding a 'rigorously defined concept', resulting in a 'situation in which p does not vary with q -in which the demand curve facing the firm is horizontal' (Stigler 1957: 5). It is the latter version of competition that Knight discusses meticulously. Knight's discussion, Stigler adds, 'so prepared the way for the widespread reaction against it in the 1930's' (ibid.: 11).

2 Schutz's second-order constructs regard the transformation of our daily, common-sense, first-order constructs into scientific constructs that are stripped of the ambiguities and inconsistencies that are of no concern in daily life (see Chapter 2).

3 This knowledge radically differs from the 'Crusoe epistemology' of the purely individualistic, isolated individual who is instrumental, exclusively scientific, and without any intellectual curiosity (Knight 1947: 207). For that matter, it is questionable whether knowledge is thinkable without intersubjectivity.

4 Chapter 2 devotes a subsection to the concept of intersubjectivity.

5 For that matter, the so-called *a priori* probability, merely regards analytical sentences that do not refer to an empirical reality. In this respect, Kaufmann (1931: 759) notes that 'die *Wahrscheinlichkeitsrechnung* aus sich heraus keine Ergebnisse für Erhahrungswissenschaften als solche, d. h. keine empirischen Erkenntnisse, liefern kann'.

6 This account of the working of the human mind emasculates Harold Demsetz's view that Knightian uncertainty excludes rational action. Demsetz argues as follows:

> Uncertainty is a strange source of profit if Knight's objective is to resuscitate the role of profit in guiding resources in a price-directed economy. Being unpredictable, it cannot rationally influence resource allocation decisions.
>
> (1995: 3)

7 In this context, Schutz's distinction of first-order versus second-order concepts would be applicable, reformulating the commonsense concepts as stripped of ambiguity.

8 A support to Knight's idea of 'indirect knowledge' based on the knowledge of others may be found in a footnote of Hayek's (1937) paper on *Economics and Knowledge*. Hayek:

> [A]ll propositions of economic theory refer to things which are defined in terms of human attitudes towards them, that is, that for instance the "sugar" about which economic theory may occasionally speak, is not defined by its "objective" qualities.
>
> (1937: 50, n. 2)

Our human attitudes and opinions toward things constitute the terms that found our social-economic life. It is a notion that belongs to the '*verstehende* social science', Hayek notes (ibid.).

References

Bergson, H., 1913, [2001], *Time and Free Will*, London, edited by G. Allen, New York: Dover Publications Inc.

Coase, R.H., 1937, The Nature of the Firm, *Economica, Vol. 4 (n.s.)*, 386–405.

Coase, R.H., 1991, The Nature of the Firm: Origin. In: O.E. Williamson, S.G. Winter, eds., 1991, [1993], *The Nature of the Firm, Origin, Evolution, and Development*, 34–47, Oxford: Oxford University Press.
Coase, R.H., 1992, The Institutional Structure of Production, *The American Economic Review, Vol. 82, No. 4*, 713–719.
Demsetz, H., 1995, [1997], *The Economics of the Business Firm*, Cambridge: Cambridge University Press.
Eatwell, J., M. Milgate, P. Newman, eds., 1987, [1991], *The New Palgrave, a Dictionary of Economics*, Vol. 3, London: The Macmillan Press Limited.
Farber, M., 1940, [1968], *Philosophical Essays*, New York: Greenwood Press, Publishers.
Hayek, F.A., 1937, Economics and Knowledge, *Economica, New Series, Vol. 4, No. 13*, 33–54.
Hayek, F.A., 1945, The Use of Knowledge in Society, *The American Economic Review, Vol. 35, No. 4*, 519–530.
Kaufmann, F., 1931, Was kann die mathematische Methode in der Nationalökonomie leisten? *Zeitschrift für Nationalökonomie, Vol. 2, No. 5*, 754–779.
Kaufmann, F., 1940, [1968], Phenomenology and Logical Empiricism. In: M. Farber, ed., 1968, *Philosophical Essays*, 124–142, New York: Greenwood Press, Publishers.
Kaufmann, F., 1944, *Methodology of the Social Sciences*, Atlantic Highlands, New Jersey: Humanities Press.
Keynes, J.M., 1933, [1972], *Essays in Biography*, London: Macmillan St. Martin's Press.
Knight, F.H., 1921, [1971], *Risk, Uncertainty and Profit*, Chicago, IL: Chicago University Press.
Knight, F.H., 1922, Ethics and the Economic Interpretation, *The Quarterly Journal of Economics, May, Vol. 36, No. 3*, 454–481.
Knight, F.H., 1924, Some Fallacies in the Interpretation of Social Cost, *The Quarterly Journal of Economics, Vol. 38, No. 4*, 582–606.
Knight, F.H., 1947, *Freedom and Reform*, New York: Harper & Brothers.
Marshall, A., 1890, [1920], *Principles of Economics*, London: Macmillan and Co., Limited.
McNulty, P.J., 1967, A Note on the History of Perfect Competition, *The Journal of Political Economy, Vol. 75, No. 4, Part 1*, 395–399.
Polanyi, M., 1966, *The Tacit Dimension*, Chicago, IL: Chicago University Press.
Schutz, A., 1932, [1967], *The Phenomenology of the Social World*, New York: Northwestern University Press; [*Der sinnhafte Aufbau der sozialen Welt*, Wien: Julius Springer].
Schuetz, A., 1953, Common-Sense and Scientific Interpretation of Human Action, *Philosophy and Phenomenological Research, Vol. 14*, 1–38.
Simmel, G., 1910, How Is Society Possible? *American Journal of Sociology, Vol. 16, No. 3*, 372–391.
Smith, A., 1776, [2005], *The Inquiry into the Nature and Causes of the Wealth of Nations*, London: W. Strahan and T. Cadell; The Electronic Classics Series, Penn State: Pennsylvania State University.
Stigler, G.J., 1957, Perfect Competition, Historically Contemplated, *The Journal of Political Economy, Vol. 65, No. 1*, 1–17.
Stigler, G.J., 1987, [1991], Frank Hyneman Knight. In: J. Eatwell, M. Milgate, P. Newman, eds., 1987, [1991], *The New Palgrave, a Dictionary of Economics*, Vol. 3, 55–59, London: The Macmillan Press Limited.
Williamson, O.E., S.G. Winter, eds., 1991, [1993], *The Nature of the Firm, Origin, Evolution, and Development*, Oxford: Oxford University Press.

5   On Coase

5.1 Introduction

Ronald Coase exhibits an almost unconceivable constancy in his intellectual career that began in 1931 at the age of twenty and encompasses approximately eight decades. In his prolific oeuvre that counts more than eighty papers, Coase brings forward an identical perspective as included in his three papers, 'The Nature of the Firm' (1937), 'The Marginal Cost Controversy' (1946), and 'The Problem of Social Cost' (1960). As stated by Coase, '[o]ther papers which extend, illustrate, or explain the arguments in these three papers are also included', embodying the same point of view (Coase 1988: 1). It is the adage '"The normal economic system works itself"', as his London School of Economics professor Arnold Plant taught him, that constitutes the prevailing tone in this viewpoint (Coase 1991: 38). The adage phrases a fundamentally analytical attitude toward investigating the working of the market and definitely not a politically inspired slogan of a laissez-faire ideologist. In this attitude, Coase concurs with Knight's explication of the presuppositions of its working, as discussed in the preceding chapter.

Coase's unaffected theme is the working of the economic system embodied in the interrelatedness between the firm, the market, and the law. The formal view renders that '"the theory is simply the logic of optimal pricing and input combination"', Coase notes, referring to Martin Slater (quoted in Coase 1988: 3). Against the formal view as engaged in an individual's choice issues stands the study of the working of the economic system ultimately engaged in institutionally endorsed exchange relationships between human beings whose behavior is led by the common-sense notion 'that, in almost all circumstances, a higher (relative) price for anything will lead to a reduction in the amount demanded' (ibid.: 4). Coase does not merely concur with James Buchanan (1979: 20), Kenneth Arrow (1974: 18), and many others that exchange is, as discussed in Chapter 3, the main subject matter of the economist. He furthermore emphasizes and explicates that it is reciprocity that imports the working of the economic system. For instance, in his 'Social Cost' paper, he identifies it as the heart of the matter of harmful effects. The real question is, Coase (1960: 2) notes: 'Should *A* be allowed to harm *B*, or should *B* be allowed to harm *A*?'

DOI: 10.4324/9781315764221-5

Attention to the concept of reciprocity determines the nature of Coase's analysis and carries, I contend, the hallmark of his unorthodox economics. It concerns a social reciprocity that also features Knight's *Risk, Uncertainty, and Profit*. As George Stigler notes in his preface to the 1971 edition of Knight's book, Knight's analysis transforms 'an economic system from a beehive into a conscious social process with error, conflict' (cited in Knight 1921: xiv). Reciprocity features 'the interpersonal relationships ... needed as part of our collective organization of society, for our mutual improvements', that is, addressing scarcity (Arrow 1974: 18). It permeates the economic system in which different layers may be distinguished. It appears initially, on one hand, as the tit-for-tat phenomenon in mundane life against and, on the other hand, as the philosophically ultimate underpinning of the origin of societal life. I elaborate this idea of reciprocal layers somewhat.

A case of the initial layer of reciprocity may be found in Coase's (1992: 718) Nobel Prize lecture when he refers to the 'two individuals exchanging nuts for berries on the edge of the forest'. It sketches the archetypical transaction and is probably interpreted by Coase as such. It pictures a state-of-nature reciprocity that ostensibly opens out without any institutional artifact.

Second, a more sophisticated view on it, however, reveals that the exchange reciprocity demands for a system of rights and obligations that anatomizes, describes, and confers actors' respective positions in the transaction. It may happen to evolve within a firm or the marketplace out of sheer habit. It primarily emerges as a fruit of legislation. Oliver Williamson (2000: 597) would refer to this layer as the 'levels of governance and institutional environment'.

A third, profound layer regards the context that enables such phenomena as bargaining, haggling, and such a thing as legislation, that is, as an institutional environment. These phenomena presuppose reason and speech, which are concepts addressed by Adam Smith. Man's propensity to exchange is the 'necessary consequence of the faculties of reason and speech', constituting 'a civilised society' in which 'he (man) stands at all times in need of the cooperation and assistance of great multitudes' (Smith 1776: 16–17). These multitudes of cooperation await further explication.

Fourth and finally, it is the phenomenological perspective that enables denoting the ultimate layer of reciprocity that founds the multitudes of cooperation and assistance. It is ultimate in the sense that it refers to man's consciousness. In this context, the relevance of Georg Simmel's (1910: 375) view returns, as discussed in Chapter 3, on society as the confrontation of the *ego* as an irreducible and unshakable identity with his *alter ego*, that is, the fact of the *thou*, that which the *ego* experiences as 'something independent of our representation, something which is just as really for itself (*genau so für sich ist*) as our own existence'. The reciprocity in this existential confrontation founds Simmel's *The Philosophy of Money* (Simmel 1976). In effect, it is the ultimate ground of the economic system of exchange at large. Phenomenology elaborates on this ultimate reciprocity.

The layers of reciprocity display a correspondence with the nature of analysis. It varies from disregarding any reciprocity, as in Robbins's scarcity definition of economics, via attention to it in straightforward evidence of it in law-and-economics analysis to a phenomenologically underpinned reciprocity that enables theoretical laws as discussed in Chapter 1.

On one hand, a number of case studies about, for example, the postal monopoly, broadcasting, and lighthouses features Coase economics, that, on the other, precedes the formulation of the theoretical concepts that 'change in the way we analyze the working of the economic system and in the way we think about economic policy' (Coase 1992: 713). This sequence corresponds to Schutz (1932: 248), who develops a 'sociology of the everyday-life' (Kurrild-Klitgaard 2001: 120) in his phenomenology of the social reality that renders 'ideal-typical constructs (in our sense) in order to delimit their subject areas and to establish an objective context of meaning', that is, theoretical propositions. This procedure happens time and again in what follows. In this respect, the present chapter is key for defining the agenda for the next two chapters that elaborate on the further theoretical development of the themes of Coase's representative papers, that is, the firm in Chapter 6 and government interference in the market in Chapter 7.

Section 5.2 covers the 'Firm' paper in which Coase (1937) introduces the concept of transaction cost. The next section discusses 'The Marginal-Cost Controversy' (Coase 1946). The paper 'provides an excellent illustration of the approach of modern economics', that is, '"blackboard economics"', assuming all information that is needed is available (Coase 1988: 19). Section 5.4 considers the 'Social Cost' paper (Coase 1960). The problem of social cost, Coase diagnoses, is the absence of property rights or the ambiguous definition of them. Property rights definition and transaction cost constitute one another's counterparts; poorly defined rights cause transaction costs.

Section 5.5 reflects on Coase's case-study methodology that, all the same, results in theoretical innovation. It reflects his ambition to cover 'essential relationships in the real world' (Mäki 1990: 319). It is opposite to prevailing nominalist economics of generating hypotheses and doing statistical analysis of big data. Contrariwise, detailed accounts of mundane economic phenomena, that is, the *Lebenswelt*, constitute Coase's starting point of the vertical route from plain concreteness to increasingly abstract concepts. It safeguards him from blackboard economics.

Section 5.6 interprets Coase's theoretical insights from a phenomenological perspective. In correspondence with Adam Smith, Coase takes self-interest as the appropriate motivation to conclude exchange between strangers; mere benevolence will not be sustainable. In phenomenological terms, it regards exchange between contemporaries who act in a typical manner, that is, to identify as homunculi. It enables the theorist to safeguard scientific objectivity and afford theoretical exactness while observing human subjectivity. The phenomenological interpretation repays the previous digression on Schutz's phenomenology of the social world. It reveals a human being's experience in the economic system, that is, one's consciousness in the reciprocity with others of exchange situations in which he finds himself.

The final section, Section 5.7, presents some conclusions.

5.2 The nature of the firm

At the outset of the 'Firm' paper, Coase brings up a tension that basically originates the new version of institutional economics. He aspires to employ a definition of the firm that should be not only realistic but also tractable in terms of marginal analysis. However, to what extent does the vigor of tractable marginal analysis allow a definition of the firm that 'corresponds to what is meant by a firm in the real world'? (Coase 1937: 386). Besides and against correspondence to the real world, Coase posits, quoting Lionel Robbins, 'our definition must, of course, "relate to formal relations which are capable of being *conceived* exactly"' (ibid.: 387). Pregnant about Coase's reference to Robbins is that, in the context of the quote, Robbins (1932: 64) profiles his critical position regarding the subject matter of economics as 'an enquiry into the causes determining the production and distribution of wealth'. Against this 'traditional approach to Economics', Robbins introduces studying the economic system 'as a series of interdependent but conceptually discrete relationship between men and economic goods' (ibid.: 64, 68). As an aside, Robbins notes to have felt,

> with Professor Schumpeter, a sense almost of shame at the incredible banalities of much of the so-called theory of production – the tedious discussions of the various *forms of peasant proprietorship, factory organization*, industrial psychology, technical education, etc. which are apt to occur in even the best treatises on general theory arranged on this plan.
>
> (ibid.: 65; emphasis added)

The fundamental objection to this procedure is that it necessarily precludes precision, Robbins comments. 'Scientific generalisations, if they are to pretend to the status of laws, must be capable of being stated exactly', he amplifies (ibid.: 66). Coase endorses this viewpoint, as his quoting in assent of Robbins shows; 'formal relations ... *conceived* exactly' (ibid.). This is remarkable as, at the same time, Coase adheres to the very substantive approach to the mundane economic reality that Robbins abhors. It is Felix Kaufmann who is relevant in this aspect.

Regarding this economics as 'formal relations and conceived exactly', Robbins, in his turn, refers to Kaufmann (1931). This arrests, as Kaufmann reconciles economics as a formal science with a substantive view, removing the purported incongruity in Coase's definition. Kaufmann identifies our economic reality as a domain of stable conduct and coherence between the relations fueled by a uniformly motivational structure that renders economics a particularly favorable ground for mathematical application (ibid.: 774). It renders economics a matter of human relationships that may be conceived exactly rather than what Robbins (1932: 68; emphasis added) claims, 'a series of interdependent but conceptually discrete relationships between *men and economic goods*'.

The painstaking definition discussion concurs with Coase's (1937: 386) goal 'to clarify the assumptions' of economic theory. In this, he finds his intellectual fellow in Frank Knight (1921: 76–81), who is likewise engaged in thinking through the assumptions that underlay the working of the economic system. In his Nobel Prize lecture, Coase associates his 'Firm' paper with the Planning Debate of the early decades of the twentieth century. He rephrases the firm issue by questioning what is wrong with Lenin's idea 'to run the economic system as one big factory' (Coase 1992: 715). How can economists' dismissal of Lenin's idea be reconciled with the 'existence of management and of apparently planned societies, that is, firms', as operating in the market economy? (ibid.). Apparently, the normal economic system requires such a thing as planning.

As discussed, the beginning point in Coase's analyses is the automatic working of the economic system. It finds its analytical elaboration of the price mechanism as a 'model of perfect decentralization' as described by Knight under the assumption of uncertainty absent (Demsetz 1988: 145). Knight provides an impression of such an imaginary society:

> The people are formally free to act as their motives prompt in the production, exchange, and consumption of goods. They "own themselves"; there is no exercise of constraint over any individual by another individual or by "society"; each controls his own activities with a view to the results which accrue to him individually.
>
> (1921: 77)

The current operation of the economic system is '"under no central control, it needs no central survey"', Coase (1937: 387) notes, quoting Sir Arthur Salter. Therefore, in this perspective, the firm is an anomaly. *Nota bene*, this elaboration refers to the working of the economic system as a *whole*.

However, Coase directs his attention to the micro level. Under this aspect, he adds that the working of the economic system,

> does not mean that there is no planning by individuals. These exercise foresight and choose between alternatives. This is necessarily so if there is to be order in the system.
>
> (1937: 387)

Apparently, he drops the assumption of actors as beings without substance. Furthermore, Coase observes planning within the firm as an alternative to the price mechanism 'akin to what is normally called economic planning' (ibid.: 388). This planning, Coase underlines, 'is quite different from the individual

planning mentioned above' (ibid.: 387). It regards planning as the very alternative to the price mechanism; for instance:

> If a workman moves from department Y to department X, he does not
> go because of a change in relative prices but because he is ordered
> to do so.
>
> (ibid.)

Therefore, what is at issue is why, in the specialized exchange economy, there is
an allocation of resources by means of an entrepreneur, that is, a firm, as an
alternative to allocation by the price mechanism. Coase's famous answer is this:

> The main reason why it is profitable to establish a firm would seem to be
> that there is a cost of using the price mechanism. The most obvious cost
> of "organising" production through the price mechanism is that of dis-
> covering what the relevant prices are.
>
> (ibid.: 390)

The latter quoted sentence is a step further away from the perfect decentralization model, that is, perfect competition, in which price is a commonly known
datum. In this context, competition is a matter of tentative interaction between
human beings who, in a behavioral process, find commonsense exactness sufficient for conducting their trades. For instance, Adam Smith notes:

> It (e.g., product quality) is adjusted, however, not by any accurate meas-
> ure, but by the higgling and bargaining of the market, according to that
> sort of rough equality which, though not exact, is sufficient for carrying
> on the business of common life.
>
> (1776: 33)

Apparently, it is the classical, open type of competition that Coase has in mind
diagnosing the cost of using the price mechanism as explaining the existence of
the firm. We are leaving the Garden of Eden, Knight (1921: 268) would say.
Knowledge is no longer fully and freely available. The price is no longer a datum. The market is a place of complicated exchange transactions raising the
cost of higgling and negotiating, writing contracts, and contract enforcement
that may render the firm, as an entrepreneur-coordinator, an advantageous
alternative. Coase concludes:

> It can, I think, be assumed that the distinguishing mark of the firm is the
> supersession of the price mechanism.
>
> (1937: 389)

It is particularly the recurring nature of negotiating and concluding separate
contracts for each exchange transaction on a market that may make it

advantageous to substitute such a series of contracts for one 'whereby the factor, for a certain remuneration (which may be fixed or fluctuating), agrees to
obey the directions of an entrepreneur *within certain limits'* (ibid.: 391). For
that matter, the concept of transaction cost is reminiscent of Carl Menger's
(1976: 189) concept of 'economic sacrifices that exchange operations demand',
as discussed in Chapter 3. Furthermore, the alternative to contract specification is to relegate the details of what the supplier is expected to do to the purchaser who directs the resources within the limits of the contract. The supplier's
dependence on the buyer renders the relationship a firm. In a footnote,
Coase adds:

> Of course, it is not possible to draw a hard and fast line which determines
> whether there is a firm of not. There may be more or less direction.
>
> (ibid.: 392, n. 1)

The outcome is that, 'by forming an organisation and allowing some authority
to direct resources', that is, by establishing a firm, 'certain marketing costs are
saved' (ibid.: 392).[1] Apparently, the costs incurred to acquire knowledge about
the market and the presence of uncertainty explain the existence of the firm.
With a reference to Knight, Coase notes: 'It seems improbable that a firm
would emerge without the existence of uncertainty' (ibid.). It is the dropped
perfect decentralization assumptions that generate the *raison d'être* of the firm,
defined as an (authority) alternative to the market. The latter point I criticize
in Chapter 6.

The supplemental question that Coase discusses regards the size of the
firm, that is, size defined as the number of transactions organized by the entrepreneur (ibid.: 393).[2] Basically, it is a trade-off between a marginal cost of
organizing a transaction within the firm versus the marginal costs of performing the same transaction via an exchange on the open market, 'or the costs of
organising in another firm' (ibid.: 395). Variables in this trade-off regard, for
example, decreasing returns to the entrepreneur function and an increased
chance of an entrepreneur's misallocation of resources when the number of
transactions organized by him increases (ibid.: 394). In this respect, 'the spatial distribution of the transactions organized' and 'the dissimilarity of the
transactions' form a part of the variables. Apart from these variables, the size
of the firm depends on its coherence with the supply price of factors of production (ibid.: 397).

In the concluding section of the 'Firm' paper, Coase returns to the two
questions as posed at the beginning regarding assumptions of economics: 'Are
they tractable? and: Do they correspond with the real world?' (ibid.: 386). Regarding the latter question Coase concludes that his definition, an employer's
direction of employees, 'approximates closely to the firm as it is considered in
the real world' (ibid.: 404). Tractability-wise, it is the principle of marginalism
that safeguards the tractability of the definition, that is, of the size of the firm.
Its application summarizes Coase's theory of the firm:

The question always is, will it pay to bring an extra transaction under the organising authority? At the margin, the costs of organising within the firm will be equal either to the costs of organising in another firm or to the costs involved in leaving the transaction to be "organised" by the price mechanism.

(ibid.)

Coase's own comment on this theoretical proposition is significant.

Business men will be constantly experimenting, controlling more or less, and in this way, equilibrium will be maintained.

(ibid.)

The latter quote substantiates the ambition discussed above to formulate "'formal relations which are capable of being *conceived* exactly'" (ibid.: 387). The marginalism template enables Coase to conclude with an exactly conceived theoretical proposition in which businessmen figure as homunculi.

The *Firm*-paper wonders what planning and authority of a firm may add to an economic system ruled by market prices. It results in its very fruit: the concept of transaction cost as "'a missing element in our models'", Coase (1991: 62) notes later, referring to Ben Klein. In retrospect, he considers the introduction of a transaction cost as 'the most important contribution of "The Nature of the Firm" to economics' (ibid.). A transaction cost renders the concrete phenomenon of exchange between individuals, for example, of 'nuts for berries on the edge of the forest', a complicated affair (Coase 1992: 718). The inclusion of a transaction cost creates the relevance of the institutional structure behind an exchange. The 'Firm' paper founds new institutional economics (NIE) as it prompts the economist to more closely examine what enables the exchanging individuals who have to cope with the transaction cost. What is at issue is the institutional structure of the market. Against this stands the firm as an alternative archetypically institutional structure to deal with a transaction cost. Together, they constitute the main proposition of the 'Firm' paper.

5.3 The marginal cost controversy

During the Conference on the Economics of Regulation of Public Utilities that was held at Northwestern University, Evanston, Illinois, in June 1966, Coase reviewed his position in the marginal cost controversy. He initiated his talk with a personal history regarding his period at the London School of Economics (LSE) during the 1930s. It was the work of Abba Lerner that first drew Coase's attention to the concept that, even when the marginal cost was lower than the average cost, marginal cost pricing would be appropriate for achieving an economic optimum (Coase 1966). Later on, Lerner (1944: xi) elaborated on it in his *The Economics of Control*: 'The prices can be made to reflect their *M*' ('marginal substitutability'). Lerner was a member of a group of LSE economists such as 'Robbins, Hayek, Hicks, Allen, Kaldor and others' who, in the 1930s, were making 'great strides ... in the development of economic theory' (Coase 1966: 97). Coase, however, was associated with Arnold Plant's LSE department, specialized in commerce and, as such, was keenly interested in the theoretical work being done on cost analysis and pricing issues but, as a member of the Plant group, 'thought of it in practical terms' (ibid.).

The anecdote states the origin of Coase's theoretically fundamental attitude: the search for the economic reality behind the theoretical concepts. Additionally, marginal cost pricing is *par excellence* a theme in which the application of theory meets practical feasibility. The marginal cost pricing doctrine is a product of pure theory that would be directly usable. Prominent advocates of it are economists who, in the Collectivist Planning Debate of the 1920s and 1930s, aimed to refute Ludwig von Mises's and Friedrich von Hayek's (1935) denial of the possibility of any economic calculus under socialism. For instance, Oskar Lange and Fred Taylor contend that the 'Central Planning Board' of the socialist economy may achieve the allocative efficiency of the competitive market with two essential conditions:

> the parametric use of prices in accounting; and the two essential rules – minimization of costs and equality of marginal cost and selling price of the product.
>
> (Lippincott 1938: 17–18)

For that matter, 'the parametric use of prices' amounts to consumers' sovereignty and freedom of choice to put resources to work. It is particularly Lerner (1937) who, as an apologist of socialism, assuming these freedoms, expands on marginal cost pricing as the very weapon to spare the socialist economy the economic chaos that the opponents of socialism foresee. Marginal cost pricing features socialist economic theory. Outside the Planning Debate, marginal cost pricing is more specifically to be associated with cases of continuing decreasing average cost production, for example, as pricing policy of public utilities such as roads and bridges. A notable theoretical advocate in this respect is Harold Hotelling (1938).

I discuss the theoretical background of the idea in both applications. Three subsections follow. I start with grounding its use in socialist economic calculus and continue with the reasoning behind its application to the decreasing average cost case. Regarding the latter, I discuss its theoretical development that precedes Hotelling's plea of the doctrine. Thereafter, I discuss Coase's critical perspective on it.

5.3.1 *Marginal cost pricing as a socialist's economic calculus*

Lerner's intellectual agenda is to elaborate on the allocation problem the socialist economy faces as identified by Friedrich von Hayek (1935) and Ludwig von Mises. 'Our (socialist) real object' that Lerner (1937: 256) aims at is *'the most economic utilization of resources*. Against this, the opponents of the socialist ideal propose that the paragon of allocative efficiency is a perfect competitive equilibrium, that is, the fruit of "'competitive individualism'" based on private property (Knight 1936: 255). It is Enrico Barone who, as an exponent of the School of Lausanne, demonstrates the applicability of the formal principles of a perfect equilibrium to a socialist economy (Hayek 1935: Appendix A). Considering the freedom of choice for consumers and workers, the socialist economy may mimic the perfectly competitive equilibrium. Barone's account of this proposition amounts to writing out an equational system à la Walras (ibid.). The Walrasian model to which Barone refers is one of the three 'expositional forms' of the basic doctrine of allocative efficiency. Besides Walras's model, there is the 'Marshallian apparatus of Supply and Demand Curves' (Durbin 1936: 677). A third exposition of the welfare optimum regards the Austrian marginal analysis. The three forms arrive at the same positive conclusion, as Evan Durbin states, 'perfect competition secures the right distribution of resources' (ibid.).

In this aspect, Lerner (1937: 254) recognizes the relevance of the 'difference between the system of analysis and the technique of administration'. It is obvious, for instance, that the daunting number of equations required to solve the allocation of resources renders the Walrasian analysis unsuitable as an administrative technique basis. In the same manner, Marshall's (1890: 838–858) supply and demand apparatus as explicated in the mathematical appendix to his *Principles* lacks the implementation fitness required as a technique of administration. Furthermore, the equilibrium models result from a static analysis of given resources and preferences, blocking any applicability to the dynamic reality. Against this, it is the Austrian marginal analysis that offers the appropriate economic calculus of allocative efficiency. Lerner:

> If we so order the economic activity of the society that no commodity is produced unless its importance is greater than that of the alternative that is sacrificed, we shall have completely achieved the ideal that the economic calculus of a socialist state sets before itself.
>
> (1937: 253)

It is the basic impossibility to oversee the economic entirety that renders the (Paretian) marginal analysis as very expedient. Lerner's solution is that

> all the officers of the economic administration equalise their revenues to their marginal costs – and this is what they would have to do if each is simply enjoined to maximise the profits of the enterprise under his control – this will suffice to set in motion all the forces necessary to achieve the equilibrium.
>
> (ibid.: 254–255)

It is strongly reminiscent of the solution that Hayek presents in his paper, 'The Use of Knowledge', to the information problems faced by the central planner.

Against the central planner who is unable to apply the economic calculus, Hayek (1945: 524) poses "'the man on the spot'" with his practical knowledge about the 'changes in the particular circumstances of time and place'. Lerner's marginal-cost-pricing rule creates an officer's situational logic, situations in which he finds himself, regarding decisions that concern a matter of '*how much more or less difficult* to procure' or 'how much more or less urgently wanted are the alternative things he produces or uses' (ibid.: 525). Apparently, the collectivist economic planning turns into its opposite, i.e., using marginal cost pricing as 'a kind of machinery for registering change', that is, a socialist imitation of the market (ibid.: 527).

In his paper 'Statics and Dynamics in Socialist Economies', Lerner (1937: 265) discusses various decision situations that the officers of economic administration may meet such as build or rebuild questions, the case of large indivisible units of input, and taking account of short term versus long term as a matter of 'degrees of "looking forward"'. Basic in the solutions of them is the maxim that bygones are bygones. 'The only costs that are relevant are the costs the incurrence of which is in question', distinguishing short-term from long-term decisions (ibid.: 264). Officers' guiding principle is that economic activity should be undertaken if the returns on it are expected to be greater than the costs (ibid.: 266). To this, Lerner adds the restriction that 'the principle applies only to each indivisible item of economic activity' (ibid.). By this, he avoids the complicated issue of common costs a complex of activities carried on by a firm would raise.

Consistent use of the (marginal-cost-pricing) rule generates counterparts. Whenever the average cost is increasing, marginal cost pricing results in a positive (quasi-)rent against a negative (quasi-)rent in the event of decreasing average cost. In the latter instance, the marginal cost pricing will incur losses. However, these losses may be compensated by the profits of the cases in which the marginal cost exceeds the average cost. In this aspect, Durbin (1936: 685) concludes that 'it might be impracticable if anything less than everything were in the hands of the State'. In this respect, Lerner (1937: 258) notes that it 'adds one more *economic* argument in favour of a speedy transition from Capitalism to Socialism'.

The theoretical concepts that are discussed support marginal cost pricing to render allocative efficiency in a socialist economy. In this aspect, Lerner makes a notable aside. The comparison between capitalism and socialism regards the 'theoretical system in both cases – i.e., leaving apart such sociological questions as incentives, etc.' (ibid.: 267, n. 1). The 'theoretical system' refers to 'the technical and economic conditions of perfect competition', that is, given prices, and price equal to average cost. Apparently, Lerner interprets economic conditions as being confined to equations 'as symptoms of perfect competition' (ibid.: 267). In the same manner, Durbin perceives the 'economic calculus in a planned economy.' The 'marginal product method does apply with equal force to either a *laissez-faire* or a planned system. ... All logical, theoretical and accountancy problems are common to both types of systems' (Durbin 1936:

678). Criticism such as "'The calculations will not be made'", is not an issue that the 'professor of economic theory is competent to discuss. They are problems of social behavior' (ibid.). 'As long as the socialized factories calculate marginal products, and resources move to the highest margins, the problem of calculus will be solved' (ibid.: 679).

For the time being, Lerner states – apparently referring to the capitalist economy – that a consistent application of marginal cost pricing brings 'about the situation to which Professor 'Pigou's scheme of taxes and bounties intended to guide the competitive economy'. Against this, Lerner considers:

> In the socialist State it is so much simpler, because there is no need for any particular firm or industry to cover its costs.
>
> (1937: 269)

This quote offers a nice bridge to the very subject of the marginal cost pricing controversy; that is, is a consistent application of marginal cost pricing appropriate under capitalism?

5.3.2 *Marginal cost pricing and decreasing average cost*

The controversy regarding marginal cost pricing regards its application to products produced under decreasing average cost, such as public utilities. It leads to a loss-making situation whereas capitalism presupposes that each firm covers its costs. Therefore, it is argued that government should subsidize production when marginal cost pricing generates a loss. Alternative solution would be, as J.E. Meade (1944: 327) contends, 'the socialization of "increasing returns" industries, ... , best accompanied by some measure of public ownership of property'. In his Comment on Meade, J.M. Fleming notes that

> Mr. 'Meade's statement of the principles which should govern the price and output policy of a state-controlled enterprise, though possibly a little over-simplified, is not, I think, open to serious objection.
>
> (ibid.: 328)

Until the 1940s, marginal cost pricing had been a received doctrine. A classic plea for the doctrine is Hotelling's (1938) paper 'The General Welfare in Relation to Problems of Taxation and of Railway and Utility Rates'. Hotelling begins with condemning the New York toll bridges as doing harm to the 'general welfare' (ibid.: 242). The paper discusses the general welfare considerations of marginal cost pricing and the taxation issues that a consistent use of it entails.

Since Adam Smith economic theory claims that competition will be the best for all, Hotelling (1938: 260) notes. It refers to the 'typical agricultural situation of rising marginal cost'. Against this, Hotelling discerns an increasing share of economic activities that require substantial investments that exhibit a decreasing cost structure. It regards enterprises such as bridges, electric power plants, and railroads for which free competition is not a sustainable formula. Competition will decrease the price of an amenity's use equal to zero as its marginal cost nears zero, that is, marginal cost pricing. Thus, 'the owners would retire in disgust to allow anyone who pleased to cross free' (ibid.). At the same time, this zero price enhances the efficient use of such an investment. Therefore, Hotelling contends, there is a case for intervention but definitely not one such as the New York reintroductions of toll bridges. These 'are inefficient reversions' (ibid.: 242). Hotelling recaps:

> The efficient way to operate a bridge – and the same applies to a railroad or a factory, if we neglect the small cost of an additional unit of product or of transportation – is to make it free to the public, so long at least as the use of it does not increase to a state of overcrowding.
>
> (ibid.: 260)

However, he also notes 'the common assumption, so often accepted uncritically ... , that "every tub must stand on its own bottom,"', that is, that total cost recovery is required (ibid.: 242). This thwarts the social welfare maximizing doctrine. Against this, Hotelling advocates government intervention.

It is the government's taxation faculty that affords it to restore prices that equate with marginal cost to maximize social welfare. In this aspect, the tariff issues of, for example, public amenities, are inextricably related to taxation issues. Hotelling proposes an integrated approach as he perceives the problems of taxation and creating utility rates as nearly identical. More generally, the taxation issues may be extended 'to the prices of the products of all industries having large fixed costs independent of the volume of output' (Hotelling 1938: 243). Actually, this is killing two birds with one stone. The graphic analysis that advocates marginal cost pricing is directly applicable to the taxation that this pricing necessitates. Referring to J. Dupuit (1844) as Marshall's precursor, Hotelling presents Figure 5.1, applying Marshall's graphic analysis.

DB depicts the demand curve. Supply curve SB coincides with the marginal cost curve, assuming perfect competition rendering market prices as given. Intersection B is a market equilibrium. A tax t per unit imposed on the sellers lifts the supply curve bodily to RL, 'at height $t = SR = NL$ above its former position' (ibid.: 244). Hotelling's graphic analysis of the general welfare effects of the imposed tax is demonstrated as follows.

At market equilibrium B, the total value of the demand is the area under the arc DB. The total sum the consumers pay then is the rectangle area $OCBA$. Therefore, the consumers' surplus is the curvilinear area ABD. Curvilinear area SBA represents the producer's surplus. At B, the uniform price per unit equals marginal cost, maximizing the sum of consumers' and producers' surpluses. However, tax t interferes with this optimum, resulting in a net loss of general welfare as represented by the shaded area NBL, i.e., a dead weight loss.[3]

Hotelling's figure, shown in Figure 5.1, is instructive in two respects. First, it substantiates that a tax in the event of increasing cost conditions does not

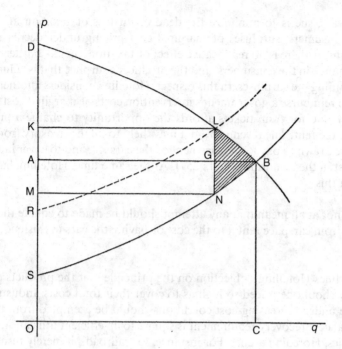

Figure 5.1 Welfare effects of a tax.
(*Source*: Hotelling 1938: 243.)

prompt general welfare, regardless of the shape of the relevant curves. On the contrary, and against Marshall, the figure illustrates that taxation harms the general welfare. It is merely in the case of decreasing cost conditions that general welfare effects may justify government intervention, that is, subsidizing, as substantiated by Marshall and Pigou. Under this aspect, taxation remains a relevant issue, that is, to fund the bounties. This renders Figure 5.1 instructive a second time. The size of the shaded area, the deadweight loss, depends on the slope of the demand and supply curves. This offers significant information for the choice of the type of taxation. It renders an excise duty on a commodity of which the demand curve is rather price-elastic and more harmful from a general welfare perspective than taxing a necessity of which the demand is price indifferent. The latter minimizes the deadweight loss compared to the former. This reasoning founds Hotelling's 'dead loss minimizing tax systems' such as 'income and inheritance taxes, and taxes on site values' (ibid.: 256–257). For instance:

> Land is the most obviously important, but not by any means the only good, whose quantity is nearly or quite unresponsive to changes in price, and which is not available in such quantities as to satisfy all demands.
>
> (ibid.)

What is at issue is to minimize the deadweight loss of taxation against the added consumers' surpluses of marginal cost pricing under decreasing cost conditions. If there is no reallocative effect of taxation, the tax burden is equal to the change in the consumers' and the producer's surplus, that is, a lump-sum tax skimming the surpluses. In this respect, Hotelling considers another opportunity to reimburse a government's intervention costs of marginal cost pricing. Peak demand for train tickets affords the opportunity to charge a price that captures the rent. The revenue from it may 'help to fill the treasury from which funds are drawn to pay for replacement of the cars ... , and to cover interest on their cost in the meantime' (ibid.: 257). At the same time, Hotelling hastens to add that this

> does not at all mean that any attempt should be made to equate the revenue from carspace rental to the cost of having the cars in existence.
>
> (ibid.)

It underlines Hotelling's objection on the principle that the products of every industry should be priced so high as to cover their total costs. Industries that produce under decreasing-cost conditions should be exempted from this rule. The total cost recovery requirement is square to an efficient utilization of public utilities, Hotelling argues. For instance, for railroads, it merely results in an 'extreme and uneconomic complexity of railway freight and passenger rate structure' (ibid.: 263). A ticket purchaser's optimization will be unaffordable as it 'requires the study of an encyclopedic railroad tariff, together with complicated trial-and-error calculations' (ibid.: 264). In this respect, tariffs and taxes exhibit a comparable arbitrariness (ibid.: 242). It is the outcome of the 'conservative criterion ... of a sufficient revenue for total costs' (ibid.: 267). This criterion urges imposing such curious and uneconomic tariffs. Against this, Hotelling formulates his assessment criterion of an investment:

> if some distribution of the burden is possible such that everyone concerned is better off than without the new investment, then there is a prima facie case for making the investment.
>
> (ibid.)

He explicitly disregards the *practicability* of such a distribution. Hotelling is engaged in the theoretical question of 'whether the aggregate of the generalized surpluses (of total benefits over marginal costs) is likely to be great enough to cover the anticipated cost of the new investment' (ibid.: 269). This is the very mathematical and economic problem regarding investment decisions. Thus, Hotelling concludes:

> This will call for a study of demand and cost functions by economists, statisticians, and engineers, and perhaps for a certain amount of large-scale experimentation for the sake of gaining information about these

functions. ... Perhaps this is the way in which we shall ultimately get the materials for a scientific economics.

(ibid.)

It is economics as the fruit of arithmetic and mathematical analyses of the economic reality of demand and cost functions. This perspective corresponds with Lerner, Barone, and others who are engaged in formulating the optimum welfare conditions of a socialist economy: economics as a technical affair. Regarding mundane economic issues, there is one rule: apply marginal cost pricing.

5.3.3 *Marginal cost pricing as a controversy*

It is the indivisibility of the distributive network of such firms that drops marginal cost below average cost, that is, marginal cost pricing consistently rendering them loss-making. Coase's (1946) elaborate example in his main paper on the marginal cost controversy is instructive in this respect. Coase's example is as follows:

> Assume that consumers are situated around a central market in which a certain product is available at constant prices. Assume that roads run out from the central market but that each road passes only one consumer of the product. Assume also that a carrier can carry on each journey additional units of the product at no additional cost (at least to a point beyond the limit of consumption of any individual consumer). Assume further that the product is sold at the point of consumption. It is clear that the cost of supplying each individual consumer would be the cost of the carrier plus the cost at the central market of the number of units consumed by that particular consumer of the product.

(ibid.: 171)

Hotelling and Lerner would price a product unit equal to the cost at the central market. Clearly, this renders the costs of carriage unpaid, or rather to be paid by the taxpayers, as Hotelling recommends. A case in point in Coase's example is that all the costs are direct costs, that is, attributable to individual consumers.[4] Coase further assumes that 'all factors are in perfectly elastic supply' (ibid.). The example illustrates nicely that marginal cost pricing produces the incongruity that consumers who generate costs directly attributable to them do not have to pay these costs. Basically, Coase argues, marginal cost pricing amounts to a supersession of the basic principle of the price system. It denies that a consumer should pay the cost of a product he buys in all cases. Against the price system, the Hotelling–Lerner solution basically presents the government as the alternative body to allocate 'the use of factors of production between consumers' (ibid.). This questioning of the price system prompts Coase 'to turn to a consideration of fundamentals' (ibid.). It features Coase's analytical style, indeed.

The commonsense rule that one should pay the cost of the product one purchases founds the economic system. A basic feature of a price is that it represents 'the value of the resources used to produce the product to some other consumer, or possibly even to the same consumer in another use', that is, the costs (Coase 1945: 112). Whenever a consumer pays less than the costs, this causes a maldistribution of resources. Actually, the effect of the loss-making pricing is that, for the same factor, various people are charged differently. In the example, consumers do not have to take into account the costs of carriage, commanding resources they do not pay for. This difference in charging for the same factor inherently upsets the income and wealth distribution. Moreover, the taxation imposed on others to recover the costs of carriage generates a redistribution of income and wealth. Furthermore, taxation will harm the marginal conditions that marginal cost pricing aims to observe.

In this analysis reemerges Coase's basic perspective: the reciprocal nature of economic exchange underlined by the definition of cost. It is the obstruction of this reciprocity ensued from marginal cost pricing that generates the inefficiency flaws and the redistribution effects. Under this aspect, Coase proposes a multipart pricing. It is not by accident that his central market example as quoted is expedient to explain the alternative pricing.

Multipart pricing is a third possibility between marginal versus average cost pricing. Apparently, both present strong arguments. The marginal cost pricing proponent argues that it is rational to charge the consumer an additional unit for merely the additional costs. Average cost pricing, the argument goes, 'would [under decreasing cost conditions] not reflect the value of the factors in another use or to another user. But, Coase continues, for the same reason it can be argued that the consumer should pay the total cost of the product' (Coase 1946: 173). What is at issue is that the consumer is not only involved in deciding about an additional unit of a product but also in 'whether it is it worth his while to consume the product at all' (ibid.). Obviously, the former implies the latter from which may be inferred that, in any way, marginal cost pricing is unsatisfactory.

It is multipart pricing that unites the best of the preceding options. On one hand, the consumer should pay the total cost of the products supplied to him. On the other, he should pay for the marginal cost that the additional units entail. Therefore, in the central market example

> the consumer should be charged one sum to cover the cost of carriage while for the additional units he should be charged the cost of the goods at the central market.
>
> (ibid.)

Actually, this is the two-part pricing as a version of the multipart pricing as 'well known to students of public utilities' such as the electric power industry and waterworks (ibid.: 173–174). In contrast to marginal cost pricing, multipart pricing offers an investment criterion, that is, whether to decide on a certain production at all. What is at issue is whether the consumer would be prepared to pay the total cost of the product. The marginal cost pricing has recourse to the 'study of demand and cost functions by economists, statisticians, and engineers', Hotelling (1938: 269) puts forward. For instance, to address the investment decision about building a bridge, he notes, referring to Dupuit,

> would be a matter of estimation of vehicular and pedestrian traffic originating and terminating in particular zones, with a comparison of distances by alternative routes in each case, and an evaluation of the savings in each class of movement.
>
> (ibid. 246–247)

The quote indicates Hotelling's alternative to the price system. Coase's (1946: 175) comment on it is that the 'possibility to make such estimates, with considerable accuracy and at low cost' might result in an abolition of the price system. Lerner, Coase adds, argues for a pricing system as such estimates would be impossible. In general, Hotelling exhibits a type of contempt for long-term investment questions and focuses on the operation of existing amenities. Hotelling:

> It will be better to operate the railroads for the benefit of living human beings, while letting dead men and dead investments rest quietly in their graves, and to establish a system of rates and services calculated to assure the most efficient operation.
>
> (1938: 269)

Hotelling disregards the very omission of the market test of marginal cost pricing compared to the multipart pricing advocated by Coase. The balance is in favor of multipart pricing. However, Hotelling and other proponents are merely engaged in comparing marginal versus average cost pricing, claiming the superiority of the former against the latter. In favor of marginal cost pricing is that it would be a welfare loss if additional units are not priced at marginal cost. Regarding the market test, the argument is more qualified. Average cost pricing determines whether consumers are willing to sacrifice the value of factors to obtain that other value in that form. However, 'the difficulty is, Hotelling points out, that the reverse is not true' (Coase 1946: 180). If the demand curve lies at all points below the average cost curve, average cost pricing will not meet the market test. At the same time, it is thinkable that the integral of consumer's surpluses would justify production. Under marginal cost pricing, such production would be undertaken. Comparing marginal versus average cost pricing is not a clear-cut case, Coase concludes. At the same time, relying on estimating the potential demand as an alternative to the pricing test remains a precarious route. Therefore, marginal cost pricing is not *per se* superior to average cost pricing.

Cost and demand functions feature the marginal cost pricing doctrine. At stake are consumer's and producer's surpluses as well as excise taxes that upset the marginal optimum conditions, although an inheritance tax leaves the marginal conditions as they are. It is '"blackboard economics"' that features the economics of the doctrine, as Coase coins it, in his retrospect on the controversy. He states:

> The policy under consideration is one which is implemented on the blackboard. All the information needed is assumed to be available and the teacher plays all the parts.
>
> (Coase 1988: 19)

This economics is not engaged in exchange relationships between negotiating partners but in formulating optimum welfare conditions in the abstract. It recaps Coase's critique of the doctrine in his 1946 paper.

In his review of the controversy, Coase refers to Paul Samuelson. Marginal cost pricing, Samuelson (quoted in Coase 1988: 17) argues, enables the economy to squeeze the maximum of outputs from its scarce resources. Continuing, he adds a significant idea:

> Because Marginal Cost has this optimality property, it can with some care be used to detect inefficiency in any institutional setup.
>
> (ibid.)

Reading 'Marginal Cost' as marginal cost pricing, the non-application of it becomes a shibboleth of institutional inefficiency. In this view, Samuelson inverts the causal relationship. However, in contrast to Samuelson's idea, it is the institutional setup that features the efficiency whether or not applying marginal cost pricing. In this respect, Coase refers to Tom Wilson who 'early on in the debate ... drew attention to the close relationship between financial autonomy and the administrative structure', that is, the import of the institutional setup (ibid.: 18).

Wilson's (1945) discussion of marginal cost pricing is the opposite of blackboard economics. Economists practice the theoretical concepts of the economics of welfare, he notes, without bothering about the 'information available to the business man and the accountant' (ibid.: 454). He directs his critique in particular to Mr. Meade and Mr. Lerner, who

> take as their starting-point the principle, called "the Rule," that marginal costs and price should be equated.
>
> (ibid.: 455)

This rule is the product, Wilson diagnoses, 'of those who, like Mr. Lerner, have been bewitched by the elegance of pure theory' (ibid.: 459). Against Lerner's idea 'to apply the Rule quite generally', Wilson elaborates in detail the practical issues that its application in cost-decreasing industries may entail (ibid.: 456). Wilson walks the route of vertical de-isolation, that is, from abstract application to working out the effects of the Rule in the specific situation, for example, in 'a large programme of socialization far beyond the public utility field' (ibid.). I return to this in Section 5.5.

Wilson's main point is that he qualifies the effects on economic behavior of subsidization and socialization that the rule entails, that is, of setting aside 'the *laissez-faire* criterion of profitability'? (ibid.: 455). Wilson enumerates a number of its effects:

- It requires a device to check the subsidized private monopoly regarding whether it would 'dutifully keep the commandments' (ibid.).
- It brings to bear the issue of 'the relative flexibility and inventiveness of public and private enterprises' (ibid.: 456).
- It deprives a balance sheet to check the efficiency of the manager.
- It deprives the socialist undertaker of the financial need to estimate what consumers would give for the product.
- It rather induces 'the managers of the socialist undertakings, entranced with some new technical project or anxious to increase their own importance by "empire-building"', declaring that the consumers would gladly pay for the proposed project.

(ibid.: 458)

Therefore, Wilson concludes:

The best advice the economist can give is that each enterprise, whether socialised or not, should be made to stand on its own feet and cover its own total costs whenever possible.

(ibid.: 459)

Financial autonomy should have precedence over the marginal cost rule. At the same time, Wilson further qualifies his advice. Whenever possible, it would be preferable to apply a two-part tariff as it unites the advantage of marginal cost pricing with that of total cost recovery. Furthermore, the rule remains appropriate in some obvious cases 'such as the provision of parks and monuments' (ibid.).

Wilson elaborates on the effects of the (partial) abolition of the pricing system as emphasized by Coase. The effects that are enumerated substantiate the effects in terms of changed incentives. In retrospect, they may be interpreted as effects of changed property rights. The subsidies and socialization of production render the property rights of the resources involved non-, or at least ill, defined, loosening the connection between benefit and cost. In this aspect, Wilson's contribution to the marginal cost controversy might be perceived as foreshadowing Coase's (1960) 'The Problem of Social Cost', the paper that drives the concept of property rights explicitly home to economists.

5.4 The problem of social cost

Edmund Kitch's (1983) 'The Fire of Truth' provides a nice glimpse into the genesis of Coase's 'Social Cost' paper. Kitch's paper is a transcript of a conference on '"Intellectual History of Law and Economics"', held in May 1981; *A Remembrance of Law and Economics at Chicago, 1932–1970*. (ibid.: 163). The conference gathered a group of distinguished economists and lawyers, such as Milton Friedman, Harold Demsetz, Armen Alchian, George Stigler, William Landes, Richard Posner, and Henry Manne, 'to create a source document that ... might gain insight into how people, ideas, universities, and societies interact' (ibid.: 163–164). The other purpose of the conference was to pay tribute to the first two editors of the *Journal of Law and Economics*, Aaron Director and Ronald Coase (ibid.: 164).

The transcript recounts a seminar at Director's home with, among others, Friedman and Stigler, to occasion Coase to defend his view on harmful effects as developed in his 'Federal Communications Commission' ('FCC') paper (Coase 1959). In this paper, Coase refutes Pigou, who approaches the problem of harmful effects 'in terms of a difference between private and social products' (ibid.: 26). Stigler recalls 'the seminar was one of the most exciting intellectual events of my life' (Kitch 1983: 221). He continues:

> At the beginning of the evening we took a vote and there were twenty votes for Pigou and one for Ronald (Coase), and if Ronald had not been allowed to vote it would have been even more one-sided. The discussion began. As usual, Milton (Friedman) did much of the talking. I think it is also fair to say that, as usual, Milton did much of the correct and deep and analytical thinking. I cannot reconstruct it. ... Milton would hit him from one side, then from another, then from another. Then to our horror, Milton missed him and hit us. At the end of that evening the vote had changed. There were twenty-one votes for Ronald and no votes for Pigou.
>
> (ibid.)

Coase remembers it. 'He (Milton) grilled me for half an hour or more, but when I was still standing at the end of that I felt I was home' (ibid.). The seminar resulted in a new version of the 'FCC' paper: 'The Problem of Social Cost' (Coase 1960).

In another part of the conference transcript, Kitch reports a dialogue that further elucidates the genesis of the *Social Cost* paper. William Landes questions Coase regarding the influence of Knight's 'Some Fallacies in the Interpretation of Social Cost' (Knight 1924). The following ensues from Landes's question:

Landes: That was in some ways a forerunner of your paper on social cost because it spells out the importance of property rights in resource allocation, and I wonder if you were familiar with Knight's article?

Coase: Oh, yes. In fact, I would say that the title of my paper came from Frank Knight, and the title of the paper was rather to indicate the topic I was talking about, because, of course, I don't think the concept of social cost is a very useful one, and I don't ever refer to it. But it did indicate to people what I was talking about. I knew it, and if there are traces of what Knight says in my work, it wouldn't surprise me.

Friedman: It would surprise you if there weren't, wouldn't it?

Coase: Yes, that's right.

(Kitch 1983: 215)

In the perspective of this dialogue, it is very remarkable that Coase in neither his 'FCC' nor in his 'Social Cost' paper refers to Knight's 1924 paper. All the more, as the transcript reads, Coase had to read Knight's (1921) *Risk, Uncertainty and Profit* as an LSE student. In addition, Coase declares: 'Knight happens to be one of the most important influences in developing my views' (Kitch 1983: 213). It is rightly in this famous book that Coase might have read Knight's explicit formulation of a central idea of Coase's 'Social Cost' paper. Knight writes in it:

If an agency is limited relatively to the need for its use, it must be appropriated by some one, to be administrated, to decide who is to have the use of it and who is to do without'.

(1921: 188–189, n. 2)

It is plausible that Coase's acknowledgment of Knight's influence on him must be interpreted in a general sense as neither the 'FCC' nor the 'Social Cost' paper quotes Knight's book. It might underline that they are kindred spirits engaged in the normal working of the system as a theoretical project. At the same time, it does Knight justice to preface the discussion of the 'Social Cost' paper with Knight's (1924: 584) two highways case in which he refutes Pigou's distinction regarding social versus private cost and product. In this, Knight pioneers Coase in another manner.

The highways case deals with Pigou's (1920: 172) contention that 'self-interest will not tend to make national dividend a maximum' when marginal private net product and marginal social net product diverge. For instance, this occurs in industries with increasing costs. Individual profit-seeking inflicts (social) costs on others who face increased cost, that is, decreased product, Pigou argues. An excellent example of decreasing product is a congested highway. Suppose there are two highways between two points, a narrow but well-maintained one and a broad, poorly graded and surfaced one. Obviously, if there is heavy traffic of trucks, congestion will develop on the narrow highway, as

any driver of any truck has an incentive to use the narrow road, until the advantage is reduced to zero for all the trucks. Thus, as the author (Pigou) contends, individual freedom results in a bad distribution of investment between industries of constant and industries of increasing cost.

(Knight 1924: 585)

This founds the rationale for social interference to levy a tax on each truck using the narrow road 'so adjusted that the number of trucks on the narrow road would be as such as to secure the maximum efficiency in the use of the two roads taken together' (ibid.: 585–586). The tax increases the private cost with the (social) cost inflicted on others due to excessive demand, Pigou reasons. It will discipline the truck drivers, enhancing national dividend.

However, Knight proposes that the flaw 'in such economic theorizing is that the assumptions diverge in essential respects from the facts of real economic situations' (ibid.: 586). It disregards that private ownership (of resources) features competition. Knight:

> If the roads are assumed to be subject to private appropriation and ex-ploitation, precisely the ideal situation which would be established by the imaginary tax will be brought about through the operation of ordinary economic motives.
>
> (ibid.: 586–587)

The conclusion of Knight's analysis is that the normal economic system of competition enabled by private property (rights) dissolves the Pigovian contrast of private versus social product. 'The transferable resources are distributed among alternative uses in such a way as to yield equal marginal value product everywhere' (ibid.: 598). These are the fruits of Knight's analysis as they reemerge in the 'FCC' and the 'Social Cost' papers. Significant in this respect is the footnote in which Knight commends the attention of 'the advocates of "inductive economics" ...; that what is needed in the case is not more refined observation or the gathering of "statistics", but simply correct theorizing' (ibid.: 586, n. 5). Clearly, this note deals a blow to Hotelling's analysis discussed in the preceding section.

5.4.1 The 'FCC' paper

In March 1910, the US Navy Department submitted a letter to the Senate in which it complained about the '"etheric bedlam produced by numerous stations all trying to communicate at once. ... Public business is hindered to the great embarrassment of the Navy Department."' (Navy letter, quoted in Coase 1959: 2). The department worried particularly about the calls of vessels in peril on the sea that go unheeded in the etheric chaos. The Navy Department raised a matter that resulted in regulating the broadcasting industry. In 1912, an act was passed that ordered radio stations to apply for a license issued by the secretary of commerce. The act created a demanding range of duties of the secretary as

> this license would include details of the ownership and location of the station, the wave length or wave lengths authorized for use, the hours for which the station was licensed for work, etc.
>
> (ibid.)

In the course of the 1910s, it was proposed to create a government monopoly that would give control of the radio industry, for instance, to the Department of Navy, comparable to the post office monopoly. Mr. Daniels, secretary of the navy, argued: "'There is a certain amount of ether, and you cannot divide it up among the people as they choose to use it; one hand must control it.'" (ibid.: 3). Later, Mr. Daniels contended that "'radio, by virtue of the interferences, is a natural monopoly'" (ibid.: 4).

During the 1920s, the number of radio stations exploded, facing the secretary of commerce with the unrewarding task of preventing interferences between them. Furthermore, several detailed conditions inserted by the secretary were destroyed by court decisions that rendered it increasingly difficult to regulate the expanding industry of radio broadcasting, telephone, and telegraph. In 1927, an act passed that brought into existence the Federal Radio Commission, which was entitled to prescribe a number of detailed conditions that the licensee would have to satisfy in order to prevent broadcasting interferences. In general, the commission was entitled to issue a license if the "'public interest, necessity or convenience would be served'" (ibid.: 6). In 1934, the Federal Radio Commission changed into the Federal Communication Commission (FCC), which was also responsible for regulating the telephone and telegraph industry (ibid.: 7).

This history of regulating broadcasting is, at the same time, a report of decisions disputed by license applicants who distrust the discretionary powers of the authorities. Moreover, regulation policy raises the reasonable fear that the discretion of the regulating authority clashes with the 'Doctrine of Freedom of the Press' (ibid.). Censorship lies in wait in interpreting the vaguely formulated license criteria.

> Furthermore, Coase concludes, the Commission has many favors to give, and few people with any substantial interests in the broadcasting industry would want to flout too flagrantly the wishes of the Commission.
>
> (ibid.: 12)

This FCC, as it acted in the 1950s, was prone to arbitrariness and censorship. Additionally, the licensing policy of the FCC generated outright arbitrary monopoly rents for the fortuitous applicants who obtained a license. These circumstances offered Coase sufficient ammunition to write the 'FCC' paper and develop the ideas in 1958–59 (Kitch 1983: 222).

The FCC has its own rationale. As referred to earlier, some conceive ether as a certain amount of something material, limited in quantity that cannot be distributed but by one agency, either by the government or an entity that owns the radio stations, that is, as a natural monopoly. Mr. Justice Frankfurter, representing the opinion of the Supreme Court in a radio law case, accounts for the Radio Act of 1927, underlining certain basic facts about radio as a means of communication -its facilities are limited; they are not available to all who may wish to use them; the radio spectrum simply is not large enough to accommodate everybody.

(Frankfurter, quoted in ibid.: 12–13)

The scarcity of the radio spectrum is Frankfurter's rationale for federal regulation. Obviously, Coase responds that, for an economist, this is an unguarded goal. The scarcity of frequencies refers to the very economic problem. Scarcity is relevant for all resources used in the economic system. What is at issue is why this frequency scarcity cannot be solved by the price mechanism, as is usually done in the American economic system (ibid.: 14) The actual cause of the trouble of the frequency scarcity, Coase argues, is the nonexistence of property rights. Probably, the proponents of government regulation of frequencies bother with the nonphysical, obscure nature of ether. Clearly, they wrestle with the concept. On one hand, the concept of the radio spectrum circulates as in physical terms, limited in quantity. On the other, it is obvious that ether does not make a good commodity that can be parceled out. At the same time, it is exactly this image of physically parceling out that is in accordance with the manner in which an economist is used to thinking of the factors of production, consumption goods, and traded commodities in physical units, such as acres of land and bottles of wine. The blind spot of the regulation proponents is that they do not recognize that the bedlam of frequencies does not result from the impossibility to divide the radio spectrum into physical parcels but from the non-definition of the rights to use them. The bedlam of radio frequencies reflects a conflict of property rights that features scarcity. All economics begins with the definition of property rights. Therefore, the exchange of commodities regards the exchange of property rights, and the production of goods presupposes the right to use or abuse resources of production. The definition of property rights renders frequencies amenable to a price mechanism, granting a frequency to its highest bidder, as Leo Herzel (1951) advanced.

Generally, the definition of property rights points to its basically reciprocal nature. The establishment of a property right as an assignment to someone is, by definition, an exclusion of others. 'All property rights interfere with the ability of people to use resources' (Coase 1959: 27). The advantage of establishing exclusive rights to use a resource is obvious. However, the exertion of property rights frequently results in actions that directly harm others. 'For example, a radio operator may use a frequency in such a way as to cause interference to those using adjacent frequencies' (Coase 1959: 26). It is, at the same time, this reciprocity that occasions the economic actors to conclude to a property rights exchange. In the property-rights perspective, there is no analytical difference between a payment for the right of the use of a resource versus a payment for the right to inflict the uses fructus of someone else's premises or radio frequency. In both emerges the reciprocal dimension that might invite a deal. This is a central concept in the 'FCC' paper.

5.4.2 The 'Social Cost' paper

The 'Social Cost' paper expands on the economics of harmful effects as discussed in the 'FCC' paper. It deals 'with the question in a more explicit way and without reference to the original problem', that is, frequency interference (Coase 1960: 1; n. 1). In the standard example of harmful effects, a factory's production generates inflicting harm on neighboring premises. This harm must be compensated by the factory is the received Pigovian answer, at least until the 'FCC' paper. Against Pigou, Coase underlines, is the reciprocal nature of an economic harm issue. If A harms B, then the avoidance of this harm would harm A. 'The problem is to avoid the more serious harm', Coase repeats in the Social Cost paper (ibid.: 2).

Coase elaborates on the reciprocity of harm in an instance in which cattle go astray and destroy crops on neighboring land. Coase's manner of presentation reveals the harm the cattle cause as a mundane economic choice problem: 'meat or crops' (ibid.). What is required is to know the value of what is obtained versus what is sacrificed. Apparently, there is a market for harmful effects, assuming that its pricing system operates smoothly, that is, without cost. First, Coase faces this idea with the conventional Pigovian solution in which the damaging business is liable for the destruction. An arithmetical example of the crops' damage illustrates the working of the market. In this respect, Coase faces the smoothly working market with the Pigovian liability for damage. Second, he expands on the working of the market for harmful effects in instances without liability for the loss.

First, suppose the cattle raiser is liable for the damage caused. Suppose further that the cost of a fence is $9 and the price of a crop per ton is $1. Obviously, if the damage amounts to more than $9, it is beneficial for the cattle raiser to put up a fence. Below the $9 damage value, the destruction is an additional cost that the cattle raiser will 'take into account along with his other costs' (ibid.: 3). Another arithmetical example presents a Pareto-efficient contract between the cattle raiser and the corps farmer. Suppose the farmer's net gain when cultivating the land is $2. Suppose further that the cattle raiser increases the number of cattle that generate damage of $3. The liability to pay this $3 to the farmer affords the opportunity to make a Pareto-efficient deal, concluding a contract in which the farmer agrees not to cultivate the land for any payment between $2 and $3. Clearly, the smoothly working market crops out a range of mutually satisficing bargains. For instance, another possibility would be that the farmer chooses a cultivation that is 'less liable to damage by cattle, but which would not be as profitable as the crop grown in the absence of damage' (ibid.: 4; n. 4). Thus, suppose the net gain of the new crops is $1 instead of the former yield of $2. Suppose further that the damage with the new crop is $1 instead of the former $3. These figures open the opportunity for the cattle raiser to offer the farmer any sum less than $2 to induce the farmer to choose the less damaging crops. What is required is that the cattle raiser offers more than $1, that is, more than the loss of net gain due to the cultivation switch. The conclusion from these simple arithmetical examples is that market transactions may forestall that liability rules would result in continuing cultivation, forcing a damage payment by the cattle raiser that exceeds the net gain of the farmer. Market transactions generate a maximized value of production.

Second, the smoothly working market generates the same maximized value of production if there are no liability rules for the damage. Suppose the cattle raiser considers increasing his herd with one steer that would add damage to crops of $3. Whether or not the cattle raiser is liable, the final result is independent of the liability issue. What is at issue is whether the additional cost incurred of $3 worth of damage is less than the increase in value of the cattle production. With 'the delimitation of property rights' as an 'essential prelude to market transactions', a net gain of the additional steer of $3 provides the cattle raiser the opportunity to entice the farmer to refrain from cultivating the land on which the cattle go astray (Coase 1959: 27). The payment will be plus $3 but less than the net gain of the steer that has been added. The property rights prelude is the stepping-stone to market transactions transferring and recombining these rights. It is needed to know 'whether or not a damaging business is liable for damage caused' but has no effect on the final result (Coase 1960: 8).

Harmful effects of economic actions emerge in countless guises. As discussed, the departing point in Coase's analysis is his ability to determine the reciprocal nature of the problem. Seemingly, it is rather simple: without cattle, there is no crop damage, and without crops, there is no cattle that damage. All the same, when brought before the court, the court decision does not always reveal this platitude. For instance, the court decisions in the case *Bryant v. Lefever* do not recognize the reciprocal nature of the matter (ibid.: 11). The case concerns a smoke nuisance issue. A plaintiff and a defendant live in adjoining houses. The former was able to light fires in his house without the chimneys smoking until the latter took down his house and rebuilt it much beyond the original height. Furthermore, the defendant stacked timber on the roof of his house. These changes caused the plaintiff's chimneys to smoke whenever he lit fires (ibid.). A jury awarded the plaintiff $40 in damages, arguing that the higher wall and the stacked timber prevented the chimneys' drawing. However, the Court of Appeals reversed the judgment, arguing as follows. The plaintiff has no legal right to claim that the defendant facilitates the egress of the plaintiff's smoke.

> He cannot sue the defendants, because the smoke made by himself, for which he has not provided any effectual means of escape, causes him annoyance.
>
> (Cotton, L.J., quoted in ibid.: 12)

The case of *Bryant v. Lefever* nicely reflects the conventional interpretation of harmful effects as a one-sided affair that inevitably result in arbitrary decisions of a jury and Court of Appeals. However, 'the smoke nuisance was caused both by the man who built the wall *and* by the man who lit the fire' (ibid.). Both undertake actions that are valuable to them. It amounts to a choice: a wall versus a drawing chimney, a choice that might result in a transaction that is beneficial to both parties.

The whole potential of mutually beneficial bargains that the harmful effects offer depends on the assumption that the market works smoothly. However, as Coase (1937: 390) notes in his 'Firm' paper: 'there is a cost of using the price mechanism'; that is, the transaction cost is positive. It is particularly the concept of positive transaction cost that makes up the theoretical innovation. Positive transaction cost renders it extremely difficult to conclude Pareto-efficient transactions in all the discussed instances. It is necessary to know who is involved in the harmful effects, to define the harm, to write a contract, to meter the terms agreed upon, and to enforce them; let alone the strategic behavior that the potential partners may exhibit. Therefore, many times, prohibitively high transaction costs thwart a transaction that would 'avoid the more serious harm' (Coase 1959: 26). To adhere to this aim, it is required to search for an alternative; that is, what may substitute the market?

As emphasized, a transaction basically concerns a transfer and or recombination of property rights. In this perspective, the question is to determine an arrangement of property rights that avoids the more serious harm. For instance, legislative regulation may substitute the market transaction to establish a relatively efficient arrangement of rights. Theoretically, the alternative arrangement is the outcome of weighing the value of what is obtained by a harmful effect versus the value that would be sacrificed. Furthermore, it is required to take into account the administrative cost of the alternative to the market. In this aspect, it might be profitable 'to do nothing about the problem at all' (Coase 1960: 18). These variables render that the economist studies a type of 'broker' who brings parties together by means of a choice out of a gamut of legally supported economic organizations. In this view, the firm as a legal alternative to the price mechanism is but an instance of substituting the market for another institutional setting, avoiding more serious harm, or concluding a positive sum contract. Coase:

> The government is, in a sense, a super-firm (but of a very special kind) since it is able to influence the use of factors of production by administrative decision.
>
> (ibid.: 17)

It is a government's legislative capacity and authority that bring law and economics together to assist or replace the working of the market. For that matter, against economists, legislators and judges are superior in recognizing 'the economic implications of their decisions and are aware ... of the reciprocal nature of the problem', Coase notes (ibid.: 19). For instance, on tort cases, judges weigh the interests of disputing parties. Particularly, American writers on tort, he notes, emphasize the element of reciprocity in their subject. William Prosser on torts, as quoted by Coase, asserts:

> It is only when his conduct is unreasonable *in the light of its utility and the harm which results* [italics added], that it becomes a nuisance.... As it was said in an ancient case in regard to candle-making in a town, "Le utility del chose excusera le noisomeness del stink."
>
> (Prosser, quoted in ibid.: 19)

An example of a sophisticated assessment of interests is illustrated in the *Adams v. Ursell* case. Defendant Ursell managing a fried fish shop, 'set up his shop near houses of "a much better character"', causing a nuisance to the direct neighbors. However, the judge commented, '"it by no means follows that because a fried fish shop is a nuisance in one place it is a nuisance in another"' (Judge, quoted in ibid.: 21). Ursell had to move to a 'premises near houses of "a much worse character", the inhabitants of which would no doubt consider the availability of fish-and-chips to outweigh the pervading odour and "fog or mist"' (ibid.: 21–22). For that matter, it was rather easy to move to the more suitable location in the neighborhood.

Coase expands on a number of court cases showing the comparisons that judges make 'between what would be gained and what lost by preventing actions which have harmful effects' (ibid.: 27–28). At the same time, the danger remains of an erroneous weighing of interests. *A fortiori*, this is valid for governments that design the intervening regulations, apart from being swayed by vested interests. For that matter, Coase's balancing of the respective harmful effects nears the assumption of interpersonal comparison of utilities, possibly making him an ally of Pigou in this respect. I further discuss this in Chapter 7.

The conclusion of both the FCC and Social Cost papers amounts to a refutation of Pigou's welfare economics regarding harmful effects. Coase (1960: 28) concludes the 'Social Cost' paper by discussing relevant elements of Pigou's (1920) *The Economics of Welfare*, that is, 'the fountainhead for the modern economic analysis' of harmful effects. The main point in Coase's review of Pigou regards the divergence of private versus social product or cost. Pigou's perception of the nature of this divergence features his economic thought.

It is the idea of a state of nature, that is, status quo in the sense of the distribution of property rights, that directs Pigou's reasoning.[5] It offers him the logically required fixed point to precisely identify any divergence. As yet, it is a concept that remains latent. Initially, Pigou founds his analysis on the fundament that the economic system of self-interest tends toward a natural economic welfare balance. So, Pigou joins to

> certain optimistic followers of the classical economists, [who] have suggested that the "free play of self-interest", if only Government refrains from interference, will automatically cause ... more economic welfare that could be attained by any arrangement other than that which comes about "naturally".
>
> (1920: 127)

In this aspect, he adds, referring to Adam Smith, that self-interest cannot function without being 'qualified and guarded by special laws, before it will promote the most productive employment of a country's resources' (ibid.: 128). As an underpinning, Pigou refers to Edwin Cannan (quoted in ibid.) who stresses that the '"working of the self-interest is generally beneficent ... because human institutions are arranged so as to compel self-interest"' to do so. For instance, states impose limitations on the absolute powers of owners of property rights, for example, rules restraining people from setting fire to their house (ibid.: 129). Herein Pigou underlines the significance of well-defined property rights as the very base of optimizing economic welfare, that is, 'the most productive employment of a country's resources' (ibid.: 128). It may be interpreted as an account of Arnold Plant's and Coase's (1991: 38) adage, '"The normal economic system works itself"'. Thus far, there is no private versus social distinction; as yet, economic theory is engaged in market transactions enabled by 'human institutions', that is, by property rights. From here, Pigou leaves the theoretical domain as we have known it since the Marginal Revolution.

Against the recognition of institutions that enhance the most productive use of resources, Pigou (1920: 129) nevertheless observes failures and imperfections 'even in the most advanced States'. So, *The Economics of Welfare*, he continues, aims to study the many obstacles that prevent the use of the community's resources in the most effective manner. 'Its purpose is essentially practical' (ibid.). Practical in Pigou's perception means to explain the way that governments can 'control the play of economic forces ... to promote the economic welfare, and through that the total welfare' (ibid.: 129–130). In a footnote, Pigou refers to Marshall, who establishes that

> much remained to be done, by a careful collection of statistics of demand and supply and a scientific interpretation of their results, in order to discover what are the limits of the work that society can with advantage do towards turning the economic actions of individuals into channels in which they will add the most to the sum total of happiness.
>
> (1890: 475)[6]

Apparently, the interpretation of statistics designs government intervention. At the same time, the quote presents 'scientific interpretation' (of government interference) as taking account of an individual's situational logic.

What is at issue is eliminating the obstacles of side effects. To grasp them, Pigou aims

> to provide a suitable definition for the concepts which are fundamental ... , namely, *the value of marginal private* and *the value of the marginal social net product*.
>
> (1920: 131)

The definition of the fundamental concepts reads as follows:

- The marginal social net product is the total net product of physical things or objective services due to the marginal increment of resources in any given use or place, no matter to whom any part of this product may accrue.
- The marginal private net product is that part of the total net product of physical things or objective services due to the marginal increment of resources in any given use or place that accrues in the first instance – *i.e.* prior to sale – to the person responsible for investing resources there.

                                                                  (Pigou 1920: 134–135)

The definitions provide statistical devices for identifying the obstacles, that is, differences between private and social net products. From a theoretical perspective, however, it is particularly significant to pay attention to Pigou's account that brings him these concepts. Here emerges the idea of a state of nature, that is, as the point of reference. He distinguishes 'between two senses in which the term marginal increment of resources may be employed' (ibid.: 131).

- The marginal social net product reflects the marginal resource increment in the context of a net addition to the sum total of resources in existence. It must be perceived as an addition executed by a type of panoptic authority, '*so to speak, from outside*' (ibid.: 131; emphasis added).
- The marginal private net product regards the marginal increment in the sense of a net resource addition 'as being transferred to the particular use or place we are studying from some other use or place', that is, the marginal calculation of reshuffling resources, initiated, so to speak, *from the inside* of the individual actor (ibid.: 131–132).

The distinction enables Pigou to identify the differences between marginal social versus marginal private net products. An increase in the use of resources by a firm in one industry may cause external economies internal to the industry or lessen the production costs of a firm in another industry. 'Everything of this kind must be counted in', Pigou underlines (ibid.: 134). For instance, the railway company should compensate for the harm done by trains to the owners of properties adjoining the railway tracks. Basically, the aim of the intervention (from outside) is to repair the economic welfare positions preceding the economic activity at hand. 'I take, Coase argues, Pigou's policy recommendations to be, first, that there should be State action to correct this "natural" situation' (Coase 1960: 29).

Coase elaborates on the case of 'sparks from engines', noting that '[i]t is not, of course, easy to imagine the construction of a railway in a state of nature' (ibid.: 31). Obviously, the railway entrepreneur finds himself in a situation profiled by legislature and regulations, that is, in an institutional environment, conceivably being liable for harmful effects. This is the very institutional environment of the economic actors to which Pigou (1920: 128–129) himself alludes in the preamble to his definition of the marginal private net product. It is the same for those who experience the positive or negative side effects of using resources that are subject to this institutional environment. They do not find themselves in the state of nature disturbed by side effects. However, in discussing the obstacles of side effects, Pigou focuses on calculating the difference in value between private and social, presuming a state of nature and, therefore, neglecting any institutional arrangement that features the relationship between the partners involved.

Apparently, Pigou's analysis labors an ambiguity that basically stems from the definition of his central twin concepts. The definition of the marginal *private* concept accords with the tradition of the marginal analysis of human behavior, referring to the relevance of property rights to self-interested actors who apply situational logic. However, in the definition of the marginal *social* concept, Pigou has recourse to someone's panoptical observations of phenomena that affect the preceding economic welfare positions in marginal terms. This explicitly declared outside view deviates fundamentally from the analytical tradition of the Marginal Revolution in spite of the use of marginal quantities. Therefore, the 'additional state action' required (of compensation) is based on calculating the difference between marginal social and marginal private net product instead of being involved in delving into the institutional details that feature and may repair the putative side effects (Coase 1960: 29). The calculation preoccupation hinders Pigou from seeing the institutional, that is, property rights nature of the problem.

To rephrase, Pigou appears to be blind to the reciprocal nature of his private–social divergences. He calculates the harm to the forester caused by the railway entrepreneur but disregards taking into account the benefit of the train service. The right to forest attenuates the right to operate a train service. Pigou 'had not thought his position through', Coase concludes (ibid.: 39). Pigou exhibits this flaw literally in his distinction of the two types of divergence between marginal private versus marginal social net product. The classic type, for example, of a factory's smoke nuisance, he classifies as follows:

one person A, in the course of rendering some service, for which payment is made, to a second person B, incidentally also renders services or disservices to other persons (not producers of like services), of such a sort that payment cannot be exacted from the benefited parties or compensation enforced on behalf of the injured parties.

(Pigou 1920; 183)

Vis-à-vis this type, Pigou distinguishes a type of private–social discrepancy

that is liable to arise in occupations where resources have to be invested in durable instruments by persons who do not own the instruments.

(ibid.)

The relevance of this type of distinction is that the latter offers opportunities to mitigate the divergence by a 'modification of contractual relation between any two contracting partners', for example, between a tenant and an owner (ibid.: 192). Regarding the former, Pigou recommends the 'most obvious forms' of state intervention, that is, 'those of bounties and taxes'. In this instance, Pigou contends, the divergence arises outside the context of contracting partners (ibid.). Pigou's qualification of his two types just misses the heart of the problem. He does not consider that a contractual flaw in one case against the lack of any contract in the other is just part of a common problem, that is, the hindrances to bargain appropriately about the divergence that harbors a potential of mutual advantages. On one hand, Pigou recognizes the opportunities for contractual modification. For the classic side effects, on the other hand, he does not recognize the contract opportunities. Therefore, he has recourse to the one-sided intervention of bounties and taxes, 'from without', that is, disregarding the individual. He lacks a concept: transaction cost. Transaction cost would align Pigou's two divergence types.

What is at issue is 'to avoid the more serious harm' (Coase 1959: 26; 1960: 2). As discussed, in such a case as the forester and the railway entrepreneur, they will conclude a Pareto-efficient bargain if the transaction cost is zero. If the train service is more valuable than foresting, the former is able to compensate the latter to refrain from his business. The market transaction results in maximizing the value of production. It means that all the parties involved in economic activity will contract with one another for the benefits and the losses the activity entails as their property rights are well defined and enforceable without cost. George Stigler (1972: 11) phrases the bearing of the zero-transaction cost assumption as the Coase Theorem: 'the manner in which legal rights were assigned would have no effect whatever upon the methods of production'.

The world of a zero-transaction cost is a rather strange place, Stigler immediately adds (ibid.: 12). Furthermore, Coase (1988: 15) does not seem to be very satisfied with the theorem as it might divert the attention from the very message of the relevance of a positive transaction cost as an indispensable notion in economic analysis. It is the positive transaction cost, as introduced in the 'Firm' paper, in combination with the concept of property rights that make up the bearing of Coase's 'Social Cost' paper. A positive transaction cost renders it an economist's exercise in finding an institutional arrangement that prevents 'more serious harm', taking into account the reciprocal nature of the problem. In this respect, Coase concludes his 'Social Cost' paper that features his practicing economics.

A better approach would seem to be to start our analysis with a situation approximating that which actually exists, to examine the effects of a proposed policy change and to attempt to decide whether the new situation would be, in total, better or worse than the original one.

(Coase 1960: 43)

It corresponds to the world we live in, the reality of a positive transaction cost and property rights that are vulnerable to be taken care of in social arrangements and supported by legislation. In Coase's approach, such a social arrangement always refers to a specific situation. A final arithmetic example may substantiate the possible complexity of such an arrangement (ibid.: 41).

A smoke-emitting factory causes damage valued at $100 per annum to the residential vicinity. A $100 tax per annum will induce the factory to install the smoke-preventing device costing $90, generating an efficiency improvement of $10. The case becomes more complicated when the adjoining residents could avoid the damage by moving to another location which would cost $40 per annum. The figures require arranging a double tax, that is, the factory tax equal to the damage caused, and a tax imposed on the community of residents that is equal to the additional cost incurred by the factory to prevent the damage. It creates the opportunity to design a Pareto-efficient arrangement between these parties, dividing up $50, that is, $90 − $40. Obviously, this is an elegant arithmetic solution. It forestalls that

> without the tax there would be too much smoke, and too few people in the vicinity of the factory; but with the tax there may be too little smoke and too many people in the vicinity of the factory.
>
> (ibid.: 42)

Arrangements that take into account the reciprocal nature of side effects aim to find an optimizing compromise, for example, an optimal smoke emittance. They form the very opposite to the uniform Pigovian rule of state intervention by bounties and taxes that amount to the calculated divergence between marginal private versus marginal social net product. At the same time, the factory smoke example makes clear that such elegant arrangements bristle with difficulties regarding the detailed data that are required and the interrelations of the damage suffered by the parties involved. The conclusion is that there is no way back to a state of nature but that side effects stem from a positive transaction cost. Side effects are a matter of reciprocally affected property rights that may be rearranged while taking into account the transaction cost they entail. It underlines that 'we are usually concerned with a particular problem', as Coase (1959: 20) notes. A '*comparative institution* approach' may avoid more serious harm, as Demsetz (1969: 1) notes. Chapter 7 discusses some examples.

5.5 Coase's methodological point of view

In his search for immutable law in economics, Knight's attention goes 'first and primary ... for "economic theory"; by this I mean only that the primary data are taken as a matter of common knowledge'. These primary data, Knight continues, are in contrast with "empirical" procedure based on specially controlled or selected observations, treated by the special techniques of statistics or of historical criticism.

(1946: 96)

This methodological position also features Coase's economics. The starting point in several of Coase's papers is mundane economic reality, that is, primary data of common knowledge, for instance, regarding a violation of the postal monopoly, practical regulation issues the FCC faces, and the problem that trespassing cattle cause for the cattle farmer with his neighboring corn farmer. In his review of the origin of the 'Firm' paper, Coase recalls that, during his stay in the United States, he read reports of the Federal Trade Commission and trade periodicals and 'used more unusual sources (for an economist),

such as the yellow pages of the telephone directory, where I was fascinated to find so many specialist firms operating within what we thought of as a single industry as well as such interesting combinations of activities as those represented by coal and ice companies.

(Coase 1991: 39)

The quote reflects Coase's methodological stance with which he eventually wrote his, for all that, theoretically innovative, 'Firm' paper in the 1930s. Comparably, the detailed study of the British pig industry precedes his theoretical position regarding the applicability of the cobweb theorem to the price cycles in this industry (Coase and Fowler 1935). It is the meticulous search for details à la investigative journalism that precedes Coase's theoretical propositions.

It provokes for instance Posner (1993) to brand this methodology as hopelessly outdated. Against Coase's economics à la Adam Smith, Posner juxtaposes formal economics as an apparatus that can uncover inconsistencies and generate hypotheses as preparing for statistical analysis to interpret big data. Modern neoclassical theorists focus on the very institution of the price mechanism of the market as their theoretical concept. They are 'theorists of "perfect competition"' who have recourse to unrealistic, yes, false assumptions which may be quite serviceable for locating causal relations (ibid.: 76). The fruit of such causal relations is prediction, for example, modeling whether an excise tax on cigarettes would indeed result in a higher price and a lower output (ibid.). Posner's critique of Coase originates from his instrumentalist perspective on economics. Basically, this view perceives economics as an instrument to predict that, as a science of rational choice, may be used in other social sciences. Posner's idea of modern economics is formal economics engaged in the search for cause-and-effect relationships and not confined to a specific domain.

Posner correctly features Coase's methodology as being in contrast with modern formal economics that is engaged in statistics and empirical analysis to formulate predictions. Uskali Mäki (1990: 318) refers to this modern economics as a 'type of orientation in explanation' that renders 'explanation essentially a matter of derivation'. In a philosophical perspective, Posner's position is the fruit of nominalism. Inference from observable particulars bears the search for causal relations. However, this is not the only research orientation, let alone that it would produce an ultimate explanation as Posner claims. Against nominalism stands realism, the philosophical attitude that renders explanation a matter of being engaged in uncovering 'essential relationships in the real world' (Mäki 1990: 319). Instructive in this respect is the controversy between Hayek and Keynes as referred to by Gregory Christainsen. In his *Prices and Production* (1931), Hayek disputes the usefulness of statistical analysis of macroeconomic data such as the relationship between total consumption and total investment (Christainsen 1994: 12). Hayek argues:

> In fact, neither aggregates nor averages do act upon one another, and it will never be possible to establish necessary connections of cause and effect between them as we can between individual phenomena, individual prices, etc.
>
> (quoted in ibid.)

An explanation based on statistical analysis lags behind economics in general, Hayek puts forward. It is 'a kind of intellectual shorthand', Schutz (Schuetz 1943: 146) notices, when social scientists abstract from the individual human activity. What counts is the economic reality of the individual actors behind the statistics. In a realist's perspective, this regards an '*ontological reduction*', that is, 'the referents of one description are being reduced to those of another' (Mäki 1990: 322). It refers to the fundamental notion that the world is constructed of 'fundamental entities' that are independent of human perception. In economics, it originates methodological individualism or 'metaphysical individualism', 'metaphysical' as it stems from the literally 'meta' view on the world (ibid.). We possess a pre-reflectivity that grants us access to the fundamental entities, the concepts that *are* meaning (Kaufmann 1944: 18). Closely related is the idea that the inferred regularities 'escape from inductive skepticism', postulating that natural laws guide human behavior like they govern the natural world. Rational laws govern the universe which renders the essences of our reality intelligible. To defend the recalcitrance of the idea of our pre-reflectivity regarding the essentialia of the world, I call in a lengthy quote from D. M. Armstrong's *What Is a Law of Nature?* As an apologia of this metaphysical position, Armstrong 'recalls Socrates' and G. E. Moore's "Paradox of Analysis"':

> If we ask what sort of thing an X is (a right act, a law of nature ...) then either we know what an X is, or we do not. If we know, then there is no need to ask the question. If we do not know, then there is no way to begin the investigation. The enquiry is either pointless or impossible.
>
> The orthodox, and I think correct, solution of this puzzle is that we do not start with blank ignorance of what an X is. Instead, we start with an

unreflective, unselfconscious or merely practical grasp of the thing. The philosophical object is to pass from this to an articulate, explicit and reasoned grasp of what an X is. We do not go from black night to daylight, but from twilight to daylight.

(1983: 5)

This pre-reflectivity enables the theorist to envision his realist ambition, that is, to understand the world he studies. The realist is engaged in *Verständnis* rather than *Erkenntnis* (Menger 1883: 14). Thus, Coase (1975: 28) shows himself to be a realist theorist in his repeatedly expressed ambition to 'understand the working of the real economic system', as also features Alfred Marshall's economics. His realism explains his disdain for formal economics à la Robbins's definition of economics as a science of human choice. For instance, 'John Maynard Keynes said that the "Theory of Economics ... is a method rather than a doctrine, an apparatus of the mind, a technique of thinking, which helps the processor to draw correct conclusions"' (Keynes, quoted in Coase 1998: 73). In this aspect, Coase opposes Milton Friedman's position that the '"ultimate goal of positive science ... is prediction about phenomena not yet observed"' (Friedman, quoted in Coase 1994: 18). Theory has implications that may correspond 'to happenings in the real economic system', Coase notes. 'But', he adds, 'a theory is not a like an airline or bus timetable. We are not interested in the accuracy of its predictions' (ibid. 16). His realist preference regards a theory that provides insight into how the system works, although it predicts badly, above a theory that predicts well but gives us little insight (ibid.: 17). Apparently, Coase adheres to a substantive view on economics as being engaged in the working of the economic system wherein the logic of choice definitely plays a role. However, insight in its working requires 'to examine the role which the firm, the market, and the law play' in it, Coase (1988: 5) specifies.

'Coase does case studies', Posner (2011: S35) notes. Clearly, for a major part, Coase's papers concern detailed information regarding the subject under investigation. The 'Lighthouse' paper (Coase 1974) is for a major part a historical account. The 'Social Cost' paper originates from the FCC case, accomplished with a number of sample calculation cases (Coase 1960). The 'Penny Post' paper (Coase 1939) gives an account of the details of the cost structure of the post industry. However, this is not just doing case studies. This is taking the investigative, vertical route from plain concreteness to increasingly abstract concepts. As emphasized, the starting point is common knowledge of our mundane economic reality while, at the same time, armed with the methodological aim to determine what is essentially occurring in the firm, in the provision of lighthouse service, and what is essential for obtaining an efficient procurement of a capital investment operating under decreasing average cost.

Therefore, it is a fallacy to interpret the case study elements in Coase's papers as a dismissal of abstraction, as Mäki (1998) demonstrates in a beneficial explanation. Mäki uses two instructive concepts: horizontal de-isolation versus vertical de-isolation. Horizontal de-isolation regards the choice of the model items, for example, wrongly excluding items such as the internal organization of a firm, as Coase (1992: 714) explicates in his Nobel Prize lecture. It is a call for a theoretically more encompassing approach. Vertical de-isolation, however, comprehends a movement from a particular item to the item in general, and inverse, in order to grasp its essence. An instance of vertical de-isolation that Coase's lecture notes regards the 'study of vertical and lateral integration of industry in the United States' (ibid.: 715). More specifically, Coase discusses in the 'Firm' paper the integration processes of the blossoming automotive industry. He visits the plants of, for example, Ford, Fisher Body, and General Motors, gathering detailed information in order to discover the nature of the firm (Coase 1991: 43). It is the combination of this horizontal de-isolation, that is, opening up the black box of the firm, together with the vertical isolation procedure, that is, the ambition 'to find the reason for the existence of the firm in factories and offices', that features the 'Firm' paper (Coase 1991: 52). Against this methodology, Coase (1992: 714) dubs modern, formal economics as '"blackboard economics"'. It is an economics that lacks the gradually vertical isolation in theory building. It renders economics a blackboard exercise without the low level of abstraction of common knowledge as an analytical starting point. On this interpretation, Mäki features it as follows.

> Blackboard economics is economics at a high level of vertical abstraction unsupported by the process of vertical abstraction.
>
> (1998: 16)

It makes economics a matter of statistics replacing the price mechanism, a blank exercise of the parameters as, for instance, Hotelling (1938: 269) underlines. Pigou practices it, Pigou who assumes the values of marginal private cost and marginal social cost as given. It enables him to determine the magnitude of the difference between the two concepts and to propose a tax or a bounty that exactly remedies the side effect. The blackboard economist 'fixes prices, imposes taxes, and distributes subsidies (on the blackboard)', Coase (1988: 19) notes. Blackboard economics stems from applying the model of competitive equilibrium as a criterion to assess economic reality. Demsetz (1989: 3) refers to it as the *nirvana* approach that 'presents the relevant choice as between an ideal norm and an existing "imperfect" institutional arrangement'.

An artificially high level of abstraction renders the formal, instrumentalist economics as blackboard economics, Mäki diagnoses. Tony Lawson (1989) also discusses the significance of abstraction. Lawson elaborates on the intimate relationship between abstracting, on one hand, versus the choice for a realist or a nominalist approach to economic analysis, on the other. It may further enlighten Coase's methodology. He develops Nicolas Kaldor's 'reference to notions of *abstraction*, *tendencies*, and *stylised facts*', concepts that partly belong to a realist approach (ibid.: 59). Kaldor's analytical point of departure is the stylized fact. It describes the problem to be investigated and formulates the preliminary theoretical conjecture. Lawson calls it an instance of abduction or 'retroduction' (ibid.: 68). Actually, the stylized fact elaborates on Knight's (1946: 96) concept of common knowledge. What is at stake in realism is to find 'the generative structures that lie behind and actually govern the flux of observed phenomena' (Lawson 1989: 62). Therefore, for Kaldor, who espouses realism, abstraction must meet two conditions. First, 'the abstraction achieved is intended to be *real* – it is not ideal, a convenient fiction, or some such' (ibid.: 69). Formal economics features the fictitious 'as-if' hypothesis referring to a restricted class of phenomena, that is, statistical data. 'For the realist, the construction of fictions is to be avoided' (ibid.: 71). The abstraction must be *real* as it concerns the discussed reality. For instance, in the 'Firm' paper, Coase (1937: 390) abstracts from the real possibility that 'the price mechanism might be superseded if the relationship which it replaces would be preferred for its own sake', for example, 'if some people preferred to work under the direction of some other person'. In the 'Penny Post' paper (Coase 1939: 428), to abstract from expense differences in the primary distribution is based on reality. More generally, Coase's use of a case study as a precedent to his theoretical insights is in accordance with the first condition that realism imposes on abstraction.

Second, the abstraction must, according to Kaldor, 'be concerned with the essential rather than merely the most general' (Lawson 1989: 69). It is not difficult to find instances in Coase's oeuvre that vindicate this idea. An example is Coase's idea regarding the maximizing rationality hypothesis. 'There is no reason to suppose that most human beings are engaged in maximizing anything unless it be unhappiness, and even this with incomplete success' (Coase 1988: 4). Against this, Coase espouses the law of demand; that is, 'in almost all circumstances, a higher (relative) price for anything will lead to a reduction in the amount demanded', an essential, although more apposite, hypothesis (ibid.). In his Nobel Prize lecture, Coase criticizes the abstraction from a firm's internal organization of production. Against this, it is essential to take into account that 'most resources in [the] modern economy are employed within firms' (Coase 1992: 714).[7] Against the dismissal of an economics in which the firm is merely a production function brings Coase the formulation of a 'generative structure' behind the economic reality, that is, institutional structures that economize on transaction cost. The following quote of Coase concurs with Lawson's analysis of a realist's abstraction:

> Realism in assumptions forces us to analyse the world that exists, not some imaginary world that does not.
>
> (Coase 1994: 18)

The quote reads as an explicit adherence to philosophical realism. Implicitly, this position is worded in the methodological ambition of the 'Firm' paper:

It is hoped to show in the following paper that a definition of a firm may be obtained which is not only realistic in that it corresponds to what is meant by a firm in the real world, but is tractable by two of the most powerful instruments of economic analysis developed by Marshall, the idea of the margin and that of substitution, together giving the idea of substitution at the margin. Our definition must, of course, "relate to formal relations which are capable of being *conceived* exactly."

(Coase 1937: 386–387)

This methodological intro to his 'Firm' paper might have been read as 'a youthful mistake' (Coase 1991: 52). However, his methodological position has not changed since the 1930s as he asserted in his 1991 reflection on it (ibid.). The account of the twofold, ostensibly contrasting methodological requirements, summarize Coase's realist position.

- The realistic definition of the central concepts, such as the firm in the 'Firm' paper, as corresponding to 'what is meant by a firm in the real world' refers to Coase's fundamentally analytic attitude as a realist theorist.
- The tractability of the analysis as obtained by substitution at the margin, that is, 'the formal relations which are capable of being *conceived* exactly', basically stems from the realist position.

As noted in Section 5.2, the quote regarding the 'relations *conceived* exactly' is from Robbins's (1932: 66) *Nature and Significance of Economic Science*. In the realist perspective, this 'being *conceived* exactly' means that the 'generative structures that lie behind and actually govern the *flux* of observed reality', as Lawson words it, that is, are amenable to exactness. By definition, exactness features realism, and realism renders economics an exact science. Apparently, it is also valid for Coase's economics that his analyses exhibit exactness. It might not be certain that this idea will pass by unquestioningly. It is the phenomenological point of view that offers the realist social scientist the exactness he requires. The next section elaborates on it, further explicating the nature of realism, as an exercise to demonstrate the significance of phenomenology as a philosophical foundation of economics à la Ronald Coase. It discusses a transition from methodology to phenomenology.

5.6 Coase's economics from a phenomenological point of view

In his paper 'The Wealth of Nations', Coase (1977) explicates the significance of self-interest for a civilized society with an advanced division of labor. Advanced division of labor generates advanced mutual dependency between citizens that requires enlightened self-interest of the concerned partners to preserve sustainable relationships. An appeal to benevolence would be inappropriate 'in bringing about the division of labour in a modern economy' (Coase 1977: 314). In this context, Coase quotes Adam Smith:

> In civilised society he stands at all times in need of the cooperation and
> assistance of great multitudes, while his whole life is scarce sufficient to
> gain the friendship of a few persons.
>
> (Smith 1776: 17)

A man reserves benevolence for relatives and practices it with one's closest
friends. Anyway, it cannot be a leading motivation for long in anonymous relationships that merely originate from the division of labor, that is, in exchange
relationships. Coase underlines this concept as the background of the central
role of self-interest in Smith's thought. Reliance on self-interest 'is the only
way' 'in which the required division of labour is achieved', Coase (1977: 314)
argues, according with Smith.

Advanced division of labor entails a disenchanted world of objective exchange relationships in which benevolence is an anomaly. Apparently, required
is a qualified concept of intersubjectivity to address the very economic problem of exchange. It is a phenomenological insight *avant la lettre* as it dovetails
with Schutz's distinction consociates versus contemporaries. The consociates
experience a We-relationship, experience mutual benevolence, and are growing
old together, as Schutz denotes. It is a domain of intersubjectivity to which the
social scientist has no access. Against this stands the relationship between contemporaries whose intersubjectivity is conceptually structured, that is, who use
conceptual constructs, typifying their anonymous partner, and the relationship
they experience.

Smith, and so Coase, correctly associate self-interest as being suitable for
anonymous relationships. In the mundane life of man, it is obvious that benevolence cannot feature in the numerous anonymous relationships that one
maintains. It is a fact of our *Lebenswelt* that, in its turn, alludes to the structured nature of social phenomena such as exchange relationships. Apparently,
we bear conceptual constructs that render the inappropriateness of benevolence in anonymous relationships a matter of common sense. As shown, phenomenology seizes on such subjectively experienced commonsense constructs
and reinterprets them objectively. Ideal types and ideal courses of action replace the commonsense constructs that structure social phenomena.

Reconstruction in terms of ideal types, that is, homunculi, precedes the phenomenological interpretation of Coase's economics as presented in his three
essential papers. This reconstruction consists of checking whether the ideal
type meets the three conditions to study social phenomena objectively; 'the
principle of relevance, the postulate of the subjective interpretation and that of
adequacy'. 'For instance historical sciences are governed by them' (Schuetz
1943: 147). For economics as a theoretical social science, the construction of
the ideal type requires a 'next step': the postulate of rationality (ibid.). I apply
the four conditions to (Coase's) economics in general.

First, it is the *principle of relevance* that features the ideal type, the homunculus, defined by the '"scientific problem under examination"' (ibid.: 145). Exchange is the very subject of economics, that is, exchange between conscious

human beings in an intersubjective relationship that features reciprocity. This reciprocity expresses itself in the tit-for-tat principle that renders an exchange mutually beneficial.

Second, the ideal type must observe the *postulate of subjective interpretation*. It refers to the intentionality that the homunculus must represent. Modest self-interest may suffice to recognize intentionality in the ideal type. Coase (1988: 4) states it as follows: 'In almost all circumstances, a higher (relative) price for anything will lead to a reduction in the amount demanded'. Another wording of intentionality that will meet the postulate of subjective interpretation is provided by Philip Wicksteed (1910: 782) – also discussed in Chapter 3 – who typifies 'the relation is really economic', when the exchange relationship as a matter of 'non-tuïsm', that is, 'the significance *to us* of what we are doing is measured not by its importance to the man for whom it is done, but by the degree to which it furthers our own ends'. The latter again emphasizes reciprocity as it prevails in Coase's analysis.

Third, Coase's ideal type will certainly come up for the *postulate of adequacy* as abstraction by vertical isolation features Coase's analysis. 'Man as he is' will recognize himself in the homunculus that represents him in this scientific discourse.

Finally, the *postulate of rationality* renders the ideal type an analytical instrument, explaining homunculi's conduct as participating in a logically interrelated system. In this aspect, it may be assumed that Coase's ideal types observe the economic principle as phrased by Kaufmann:

> not to give up more commodities than is necessary to acquire a given set of commodities.
>
> (1933: 391)

The homunculus as *Homo economicus* features an economist's thought. More precisely, it is the homunculus's thought that uncovers the economic problem in scientifically exact relationships. The postulates and principles as approved safeguard Coase's analysis of his homunculi's thought as a realist approach demonstrating generative causality. It is homunculus's mind that unravels the essentialia, the universals in economics. I show this in the 'Firm' paper.

The clue to the 'Firm' paper may be found in Coase's footnote reference to Evan Durbin's (1936) paper 'Economic Calculation in a Planned Economy'. Coase concurs with Durbin that economic planning involves problems both in the planned economy and the competitive system. 'The important difference', Coase continues,

> between these two cases is that economic planning is imposed on industry, while firms arise voluntarily because they represent a more efficient method of organizing production. In a competitive system, there is an "optimum" amount of planning!
>
> (1937: 389, n. 3)

In Durbin's (1936: 679) economics, 'imposition' is a nonissue 'as long as the socialized factories calculate marginal products'. 'Problems of social behavior', Durbin underlines, 'are not the problems that the professor of economic theory is competent to discuss' (ibid.: 678). For Coase, however, the footnote contains the puzzle of the 'Firm' paper. In ideal-type vocabulary, evidently, the homunculi voluntarily abandon the price mechanism that enables them to conclude mutually beneficial exchange relations. What is the homunculi's rationale for sacrificing their beneficial freedom of choice? Apparently, the price mechanism model hides a variable that originates homunculi to have recourse to economic planning as a rational optimum. Coase (1937: 390) states that the missing variable is the 'cost of using the price mechanism', that is, transaction cost. He conceives the introduction of this concept as his major contribution to economics (Coase 1992: 713, 716). In a realist perspective, it is the identification of a universal in economics. Coase's economic thought is that its introduction is directly related to the central place that the concept of reciprocity occupies. The phenomenological point of view may further substantiate the significance of transaction cost as an economics' universal. Within the domain of the price mechanism, the homunculi experience reciprocity in their exchange relationships. In this domain, they discover one another as contemporaries, as anonymous potential trading partners to conclude transactions. In mundane pursuit, it is a number of constructs that accompany us in participating in the price mechanism with partners who are more or less anonymous to us, for example, price lists, ads, contracts, sell-by date, reputation, inspection, reviewing the potential partner, and routine trust in one another's behavior in a situation of transacting. Coase (1937: 390–391) enumerates a few transaction-cost-generating variables that feature the exchange reciprocity. It regards the cost of discovering the relevant prices, the cost of negotiating and concluding an exchange contract, and the replacement of a series of contracts by one that lowers the transaction cost.

Finally, the Coase Theorem generalizes the role of transaction cost versus property rights as universals in exchange relationships. However, versions of it circulate as theorems originate from a necessary conclusion as deduced from the analysis of meaning and the *ceteris paribus* clauses that are assumed. Robert Cooter (1987) distinguishes three versions in his *New Palgrave* entry, 'Coase Theorem', Cooter words them as follows:

The initial allocation of legal entitlements does not matter from an efficiency perspective so long as

1. *they can be freely exchanged;*
2. *the transaction costs of exchange are nil;*
3. *they can be exchanged in a perfectly competitive market.*

(ibid.: 457)

The first version assumes unambiguously formulated legal entitlements. The second underlines the frictionless nature of exchange as a prerequisite.

The third implies that the well-known, perfect market conditions hold. In Kaufmann's methodological perspective, these versions concern varying *ceteris paribus* conditions resulting in different theoretical propositions.

From a phenomenological point of view, an interesting basic point that Cooter refers to is that strategic behavior may hinder concluding a potentially mutually beneficial transaction in spite of a zero-transaction cost. As 'a rule of thumb', Cooter comments, 'the transaction cost interpretation is not strictly true' (ibid.: 459). 'The Coase Theorem errs in the direction of optimism', Cooter diagnoses (ibid.). Applied to the problem of externalities, the theorem presupposes a government that creates property rights and then, 'like a deist god', retires from the scene whereupon mutually beneficial exchanges conclude (Cooter 1982: 19). Against this, Cooter (1987: 459) poses the 'Hobbes Theorem that errs in the direction pessimism by assuming that the problem of dividing the surplus can only be solved by coercive force'. A successful exchange requires a permanently acting leviathan, like theist god (Cooter 1982: 19). Reality lies somewhere between these poles, Cooter concludes. This conclusion, however, is in conflict with the phenomenological perspective and the nature of homunculi that represent a society that consists of a basic intersubjectivity between the 'I' and the 'alter *ego*'. Actually, Cooter confounds here the analysis of meaning with an explanation of facts. It is an example of 'misplaced concreteness' to conclude that reality is somewhere between the opposites. In the realist perspective, intersubjectivity as society's foundation enables the reciprocity that features economics without which any institutional setting would be literally meaningless. In the Hobbesian, atomistic world, this intersubjectivity is absent. A compromise à la Cooter between the idea of human beings as intersubjective creatures versus man as an atomistic entity is unthinkable. The homunculi who people Coase's economics experience intersubjectivity, recognize one another in their rationality, exchange property rights, and have recourse to institutional devices to economize on transaction costs. Moreover, they cannot escape from their rationality.

5.7 Conclusion

The coherence in Coase's economics may be summarized as follows:

- First, it consists of substantiating that 'the normal economic system works itself' (Coase 1991: 38). It is the zero hypothesis, whose assumptions invite further research.
- Second, against formal economics, he practices its substantive pendant as engaged in exchange relations between men on the spot who find themselves in situations that ask for their rational attention.
- Third, as economics from within, the study of exchange situations directs attention to reciprocity as an economic manifestation of intersubjectivity.
- Fourth, he implicitly follows phenomenology that demonstrates that intersubjectivity as the existential experience of the '*ego*' and the '*thou*',

constitutes the social reality economist's study. He is engaged in the reciprocity of tit-for-tat relationships of contemporaries. This may be further qualified.

a. It results in a search for markets and other institutional arrangements as alternative tit-for-tat relationships;

b. Coase (1992: 719) delves into the details of his subject, studying 'man as he is' and questioning 'how the real economic system works', as he notes in his Nobel Prize lecture. It is reminiscent of Adam Smith's (1776: 33) eye for reality as that 'sort of rough equality ... sufficient for carrying on the business of common life'.

c. At the same time, he espouses the 'logic of choice', employing it to examine 'the role of the firm, the market, and the law in the working of the economic system' (Coase 1988: 5).

d. Finally, it affords him to arrive at 'formal relationships which are capable of being *conceived* exactly' (Coase 1937: 387).

Phenomenology offers a philosophical interpretation that removes the ostensible contrast in Coase's economics between an almost anecdotical concreteness versus an exactness as aspired in formal relationships. Phenomenology shows that we experience an intersubjectively structured social reality in which more or less inexact concepts are amenable to reformulation in scientifically exact terms. This procedure bridges Coase's eye for details in daily economic pursuit against his theoretical ambitions. It finds its methodological counterpart in the process of vertical (de-)isolation, in search of the essentialia that feature the problem. Corresponding to the substantive view, Coase's economics is a search for 'generative causality' against the 'logical causality', the latter stemming from modelling based on abstract assumptions that, for instance, the perfect competition model feature (Jaffé 1976).

Coase's three main papers underpin that there is such a thing as an economic system that possesses objectivity. It illustrates the realist position of the theorist. All the same, the starting point is the situation in which people find themselves; for example, a farmer whose cattle go astray faces a new economic logic of a neighbor who experiences harm from it. Coase directs his attention to the microeconomic level on which the economic system demonstrates its objectivity. The three papers exhibit his theoretical constants in their interwovenness. The 'Social Cost' paper (and the 'FCC' paper) generalizes the 'Firm' paper. Private property rights as a key concept in the former two may explain the choice issue that the latter raises. The transaction cost that determines the choice of firm versus price mechanism actually regards the relative efficiency of transacting property rights. However, the 'Marginal Cost Controversy' paper preludes the 'FCC' and the 'Social Cost' papers. Pecuniary diseconomies of an extended production of an individual cause an increasing average cost to others in the industry. It motivates Marshall and Pigou to argue for taxing the extending producer in order to enhance the general welfare. It is an instance of a mismatch between private and social marginal costs that requires a repair from outside, they contend. Knight demonstrates that it is rightly a matter of property rights that causes a changing scenario of costs that the participants in the industry face. Accordingly, these property rights register the changed scarcity and demonstrate the working of the economic system, inducing the participants to reconsider their choices. Coase further develops this idea in the 'FCC' and the 'Social Cost' papers. A rule such as marginal cost pricing is not required as an intervention as long as property rights are univocally defined. Accordingly, attenuation of property rights finds its conceptual counterpart in a transaction cost. The firm is Coase's first endogenously explained institution, although it actually regards its size. Property rights generalize the theme of institutions. A transaction cost lends an exactness to the economics of institutions.

Finally, Coase does case studies as an economist who is basically antitheoretical, Posner (1993: 80) argues. The critique nicely articulates Coase's methodological position against Posner's. Posner is a champion of instrumentalist economics, engaged in statistical data analysis in search of causal relationships that have predictive value. Against this, Coase espouses realism, studying the economic system as an objective reality. Thus, he applies vertical isolation from concrete phenomena to concepts representing their essentialia. 'At stake is', Lawson (1989: 62) notes, 'to find the generative structures that lie behind and actually govern the flux of observed phenomena'. They concern tendencies, stylized facts, that the theorist may discover pre-scientifically. It is as Armstrong (1983: 5) states it: 'We do not go from black night to daylight, but from twilight to daylight'.

The realist position recognizes the determinateness of the world. In this perspective, the economic system exhibits exactness. It is a further phenomenological interpretation of Coase's economics that may explain this exactness, that is, exact types and exact laws. First, founding in this interpretation is Kaufmann's distinction between analysis of meaning versus causal explanation of facts. The former regards the search for concepts that *are* meaning, universals that are exact types. It reflects the formulation of a null hypothesis as an economist's starting point. Against this, the latter concerns the empirical counterpart of the theoretical propositions as based on the analysis of meaning. In economics, the empirical part consists of reformulating the *ceteris paribus* clause (of the null hypothesis) whenever the theoretical proposition turns out to lack an empirical basis. Therefore, in economics, the emphasis is on the analysis of meaning. Second, Schutz's phenomenology elaborates on this analysis of meaning. In their intersubjectivity, human beings come to terms with one another. It is based on concepts that structure our *Lebenswelt*. Social life would otherwise be unthinkable and certainly unlivable. The '*ego*' and the '*thou*' experience one another in meaningful actions. It is humans' *Lebenswelt*, that is, the pre-reflective mundane life of men, from which it is a social scientist's task to transform a man's commonsense constructs into 'second-level constructs' (Schutz 1954.: 266). In this emerges reciprocity, the very feature of economics. Third, in this reciprocity, Schutz distinguishes levels of intimacy versus anonymity. Our relatives and friends with whom we are growing old together are our consociates. These reciprocal relationships are inaccessible to the social scientist. However, the greater part of our social relationships is more or less anonymous. It is in these anonymous relationships between contemporaries with whom we share time that we find in economics. As contemporaries, we behave typically as a buyer, a traveler, a postman. Fourth, it is at issue to reconstruct such contemporaries as ideal types that people the domain of economics. In this aspect, Schutz formulates four postulates that safeguard the economic ideal type, that is, *the Homo economicus*, as a homunculus. The homunculus complies with the postulate of subjective interpretation and rationality. The rationality of the homunculus expresses a subject's meaning as it *is*. At the same time, it is recognizable for the actors in the *Lebenswelt*; that is, the homunculus meets the postulate of adequacy. In terms of the principle of relevance, the homunculus figures in exchange relationships as the very economic domain. It is this homunculus who assists the theorist in discovering the essentialia and exact laws in economics. As shown, the four conditions that feature the homunculus may easily be found in Coase's economics. It justifies the phenomenological interpretation of the discussed three main papers. In this interpretation, it is the homunculus's thought that directs the analysis. In the 'Firm' paper, the homunculus takes into account the transaction cost in his choice between the price mechanism and the firm in managing its production. In a causal explanation of facts, this theoretical proposition will induce formulating *ceteris paribus* clauses to assess its empirical value. The 'Marginal Cost Controversy' is nicely eligible for a phenomenological interpretation. The rule of marginal cost pricing is a clear example of blackboard economics. It stems from the Marginal Revolution, and the Austrian version is a realist approach that allows a phenomenological interpretation. The advocates of the rule forget the *Lebenswelt* origin of the marginal analysis. They return to the *Lebenswelt* with the rule applied by an authority, disregarding the homunculi who inspired the formulation of the marginal analysis. Therefore, its application is doomed to fail and generate inefficiencies due to loosening the tit-for-tat reciprocity. Finally, the 'Social Cost' paper further equips homunculus's rationality with the concept of private property rights that regard the heart of economics as it is the legally institutional expression of scarcity. It enables the formulation of the Coase Theorem which 'logic cannot be questioned' (Coase 1992: 717). Together with the idea of a transaction cost, private property rights constitute the foundation of new institutional economics that is amenable to theoretical laws. It is the homunculus armed with the concepts of transaction cost and private property rights who reflects the logic of his situation, substantiating the generative causality it represents. I continue this phenomenological interpretation in the next chapters, following the homunculus's thought in discussing theories inspired by Coase's papers on the firm, marginal cost pricing, and the problem of social cost.

Notes

1 In a comment on his 'Firm' paper, Coase casts doubt on his inference that risky contingencies cause firm-like arrangements such as long-term contracting. This doubt was raised in 1945 by examining a number of long-term contracts. Coase ascertains:

> I found that they commonly did not specify such items as times of delivery, quantities (except in total), or the places to which the commodity should be delivered. These were matters to be determined later. And yet there was no question that I was dealing with transactions between independent firms.
>
> (1991: 68)

In this, Coase encounters a phenomenon that does not fit very well in an exchange relationship fixed in strictly defined, unmistakable contract conditions. Apparently, there exist broader forms of mutual dependency that possess viability. I discuss this in a broader context, dealing with the opportunism axiom as put forward by Oliver Williamson (1975: 4).

2 'A firm becomes larger as additional transactions are organized by the entrepreneur', Coase (1937: 393) notes. It accords with Coase's analysis, although this is a rather curious definition of firm size as it is thinkable that the number of transactions decreases and, at the same time, the size of the firm in other terms increases, for example, due to an increased value per transaction and/or increased scale of production.

3 In his conclusion, Hotelling accordingly deviates from Marshall's graphic analysis of the general welfare effects of a tax under an increasing cost condition. Marshall (1890: 468, n. 2; Fig. 31) claims that, under a certain configuration of the demand and supply curves, a tax will increase general welfare. However, Marshall arrives at this erroneous conclusion because he does not take a producer's surplus into account.

4 By this, Coase avoids the issue of common cost assignment.

5 The concept of the state of nature does here not refer to what Thomas Hobbes means to denote. Contrariwise, it refers to a pregiven, initial distribution of property rights.

6 The context of Marshall's quote regards the *theoretical* question of marginal cost pricing as discussed in the preceding section. Marshall's (1890: 468–469) graphic analyses indicate that taxes and bounties would be appropriate means to prompt a national dividend. However, Marshall adds, 'by themselves [these conclusions] do not afford a valid ground for government intervention' and then follows with 'much remains to be done' (ibid.: 475).

7 As discussed earlier, Demsetz (1995) proposes that neoclassical economics is engaged in explaining the working of decentralized coordination of production and, therefore, correctly abstracts from the internal organization.

References

Armstrong, D.M., 1983, *What Is a Law of Nature?*, Cambridge: Cambridge University Press.

Arrow, K.J., 1974, *The Limits of Organization*, New York: W.W. Norton & Company.

Arrow, K.J., T. Scitovsky, eds., 1969, [1972], *Readings in Welfare Economics*, London: George Allen and Unwin Ltd.

Boettke, P.J., ed., 1994, *The Elgar Companion to Austrian Economics*, Aldershot: Edward Elgar.

Buchanan, J.M., 1979, *What Should Economists Do?* Indianapolis, IN: Liberty Fund.

Christainsen, G.B., 1994, Methodological Individualism. In: P.J. Boettke, ed., 1994, *The Elgar Companion to Austrian Economics*, 11–16, Aldershot: Edward Elgar.

Coase, R.H., 1937, The Nature of the Firm, *Economica, Vol. 4 (n.s.)*, 386–405.

Coase, R.H., 1939, Rowland Hill and the Penny Post, *Economica, New Series, Vol. 6, No. 24*, 423–435.

Coase, R.H., 1945, Price and Output Policy of State Enterprise: A Comment, *The Economic Journal, Vol. 55, No. 217*, 112–113.

Coase, R.H., 1946, Marginal Cost Controversy, *Economica, New Series, Vol. 13, No. 51*, 169–182.

Coase, R.H., 1959, The Federal Communications Commission, *The Journal of Law and Economics, Vol. 2*, 1–40.

Coase, R.H., 1960, The Problem of Social Cost, *The Journal of Law and Economics, Vol. 3*, 1–44.

Coase, R.H., 1966, The Theory of Public Utility Pricing, *Papers presented at a Conference Held at Northwestern University June 19-24, 1966*, 96–106.

Coase, R.H., 1974, The Lighthouse in Economics, *The Journal of Law & Economics, Vol. 17, No. 2*, 357–376.

Coase, R.H., 1975, Marshall on Method, *The Journal of Law & Economics, Vol. 18, No. 1*, 25–31.

Coase, R.H., 1977, The Wealth of Nations, *Economic Inquiry, July, Vol. XV*, 309–324.

Coase, R.H., 1988, *The Firm, the Market, and the Law*, Chicago, IL: The University of Chicago Press.

Coase, R.H., 1991, [1993], *The Nature of the Firm: Origins, Evolution, and Development*. Edited by O.E. Williamson, S.G. Winter, Oxford: Oxford University Press.

Coase, R.H., 1992, The Institutional Structure of Production, *The American Economic Review, Vol. 82, No. 4*, 713–719.

Coase, R.H., 1994, *Essays on Economics and Economists*, Chicago, IL: The University of Chicago Press.

Coase, R.H., 1998, The New Institutional Economics, *The American Economic Review, Vol. 88, No. 2, Papers and Proceedings*, 72–74.

Coase, R.H., R.F. Fowler, 1935, Bacon Production and the Pig-Cycle in Great Britain, *Economica, New Series, Vol. 2, No. 6*, 142–167.

Cooter, R., 1982, The Cost of Coase, *The Journal of Legal Studies, Vol. 11, No. 1*, 1–33.

Cooter, R. 1987, [1991], Coase Theorem. In: J. Eatwell, M. Milgate, P. Newman, eds., 1987, [1991], *The New Palgrave, A Dictionary of Economics*, Vol. I, 457–460, London: The Macmillan Press Limited.

Demsetz, H., 1969, Information and Efficiency: Another Viewpoint, *The Journal of Law & Economics, Vol. 12, No. 1*, 1–22

Demsetz, H., 1989, [1991], *Efficiency, Competition, and Policy*, Oxford: Bail Blackwell.

Demsetz, H., 1988, [1990], *Ownership, Control, and the Firm*, Oxford: Basil Blackwell.

Demsetz, H., 1995, [1997], *The Economics of the Business Firm*, Cambridge: Cambridge University Press.

Dupuit, J., 1844, De la Mesure de l'Utilité des Travaux Publics, translated in *International Economic Papers, 2, 1952*. Reprinted in: K.J. Arrow, T. Scitovsky, eds., 1969, [1972], *Readings in Welfare Economics*, 83–110, London: George Allen and Unwin Ltd.

Durbin, E.F.M., 1936, Economic Calculus in a Planned Economy, *The Economic Journal, Vol. 46, No. 184*, 676–690.

Hayek, F.A. von, ed., 1935, *Collectivist Economic Planning*, London: Routledge & Kegan Paul Ltd.

Hayek, F.A., 1945, The Use of Knowledge in Society, *The American Economic Review, Vol. 35, No. 4*, 519–530.

Herzel, L., 1951, "Public Interest" and the Market in Color Television Regulation, *The University of Chicago Law Review, Vol. 18, No. 4*, 802–816.

Hotelling, H., 1938, The General Welfare in Relation to Problems of Taxation and of Railway and Utility Rates, *Econometrica, Vol. 6, No. 3*, 242–269.

Jaffé, W., 1976, Menger, Jevons and Walras De-homogenized, *Economic Inquiry, Vol. XIV*, 511–524.

Kaufmann, F., 1931, Was kann die mathematische Methode in der Nationalökonomie leisten? *Zeitschrift für Nationalökonomie, Vol. 2, nr. 5*, 754–779.

Kaufmann, F., 1933, On the Subject-Matter and Method of Economic Science, *Economica, No. 42*, 381–401.

Kaufmann, F., 1944, *Methodology of the Social Sciences*, Atlantic Highlands, New Jersey: Humanities Press.

Kitch, E.W., 1983, The Fire of Truth: A Remembrance of Law and Economics at Chicago, 1932-1970, *The Journal of Law and Economics, Vol. 26, No. 1*, 163–234.

Knight, F.H., 1921, [1971], *Risk, Uncertainty and Profit*, Chicago, IL: Chicago University Press.

Knight, F.H., 1924, Some Fallacies in the Interpretation of Social Cost, *The Quarterly Journal of Economics, Vol. 38, No. 4*, 582–606.

Knight, F.H., 1936, The Place of Marginal Economics in a Collectivist System, *The American Economic Review, Vol. 26, No. 1, Supplement, Papers and Proceedings*, 255–266.

Knight, F.H., 1946, Immutable Law in Economics: Its Reality and Limitations, *The American Economic Review, Vol. 36, No. 2*, 93–111.

Kurrild-Klitgaard, P., 2001, On Rationality, Ideal Types and Economics: Alfred Schütz and the Austrian School, *The Review of Austrian Economics, Vol. 14, No. 2/3*, 119–143.

Lawson, T., 1989, Abstraction, Tendencies and Stylised Facts: A Realist Approach to Economic Analysis, *Cambridge Journal of Economics, 13*, 59–78.

Lerner, A.P., 1937, Statics and Dynamics in Socialist Economics, *The Economic Journal, Vol. 47, No. 186*, 253–270.

Lerner, A.P., 1944, *The Economics of Control*, New York: The Macmillan Company.

Lippincott, B.E., 1938, *On the Economic Theory of Socialism; Oskar Lange, Fred M Taylor*. New York: McGraw-Hill Book Company.

Mäki, U., 1990, Scientific Realism and Austrian Explanation, *Review of Political Economy, Vol. 2, Issue 3*, 310–344.

Mäki, U., 1998, Is Coase a Realist?, *Philosophy of the Social Sciences, Vol. 28, No. I*, 5–31.

Marshall, A., 1890, [1920], *Principles of Economics*, 8th ed., London: Macmillan and Co., Limited.

Meade, J.E., 1944, Price and Output Policy of State Enterprise, *The Economic Journal, Vol. 54, No. 215/216*, 321–339.

Menger, C., 1883, [2005], *Untersuchungen über die Methode der Socialwissenschaften und der Politischen Oekonomie insbesodere*, Leipzig: Verlag von Duncker & Humblot; [Elibron Classics series].

Menger, C., 1976, [2007], *Principles of Economics*, translated by J. Dingwall, B.F. Hoselitz, Auburn, AL: Ludwig von Mises Institute; original title: *Grundsätze der Volkswirtschaftslehre*, 1871.

Posner, R.A., 1993, The New Institutional Economics Meets Law and Economics, *Journal of Institutional and Theoretical Economics (JITE), Vol. 149, No. 1*, 73–87.

Posner, R.A., 2011, Keynes and Coase, *The Journal of Law & Economics, Vol. 54, No. 4*, S31–S40.

Pigou, A.C., 1920, [1950], *The Economics of Welfare*, London: Macmillan and Co., Limited.

Robbins, L., 1932, [1962], *An Essay on the Nature and Significance of Economic Science*, 2nd ed., London: MacMillan & Co, Ltd.

Schutz, A., 1932, [1967], *The Phenomenology of the Social World*, New York: Northwestern University Press; [*Der sinnhafte Aufbau der sozialen Welt*, Wien: Julius Springer].

Schuetz, A., 1943, The Problem of Rationality in the Social World, *Economica, New Series, Vol. 10, No. 38*, 130–149.

Schutz, A., 1954, Concept and Theory Formation in the Social Sciences, *The Journal of Philosophy, Vol. 51, No. 9*, 257–273.

Simmel, G., 1910, How Is Society Possible? *American Journal of Sociology, Vol. 16, No. 3*, 372–391.

Simmel, G., 1976, [1990], *The Philosophy of Money*, (Philosophie de Geldes, 1907), edited by D. Frisby, translated by T. Bottomore, D. Frisby, 2nd ed., London: Routledge.

Smith, A., 1776, [2005], *The Inquiry into the Nature and Causes of the Wealth of Nations*, London: W. Strahan and T. Cadell; The Electronic Classics Series, Penn State: Pennsylvania State University.

Stigler, G.J., 1972, The Law and Economics of Public Policy: A Plea to the Scholars, *The Journal of Legal Studies, Vol. 1, No. 1*, 1–12.

Wicksteed, P.H., 1910, *The Common Sense of Political Economy*, edited by L. Robbins, 1933, Vol. II, London: Routledge & Kegan Paul Limited.

Williamson, O.E., 1975, *Markets and Hierarchies*, New York: The Free Press.

Williamson, O.E., 2000, The New Institutional Economics: Taking Stock, Looking Ahead, *Journal of Economic Literature, Vol. 38, No. 3*, 595–613.

Wilson, T., 1945, Price and Outlay Policy of State Enterprise, *The Economic Journal, Vol. 55, No. 220*, 454–461.

6 Theory of the firm

6.1 Introduction

According to Carl von Clausewitz, war is a continuation of the political process by other means, and so is the firm a hierarchy according to Oliver Williamson (1994: 3), 'a continuation of market relations by other means'. In this, Williamson effectively rephrases the central postulate of Coase's (1937: 389) 'Firm' paper, that is, 'the distinguishing mark of the firm is the supersession of the price mechanism'. In Coase's analysis, the firm as a hierarchy and the market as a domain of voluntary exchange become one another's alternative in coordinating production that is presented as an economic choice. As alluded to in Chapter 5, this parity is doubtful.

Anyway, Adam Smith does not pay attention to the coordinating role of the firm as a hierarchy. It is true that *The Wealth of Nations* (Smith 1776) begins with a firm that makes the most of the excellences of division of labor. Economic efficiency prompts the pin maker to subdivide his trifling manufacturing into a great number of parts. Smith:

> the important business of making a pin is, in this manner, divided into about eighteen distinct operations, which, in some manufactories, are all performed by distinct hands, though in others the same man will sometimes perform two or three of them.
>
> (ibid.: 8)

The view of the inside of the pin factory aims to substantiate the impressive advantages of labor division. Smith pays no attention to the further organization of the distinct operations within the factory. The example of the pin factory is merely used to signify the importance of the division of labor for society at large. Its unlimited application founds the 'civilized and thriving nation' that renders economic life amazingly complicated (ibid.: 3).

DOI: 10.4324/9781315764221-6

How many different trades are employed in each branch of the linen and woolen manufactures from the growers of the flax and the wool, to the bleachers and smoothers of the linen, or to the dyers and dressers of the cloth!

(ibid.: 9)

In this perspective, the firm as a manufacturer or as a grower of flax is merely a complement, a *sine qua non*, or rather the outcome of what has Smith's genuine theoretical interest: the exchanges between independent agents who unintendedly clear markets. Basically, the division of labor is, in its turn, the fruit of man's 'propensity to truck, barter, and exchange one thing for another' (ibid.: 16). Therefore, it has been since Adam Smith that the market is the basic institution of economics that is attendant on man's propensity to trade, that is, to escape from self-sufficiency. It is the marvel of the working of the market as a system of extremely decentralized, although interdependent, agents that dominates economists' agenda. Economists study a commercial society in which 'every man thus lives by exchanging, or becomes in some measure a merchant' (ibid.: 25). With such a view, the single role of the 'concept of the firm is to *separate production from consumption*' (Demsetz 1995: 8). In this economics, the households of consumers and the firm as a specialized production unit do not have substance; they are '"black boxes"' (ibid.). Obviously, the explanation of the working of the market economy does not need a view of the inside of its participants.

The market as a subject also founds neoclassical economics generating a morphology of markets varying from perfect competition to monopoly. Given the market conditions, each firm is engaged in an allocatively efficient reshuffling of its resources. This is all based on a known production function and known resource prices. It happens within a safe theoretical domain that occasions the further disregard of the issue of an efficient allocation of resources, as within the firm the production frontier is assumed to be neared as far as possible. It is not a firm's production but the market situation that is the crucial issue and dependent on factors such as the number of buyers and sellers, barriers to entry, market transparency, and product homogeneity. It is as Paul McNulty (1967: 1250) notes, this 'so-called theory of the firm is, strictly speaking, ... a theory of market structure'.

Basically, this economics of markets is the fruit of Smith's political stance against the mercantilism of his days, or rather its inverse. It opposes intervention as the normal economic system works itself. Against this established economic thought appeared during the first decades of the twentieth century its counterpart in vogue: central economic planning, witnessed the Planning Debate of the 1920s, resulting from the surging socialist movement by the end of the nineteenth century (Hayek 1935). Before that time, it was considered that market prices allocated the resources as used by firms and consumers. It is in this context that Coase asks the main question of his 'Firm' paper:

[I]n the view of the fact that it is usually argued that co-ordination will be done by the price mechanism, why is such organization [entrepreneur, or managers who co-ordinate] necessary?

(1937: 388)

Referring to the Planning Debate, he proposes:

Those who object to economic planning on the grounds that the problem is solved by price movements can be answered by pointing out that there is planning within our economic system ... which is akin to what is normally called economic planning.

(ibid.: 387–388)

Apparently, some in the market economy have recourse to the opponent system: economic planning of firms. In this perspective, the firm that is, thus far, a merely passive complement to the market transforms into a valuable alternative to it. For that matter, in this observation, Coase tacitly places the planning of a firm or an entrepreneur on par with the planning of a collectivist economy; at least it 'is akin to' the latter. Their allied status is justified as far as it refers to a firm's disregarding the role of prices. It prompts Coase to reformulate the main question quoted as follows:

Our task is to attempt to discover why a firm emerges at all in a specialized exchange economy.

(ibid.: 390)

Coase's answer is well known. Transaction cost generates a firm.

The main reason ... to establish a firm would seem to be that there is a cost of using the price mechanism.

(ibid.)

As a young socialist, Coase (1988a: 5) now theoretically infers on grounds that the market does not work itself. The firm as a hierarchy renders an alternative to the market. Coase:

Now since these are alternative methods of "organization" – by the price mechanism or by the entrepreneur – such a regulation would bring into existence firms which otherwise would have no *raison d'être*.

(1937: 393)

Definitely, firms do have a *raison d'être* since the 'specialized exchange economy' presupposes them. It is Frank Knight who, before Coase, uncovered the assumption behind the extremely decentralized economy that embezzles the firm as merely a black-box production function. It is Knight, Harold Demsetz notes, who 'seeks to understand why firms exist', depriving the firm of its '"black box" status it occupies in traditional price theory'. Demsetz continues,

> With apologies to R.H. Coase, ... Knight launched the modern theory of the firm in 1921.
>
> (1988b: 243–244)

For Coase, it is the cost of using the price mechanism, that is, transaction cost, that opens the perspective on the firm, or rather on

> the *entrepreneur* to refer to the person or persons who, in a competitive system, take the place of the price mechanism in the direction of resources.
>
> (1937: 388, n. 2; emphasis added)

This entrepreneur features in Knight's classic on the analysis of the economic system, although rather complementing than taking the place of the price mechanism. As the pioneer of new institutional economics (NIE), Knight (1921: 3) profoundly thinks through the assumptions that found theoretical economics' 'distinction of an exact science'. Basically, he is engaged in the overpowering assumption regarding the transition from certainty toward (Knightian) uncertainty that the economic theorist must address to fulfill his aspiration to study economics as an exact science. As discussed in Chapter 4, in the domain of certainty the economic system affords the rational agents the opportunity to solve the basic problems of division of labor, that is, assignment of tasks and appointment of rewards, by voluntary exchange and to do this immediately; *'together, as one'*, as Frank Knight words it (ibid.: 56). Not until the analysis assumes uncertainty change the shadow figures of rational agents into human beings who have to take decisions based on incomplete information and conjectures. Knight's uncertainty assumption encompasses Coase's positive transaction cost assumption as the former immediately lays claim to the economic agent's rationality capacity. He finds himself in an uncertain situation in which he becomes conscious. Referring to D.H. Robertson (1923: 85), the uncertainty assumption affords opportunity for the firms of entrepreneurs who act as '"islands of conscious power"'. Obviously, corresponding to this uncertain world, people face Coase's (1937: 390) 'cost of using the price mechanism'. For that matter, Knightian uncertainty requires flexible contracts, if there is contractability at all.[1] Indeed, it shows that Knight's uncertainty encompasses Coase's transaction cost. Coase's entrepreneur contracts factors that obey him *'within certain limits'* (ibid.: 391). Flexibility in contracting addresses uncertainty. In Coase's 'Firm' paper, on one hand, uncertainty and its information issues constitute *constraints* on the working of the normal economic system that causes transaction costs. In Knight's analysis, on the other hand, the entrepreneur *discovers* in the uncertain, dynamic world new, unknown situations that offer him challenging ventures whereas

Coase's pendant is engaged in economizing transaction cost and flexible contracting, basically more static. Furthermore, Knight analyses an economic agent's situation in which contracting cannot always address the uncertainty. Therefore, it is Knight who introduces the concept of *'moral hazard'* evoked by non-contractability. It makes the entrepreneur assume the uncertainty from others, neutralizing it as risk.

The introduction of uncertainty changes the mechanic economic system into the product of economic thought of conscious human beings in which "'judgment," "common sense," or "intuition."' constitute the complement of 'reasoned knowledge' (Knight 1921: 211). The mechanics of economics as afforded by certainty make place for what Knight denotes as 'a process of "cephalization"' to decide 'what to do and how to do it' when uncertainty is present (ibid.: 268). Tokens of this process abound. For instance, market intelligence and industrious competence feature the competence of the Knightian entrepreneurs 'acting, competing on the basis of what they *think* of the *future*' (ibid.: 273). An entrepreneur's conduct is based on 'human judgment … involving a proportion of failures or errors' (ibid.: 272). Similarly, Coase's entrepreneur defrays costs to *discover* prices. Additionally, due to uncertainty, it happens that 'the details of what the supplier is expected to do is not stated in the contract but is decided later by the purchaser' (Coase 1937: 392). This nears Coase's initial definition of the firm, of a contract whereby a factor 'agrees to obey the directions of an entrepreneur *within certain limits*' (ibid.: 391). Conscious conduct and its discretionary room, that is, intentionality in economics carries back to Adam Smith (Smith 1776: 7, 745), whose chapter 1 begins by accentuating the economic importance of 'skill, dexterity, and judgment' of the productive powers of labor, qualities also indispensable 'to buy in one market, in order to sell, with profit, in another'. In this aspect, G.B. Richardson (1959: 234) refers to Alfred Marshall, who denotes that firms may profit from "'economies of experience" … by virtue of goodwill or other ties'. In general, Richardson contends, it is rightly, unequally distributed knowledge as caused by the Knightian uncertainty that challenges the entrepreneurs to generate potentially profitable ventures (ibid.: 237). Intuition and a sense of market opportunities are indispensable ingredients of commercial success. Clearly, judgment and intuition are also involved in executing and coordinating production processes within the firm. It is the idiosyncratic knowledge of firms and their personnel with different capabilities, and definitely not identical production functions, that fuels competition. For that matter, a firm's capabilities form an asset that is difficult to define and so hard to contract. Edith Penrose (1959) identifies a firm's growth as an organic process of internal development rather than a reformulation of the production frontier in mathematical terms.

The uncertainty assumption evicts the economic theorist from the 'Garden of Eden' of his formal economic edifice (Knight 1921: 268). For some economists, this is a reason to drop the postulate of economic rationality as the economic agent faces unsurmountable information issues that make them unfit for figuring in exact propositions. Bounded rationality and behavioral assumptions are required to describe economic conduct in the unruly reality. It represents nominalism as a search for regularities based on statistical analysis. The opposite approach, representing realism, adheres to the rationality postulate that affords distinguishing economics as an exact science. Instances of both approaches emerge in the account of theories of the firm that follows.

Finally, in light of the numerous instances in which common sense and intuition prevail in economic decisions, it seems at least rather unlikely that economics might persist as an exact science. Judgment, common sense, and intuition constitute companions to nominalism. Michael Polanyi, however, demonstrates that such 'tacit knowledge' as judgment and common sense is an initial and central part of knowledge in general. Tacit knowledge provides us with '(1) know what to look for, and (2) … some idea about what else we may want to know', as Amartya Sen qualifies in his foreword to the 2009 edition of Polanyi's (1966: xi) *The Tacit Dimension*. In this perspective, 'the process of formalizing all knowledge to the exclusion of any tacit knowledge is self-defeating"', Sen adds, quoting Polanyi (ibid.).[2] 'Therefore, Polanyi concludes,

> a mathematical theory can be constructed only by relying on *prior* tacit knowing and can function as a theory only *within* an act of tacit knowing, which consists in our attending *from* it to the previously established experience on which it bears.
>
> (ibid.: 21)

For economics, the implication of this insight is that judgment and common sense are indispensable to the formalized model of perfect competition under certainty as they are also plausible assistance to economic conduct in a world of Knightian uncertainty. In both the perfect competition model and the Knightian entrepreneurial theory figure homunculi who originate from a theorist's analytical intuition. Therefore, Knight (1921: 3) correctly announces to keep up the distinction of economics as an exact science notwithstanding the allowance of an assumption of uncertainty that refuses statistical stipulation. This accords with the phenomenological approach à la Alfred Schutz that transforms the fluid and vague concepts we use in our mundane pursuit to come to terms with our fellow men into second-order constructs to arrive at an objective account of human conduct as based on hunches and commonsense thought. Men act like Fritz Machlup's (1967: 6, n. 2) actual driver who 'simply "sizes up" the situation and goes ahead'. Our conduct in the social world is partly based on judgment and intuition that is inherently related to the uncertain reality we live in. At the same time, it is the stability of our own social conduct (*Verhalten*) as inextricably related to that of our fellow men that founds our entire social life. In this context, Felix Kaufmann (1931: 773) concludes, '*dass auch die soziale Welt Gesetze kennt, die einen sehr geringen Ausnahmenpersentsatz besitzen*'. Further elaboration and application of the realist perspective follow in Section 6.5 on the phenomenological interpretation. As yet, nominalist and realist approaches both follow and are discussed. Prior to the theories of the firm, I discuss the interwovenness between the existence of the firm and the market as one another's complement. The sections are organized as follows.

Exchange originates firms and markets. Production renders production for others, that is, 'strangers', granting economics the social dimension that the scarcity problem of Robinson Crusoe economics lacks (Demsetz 1995: 7). This social dimension is the seat of the Knightian uncertainty as it is particularly present in the interaction between firms and markets, constituting the basic institutions of the specialized exchange economy. The first and the second sections discuss them as a prelude to the next. Section 6.2 discusses the existence of the firm as originating from exchange. It refutes the idea of the firm as a substitute for markets, as Coase's 'Firm' paper argues. The firm has its own *raison d'être*. Obviously, this is contrary to Coase's (1937: 390) 'task is to attempt to discover why a firm emerges at all in a specialized exchange economy'. The purpose of this section is rather to address the other task that Coase sets himself, that is, to show

> a definition of a firm may be obtained which is not only realistic in that
> it corresponds to what is meant by a firm in the real world.
>
> (ibid.: 386)

Coase's additional conditions that 'our definition must, of course, "relate to formal relations which are capable of being *conceived* exactly"', correspond to Knight's aspiration to practice economics as an exact science (ibid.: 387). At the same time, it is shown that Coase's idea of the firm as a planning alternative to the market precludes a proper definition of the firm.

Section 6.3 presents the market as the complement of the firm. The market is the domain of transactions that create costs. This NIE perspective may make the market an institution, conceivably a partial alternative instrument to the firm to exploit the relative transaction cost differences. However, the uncertainty offers opportunities for profitable ventures. In this aspect, I hereafter devote Section 6.4 to the NIE of organization as originating from Coase's 'Firm' paper and devote Section 6.5 to the production theory of the firm. The latter is more engaged in opportunities as offered by uncertainty and is more directed at dynamic processes as associated with Knight's analysis. Section 6.6 presents some conclusions in reference to the phenomenological perspective.

6.2 The existence of the firm

Coase faces the neoclassical model of perfect markets with this question: Why is there such a thing as a firm to plan and organize production? Apparently, the decentralized exchange economy shows a correspondence with the planned economy; anyway, it is akin to it. Coase (1937: 387) refers to planning within the firm, for instance, ordering a workman to move from department Y to department X and substituting such a move because of a change in prices.

The cost of using the price mechanism determines the use of planning or prices. In brief, this reasoning originates the markets-versus-hierarchies choice as a central NIE theme.

First, however, a firm's planning is not akin to the central planning of a socialist economy. The latter particularly refers to planning and coordination between firms whereas Coase refers to planning within firms. Second, the choice itself between planning and prices presupposes an authority that deliberates it. Furthermore, socialist economic planning apparently presupposes the existence of firms. For instance, introductory textbooks use the expository qualities of a circular flow in which producers and households figure interrelated by markets or a planning agency. Firms appear both in decentralized and centrally planned economies as soon as production for others, that is, strangers, replaces self-subsistence. The very problem of the market-versus-hierarchies choice is, as Harold Demsetz (1995: 1) states, that it disregards the question of the existence of the firm.

It is the domain of certainty and perfect information as a commencement in both Knight's and Coase's analyses that compels them to disregard the autonomous *raison d'être* of the entrepreneur and the firm, respectively. A zero-transaction cost makes the price mechanism 'a pseudonym for self-management', Demsetz (1995: 9) notes. 'All one needs for this firm are fully informed owners of *inputs* who respond to relevant prices' (ibid.: 12). In this 'model of perfect competition of neoclassical theory', he continues, 'prices seem to do everything' (ibid.: 13).

> The prices for joining an inappropriate mix are lower than for joining an appropriate mix, and all households use these inputs correctly because there is full knowledge of technologies.
>
> (ibid.: 12)

The perfect information assumption, and so a zero-transaction cost, produces an imaginary world in which there is no place for human beings. There is no room for Knight's (1921: 268) concept of 'a process of "cephalization"'. Apart from the logic that the assumption entails, it remains difficult to imagine such a world in which there is a place for neither an entrepreneur nor such a thing as a firm. Apparently, on reflection, Coase also struggles with these questions. He states:

> How matters would work out in detail is not easy to describe or even imagine. One of the factors could be responsible for the sale of the product to consumers, or it could be that one would be responsible for the sale of the component, made by some factors, to other factors, ... , or alternatively, the consumer could contract with all the factors which provide the services to make the product. There are a vast number of possible contractual arrangements but, absent firms, *none would involve the direction* of factors of production.
>
> (Coase 1988c: 38; emphasis added)

In this retrospect, Coase recognizes that there could be some type of responsibility 'for the sale of the product to consumers' to be assumed, for example, by a firm. At the same time, he realizes that such a responsibility contradicts the perfect competition model in which the perfectly informed, price-sensitive actors admit no direction. Obviously, there is a latent inconsistency in this world of perfect information and competition. Neoclassical theory seemingly irons it out. The firm figures in neoclassical price theory as a production function that is attendant on the modeling. A mathematical equation brings, as it were, the productive resources together, belittling the responsibility issue: the firm as 'a verbal convenience' or rather a mathematical one (Demsetz 1995: 12). It is the theoretical exercise to demonstrate the working of the market that warrants the firm as a nobody in neoclassical theory. Apparently, Coase follows this theoretical narrative.

Thus, direction and planning feature Coase's concept of the firm, if and only if to replace the relatively costly market. This market–firm dichotomy raises some serious issues. First, it disregards the basic issue that the market presupposes the firm as a body that produces for others. Second, it disregards specialized production for others that is done by someone without personnel. Third, the direction characteristic, as a substitute of the market, would consider the private household with a domestic staff as a firm. Fourth, it is well conceivable that a market transaction in its execution requires some form of direction and planning. Apparently, direction and planning are neither necessary nor sufficient conditions for defining the firm. Fifth, another fundamental objection, however, regards the very fact of presenting planning as an alternative management instrument to the market. In the dilemma of market versus firm, the responsibility issue is manifested to the full extent: Who broaches the dilemma? Who reflects about setting aside a market relation and substituting 'a series of contracts' for one? (Coase 1937: 391). Apparently, there is such a thing as a body, an authority that asks the concerned questions. Would it not betray an authority? Obviously, Coase's following of neoclassical conceptions makes itself felt. Under the neoclassical assumption of perfect information, the Coase (1988c: 38; emphasis added) quote holds: 'absent firms, *none would involve the direction* of factors of production'. As noted, in the logic of the assumption, it is sound. However, it leaves aside the very beginning of such a thing as production for others. Who initiates 'the coming together of inputs [that] qualifies as a firm' (Demsetz 1995: 13)? Behind this coming together, there must be a uniting force or an authority, that is, such a thing as a firm, that brings it about. Obviously, the neoclassical perfect competition model hides a latent inconsistency. On one hand, market relations suffice. On the other hand, there must be 'something' that broaches the idea of production for others. It is, for instance, as Steven Cheung (1983: 7) wonders, who coalesces the information of the product parts to produce a camera? Clearly, transaction and information costs may cause the firm to become for some specific transactions. However, who takes it up in a regime of market relations that admits no direction? In this respect, Coase does not distinguish himself from the neoclassical theorists. As little as the neoclassical theorist, Coase proves to be engaged in the responsibility issue.

Apparently, the firm versus market dilemma presupposes the existence of a firm as a responsible agent. Therefore, it is not a positive transaction cost that explains the existence of the firm. A transaction cost may definitely play a role in the theory of the firm as far as it occurs in an economy in which firms are interrelated by markets, that is, in which firms and markets are one another's complement. As yet, it is the *raison d'être* of the firm that demands attention.

Due to Adam Smith, the firm is an inalienable economic concept that is irreducible to anything else. As noted, it is a specialized production entity that produces for other people. It features an economy based on a division of labor 'from which so many advantages are derived' (Smith 1776: 16). However, Smith warns,

> it is not originally the effect of any human wisdom, which foresees and intends that general opulence to which it gives occasion.
>
> (ibid.)

The division of labor and the inherent production by firms are the necessary consequence of 'a certain propensity in human nature to truck, barter, and exchange one thing for another', explicitly not the effect of an intentionally pursued utility. Basically, this propensity, in its turn, Smith puts forward, 'as seems more probable, it be the necessary consequence of the faculties of reason and speech' (ibid.).

In this perspective, the background of the division of labor and firms refers to what basically features human beings: reason and speech. Division of labor, production by firms, and exchange constitute the very subject of economic inquiry. It is intriguing that Smith disregards the obvious explanation that economic advantage evokes division of labor and the like. Against this plausibility, Smith identifies human reason and speech as the noneconomic bottom of economics as engaged in labor division, firms, and exchange. It protects him from being faced with an infinite regress. An economic explanation of humans' propensity to exchange that constitutes the economic problem would be invalid. It is as Joseph Schumpeter words it in his 'inquiry about the general forms of economic phenomena':

> If, ... , the causal factor is itself economic in nature, we must continue our explanatory efforts until we ground upon a non-economic bottom.
>
> (1934: 4–5)

Economics cannot explain itself. Basically, this maxim asserts itself in the economic explanation via the transaction cost of the firm. The transaction cost explanation disregards the existence of the firm as stemming from human's propensity to exchange. The assumption of a zero-transaction cost and the presence of certainty produce the mere existence of an extremely decentralized model. 'The actors in this model maximize utility or wealth, and they do so in complete disregard of the decisions of others or, indeed, of even the existence of others' (Demsetz 1988a: 142).

The model actually dehumanizes economics Additionally, the archetypical nature of the firm as a starting point of economics as engaged in exchange is also ignored, causing the inconsistency noted.

It is furthermore intriguing that Smith exactly identifies man's faculties of reason and speech as founding the world of economics. It accords with the phenomenological view as discussed in Chapter 2. I return to it hereafter. In this context, it is significant to note that the concept of the firm is directly related to what grounds economics, that is, the propensity to exchange. The firm stems from man's motive to abandon self-sufficiency and give in to his longing for exchanging with others with whom he is intersubjectively related. The firm is a fundamental concept in economics, as its *raison d'être* denotes.

The basic nature of the firm concept returns in, for instance, Demsetz's approach to it. In the history of economic theory, he finds two universally applicable propositions, that is, 'that are not specific to a type of economic system'. First, it regards 'the first law of demand', expressing economic rationality (Demsetz 2008: 1). The second proposition that holds universally regards the (technological)

> relationship between the cost of producing a good, measured in terms of amount of resources committed to its production, and the total number of units of the good produced.
>
> (ibid.)

Within the economic world of exchange, human economic rationality prompts people to take advantage of the economies of scale as the technological laws of production exhibit. This universal reality renders the firm as a specialized production entity, a sustainable outcome of humans' propensity to exchange, that is, to produce for others. All the same holds humans' faculty to speech and reason as the noneconomic bottom of economic explanation. The existence of the firm is a universal in economics.

How can the firm be further defined? As yet, it is 'simply *presumed*' that the firm as a specialized production entity refers to 'an economy based on private ownership of resources' (ibid.: 2). Clearly, this accords with the definition of economics since Adam Smith and disregards the specialized production in a central planned economy.

Against J.A. Salter's adage, as repeatedly quoted by Coase, '"The normal economic system works itself."', D.H. Robertson brings in:

> Here and there, it is true, we have found islands of conscious power in this ocean of unconscious co-operation, like lumps of butter coagulating in a pail of buttermilk. The factory system itself, while it involves endless

specialization of the work of ordinary men, involves also deliberate co-ordination of their diverse activities by the capitalist employer.

(1923: 85)

The name of a part of this quote owes it to Coase, who refers to it in the 'Firm' paper. The quote particularly denotes the invariable responsibility of the capitalist employer for the coordination issues in 'the factory system itself'. Against this invariability, Coase (1937: 386) poses a rather loose description in spite of noting that a 'clear definition of the word "firm" should be given'.

> Of course, it is not possible to draw a hard and fast line which determines whether there is a firm of not. There may be more or less direction.
>
> (ibid.: 392, n. 1)

Basically, the firm is a contract 'whereby the factor, ... , agrees to obey the directions of an entrepreneur *within certain limits*' (ibid.: 391). Contractual contingency causes this firm's lack of distinctiveness. As discussed, Demsetz recognizes the firm's autonomous existence as a specialized production entity. At the same time, he concurs with Coase in viewing it foremost as a contractual matter. 'The firm properly viewed is a "nexus" of contracts', he opens his discussion on the definition of the firm (Demsetz 1988a: 154). It affords the firm a rather variable character. Therefore, Demsetz prefers to state it as a 'firm-like organization'. Instead of addressing the question of what type of nexus makes a firm, he poses the question, 'When is a nexus of contracts *more firm-like?*' (ibid.).

The problem with the nexus of contracts view is that it cannot appropriately position the authority that bears the responsibility to initiate and further organize production. Contracts suggest a transient, partial arrangement of rights and duties that conflicts with the durability that a possible appeal to organizational responsibility presumes. Furthermore, the concept of a nexus presupposes an idea of an assembly that cannot be addressed by the nexus itself. Apparently, as a nexus of contracts, the firm remains a verbal and transient entity without substance. Therefore, the definition must present the firm as an authority that initiates and substantiates production ideas for which responsibility might be experienced as coherent and durable. It is not without significance that 'the word 'firm' derives from the Latin adjective *firmus*, meaning strong, powerful, durable and lasting', as Geoffrey Hodgson (2002: 40) notices. It makes the firm a recognizable social structure whose role is identifiable in the circular flow of the economy. For instance, Frederick Fourie underlines particularly the durability of the firm as a social structure in his definition. Fourie:

> firms as cohesive, durable institutions with members (individuals) who are bound together in a solidary whole that has a durability of existence amidst changes in membership.
>
> (1993: 54)

However, this definition lacks the legal nature of the firm. The firm is, as Hodgson (2002: 56) argues, a 'distinct legal entity. ... It owns its products and sells or hires them to others'. The inalienable legal dimension of the firm accords with the very NIE idea of the transaction as an exchange of property rights. It furthermore dimensions the nature of the relationship between the firm owner and his 'workmen' whom he may order '*between certain limits*' (Coase 1937: 391). Opposite to Coase, who makes little of the definition of the firm, denoting it as 'more or less direction', Hodgson (2002: 42) presents himself in this aspect as a philosophical realist arguing that 'definitions are not merely convenient instruments of thought but attempts to carve reality at the joints so that it can be understood and explained'. Hodgson's position accords with the concept of the firm as universal, as derived earlier, through Adam Smith. With a slight adaptation, Hodgson's definition reads as follows.

> A firm is defined as an integrated and durable organization involving [one person] or more people, acting openly or tacitly as a 'legal person', capable of owning assets, set up for the purpose of producing goods or services, with the capacity to sell or hire these goods or services to customers.
>
> (ibid.: 56)

According to Hodgson's definition, at least two people are involved in a firm. However, as Demsetz (1995: 9) argues, 'a *specialized unit of production*, ... can be a one-person unit'. A single person may found a firm as a legal person who owes assets, integrating and organizing resources to sell or hire these goods or services to customers. As an entrepreneur without personnel, he takes initiative regarding products or services, brings factors together, and substantiates the division of labor. This definition encompasses the one-person enterprise. The legal nature of the firm is essential. The notion of durability and the idea of initiative and responsibility remain unaffected. The latter reflects the firm as an instance of meaning that, for that matter, entails risk. The element of responsibility concurs with Knight's perception of the firm. Knight:

> The essence of enterprise is the specialization of the function of *responsible direction* of economic life.
>
> (1921: 271)

A few sentences earlier he notes:

> Its existence in the world is a direct result of the fact of uncertainty.
>
> (ibid.)

Actually, firm and uncertainty are intimately related to one another. Taking the responsibility of production for other, strange people, generates (Knightian) uncertainty. So, the firm is both the origin and the effect of the presence of uncertainty. As such this concept of the firm encompasses the Coasean firm as device to economize on transaction cost, an apparently too restrictive concept.

6.3 The firm's complement: the market

Without the cost of using the price mechanism, the firm as a seat of authority is superfluous. As noted, this is a neoclassical trait in Coase's (1937: 386) 'Firm' paper though it contrasts with his further insistence on realism in assumptions. Israel Kirzner (1999: 4) refers to such a neoclassical relict as 'the illusion of perennial optimality'. In the neoclassical anarchistic context, it holds that all the opportunities of mutually beneficial trades have been grasped since the cost of transaction is zero; witness the Coase Theorem.[3] However, as Kirzner emphasizes, in spite of an absent transaction cost actors may miss noticing a beneficial opportunity *simply because of lack of awareness of its availability* (ibid.: 5). *A fortiori* it is questionable to presume that actors grasp the beneficial opportunities in an imperfect information regime. Neoclassical economic rationality presupposes clear-cut choices regarding potentially, mutually beneficial arrangements that will be completed. However, the very thing is to prearrange the potentially beneficial bargain, that is, to present to the rational agent the situational logic in which he finds himself. It is the institutional setting of the market that makes the economic agent aware of the opportunities to create and present appealing choices. However, it is, in its turn, the firm as a production authority that enters the market with its prearranged offer.

This representation demonstrates the intimate relationship between the firm and market. They are not merely one another's pendant. Above all, it shows that the market enables the entrepreneur to offer new beneficial opportunities for sale as created by his imaginative power. According to Kirzner, this fundamental economic process stems from 'the entrepreneurial element in human action' that, in its turn, is reminiscent of what Adam Smith recognizes as humans' propensity to exchange. Kirzner:

> Within the setting of the market the entrepreneurial element in human action can be expected to set in motion a process of mutual discovery.
>
> (ibid.: 11)

The market informs the entrepreneur about prices, showing him opportunities to arbitrage prices, form new combinations of resources, and thus take advantage of *the possibility of buying at a low price in order to resell at a higher price* (ibid.: 7). In the market, supply and demand meet one another, exchanging property rights and revealing the prices that accomplish the trades under varying grades of competition. Clearly, this perspective refers to Knight's account of the entrepreneur, who, particularly in his production for others' experiences, may make the most of the Knightian uncertainty. Furthermore, in the market notion reemerges the difference between Coase and Knight in addressing

uncertainty and information issues. Coase's entrepreneur economizes on transaction costs, whereas Knight's entrepreneur ventures opportunities.

In the function of the market, returns the relevance of the distinction between logical and generative causality as discussed in Chapter 3. The latter
type concerns a causality that stems from human consciousness. 'One's own
person, moreover, and any of its states are links in this great universal structure
of relationships', Menger (1976: 51) argues. In this perspective, the market refers to relationships between conscious human beings as sources of causality
generating competition and the market as unintended outcomes of their purposiveness. In the Austrian perspective, the intentionality of the economic subject replaces the presupposed omniscience of neoclassical economics. This
perspective views purposive agents who create beneficial opportunities enabled
by the market as an informational device. Therefore, further elaboration on the
firm requires theoretical attention to the concept of the market. The institutional structure of the market that may vary has significance, particularly for
the Knightian entrepreneur and, to a lesser degree, for Coase's market-versus-firm choice.

The firm produces commodities for strangers whose demand may be uncertain in a Knightian sense. In Knight's view, this is the *raison d'être* of the entrepreneur who is inextricably related to the market. At the same time, the firm
and the market may be perceived as two, although different, domains of human interaction that complement one another. However, according to
G.B. Richardson the degree of interrelatedness justifies questioning the strict
division between firm and market. Ricardson notes:

> What kinds of co-ordination have to be secured through conscious direc-
> tion within firms and what can be left to the working of the invisible
> hand? One might reasonably maintain that this was a key question -per-
> haps the key question- in the theory of industrial organisation, the most
> important matter that the Divine Maker of market economies on the first
> day of creation would have to decide. And yet, as I hope soon to show, it
> is a matter upon which our standard theories, which merely assume but
> do not explain a division between firm and market, throw little light. ...
> What I have in mind is the dense network of co-operation and affiliation
> by which firms are inter-related.
>
> (1972: 883)

Richardson recognizes a network of cooperation as a third domain of relations, besides firms and markets. I return to it hereafter, in Section 6.5. All the
same, the institutional setting of the market, that is, basically the rule of law,
and the organization of the market affect a firm's relationship to the market. In
this respect, I refer to Menger and Alfred Marshall, as suggested by Richard
Arena (1999).

In his discussion, 'The Marketability of Commodities', Menger (1976: 241)
precedes Knight's uncertainty issue as raised by production for an imperfectly

known market. Attained at the higher level of civilization, Menger argues, people are increasingly engaged in specialized production of '*(economic) goods of any kind that are intended for sale*', that is, commodities (ibid.: 239). As Knight is engaged in addressing the uncertainty this production mode entails, before him, Menger comparably discussed the vulnerability of this production mode in terms of marketability. Under this aspect, Menger explicitly shifts the attention from 'treatises into theories of prices' to 'the far-reaching *practical* importance' of the differences in the marketability of commodities (ibid.: 242; emphasis added). The concept of marketability is closely related to his concept 'saleableness' (Menger 1892: 245). The concepts may be interpreted as predecessors of Coase's concept of transaction costs even though Menger's marketability translates itself in degrees of economic pricing, that is, sale 'at prices that correspond to the *general* economic situation' (ibid.: 248) The marketability of commodities varies depending on causes such as the number of potential market partners, geographic reach, and opportunities to speculate (ibid.: 243–246). Menger emphasizes that it is the organization of markets, for example, by fairs, exchanges, and public auctions, that 'ensure[s] the establishment of economic prices' (ibid.: 249). He adds several instances to substantiate the concept. An example regards dealers in a commodity who locate 'their warehouses as near to other as possible in order to evoke, by their concentration, a similar concentration of customers' (ibid.). In transaction-cost terms, it is a market practice that economizes on consumers' inspection costs of 'search goods', such as furniture (Nelson 1970). Menger also pays attention to a marketability issue that might be associated with asset specificity. It regards the marketability of 'commodities that have no independent use and are wanted only as parts of other commodities' such as watch springs or pressure gauges, Menger suggests (ibid.: 251). Furthermore, he recognizes a difference in the marketability of commodities that depends on the person who offers a commodity or the manner in which it is offered. For instance,

> [s]hoes, hats and similar articles, … are always fairly saleable in the hands of a shoe merchant or a hatter. In the hands of another person, these commodities can be sold only with difficulty and almost always only at a heavy loss.
>
> (ibid.: 255)

The latter situation is directly interpretable in the phenomenological perspective of ideal types that accompany market transactions. However, the marketability dependence on the person who offers the commodity does not hold for commodities for which the qualifications are solid. 'Gold nuggets extracted from the Aranyos River' retain the same degree of sale-ableness, whosoever them offers (ibid.: 254).[4]

Menger's marketability discussion underlines the interwovenness between the (entrepreneurial) firm and the market. Firms may organize a market (practice); an entrepreneur may organize markets such as an auction or a fair, enhancing marketability; and public organization and institutional arrangement of markets serve the exchanging agents. Entrepreneurs conjecture about the marketability of a production initiative and take account of it, for example, in the design of the product to create a niche. The examples substantiate Menger's generative causality as being founded on conscious human beings who act purposively in an uncertain world of firms and markets, beings who conjecture about production opportunities and who might err (ibid.: 148). The subjectivist nature of the analysis renders it amenable to the phenomenological interpretation I return to later.

Similar to Menger, Marshall also adheres to an economics that aims at generative causality and departs from purposive human subjects. It corresponds with his definition of economics as 'engaged in the study of mankind in ordinary business of life' (Marshall 1890: 1). In this view, it suits that he is not interested in an exact definition of a market equilibrium à la neoclassical theory. '"Equilibrium" [is a term] in common use and may be used for the present without special explanation' (ibid.: 323). Rather, Marshall formulates tendencies that feature a market.

> Thus the more nearly perfect a market is, the stronger is the tendency for the same price to be paid for the same thing at the same time in all parts of the market.
>
> (ibid.: 325)

Relevant is Marshall's spectrum of general markets versus specific markets. Market conditions that determine the generality of the market concern the universality of a commodity and the degree to which it is cognizable and portable. 'Cognizable' may be interpreted as not susceptible to attenuation of the property rights that a commodity exchange defines. Clearly, portability refers to the transport cost that determines the geographical scope of the market. The conditions correspond with Menger's marketability causes, as discussed. Regarding the general market, the 'strongest case of all is that of securities which are called "international"' (ibid.: 327).

Against the general market, Marshall gives an impression of its very opposite:

> At the opposite extremity to international stock exchange securities and the more valuable value metals are, firstly, things which must be made to order to suit particular individuals, such as well-fitting clothes; and, secondly, perishable and bulky goods, such as fresh vegetables, which can seldom be profitable carried long distances.
>
> (ibid.: 328)

Obviously, in such specific markets, a host of details and peculiarities will affect the pricing. At the same time, some competitive pressure will be felt. In this aspect, 'the element of Time requires more careful attention just now than does that of Space' (ibid.: 330). Particularly, the cost of producing will influence the supply if the period is longer.

Marshall's juxtaposition of the general versus the specific market is significant for the further discussion of the firm. The general market corresponds particularly well to the neoclassical theory of competition as its conditions are near to those of perfect competition. From a phenomenological perspective, market participants regard strangers to one another who may be represented as homunculi. Against the anonymity of the general market, specific markets may be embedded in a more idiosyncratic social fabric that structures the market relations. Reputation, goodwill, and relational contracts are relevant in local, and niche markets, briefly, markets in which (inter)dependence prevails. It concerns market situations in which human subjectivity is manifestly present, inviting it to be interpreted phenomenologically.

It is when markets are non-general that there emerges an interface of markets and firms as domains of economic relationships. It reflects the competitiveness of the market as known from the market morphology profiled by the number of buyers and sellers, degree of homogeneity, and so on. Within the domain of certainty and the presence of perfect competition, the firm has no substance. It is not until the appearance of an entrepreneur who creates production for others by bringing together resources fueled by his propensity to exchange that economics acquires meaning. Basically, this initial momentum refers to an imaginary noneconomic domain to which the economist apparently has no access, as the noneconomic bottom on which he bases his analytical starting point. It is first outside the imaginary domain of certainty that the Knightian entrepreneur may discover potentially profitable ventures, and his Coasean companion, economizing on transaction costs, may deliberate on make or buy, that is, on the market-versus-firm choice. The next section particularly elaborates on the latter. Section 6.5 discusses the predominant entrepreneurial challenges offered by (Knightian) uncertainty.

6.4 NIE of organizations

The 'Social Cost' paper is a restatement of the 'Firm' paper, Benjamin Klein notes (Kitch 1983: 202). It is the reformulation of the 'Firm' paper in the 'Social Cost' paper that makes Coase (1937; 1960) the founding father of NIE of organizations. The 'Social Cost' paper identifies that 'the cost of using the price mechanism', that is, transaction cost, basically concerns the cost of exchanging property rights (Coase 1937: 390; 1960). It announces market versus hierarchy as the very theme of NIE, that is, the economics of organization. This section is divided into subsections. The first subsection discusses the concept of transaction cost. It is NIE's key concept that requires a clear definition. At the same time, this is a challenge as its introduction converts the economy in all its branches. The second subsection highlights the elaboration of the theme markets versus hierarchies based on the degree of asset specificity.

As initiated by Oliver Williamson it deviates from mainstream economics. The third subsection, however, holds on to the principles of economic rationality. It elaborates on the residual claimant as central to the theory of the firm. The final subsection lists the features that summarize a description of the concept of the firm.

6.4.1 *The concept of transaction cost*

Obviously, the concept of transaction costs contains such things as the cost of preparation of the deal by the trading parties, for example, of comparing prices, negotiating, the cost of writing the contract, and its enforcement. It comprehends the costs that stem from the additional activities of a transaction.

> The most obvious cost of "organising" production through the price mechanism is that of discovering what the relevant prices are.
>
> (Coase 1937: 390)

However, the consequences of introducing the 'cost of using the price mechanism' do not remain limited to these plain costs of contracting. We have apparently left the domain of perfect competition in which prices are known and enter the world of imperfect knowledge and uncertainty. It redirects the attention from just concluding a contract to what really counts in an exchange: the transfer of property rights. In principle, it is the definition of property rights in terms of *usus*, *usus fructus*, and *abuses* that substantiates a transaction. Their definition determines to what extent the perceived gains from trade might be realized. However, given imperfect knowledge, it may easily turn out that the expectations raised by the definition fail, that is, an attenuation of one party's or both parties' property rights as established beforehand. It is difficult to forestall these types of failures. Commonly, in a world of imperfect knowledge, the incomplete contract prevails. For instance, the quality of a commodity may be insecure and, therefore, if possible, entails a cost of inspection that is detrimental to the gain from trade. Experience goods, such as services, cannot even be inspected in advance. It may forestall a trade. Besides imperfect information, it is information asymmetry, causing moral hazard and adverse selection, that complicates the exchange relationship. Briefly, information issues severely complicate the exchange both *ex ante*, that is, before concluding a contract, and *ex post*, that is, in enforcing the execution of a contract, or due to an *ex post* transformation of the relationship, for example, by a long-term commitment. Evidently, the market exchange relations do not work themselves. Information issues prompt economic agents to search for their supersession. The firm assists, setting aside the simplicity of the purely reciprocal relations of the market in order to economize on transaction cost, and using authority, and its flexibility, to address uncertainties. This is the theoretical narrative that has inspired economists to elaborate on the organization of firms as authorities/ hierarchies and markets in their interrelatedness.

As discussed, the 'Firm' paper proposes that 'to obey the directions of an entrepreneur *within certain limits*' economizes on transaction costs, as for 'a series of contracts is substituted one' (ibid.: 391). Apparently, the firm does not imply the elimination of contracts. Rather, the issue of imperfect information may make it desirable to conclude 'a long-term contract for the supply of some article or service'. It may avoid the costs of 'several shorter contracts'. Moreover, 'owing to the difficulty of forecasting', the longer period may offer the purchasing party flexibility, which 'may well be a matter of indifference to' the supplying party, 'but not to the purchaser of that service or commodity' (ibid.: 391).

> Therefore, the service which is being provided is expressed in general terms, the exact details being left until a later date.
>
> (ibid.: 392)

It is the flexibility in the direction of resources that Coase associates with the 'firm'. In a footnote, he adds:

> Of course, it is not possible to draw a hard and fast line which determines whether there is a firm or not. There may be more or less direction.
>
> (ibid.: 392, n. 1)

Obviously, it is not merely the plain transaction costs of the contracting that lead to a firm as defined. Rather, it is the flexibility of direction – within certain limits – of the contracted resources that is decisive in superseding the strict tit-for-tat-market transactions. In this aspect, the entrepreneur is engaged in organizing those transactions that are not suitable for explicitly contracting that would entail costly and probably unworkable contract specification or would be impossible, given the uncertainty of the transactions. Voilà, the firm attends to incomplete contracts.

The second key question of the 'Firm' paper is this: 'Why is not all production carried on by one big firm?' (ibid.: 394). 'The size of the firm is limited the '"diminishing returns to management"' (ibid.: 395). In this respect, Coase refers to Austin Robinson, who holds

> the view that the limit to the optimum size of an undertaking is to be found in the increasing costs of co-ordination required for the management of larger units.
>
> (1934: 242)

In Coase's view, the size of the firm refers to the number of transactions organized by the entrepreneur. An increasing number of transactions will imply more diversity of them, furnishing 'an additional reason why efficiency will tend to decrease as the firm gets larger' (Coase 1937: 397). Eventually, it is the trade-off between the cost of organizing within the firm versus the marketing cost that will 'generally determine why firms get larger and smaller' (ibid.: 405). 'Business men will be constantly experimenting, controlling more or less' (ibid.: 404). In this aspect, the 'Firm' paper is engaged in a definition of the firm that '"relate[s] to formal relations which are capable of being *conceived* exactly"', as intended from the outset (ibid.: 387).

Basically, Coase's firm is an agglomerate of contractually incomplete contracts to address two issues:

- The cost of contracting;
- Flexibility in resource direction.

This is a remarkably modest harvest from the perspective of the further development of NIE theory. In Coase's retrospect of the 'Firm' paper reemerges these two issues. First, 'the basic reason for the existence of firms' is 'the avoidance of costs of contracting between factors of production considers' (Coase 1988c: 40). Second, Coase

> append[s] an argument about long-term contracts not in their role as an alternative to coordination within a firm but as something which could bring the firm into existence.
>
> (ibid.)

If a contract covers a long period, the buying party will prefer flexibility, awaiting the prospective contingencies before specifying the contract. Therefore, besides economizing on the cost of contracting, it is particularly the flexibility regarding 'transactions between the organizers of the firm and the factors of production it uses' that counts as the rationale for the existence of the firm (ibid.: 41). Coase concludes in his retrospect:

> So far what I said still seems to me to be correct. But I conclude: "When the direction of resources (within the limits of the contract) becomes dependent on the buyer in this way, that relationship that I term a 'firm' may be obtained".
>
> (ibid.)

The quote is from his 'Firm' paper (Coase 1937: 392). In a note he specifies the direction of resources as regarding the relationship between 'master and servant' (ibid.: 392, n. 1). In retrospect, however, Coase (1988c: 41; emphasis added) adds that he 'would prefer now to say' that the firm as organizer would arise when there are '*several* factors' whose activities are to be coordinated. All the same, the bearing of the paper itself remains seemingly rather limited, with nothing about such a thing as incentive alignment. At the same time, the long-term nature of the contracts that feature the firm concurs with the '*solidary whole that has a durability of existence*' as a defining trait of Fourie's (1993: 54) concept of the firm quoted earlier. Moreover, notwithstanding his rather vague formulation, Coase apparently takes the firm as a legal entity concluding contracts that afford 'direction within certain limits'. In the end, Coase's concept of the firm accords with the definition stated earlier.

As yet, unanswered remains the definition of transaction cost. Apparently, the bearing of the transaction cost concept is profound. This easily may change it into a catchall concept without substance. To safeguard it, Demsetz distinguishes

> transaction cost and management cost to refer to the costs of organizing resources, respectively, across markets and within firms. This accords with Coase's terminology.
>
> (1988a: 144)

The central Coasean choice of market versus firm amounts to comparing these twin costs. However, in contrast to the clarity the distinction itself suggests is its application rather awkward. For instance, production within the firm, as prompted by relatively high transaction costs, uses resources that have been purchased via the market. So, transaction cost reemerges. However, the price of a good purchased will contain the management cost of the other firm that produced the good. Therefore, the market-versus-firm choice requires comparing the sum of both costs of the alternatives. In this aspect returns the issue regarding the existence of the firm. The relevance of the costs added implies that if the transaction cost is zero, the management cost remains, as there is, in contrast to Coase's position, still a firm. So, Demsetz identifies further, that a zero-transaction cost does not imply that all production is individualized, as the 'Firm' paper claims. Individualized or multi-person management of production is a matter of management (dis)economies of scale. Demsetz:

> Zero transaction cost informs us only that these cooperating efforts will be organized with greater reliance on explicit negotiations than would be true if transaction cost were positive.
>
> (ibid.: 146)

The essence of the firm as a management device may vary; besides incomplete contracting, it is engaged in explicitly written contracts. Moreover, besides transaction and management costs, it is production cost that counts in considering a make-or-buy choice. Basically, this choice is not restricted to buying versus producing a commodity. It may also imply considering taking over the firm that produces the commodity concerned, for example, when economies of scale are in sight. Furthermore, expansion of in-house production at the expense of outsourcing may have scale effects. Obviously, both transaction, management, and production cost are relevant in the marginal area of market versus firm.[5] As denoted, this perspective refutes the proposition of the transaction cost theory that a zero-transaction cost renders the firm superfluous. The relative level of the remaining costs may justify production within the firm. The exclusive attention to transaction costs stems from holding on the theoretical idea of an extremely decentralized model of the economy in which 'information remains full and free' (ibid.: 148). However, given positive trans-action and management cost the firm rather is, as Demsetz it recaps,

> a bundle of commitments to technology, personnel, and methods, all contained and constrained by an insulating layer of information that is specific to the firm, and this bundle cannot be altered or imitated easily or quickly.
>
> (ibid.)

In this recurs the notions of cohesion and durability of the firm. Particularly, this description renders the firm a repository of information regarding the business it is engaged in. In this respect, it is relevant to distinguish between 'the economics of acquiring and using knowledge' (ibid.: 157). The firm pre-dominantly uses knowledge by directing agents who possess the relevant knowledge. It reminds of Knight's concept of indirect knowledge. 'We know things by knowledge of men who know them', and '"control" things by select-ing someone else to do the "controlling"' (Knight 1921: 291). As a bundle of commitments the firm cannot easily be altered or imitated as its repository of knowledge particularly refers to information that is hard to communicate, hence the prevalence of incomplete contracts. Moreover, it refers to a firm's identity. This information dimension affects the boundary issues of the firm, for example, regarding specialization and integration. For that matter, the in-formation dimension features the capabilities approach, offering challenging opportunities, as discussed in Section 6.5.

6.4.2 Further elaboration on Coase's theory of the firm (1): the hierarchy

The cost of organizing an additional transaction determines whether it is car-ried out within the firm, or through the market. 'This statement has been called a "tautology"', Coase (1988b: 19) notes, adding that '[i]t is the criticism people make of a proposition which is clearly right'. It is, as Armen Alchian and Har-old Demsetz (1972: 783) pose, hard to disagree with, or to refute the proposi-tion 'that, *ceteris paribus*, the higher is the cost of transacting across markets the greater will be the comparative advantage of organizing resources within the firm'. At issue is operationalizing the conditions that determine the cost of organizing the resources either in this or that way, substantiating the institu-tional options that are available. Actually, the further development of the NIE of organization may be seen as an elaboration on Coase's central tenet on firm versus market as witnessed in the theoretical contributions of, for example, Williamson (1971), Alchian and Demsetz (1972), Steven Cheung (1983), Yo-ram Barzel (1987), Sanford Grossman and Oliver Hart (1986), and Demsetz (1988c). In this aspect, it must immediately be added that, in the years preced-ing the publication of the 'Firm' paper in 1937, Coase himself also recognized the need of operationalization of the transaction cost proposition. In his retrospect, he recalls the relevant questions. Coase states:

> Why was it that what seemed to be a movement away from specialization was more efficient? Why should we make a distinction between vertical and horizontal integration? And why was it that costs could be lowered by grouping together certain activities under one control? I was very conscious that I had not got a handle on these problems. In my letter of March 24, 1932, after characterizing my own approach via the effect on costs of putting different functions under one control as "very weak" ...
>
> (1988a: 11)

In his further correspondence with his friend, Ronald Fowler, in the early 1930s, Coase explained the relatively substantial capital cost due to the 'risks inherent in this condition of bilateral monopoly'. Without mentioning it, he alluded to the relationship between the Duquesne Power and Light Company of Pittsburgh that had integrated in order to avoid the risks of what would be called asset specificity (ibid.: 13). Fowler did not understand the argument about bilateral monopoly, so Coase explicated it in a next letter. He wrote:

> Suppose the production of a particular product requires a large capital equipment which is, however, specialized insofar that it can only be used for the particular product concerned or can only be readapted at great cost. Then the firm producing such a product for one consumer finds itself faced with one great risk – that the consumer may transfer his demand elsewhere or that he may exercise his monopoly power to force down the price – the machinery has no supply price. Now this risk must mean that the rate of interest paid on this capital is that much higher. Now, if the consuming firm decides to make this product this risk is absent and it may well be that this difference in capital costs may well offset the relative inefficiency in actual operating.
>
> (ibid.)

It is important to note that this explanation basically stems from Coase's (1988b: 26) 'basic position [that] was (and is) the same as Plant's, that our economic system is in the main competitive'. The explanation has to be found in the competitive conditions that channel the repair of an inefficient situation caused by transaction issues. Therefore, the prominence of the firm reflects the normal working of the economic system. This perspective explains the vertical integration instance as addressing a potential impediment to transact. It stands out against the position of integration as a competition restricting device. The upshot is that the analysis in terms of transaction costs amounts to a search for alternative institutional routes in the working of the economic system. Coase's basic position of an economic system that is in the main competitive enables him to formulate theoretical laws à la Kaufmann, for example, of equalizing the marginal cost of Coase's organizing between alternative institutional set-tings of a transaction.

The long Coase quote prefigures what would become a central theme in transaction cost economics: asset specificity. Apparently, Coase may be a pio-neer in more than just one respect. Interdependence, particularly technologi-cal, might make partners who conclude an incomplete contract vulnerable to attenuation of their property rights. Asset specificity would promise to liberate the transaction cost theory from its tautological image, explaining vertical in-tegration. Hereafter, I discuss contributions to it from Williamson (1975, 1985); Klein, Crawford, and Alchian (1978); Klein (1988, 1998); and Coase (1988c, 2000, 2006).

Clearly, the asset specificity factor originates from interdependency in rela-tionships that are inherent to any production process. The interdependency is qualified by the degree of the division of labor. As discussed, it is humans' propensity to exchange and their preference to be engaged in the production for others that founds the division of labor. Additionally, therefore, it founds the firm as engaged in a definite type of production process that establishes its identity. The specificity of a firm results from a (de)composition of a produc-tion process that might be carried out extremely. Economies of scale and spe-cialization efficiency à la Adam Smith are driving forces behind it. In particular, industrial production processes seem to be almost endlessly decomposable and simultaneously causing (technological) interdependencies. The decomposition features a good or a service. The asset specificity discussion in new institutional economics addresses the question of whether a decomposition happens within a firm or across markets. Leading in this discussion is the idea of positive trans-action cost. Apparently, Williamson's description of a transaction corresponds to this decomposition perspective on the production process. Williamson:

> A transaction may thus be said to occur when a good or service is trans-ferred across a technologically separable interface.
>
> (1981: 1544)

It probably is Williamson's preoccupation with transaction cost that makes him confound the legal concept of 'transaction' with a switch of a good or service across production processes. However, insofar as the technologically separable interface refers to the intermediate production of two producers, a transaction refers to a preceding decomposition of a production process. Therefore, technological (de)composition questions such as specialization and integration precede the issues put on the agenda by transaction cost econo-mists. Technology, first of all, determines the structure and the working of the economy; that is, which forces determine the division of labor within and be-tween firms? In this respect, George Stigler refers to Adam Smith's (1776: 20) famous title of chapter 3 of *The Wealth of Nations*: 'That the Division of La-bour is limited by the Extent of the Market'. Specialization and scale econo-mies prompt efficiency, however, the extent of the market limits their opportunities. Clearly, a patisserie cannot survive in a sparsely populated area. Stigler points at the significance of Smith's theorem for our perspective on the firm that is engaged in a series of distinct operations:

> purchasing and storing materials; transforming materials into semifinished products and semi-finished products into finished products; storing and selling the outputs; extending credit to buyers; etc.

(1951: 187)

This view on the firm corresponds to Demsetz's (1988a: 148) concept of the 'firm as a bundle of commitments' as discussed earlier. Nevertheless, it radically differs from the perception of the firm as defined by the production function. It directs the attention to the structure of the production process of the firm. It provides a micro-microeconomic view. Obviously, this structure of production resulting from labor division has its technological rationales, and considerations of competition may affect the production structure within and between firms. Therefore, it is appropriate to discuss (technological) production structure variables before embarking on the asset specificity issue of transaction cost theory. In this aspect, I refer to Stigler's perspective on integration and disintegration that uses a simple graphic to show the cost structure of a production.

The graphic, Figure 6.1, depicts three cost functions; Y_1 decreasing, Y_2 increasing, and Y_3 as U-shaped; P = money; Q = production output. It disregards the interrelationships of the cost functions. Moreover, 'if there is a

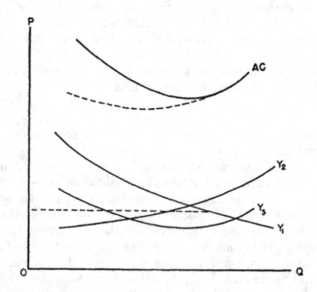

Figure 6.1 Production structure.

Source: Stigler (1951: 187).

constant proportion between the rate of output of each function and the rate of output of the final product ... we may draw the cost curves of all functions on one graph' (ibid.). The usual average cost (AC) is the vertical sum of the cost functions.

It shows that the production structure is, first of all, a technological affair. Each function, such as enumerated earlier, has its own cost structure: AC is the vertical sum of Y_1, Y_2, and Y_3. If, for instance, an auxiliary function exhibits increasing returns over a relevant range, a firm may abandon that function, 'allowing another firm (and industry) to specialize in them to take the full advantage of increasing returns' as the broken lines in Figure 6.1 depict (ibid.: 188). However, if, from a certain point of output Q, a particular function, Y_3 is subject to decreasing returns to scale, the firm may opt for outsourcing a part of the function, that is, beyond the minimum of Y_3. Furthermore, managerial rivalry between functions in the production may affect the production structure. The range of functions may overstrain a firm's coordinating capacity. Stigler notes that, if functions are rival, 'then usually the firm will increase its rate of output when it abandons a function' (ibid.: 189).

In accordance with Smith's theorem, it holds that a growing industry generates vertical disintegration. For that matter, industries exhibit a life cycle. Young industries with innovative products often require new types of materials and services and hence produce them in-house. When industries become mature and increase in size, a disintegration of functions will occur. It is the mature phase of an industry that exhibits 'progressive specialism, horizontal as well as vertical'. Finally, a decline of the industry resorts reintegrating functions and compensating lost business by taking advantage of economies of scope (ibid.: 190).

Competition versus monopoly is, besides technology, another 'earlier conception' that explains the structure of production (Williamson 1985: 1).[6] Firms integrate in order to circumvent price control by a supplying company. Non-price rationing of raw material cartels evokes their customers to integrate backward. In this respect, Stigler refers to a nineteenth-century example of backward linkage integration that occurred in Germany:

> the operation of the coal syndicate, now caused the steel companies to seek to free themselves from dependence upon the syndicate. ... Some of the large industrial consumers ... acquired their own mines individually or in groups. Among these were such important companies as the Vereinigte Stahlwerke, Rhenische Stahlwerk-Admiral, Badische Anilin- und Sodafabrik, Norddeutsche Lloyd, Friedrich Krupp.
>
> (ibid.: 191)

Another competition consideration to integrate regards the opportunity of price discrimination offered by integrating the next production phase. The diversification of products in the next phase may afford the opportunity to take advantage of the differences in demand price elasticity, for example, a transport company taking over a warehousing firm.

Stigler refers to relationships that may explain the functional structure of an industry. For instance, structural reductions in transportation costs are a major factor of disintegration. Furthermore, 'localization is one method of increasing the economic size of an industry and achieving the gains of specialization' (ibid.: 192). The latter refers to Marshall's (1890: 277) external economies.

All of these points provide some insight into the relationships that determine the structure of production. At the same time, Stigler is not very hopeful about a theoretical framework explaining the production functions of the firm. He concludes:

> As soon as one tries to classify the variegated details of production, one finds how artificial and arbitrary "vertical" relationships are.
>
> (ibid.: 191)

The extent of the market as a basic force that features the structure of the economy still remains.

Finally, Stigler alludes to the very issue of transaction cost theory as he refers to the positive cost of transactions between firms against the idea that, within firms, the transactions would be free. An example borrowed from the Birmingham small-arms industry in 1860 argues against the alleged difference.

> The master gun-maker – the entrepreneur – seldom possessed a factory or workshop. ... Usually he owned merely a warehouse in the gun quarter, and his function was to acquire semi-finished parts and to give these out to specialized craftsmen, who undertook the assembly and finishing of the gun. He purchased materials from the barrel-makers, lock-makers, sight-stampers, trigger-makers, ramrod-forgers, gun-furniture makers, and, if he were engaged in the military branch, from bayonet-forgers. All of these were independent manufacturers executing the orders of several master gun-makers. ... Once the parts had been purchased from the "material-makers," as they were called, the next task was to hand them out to a long succession of "setters-up," each of whom performed a specific operation in connection with the assembly and finishing of the gun.
>
> (Allen 1929; quoted in ibid.: 192–193)

Apparently, the transaction cost between all those independent specialized craftsmen turn out to be lower than the management cost that the master gun-maker would incur in integrated production. The quote pictures a detail from an industry that, during the 1860s, employed 5800 people within Birmingham of whom "'the majority worked within a small district round St Mary's Church'" (ibid.). The immediate vicinity of industry members suggests a close-knit society that, without a doubt, serves as a catalyst of the relative efficiency of the numerous market relationships. It emphasizes the versatility of the problem of determining the variables of an economy's production structure. The localized industries afford, as Marshall denotes, important external economies ... secured by the concentration of many small businesses of a similar character in particular locations.

(1890: 266)

Therefore, without such a substantial degree of localization, a different pattern of production relationships in the small-arms industry might be observed. Apparently, other production-structure variables exist besides technology and competition considerations. It alludes to the relevance of a social fabric as Marshall expressively sketches:

> When an industry has thus chosen a locality for itself, is likely to stay there long: so great are the advantages which people following the same skilled trade get from the neighbourhood to one another. ... Good work is rightly appreciated, inventions and improvements in machinery, in processes and the general organization of the business have their merits promptly discussed: if one man starts a new idea, it is taken up by others ...
>
> (ibid.: 271)

As yet, technological interdependence between resources holds as a solid starting point to deliberate the production structure.

From this, I return to the new institutional economics elaboration on this structure in a Coasean vein, that is, that brings in the perception of the transaction as a transfer of property rights between economic agents. In Section 6.5, I return to the significance of production issues elaborating on items such as the firm as a repository of knowledge, skills, and competence, affording the Knightian entrepreneur his profitable ventures that fuel competition in an uncertain world. First, I embark on the further elaboration of the transaction cost approach.

Against Stigler, who finds that vertical relationships are ultimately artificial and arbitrary, poses Williamson (1971: 113) 'a complete treatment of vertical integration[, that merely] requires that the limits as well as the powers of internal organization be assessed'. Against Stigler, he poses: 'technology is no bar to contracting; it is transactional considerations that are decisive' (Williamson 1975: 17). The concept of transaction cost offers the required theoretical framework to remove the seeming arbitrariness of vertical integration and actually of the organization of economic activity in general. Williamson:

> Indeed, if transaction costs are negligible, the organization of economic activity is irrelevant, since advantages one mode of organization appears to hold over another will simply be eliminated by costless contracting.[7]
>
> (1979: 233)

Apparently, Williamson (1971: 113) disregards, in this tenet, the relevance of production cost that features the organization of the production by means of 'usual scale economies and least-cost factor proportions'.[8] As demonstrated in the preliminary earlier, this is basically untenable. As yet, I follow Williamson in his emphasis on transaction cost, disregarding production cost and management cost as identified by Demsetz (1988a). It is true, Williamson (1979: 245) recognizes that 'the object is to economize on the *sum* of production and transaction costs'. At the same time, he justifies the theoretical neglect of the production cost as follows.

> To the degree production-cost economies of external procurement are small and/or the transaction costs associated with external procurement are great, alternative supply arrangements deserve serious consideration.
>
> (ibid.)

In this manner, Williamson begins elaborating the problem of the vertical integration of production as initially raised by Coase in the early 1930s in his correspondence with Fowler. For that matter, Williamson does not refer to Coase in this respect. On the contrary, he presents the awkward combination of asset specificity (i.e., idiosyncratic attributes) and vertical integration as introduced by himself. Williamson, referring a 1971 paper by himself, states:

> The proposition that the idiosyncratic attributes of transactions have large and systematic organizational ramifications first appeared in conjunction with the study of vertical integration (Williamson 1971).[9]
>
> (1985: 53)

In his elaboration of the vertical integration theme, Williamson takes three steps. The first, and fundamental in Williamson's transaction cost economics, regards his adherence to two behavioral assumptions: bounded rationality and opportunism. The latter is defined as 'a condition of self-interest seeking with guile' (Williamson 1985: 30). It is a token of a Machiavellian portrayal of man, as Williamson, together with Scott Masten, explicitly refer to elsewhere (Williamson, Masten 1999: xiii). Opportunism and humans' cognitive limitations feature Williamson's economics. He presents this perspective in an early paper on Coase's firm-versus-market alternatives (Williamson 1971). On one hand, there exists, 'on account of the bounded rationality', a greater confidence in the objectivity of market exchange when markets work well compared to the bureaucratic processes of a firm (ibid.: 113). On the other hand, when markets do not work so well, the firm renders a relatively efficient alternative as its internal organization commends: 'incentives, controls, and what may be referred to broadly as "inherent structural advantages"' (ibid.). Against an imperfectly working market in which the boundedly rational agents are doubtful, the firm is a remedy to address opportunism and offers the most distinctive advantage of the firm, that is,

> the wider variety and greater sensitivity of control instruments that are available for enforcing intrafirm in comparison with interfirm activities.
>
> (ibid.)

Furthermore, Williamson continues, the 'firm has constitutional authority', which is inexpensive access to the requisite data to monitor and the opportunity of '*intra*organizational settlement by fiat', replacing costly negotiation or litigation in the event of '*inter*organizational conflict' which 'can be settled by fiat only rarely, if at all' (ibid.: 114). To these qualities of the firm, he adds that repeated interpersonal interactions may further the economies of communication. Obviously, Williamson expands on Coase, representing a gamut of opportunities to accomplish a transaction as the basic unit of analysis. At the same time, he dismisses the overpowering role of economic rationality as defined by, for example, Kaufmann, replacing it for organizational management concepts.

The second step in the study of vertical integration is defining the critical dimensions of a transaction. Williamson distinguishes three of them:

1. Uncertainty;
2. Frequency;
3. Asset specificity.

Uncertainty reflects the world of imperfect information and markets that generate transaction costs. Frequency refers to the degree of recurrence of a transaction. The very critical dimension regards the third about 'the degree to which durable transaction-specific investments are incurred' (Williamson 1979: 239). It is the combination of uncertainty and frequency that substantiates the transaction-dimensioning impact of asset specificity. Uncertainty might be obviated by contractual arrangements for contingencies. Frequently recurring transactions may generate a mutual dependency. However, a transaction-specific investment generates a dependency that may be exploited opportunistically whenever a contingency occasions it. Transaction-specific expenses are nonmarketable in the event of severance of the business relation. They render a transaction 'idiosyncratic' (ibid.: 240). Besides physical investments that render a transaction idiosyncratic, it is human investment, for example, personal knowledge and skillfulness acquired during the job, that may generate dependency. Later on, Williamson (1983: 526) distinguishes site specificity and dedicated specificity, that is, capacity dedicated to a single customer.

Williamson provides some illustrations of idiosyncratic transactions caused by physical asset investment that are reminiscent of the American car industry issues that Coase investigated in preparation of his 'Firm' paper. Williamson states:

> Examples are (1) the purchase of a specialized component from an outside supplier or (2) the location of a specialized plant in a unique, proximate relation to a downstream processing stage to which it supplies vital input.
>
> (1979: 242)

Specific investments, scale economies, and the absence of alternative buyers effectively lock the parties into a bilateral monopoly. It exemplifies the idiosyncratic transaction as the extreme of a spectrum on which the very opposite concerns a transaction that is feasible for standardization and subjected to large numbers of competition. The intermediate regards transactions that contain contractual ambiguities that are susceptible to contingencies, that is, more or less incomplete contracts. Apparently, the critical dimensions generate a broad spectrum of different transactions.

The third and final step in Williamson's analysis is determining what he refers to as the governance structure that is appropriate to economize on transaction cost in order to limit the effects of bounded rationality and the harmful effects that opportunism has on efficiency; a governance structure that matches a transaction. In his 1979 *Journal of Law and Economics* paper, he considers three broad governance structures: 'non-transaction specific, semi-specific, and highly specific' (ibid.: 247). First, '*Market Governance: Classical Contracting*' is the appropriate structure to govern the non-specific transaction. Its non-specificity and the presence of competing suppliers forestall harmful opportunism. The contracting is attendant on cashing mutual benefit. Second, '*Trilateral Governance: Neoclassical Contracting*' is an intermediate institutional form that focuses on completing contracts that involved specialized investments, for example, by means of '*third-party assistance* (arbitration) in resolving disputes' rather than restoring reliance on litigation as used in classical contracting. Third, '*Transaction-specific Governance: Relational Contracting*' applies to 'recurring transactions of mixed and highly idiosyncratic kinds'. In this respect, Williamson further distinguishes two types of governance structures. One is '*(a) Bilateral Governance: Obligational Contracting*' that is applicable to transactions when production requires extensively specialized human and physical assets. The buyer depends on interfirm supply as he cannot realize scale economies himself (through vertical integration). The transaction specificity gains relevance when the adaptation of a contract is at issue. Adaptation across a market interface may be susceptible to opportunism and 'can be accomplished only by mutual, follow-on agreements'. In this respect, Williamson recognizes, in considering a contract adaptation, a trade-off between, on one hand, the incentive of a party to sustain the relationship and, on the other, preserving the separate profit stream that a party appropriates from the existing contract. Finally, transactions that become increasingly idiosyncratic weaken the incentives for trading across the market interface. It prompts: '*(b) Unified Governance: Internal Organization*', that is, vertical integration,

> as the specialized human and physical assets become more specialized to a single use, and hence less transferable to other uses, economies of scale can be as fully realized by the buyer as by an outside supplier ... vertical integration will invariably appear in these circumstances.
>
> (ibid.: 252–253)

Stated differently, the governance choice becomes indifferent regarding production cost. Apparently, Williamson holds opportunism as decisive. What counts are the adaptive properties of the governance mode that are required for idiosyncratic transactions. To substantiate the case for vertical integration, Williamson enumerates the advantages of internal organizations. For instance, adaptations do not require 'to consult, complete, and revise interfirm agreements'. Extensive adaptability of the highly idiosyncratic transactions by fiat and administration features the vertically integrated interface. Additionally, single ownership warrants joint profit maximization (ibid.: 248–253).

The upshot of the tripartite analysis – behavioral assumptions, transaction dimensions, and governance structures – is the exploration of hazards of opportunism that manifest in transaction-specific relationships followed by the formulation of bilateral contracts or proposing integration to address opportunism. Actually, classical contracting as market governance for nonspecific transactions is a nonissue in Williamson's analysis. Rating services, the experiences of others of the standardized good, and other alternative purchase and supply arrangements constitute a whole of market practices that 'protect[s] each party against opportunism by his opposite' (ibid.: 249). Williamson's main behavioral concept is opportunism, which renders the idiosyncrasy of the transaction, that is, the degree of asset specificity, the very explaining variable in Williamson's transaction cost theory. In his *The Economic Institutions of Capitalism*, he recaps it as follows, assuming that the economies of scale and scope are negligible:

> Thus market procurement is the preferred supply where asset specificity is slight. … But internal organization is favored where asset specificity is great. … the switchover value, where the choice between firm and market is one of indifference, occurs at $\bar{k}$.
>
> (Williamson 1985: 91)

Obviously, the crucial variable is k, that is, 'an index of asset specificity' (ibid.: 91). Williamson presents k as a quantified variable depicted on the x-axis of Figures 4.1 and 4.2 in his book (ibid.: 91, 93). Apart from changing symbol A into a k, and a slightly different shape of the $\Delta C + \Delta G$ line, Figure 4.2 corresponds to Figure 2 used in a 1984 paper (Williamson 1984: 213). Like the latter two figures, Figure 6.2 takes account of the economies of scale that the market offers relative to in-house production.[10] It takes into account both production and governance costs. The relative production-cost disadvantages of internal organizations for standardized, nonspecific transactions are high as market procurement may benefit from economies of scale and scope. The difference is denoted as ΔC. The disadvantage decreases when asset specificity increases but remains positive. Against this relationship stands the governance-cost differences between internal organization versus market procurement, denoted as ΔG. When asset specificity increases, market-procurement cost increases likewise and will finally outstrip the internal-organization cost, rendering a negative

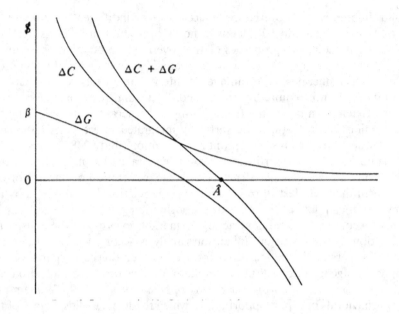

Figure 6.2 Representative Net Production and Governance Cost Difference.
(*Source:* Williamson 1984: 213)

cost difference between internal organizations and market procurement, that is, $\Delta G < 0$. At a certain value of the increasing A, $\hat{A}$ in Figure 6.2, the vertical sum of production-cost and governance-cost differences becomes negative, $\Delta C + \Delta G < 0$, that is, the switchover value for opting for vertical integration. It is relevant to note that these cost relationships concern, on one hand, the production cost of a discernable stage as part of 'successive production stages'. For convenience, 'the output is assumed to be constant' (ibid.: 212). On the other hand, the analytical problem concerns the transaction, that is, whether this specific stage of the production process should be outsourced. The sum of differences in production and (transaction) procurement costs is decisive.

The three implications that Williamson links to this exposition are the threesome he repeatedly presents: market procurement versus internal organization with mixed governance as the intermediate option (ibid.: 214). Mindful of Williamson's adage, 'In the beginning there were markets', Figure 6.2 basically represents market transactions except for instances in which asset specificity exceeds $\hat{A}$ (Williamson 1975: 20, 1985: 87). It is reminiscent of Adam Smith as the exponent of division of labor.

Rightly, Williamson (1984: 212) refers to his exposition as depicted in Figure 6.2 as 'a heuristic display of what is at stake' in the choice between internal organization versus market procurement. Asset specificity is central to it. For that matter, he omits the other critical dimensions of the transaction, that is, uncertainty and frequency. A variation in these would further complicate the analysis.

As yet, Figure 6.2 cannot serve but for heuristic purposes indeed as Williamson does not operationalize key variable asset specificity, that is, A. Therefore, it is not possible to substantiate the functions as depicted in Figure 6.2, that is, $\Delta C = f(A)$, and $\Delta G = f(A)$. Furthermore, assuming that A might be determined, the concepts of ΔC and ΔG demand to be calculated for which the theorist is faced with additional, and unbridgeable, issues. The calculation of ΔC results from comparing internal-production versus market-procurement cost. And so, the calculation of ΔG refers to the governance-cost differences between internal versus market procurements. It suggests that the internal-production cost can be calculated separately from the governance cost of internal production. Besides this, it presupposes that the governance cost of the single transaction regarding a separate stage of a successive production process can be separated from the overall governance cost of production that undoubtedly consists of several, what Stigler refers to as 'operations', as depicted in Figure 6.1 by the separate cost functions.[11] Furthermore, it is highly questionable whether such separations of cost categories are feasible. ΔC assumes that the production cost of market procurement does not coincide with the market price as its governance cost will assumingly be calculated separately. As discussed, Demsetz (1988a: 145) notes that any production mode entails both internal organization and market transactions, that is, management and transaction cost. Moreover, it is the integral sum of management, transaction, *and* production cost that is decisive. In this aspect, Williamson's exclusive focus on economies of scale and scope as determining the production cost in the trade-off between internal versus market production is not sound. Williamson poses:

> The production cost penalty of using internal organization is great for standardized transactions for which market aggregation economies are great, whence ΔC is large where A is low.
>
> (1984: 213)

As Figure 6.2 depicts, the line segment left of the $\hat{A}$ market procurement is relatively efficient. However, the cost structure refers to a single, unique transaction regarding an assumingly given output representing a production stage, that is, an operation, as implied by the variable definition of A. However, as noted, the nonspecific, standardized transaction is one out of a number of transactions regarding operations that are required for production. Therefore, for production-technological reasons, that is, production-cost reasons, may be refrained from market procurement of the nonspecific transaction. Furthermore, the varying production structure as depicted in Figure 2 in the 1984 paper (ibid.) makes it hard to reconcile with 'the output is assumed to be constant' (ibid.: 212). The plausible interpretation of the assumption as referring to the output quantity does not clarify the presentation, as an allowed qualitative variation of output makes it unfit for further comparative analysis. The *non sequitur* is that a varying production structure, that is, varying asset specificity, would leave the qualitative nature of the output undisturbed.

Finally, it is rather difficult to understand the negative component of the ΔG curve. The governance cost differences between internal and market organization may become negative in terms of costs. For the line segment to the right of $\hat{A}$, there is no cost of market organization, reads Williamson's analysis. From point $\hat{A}$, the negative ΔG must be interpreted as a negative bureaucratic cost. Yet, it seems rather difficult to quantify such a change of positive bureaucratic cost disadvantage from, initially β in Figure 6.2, into a negative bureaucratic cost disadvantage, that is, into bureaucratic revenue, an actually heuristic use of cost categories explicating a presupposed explanation.

Obviously, the final step in Williamson's analysis, that is, the search for a match between governance structure and transaction, does not yield undisputable outcomes. Furthermore, the several issues that the theorist faces in his attempt to substantiate the presumed relationships raise serious doubt about Williamson's promise that his analysis would yield 'refutable implications' (ibid.: 196).

Finally, I return to the first step in the analysis, that is, Williamson's behavioral assumptions: bounded rationality and opportunism. An agent's bounded rationality manifests in the uncertainty dimension of the transaction and might find mitigation in its frequent recurrence; however, frequency is no warrant against future failures. Bounded rationality emphasizes the information issues of incomplete contracting that may involve future adaptations. However, the more prominent human trait in the analysis is opportunism, which comprises the significance of the key variable transaction specificity of human and physical assets. The dependency that the specific assets generate occasions the independent party to follow Machiavelli's advice to breach the contract with impunity "'*whenever* the reasons which him bind himself no longer exist'" (Machiavelli, quoted in Williamson, Masten 1999: xiii; emphasis added). However, Williamson and Masten assert that, 'through the lens of governance', hazards of opportunism such nonstandard contracting 'can be mitigated by those who look ahead, perceive potential conflict, and craft private ordering supports which infuse confidence' (ibid.). A variety of relational contracting presents itself 'to serve efficiency purposes when viewed through the lens of governance' (ibid.). At the same time, these excellences of the lens of governance raise the question of whether they are consistent with the bounded rationality that is assumed, *quod non*. All the same, opportunism appears to be an inspiring idea, to which I return later.

An internal organization is a safe haven against the market where opportunism lies in wait to put the dependent, ill-informed, and boundedly rational trading partner at a disadvantage. Integration addresses opportunism. In his *Markets and Hierarchies*, Williamson expands on his organizational management concepts. He proposes:

> Internal organization enjoys advantages of three kinds over market modes of contracting in circumstances where opportunism and small numbers conditions are joined.[12]

(Williamson 1975: 29)

The first advantage is that the parties within the organization compared to autonomous contractors are less able to appropriate subgoal gains at the expense of the overall organization. Second, and related, the internal organization has a greater number of effective monitoring opportunities. Third, the internal organization is relatively advantageous in settling disputes and conflicts in an informal manner (ibid.).

> The upshot is that internal organization is less vulnerable to the hazards of opportunism when – either from the outset, or as is more commonly the case, as a result of idiosyncratic experience during contract execution – a small numbers exchange condition obtains.
>
> (ibid.: 30)

Williamson finds further support for the superiority of internal organization in its 'language advantages', which is significant in two respects. First, an efficient internal code permits communicating idiosyncratic conditions to overcome information impactedness. Second, internal parties face the prospect of being experience-rated, which will discourage opportunistic representations regarding, for instance, their qualifications to perform (ibid.: 35–36).

> The upshot is that, however well-developed experience-rating is in interfirm contracting respects, intrafirm evaluations are apt to be even more refined. Both horizontal and vertical integration may occur for this reason.
>
> (ibid.: 37)

Apparently, the authority of internal organization is Williamson's very weapon against opportunism and rent seeking with guile. It is a panacea: 'integration harmonizes interests (or reconciles differences, often by fiat) and permit an efficient (adaptive, sequential) decision process to be utilized' (ibid.: 95). The virtues of 'an authoritative order' explain the integration of businesses (ibid.: 101).

However, Williamson's appreciation of the internal organization needs to be qualified. First, the integration of firms widens the span of control. Assuming bounded rationality, this challenges the information issues. For instance, additional organizational layers threaten the effectiveness of the authoritative order. Second, an increase in information asymmetries will accompany an integration. Stated differently, new opportunism possibilities announce themselves. For instance, Alchian and Demsetz (1972) identify the problem of shirking within the firm. Moreover, the firm as an authority is not a monolith but may conceal conflicting interests, for example, between managers and owners (Berle, Means 1932). It is as Frank Knight already noted before Berle and Means regarding an organization's superiority as an

> effective unification of interest which reduces the moral hazard connected with the assumption by one person of the consequences of another's person decisions', … 'there is still much to be desired. Doubtless the task is impossible, in any absolute sense.
>
> (1921: 253)

Third, as Gregory Dow (1987: 20) notes, 'transaction cost theorists tend to see authority primarily as a *remedy* for opportunism, rather than as a device which might be *abused* in an opportunistic fashion'. Under conditions such as information advantage and dependency, an authority's tool of decision by fiat is 'tailor-made for unilateral pursuit of [a firm's manager's] self-interest' (ibid.: 21). Fourth, authority as the remedy for opportunism and conflicts accords with a Machiavellian world view. Another aspect is that opportunism-restraining authority requires monitoring and 'a capacity to impose sanctions when abuses are detected' (ibid.: 22). Therefore, against wielding power as authority, participation of employees in control issues that attenuates authority may offer management advantages.

The upshot of Williamson's analysis is that opportunism appears to be the decisive behavioral assumption. Whenever asset specificity acquires a specific value, $\hat{A}$, vertical integration is the appropriate response to opportunism. However, it appears that vertical integration cannot always secure removing opportunism. On the contrary, new instances of opportunism and the effects of bounded rationality announce themselves. Williamson introduces the authority of a hierarchical organization as a *deus ex machina* in his theory that apparently does not succeed in completely finishing opportunism. Methodologically, this is a significant caesura that I return to.

It is now appropriate to direct attention to Williamson's (1984: 196) promise to 'develop refutable implications' of the organizational insights deepened in the paper discussed. It is doubtful whether this promise of his positivist ambition may be redeemed. The empirical research of his declared heuristic model faces issues such as operationalizing asset specificity, identifying governance cost in general, and insulating production and governance cost of the concerned transaction. However, as Paul Joskow notes, referring to the lack of a rigorous mathematical foundation of the determinants of vertical integration, that

> [w]hat passes as "theory" is little more than toy models with no obvious value in explaining real economic phenomena. Really good theory is too rare but is of fundamental importance to our *understanding* of these phenomena.
>
> (Joskow 1988: 101, n. 11; emphasis added)

Taking the methodological details of Joskow's note for granted as far as it regards refutable implications, I discuss some empirical research on the central tenet regarding asset specificity and the organization of economic activity. What may this transaction-cost theory add to the understanding of the 'institutional structure of production'? (Coase 1992). In general, transaction-cost theory exhibits its appealingly empirical relevance as an alternative to the neoclassical perfect-competition model in explaining the variety of institutional arrangements such as franchising, vertical and horizontal integration, contractual vertical restraints, joint ventures, and certain other horizontal agreements.

The concept of transaction cost and the idea of attendant information imperfections offer a new perspective on integration phenomena that neoclassical theory can explain only as effects of scale economies or efforts to curb competition and founding monopolism.

However, what is at issue is the empirical question to confirm this refutable implication: If assets become more specific and appropriable quasi-rents are increasingly created (and therefore the opportunistic behavior increases), then the costs of market procurement increase more than the costs of vertical integration. Besides Williamson, for instance, Benjamin Klein, Robert Crawford, and Armen Alchian arrive at a corresponding proposition (Klein et al. 1978). Before further elaborating on the empirical counterpart of it, I recap Klein et al.'s approach.

Klein et al. show how the market for long-term contracts takes account of opportunism. It concerns a so-called implicit contractual guarantee against opportunism enforced by the market mechanism. It is the opposite of 'an explicitly stated contractual guarantee' that is particularly legally enforceable (ibid.: 303). The latter raises the costs of policing and litigation and, potentially, the enforcement cost in court. It refers to Williamson's (1979: 249) trilateral governance. Klein at al.'s discussion of the implicit contractual guarantee is sophisticated. Herein, opportunism finds its pendant in reputation that is the wager of self-interest-maximizing conduct of agents who are rent seeking with guile. A way in which the implicit market guarantee works as explained by Klein et al. follows. It offers

> to the potential cheater a future "premium," more precisely, a price sufficiently greater than average variable (that is, avoidable) cost to assure a quasi-rent stream that will exceed the potential gain from cheating.
>
> (Klein et al.: 304)

It is a trade-off between the present-discounted value of the benefits of one's reputation against the once-only gain of cheating. As long as the party who is vulnerable to opportunism offers the premium as defined, he is protected against opportunism.

First of all, Klein et al. exhibit the opportunism assumption in their elaboration which is a paragon of the Machiavellian worldview, to wit, that whenever it is profitable to cheat, just cheat. Opportunism prevails. At the same time, calculating such a sophisticated trade-off again questions the bounded rationality assumption. Obviously, it is the bounded rationality of the economic agents in a world of imperfect information that occasions opportunism. Therefore, this exercise on the feasibility of long-term contracts in the analysis of Klein et al. is rather a prelude to the ultimate solution to opportunism: vertical integration. They acknowledge that, the larger the appropriable specialized quasi-rents (degrees of asset specificity) become, the more inappropriate becomes the transaction contract of the implicit guarantee against opportunism as a solution, as 'the larger the premium payments necessary to prevent contractual reneging' must be (ibid.: 307). Against this, 'it is reasonable to assume', Klein et al. posit,

> that any internal coordination or other ownership costs are not systematically related to the extent of the appropriable specialized quasi rent of the physical asset owned.
>
> > (ibid.)

Therefore, in accordance with Williamson, Klein et al. conclude that manifesting asset specificity results in 'integration by common or joint ownership' (ibid.). In its completeness the proposition as derived by Williamson and Klein et al. reads as follows:

> Hence we can reasonably expect the following general empirical regularity to be true: the lower the appropriable specialized quasi rents, the more likely that transactors will rely on a contractual relationship rather than common ownership. And conversely, integration by common or joint ownership is more likely, the higher the appropriable specialized quasi rents of the assets involved.
>
> > (ibid.)

Aside, a slight difference between them may be noted. Williamson deems the authority of the internal organization the remedy against opportunism as caused by asset specificity. Contrariwise, Klein et al. apparently rely on ownership as the incentive-generating device to address opportunism, implicitly alluding to the concept of residual claimant to which I return later.

As noted, it is no sinecure to ascertain the empirical evidence of Williamson's and Klein et al.'s refutable implication. First, a number of interfering variables thwarts the *ceteris paribus* conditions it entails. For instance, the analysis of Stigler as discussed above generates variables that complicate the hypotheses of the transaction cost theory. The search for empirical evidence of a relationship as concerned amounts to a type of hypothesis testing 'that is quite common in economics', that is, whether the single relationship that is postulated is consistent with the data. The alternative to the null hypothesis is that the likeliness of vertical integration increases when the transaction is increasingly specific. The problem is, Joskow (1988: 108) notes, that 'an alternative theory is not provided here'. In this context, Coase states the problem as follows:

> What readers were no doubt hoping to discover about the relation of the costs of contracting and of vertical integration appears as an assumption.
>
> > (1988b: 43)

Second, as noted, it is quite an issue to provide an empirical measurement of both the dependent and the independent variables of the concerned relationship. It concerns issues that are inherent to the methodologically instrumentalist view to which I return in Section 6.6, on methodology. After an enumeration of empirical issues, Paul Joskow concludes:

> The best we can hope for more qualitative information on variation in the importance of asset specificity.
>
> (1988: 106)

The almost canonical instance of empirical research to substantiate that opportunism leads to vertical integration is General Motors' (GM's) take-over of Fisher Body. *Nota bene*, it is opportunism rather than asset specificity that is the explanatory variable in the following. Fisher Body's investment in dies for stamping body parts for GM models makes the supply agreement between Fisher Body and GM the very illustration of asset specificity. This concept constitutes the background of Klein's et al. account of the GM–Fisher-Body relationship during the early decades of the twentieth century (Klein et al. 1978). The points Klein et al. refer to must be conceived as the buildup to the merger of 1926. In 1919, GM concluded 'a ten-year contractual agreement with Fisher Body for the supply of closed auto bodies' (ibid.: 308). The exclusive contractual conditions eliminated GM's post-contractual threats toward Fisher Body. However, this exclusiveness would offer Fisher Body a monopoly position. 'The price was set on a cost plus 17.6 per cent basis (where cost was defined exclusive of interest on invested capital)' and should be comparable to prices charged to GM's competitors (ibid.: 309). In the years after 1919, the shift from open to closed bodies generated a strong increase in the demand for the latter. 'Meanwhile GM was very unhappy with the price it was being charged by its now important supplier Fisher' (ibid.). GM believed that Fisher Body's price increases stemmed, for a substantial part, from capital cost that was not included in the original contract. Moreover, Fisher Body refused to meet GM's wish to locate their body plants adjacent to GM' assembly plants. Klein et al. conclude that

> [b]y 1924, GM had found the Fisher contractual relationship intolerable and began negotiations for purchase of the remaining stock in Fisher Body, culminating in a final merger agreement in 1926.
>
> (ibid.: 310)

Fisher Body's opportunism resulted in a vertical integration, Klein et al. argue. In his comment on Coase's critique of the Klein et al. paper, Klein (1988: 202) contends that GM's dramatic increase in demand for closed metal bodies 'moved the contractual arrangement outside of the self-enforcing range and made it profitable for Fisher to hold up General Motors'. Klein substantiates his claim as follows:

Fisher effectively held up General Motors by adopting a relatively ineffi-cient, highly labor-intensive technology and by refusing to locate the body-producing plants adjacent to General Motors assembly plant.

(ibid.)

In his *New Palgrave* entry, 'Hold-Up Problem', Klein repeats and further un-derpins this. According to him, it is the 'contractually induced hold-up poten-tial' that led to GM' takeover action of 1926 (ibid.: 203). In this manner, new effects of incomplete contracting appear that are not mentioned in the original 1978 paper. In a special issue of *The Journal of Law and Economics* on vertical integration of 2000, Klein's contribution is another defense of the original po-sition taken by Klein et al. in 1978. Admittedly, Klein (2000: 106) notes, it is true that the 1919 contract between GM and Fisher Body 'initially worked well, [but] broke down in 1925 when GM' demand for Fisher bodies increased dramatically. Compared to the 1978 paper, it is another new dimension in the argument. The additional demand led to an increase in Fisher's sales-to-capital ratio stemming from Fisher's refusal 'to make the necessary capital investments required to produce bodies efficiently for GM' (ibid). In this respect, Klein re-fers to Alfred Sloan, who testifies that

the contractually fixed percentage upcharge on noncapital costs (17.6 per-cent) resulted in prices that were too high because it implied a margin that was more than sufficient to provide a normal rate of return on capital.

(ibid.: 115)

The unanticipated demand increase for bodies by GM that occurred in 1925–1926 generated the 'malincentives associated with the cost-plus contract terms' (ibid.: 129). The main point was the dispute about Fisher Body's refusal to locate a new body plant near GM's Flint assembly plant. A persistent frus-tration for GM was the shipping cost of transporting the bodies from Detroit to Flint (57 miles) plus the cost of loading and unloading. On these costs, 'could Fisher add 17.6 percent', Klein puts forward (ibid.: 116).

Contingencies such as an unanticipated rise in demand increase the value of the hold-up option as present in every imperfect contract make vertical inte-gration more likely. *A fortiori*, Klein argues, this holds when 'sufficient reputa-tional capital' lacks to sustain a flexible contractual arrangement (ibid.: 139). It explains GM's takeover action as it shifts the operating control of Fisher Body from the Fisher brothers to GM, avoiding 'the difficulties created by the alternative mechanism of control, the imperfect long-term, fixed-price-for-mula body supply contract' (ibid.: 133). Therefore, Klein concludes,

it is important to consider more than the narrow transaction costs of spot contracting (discovering prices and executing contracts) upon which Coase focuses.

(ibid.: 138)

This comment on Coase balances Klein's (2000) paper that defends his position in the GM–Fisher Body debate as it also reads in the Klein et al. paper of 1978. Particularly, the comment is a defense against Coase's vehemently criticizing the claim that opportunism led to GM's 1926 takeover of Fisher Body. In one of his last papers, Coase (2006) recaps his critique, attaching a methodological subsection.

In the ten years after its publication, the 1978 paper of Klein et al. 'was much cited (226 times)', although the Fisher Body versus GM case attracted little further attention, Coase (2006: 256) notes. At the same time, the Fisher Body–GM case has acquired a canonical status in the new institutional economics of organization and contract theory. Williamson's (1985: 115) *The Economic Institutions of Capitalism* refers to the Fisher Body–GM relationship as 'consistent with the overarching argument' that deepening of transaction-specific investments eventually yields to 'unified governance'. Bengt Holmström and John Roberts recap 'the classic hold-up story told by Klein et al. as follows:

> In either case, inefficiency results: either the market does not bring about optimal investment, or resources are expended on socially wasteful defensive measures. Having the auto company own the dies solves the problem.
>
> (1998: 74)

Coase (2006: 263) refers to a number of other publications that repeat the account of the Klein et al. paper. However, the 'tale told by Klein' and by Klein et al. is not just mostly improbable, but it is, in fact, also untrue, Coase (2000: 27) argues. The injurious behavior of Fisher Body against GM is improbable as the years preceding the 1926 takeover form a period of close relationships between the two companies. For instance, Fred Fisher was, in 1922, 'appointed as a member of the executive committee of General Motors' (ibid.: 24). The aim was to ensure effective communication between the companies by Fred Fisher becoming involved in GM's '"broad decisions production, products design, output and pricing that inevitably affected the work of his own organization"' (Fisher Body's work), as noted by Alfred Chandler and Stephen Salsbury (1971: 576; quoted in Coase 2000: 24). In his 2000 paper, Coase reports the details of the personal relationships between GM executives and the Fisher brothers, concluding that

> [i]Indeed, it is ludicrous to suppose that the Fisher brothers, occupying the most senior positions in the General Motors organization, would have engaged in the practices injurious to General Motors that are described by Klein.
>
> (2000: 26)

Moreover, Coase demonstrates that it is patently untrue that the plant location issue, as put forward by Klein et al., would be a matter of opportunism.

Obviously, location was not an issue in the Fisher Body–GM relationship in the period between 1921 and 1925 as approximately ten body plants of Fisher Body were built near GM assembly plants. Klein et al.'s claim that Fisher Body 'refused to locate their body plants adjacent to General Motors plants' is based on a specific dispute between GM and Fisher Body about a new body plant that GM wanted constructed in Flint, Michigan, to meet the growing Buick sales 'while Fisher Body wanted to expand production in its Detroit plant' (Coase 2006: 267). Apparently, the dispute merely concerns a matter of diverging interests and not a *per se* witness of a hold-up by Fisher Body. As Coase wonders: 'Are the coach passengers who resist the highwayman holding up the highwayman?' (ibid.: 270).

Therefore, asset specificity does not *per se* entail vertical integration as the business history between A. O. Smith and GM demonstrates. When Coase (1988c: 45) visited the A. O. Smith plant in Milwaukee in 1932, the firm manufactured important automobile parts made 'with expensive and highly specific equipment' and 'shipped over hundreds of miles to the GM assembly plants'. In 1979, A. O. Smith was said to still be one of the world's largest independent producers of automobile frames, and GM was still a major customer (ibid.). In this respect, Coase refers to his incidental discovery during research as an employee of the British Central Statistical Office. Information in long-term contracts could not help forecast the demand for labor as they were incomplete. Remembering this, Coase (2006: 261) adds, 'made me more confident in my view that opportunism was not a major factor determining how industry was organized'.

Furthermore, contractual provisions may forestall the presumed opportunism that asset specificity would generate. For instance, the 1919 GM–Fisher Body contract states 'that "a die and special tools shall be manufactured for GM at cost plus 17.6% of such cost."' (ibid.: 267). In this aspect, Coase (2000: 29) refers to a memorandum stating that, for financing reasons, '"it would be better for General Motors Corporation to own the assembly plants, leasing them to the Fisher Company."' It would be better that GM would finance the huge investment and that Fisher Company would not 'issue further senior securities' (ibid.). This makes the favorable pricing conditions an outcome of mutual benefit, not a plausible occasion for the opportunism as put forward by Klein et al.

More points may be added to the argument that Coase puts forward that undermines opportunism as GM's ultimate reason for the 1926 takeover. The GM–Fisher Body case is as misleading as it is classic in confirming that asset specificity would lead to vertical integration to remove opportunism. Against the number of prominent exponents of new institutional economics of organizations who adhere to the GM–Fisher Body account as a reliable substantiation of the opportunism tenet appeared in three papers in 2000 that, as a remarkable coincidence, concurrently refute the Klein (and Klein et al.) account (Coase 2006: 264–268).[13] They corroborate the abundant empirical evidence that Coase opposes regarding the GM–Fisher tale of Klein et al. and

Klein. 'The linkage is weak' between asset specificity and higher cost of market governance of activities, Demsetz (1988a: 147) establishes, criticizing Williamson's book on the institutions of capitalism. For instance, asset specificity may decrease the coordination costs associated with integrating knowledge effectively, lessening the need for vertical integration (Demsetz 1988b: 169).

How to explain the canonical status of the GM–Fisher Body narrative that appears to be patently wrong? Why do several distinguished economists adhere to the narrative that vertical integration is the very remedy against opportunism? Why does Klein, in good faith, persist in defending his initial position while always adducing new dimensions to his argument? In the final part of his 2006 paper, Coase provides a methodological explanation of these questions. 'Economics as having become a theory-driven subject' does not prompt economists to '"anxiously seek the challenge of the facts"', Coase (2006: 275) notes, referring to Stigler. Coase diagnoses:

> The argument of Klein et al. was certainly logical. But it inhibited thought and, as a result, the truth was not discovered.
>
> (ibid.)

In this context, Coase's idea of blackboard economics returns, that is, a '*high level of vertical abstraction unsupported by the process of vertical abstraction*' (Mäki 1998: 16). Klein's persistent defense of his position contrary to the facts stems from practicing logical causality instead of the generative causality that departs from the economic reality of agents' mundane pursuits. Coase practices economics from within, analyzing human beings whose conduct follows the economic rationality of homunculi. This methodological stance opposes positivist economics, staging boundedly rational agents who, at the same time, are engaged in rent seeking without scruples. Section 6.6 further discusses the methodological differences.

To recap, it may be inferred that the evidence is poor that, also in plain cases of asset specificity, integration is the obvious means to remedy transaction cost issues. The concept of asset specificity fails to give structure to transaction costs as an explanatory variable. Another problematic issue in the asset specificity account is the claim that vertical integration, that is, the firm, would defuse the hazards of opportunism. As discussed, particularly Williamson (1975: 29) expands on the excellence of the firm as an internal organization device being preferred 'over market modes of contracting in circumstances where opportunism and small numbers conditions are joined'. However, it remains unclear why and how the opportunistic conduct of agents who are seeking self-interest with guile would be addressed in the internal organization. In this aspect, Williamson contends that internal organization offers the opportunity to settle 'disputes and conflicts, in an informal way' (ibid.). In the methodological individualism perspective that bears the transaction cost theory, this is a rather unsatisfactory escape. Therefore, for instance, Grossman and Hart (1986: 693, n. 1) wonder why 'integration transforms a hostile supplier into a docile employee'.[14] Presenting the advantages of internal organization as the remedy against the hazards of transaction cost issues accords with Coase's basic and seminal idea of his 'Firm' paper as founding the transaction cost theory.

6.4.3 Further elaboration on Coase's theory of the firm (2): the residual claimant

The firm is a type of intruder in the economic system that must find its explanation in the mundane reality that the prearranged mutual benefits of the property rights exchange do not come true. The origin of this failure is transaction cost, the 'Firm' paper diagnoses. The nature of this failure is a wavering exchange of property rights. Therefore, as Klein notes, the 'Social Cost' paper is a restatement of the 'Firm' paper (Kitch 1983: 202). Property rights state the substance of an economic agent's self-interest as it features in the history of economic thought. Therefore, the new institutional economic explanation of the firm as an organization and its limits must be read in terms of property rights that are safeguarded by their owner's economic rationality. This economics carelessly ignores, for instance, Williamson's organizational management as an alternative instrument to discipline the transactions. Collaterally, this economics disregards Williamson's (1985: 31) 'behavioral assumptions, i.e., bounded rationality and opportunism'.[15] Against Williamson who presents his 'organizational imperative' as 'a different and larger conception of the economic problem than does the imperative "Maximize profits!"', I hereafter discuss exponents of new institutional economics who rightly cling to what Williamson caricatures: the economic rationality as phrased by Kaufmann (1933: 391; Williamson 1985: 32).

This subsection elaborates further on new institutional economics from within with agents who act economically rational. In this aspect, the concept of a contract stipulates economic rationality. This approach accords with Coase (1937: 391), whose firm substitutes 'a series of contracts for one ... whereby a factor agrees to obey the directions of an entrepreneur *within certain limits*'. Rephrased, Coase's firm refers to a contractual transfer of property rights that offers the firm some flexibility. This flexibility is a manifestation of a firm's authority. In the analysis of Coase, the authority merely regards this flexibility; as far as strict tit-for-tat market relations do not work, a firm's direction appears within certain limits. Without the cost of using the market, the firm has no *raison d'être*. The further elaborations on Coase's analysis in this subsection take this notion for granted. However, as discussed, the authority of the firm is not restricted to the interpretation of flexible contracts. On the contrary, as noted in a reference to Adam Smith, the firm is an authority that traces back to humans' propensity to exchange one thing for another. The firm exists as an authority that is irreducible to economic categories and brings resources together in autonomous flexibility. Therefore, in the following, this is the definition of the firm that remains unimpaired:

a cohesive, durable legal entity of an entrepreneur not per se with employees, who brings together resources to substantiate an idea of production, and to sell its product to others.

The firm combines the resources of several owners who exchange their property rights. In this aspect, Steven Cheung denotes an important distinction. On one hand, the firm is engaged in partial transfers of property rights such as a lease or a hire as opposites of an outright transfer of them (Cheung 1969: 23). On the other hand, in contrast to those agents who partially transfer their property rights stands the owner of the firm who aims to govern the use of the contractually stipulated property rights as a residual claimant. The analysis concerns the '*structure*' of the partial transfer of rights against those of the owner. Cheung recaps this contract structure as follows:

> The stipulations, or terms, which constitute the structure of the contract are, as a rule, designed to specify (a) the distribution of income among the participants, and (b) the conditions of resource use.
>
> (1970: 50)

In the zero-transaction-cost world, the remuneration among the members of the firm enhances efficient use of resources. Furthermore, if the output varies due to a natural risk such as weather conditions, the members may nevertheless conclude an optimal risk allocation. It is the world in which the Coase Theorem holds and perfect competition prevails. The distribution of the rewards among the members corresponds with their respective marginal contribution to the production. The zero-transaction-cost assumption assures what John B. Clark explicated two decades after the Marginal Revolution of the 1870s. Clark:

> The farmer is here the master of the situation, and he hires men from other employments till the product that he gets by means of their labor only offsets the sums that he must pay to them.
>
> (1891: 307)

The productivity of the production factors translates itself into a corresponding distribution of income. However, positive transaction cost fractures this correspondence and generates inefficiency as it thwarts agents' economic rationality. Apparently, the contractually arranged transfer of property rights fails. The endeavor to push back the inefficiency renders that 'the direction of causation is the reverse', as Alchian and Demsetz (1972: 778) succinctly note. Appropriate rewards prompt productivity. Obviously, tightening the connection between reward and productivity improves the efficiency of production. Incentive alignment becomes the denominator of new institutional economic theories. How to safeguard the prearranged mutual benefits of the rights transfer under the conditions of positive transaction cost risks regarding the input–output relationships and the legal-institutional setting. An additional question is how to maximize efficiency of resources that omit definition of property rights. Hereafter, I pass in review some theories that address this question.

Cheung (1970: 51) frames the issue of incentive alignment in terms of '"externalities" [which are] attributable to either (1) the absence of the right to contract', for example, marine fishing grounds; (2) incomplete contracting; or (3) to a contract stipulation that is inconsistent with marginal equalities, for example, a lump-sum remuneration. The differences between the cases are only a matter of degree. Directly relevant to the firm are the second and third cases. The firm may reap the fruit of production efficiency when combining resources of different owners. It requires partially transferring property rights, incurring a cost of negotiating, and enforcing the stipulation of the contract. Furthermore, it is rightly the partial nature of the transfer of property rights that may expose the contractual members to uncalculated, although economically relevant, effects, for example, a lessee's careless use of the leased asset may impair a lessor's present value of the asset. Apparently, the former generates an externality, deteriorating the latter's property rights without compensating him. These insights accompany Cheung in discussing contract choices in (Asian) agriculture.

Three main forms of contract circulate in agriculture, 'namely, a fixed-rent contract (rent per acre stated in cash or in crop), a share contract and a wage contract' (Cheung 1969: 25). Apart from transaction cost, output risk is an item that, in agriculture, may affect the contract choice. In this aspect, Cheung advances this hypothesis:

> the choice of contractual arrangement is made so as to maximize the gain from risk dispersion subject to the constraint of transaction costs.
>
> (ibid.)

It is risk aversion that prompts the choice of a share contract. It disperses the income variances due to the risk of the nature or state of the world to which agriculture is exposed. Insurance theory instructs that, considering risk aversion and taking account of the insurance cost, there may be an efficiency gain of risk dispersion. Besides, transaction cost will further profile the contract choice as physical features of input and output differ and require sets of stipulations that demand varying efforts in negotiation and enforcement (ibid.). It is required to juxtapose the efficiency gain of a dispersion of income variances against the relatively high transaction cost of a share contract and compare its assessment to a fixed-rent or a wage contract. A share contract contains stipulations concerning rental percentage, 'the ratio of non-land input to land, and the types of crops to be grown' (ibid.). They require negotiations between landowner and tenant whose interests do not converge in all respects. Furthermore, the landowner must ascertain the actual harvest yield on which his share is based. Shortly, the negotiation and enforcement cost of a share contract in comparison with a fixed-rent or a wage contract are substantial (ibid.: 25–26).

A landowner's choice between a fixed-rent and a wage contract is ambiguous. On one hand, a fixed-rent contract incentivizes the labor input whereas the cost of enforcing the land input is low, if any. On the other hand, a wage contract is relatively difficult to enforce whereas it is conducive to 'policing (or enforcing) the maintenance of soil and other assets owned by the landlord' ibid.: 26). The difference in risk allocation is clear. The wage contract allocates the yield risk to the landlord; the fixed-rent contract to the tenant. As dispersion of risk may offer efficiency, a share contract is a third contract option. As such, they exhibit their tautological value.

These considerations, Cheung proposes, tailor the contract stipulations in agriculture. The nature of the industry urges the theorist to take account of risk allocation. At the same time, Cheung's main analytical perspective is the externality frame, as noted earlier. The recurring questions in stipulating a contract are, Does it offer opportunities to deviate from the prearranged mutual benefits that would result from everyone's contribution that is agreed on? and How can one another's property rights be safeguarded when executing the contract? Cheung illustrates his analysis with some agricultural evidence that may be interpreted in terms of a trade-off between risk allocation and transaction cost. I discuss two instances.

The first is an interesting example that he borrows from the French landed gentry. French *seigneurs*

> let out their lands in *gros* to middlemen or *fermiers* (to be distinguished from *fermiers exploitants*), who paid a fixed sum to the proprietor and gathered the rents from *metayage* or from *censitaires* at their own risk for a personal profit.[16]
>
> (Maxwell, quoted in Cheung 1969: 28)

A *fermier* as a third party, on one hand, circumvents the high transaction cost of a share contract and, on the other, insures the proprietor of a fixed yield of the crop. Above the saving on transaction cost, the *fermier* offers the increased utility of a fixed income compared to the income variance of a share crop. The *fermier* who extracts his remuneration from the advantages he creates is reminiscent of Knight's entrepreneur. For a general insurance company, the transaction cost to insure crop yields would be prohibitively high. It would have to check both the inputs and the actual crop yields. Contrary to the insurance company's lack of information, the local *fermier* commands what Knight (1921: 292) would refer to as indirect knowledge, that is, 'the knowledge of other men's knowledge of these things'. Knight adds:

> So fundamental to our problem is the fact that human judgment of things has in an effective sense a "true value" which can be estimated

more or less correctly by men possessing it and by others – so fundamental is it for understanding the control of organized activity, that the problem of judging men's powers of judgment overshadows the problem of judging the facts of the situation to be dealt with.

(ibid.)

The *fermier* economizes on the transaction cost of insurance due to specialized 'indirect' knowledge. Moreover, the fixed sum paid to the proprietor dramatically heightens his incentive to prompt the rents from *metayage* or the *censitaires*. In this respect, Cheung reports in a footnote that Coase pointed him at the British practice to farm out the tax collection for the Crown. The payment of the "farmers" to collect taxes strongly incentivizes their tax collection compared to that of the collecting agents in employment. Both the *fermier* and the tax farmers economize on enforcement cost (Cheung 1969: 28, n. 15).

A second instance that substantiates Cheung's transaction cost theory regards the observation on the Chinese perpetual leases. Under this lease practice "'the landowner holds ownership right to the [bottom of] land, and the tenant owns the right to the soil. ... These two rights are separate'" (Chang, Wang, quoted in ibid.: 38). This distinction is particularly opportune when a tenant invests in changing wasteland into soil to be tilled. A transfer of the outright improvement of the value of the land from tenant to landowner would raise intractable measurement and negotiation costs. Against this, a tenant's right to the soil permitting him to sell this property right either to the landowner or to another tenant is the very incentive to initiate such a potentially efficient land improvement. Furthermore, the "'right to the soil'" creates a market for what otherwise would cause an externality, that is, an uncompensated transfer of wealth from tenant to owner (ibid.).

Cheung's analysis is an instrument to denote the economic rationality behind the diversity of contractual stipulations, allocating a yield risk given the transaction cost. At the same time, the evidence that he proposes shows that the theoretical concepts do not result in univocal contract choices. It 'has perhaps raised more questions than it has answered', Cheung adds (ibid.: 41). As yet, his analysis unwittingly underlines the contractual nature of the firm. Cheung is instructive in investigating the '*structure*' of the partial transfer of rights against those of the owner as an elaboration of Coase's (1960) 'Social Cost' paper. In this perspective, the firm appears to become a fluid concept, entailing a repetition of the definition question of the firm as dealt with in Section 6.2.

Referring to the tripartite contract forms that Cheung discusses, the wage contract alludes to the existence of a firm; someone obeys the directions of the landowner *within certain limits*. The landowner who employs a farmworker represents a firm, offering its yield on the product market. It accords with Demsetz's (1988a: 148) description of the firm as 'a bundle of commitments (although limited in number) ... , all contained and constrained by an insulating layer of information that is specific to the firm'. However, the fixed-rent and the share contract make it rather difficult to perceive the contracts between the landowner and the tenant as representing firms. Neither the fixed-rent nor the share contract is part of a bundle of commitments. Neither is there such a thing as direction within certain limits that would justify naming these contractual relationships as a firm. The next question is, May the landowner, the tenant, and therefore the *fermier* and the tax farmer, be perceived as firms?

Cheung (1983: 16) raises the same question about the orchard owner who contracts a beekeeper to pollinate his fruit trees. It may be

> a hive-rental contract, a wage contract, a contract sharing the apple yield, or, in principle, some combination and still other arrangements.
>
> (ibid.: 17)

Prima facie, the rental contract and the share contract denote contracts between two firms. At the same time, however, neither the rental contract nor the share contract excludes the firm hallmark, that is, some direction within certain limits. Likewise, such direction may happen between the landowner and the tenant, although the latter is no employee of the former. Apparently, 'direction within certain limits' is no reliable criterion to discern firm from market. This accords with Demsetz's (1988a: 144) point that management and transaction cost are difficult to separate in a transaction.

The puzzle originates from the polar cases as presented in the 'Firm' paper. 'Outside the firm', Coase (1937: 388) argues, 'price movements direct production. ... Within a firm, ... the entrepreneur-co-ordinator ... directs production'. It suggests, as Cheung (1983: 3) notes, on one hand, product market transactions and 'on the other, "firm transactions" [that] involve factors of production'. However, reality appears to be more complex. For instance, the firm that contracts a factor that it directs within limits may also contract market relations that contribute to a firm's production. As Coase (1937: 388) states, 'the degree to which the price mechanism is superseded varies greatly'.

The fundamental element that originates the market-versus-firm dilemma is the measurement problem that thwarts a univocally contractual delineation of property rights. This measurement problem varies and so the degree in which a contractual stipulation must have recourse to 'direction within certain limits' also deviates. Thus, in a department store, the location of an independent shop within the building, 'may be the result of competitive price bidding for space', Coase puts forward (ibid.). Obviously, the market mechanism directs the relationship between the store and the shop. At the same time, the shop must certainly observe the rules of conduct as prescribed by the department store. The essential point behind this unruly mix of market and firm elements is that it all depends on Coase's trouvaille, that is, the measurement problem, particularly on 'the most obvious cost of "organizing" production through the price mechanism [that is] of discovering what the relevant prices are' (ibid.: 390).

This 'discovering prices' requires a broader interpretation than just uncovering the relevant prices. It refers to several aspects of the question of whether an efficient opportunity exists to appropriately delimitate the partial transfer of property rights constituting 'the structure of a contract' (Cheung 1970: 50). First, Coase (1937: 391) proposes that it may be efficient to replace a number of separate contracts for one, for example, an employment contract. Second, it may be advantageous to express the service or commodity to be provided in general terms, that is, 'details being left until a later date' (ibid.: 392). It offers the purchaser flexibility, for instance, when he 'will not know which of these several courses he will want the supplier to take' (ibid.: 391–392). Cheung recognizes two other dimensions of the pricing issue. Thus, a third aspect is that commodities frequently consist of a number of components that acquire their value in relation to the final product. An agreement on the price of a component between its producer and the consumer of the final product would be an awkward affair. Cheung (1983: 6–7) refers to it as 'the information cost of knowing a problem' on which the producer of the final product can economize compared to the consumer. The supply of components will be based on piece-rate contracts that are directly measured and priced that, however, result from 'negotiations between specialist agents and input owners' (ibid.: 7). For that matter, this states the unmistakable coordinating role of the firm that tends to be neglected in the contractual perspective. As a fourth aspect of 'discovering prices', Cheung notes that, if individual contributions are inextricable, such as in teamwork, one-on-one price agreements are not feasible. The remuneration will be a proxy. Furthermore, it may be Pareto-efficient to appoint a monitor who has authority to sanction each member's contribution. The question refers to Alchian and Demsetz (1972) who consider a monitor's role as the very rationale of the firm.

The four aspects dimension the 'cost of using the price mechanism' (Coase 1937: 390). They further profile the structure of the contracts that may vary, for example, in term length, completeness, flexibility, and incentives. The measuring difficulties prompt the entrepreneur to have recourse to proxies that relate the remuneration to input contribution. At the same time, the firm owner will have opportunities to conclude piece-rated contracts with other input owners. Furthermore, a series of contractors and subcontractors may be involved in the production process. In particular, the construction industry offers countless opportunities for subcontracting building activities as many of them are amenable to being measured univocally. Cheung presents a nice instance of (sub)contracting that happened in Hong Kong. Cheung:

> The transmission of price signals through specialization in contracts and price information may involve several steps. Consider the laying of hardwood floors. A landlord who wants to build a high-rise finds a building contractor. This contractor subcontracts with a hardwood floor contractor on an agreed price per square foot – a piece count. The subcontractor, who imports the wood materials and adds finishing work to the wood on a piece-rate basis, in turn finds a sub-subcontractor, provides him wood, and offers him a price per square foot laid. Finally, the sub-subcontractor hires workers and again pays them per square foot laid.
>
> (1983: 11)

The measurement problem is left to the competitive market. Furthermore, it demonstrates the efficiency potential of piece-rate contracting. For instance, the floor layer does not need to be monitored, although inspection is required as the piece rate prompts him to rush. On balance, piece-rate contracts economize on management cost. However, for a number of productive activities, a piece rate is inappropriate as stipulating a price is impossible. A diversity of quality dimensions and a number of other incommensurables of inputs and input owners generate contracts that demand direction and coordination and particularly knowledge of product and production processes. It renders the firm a repository of information, as I will return to in later information. Contrariwise, market relations feature the sequence of contracts in the Hong Kong floor construction industry in which individuals conclude piece rate contracts. Apparently, as Coase states,

> Of course, it is not possible to draw a hard and fast line which determines whether there is a firm or not. There may be more or less direction.
> (1937: 392, n. 1)

The firm is simply, Cheung (1983: 3) notes, a manner of organizing 'activities under contractual arrangements that differ from those of ordinary product markets'. Adhering to Coase, it is the cost of using the price mechanism that delimits the firm. At the same time, it is rightly this idea that causes Cheung's puzzling with the definition of the firm. Like Coase, Cheung ignores the existence of the firm as the analytical starting point, as an archetypical concept, independent of whether there are costs for using the price mechanism. However, as far as the tenant, the landlord, the beekeeper, and the sub-subcontractor represent legal entities who exchange property rights, under conditions that may vary, to combine resources to be sold or hired, they meet the definition given earlier.

Alchian and Demsetz's (1972) paper 'Production, Information Cost, and Economic Organization' is a classic in NIE. It concurs with Coase's (and Cheung's) idea of the firm as basically a complexity of contracts about property rights. This idea contrasts with the concept of the firm as an essentially organizational device that exercises authority as put forward by Williamson. The one who owns the firm 'hires, fires, changes, promotes, [demotes], and renegotiates' and is incentivized by the residual value of the firm (ibid.: 786). Thus, Alchian and Demsetz see no difference in the relationship between a grocer and a customer versus that between an employer and an employee. In this perspective, Coase's (1937: 391), 'directions ... *within certain limits*', that is, 'managing, directing, or assigning workers to various tasks' actually amounts to

> noting that the employer continually is involved in renegotiation of contracts on terms that must be acceptable to both parties.
> (Alchian, Demsetz 1972: 777)

Accordingly, the analysis remains within the domain of the exchange of property rights, underlining the reciprocal nature of economic relations as they also exist within the firm. However, Alchian and Demsetz perceive their paper as 'a step down the path pointed out by Coase toward' a theory of the firm (ibid.: 784). They substantiate Coase's transaction cost explanation of the firm. According to Alchian and Demsetz, it is team production and the transaction cost issues this entails that explain the existence of the firm. Team production reaps the synergetic efficiency fruits of cooperation. At the same time, it renders the individual contribution to the production inextricable. Consequently, this generates an incentive issue as it invites shirking which is detrimental to the productivity of the team. This shirking bias is inherent to team production as the utility increase of the shirking team member exceeds the disadvantage he experiences of the productivity loss as the latter is spread out over all the team members. The shirking member imposes a negative external effect on the other members, enticing them to imitate him. Therefore, they find themselves in a prisoner's dilemma. Apparently, team production causes an attenuation of property rights that is detrimental to the benefits of the team. A repair of the definition of a team member's rights will result in a Paretian-efficiency improvement for all. A monitor who forestalls shirking, that is, an efficient monitor whose cost of monitoring does not offset the productivity gain of reduced shirking, is required. The aggregated benefits of refraining from shirking enables the monitor to incentivize the team members by tightening the relationship between (monitored) productivity and reward. The prospect of increased residual value of the firm prompts the outright owner of the firm to restore efficiency by means of articulating the mutual benefits of team production, changing the predicament of a prisoner's dilemma into the payoff of another-regarding game. The firm owner as a residual claimant is the leading figure in the capitalist enterprise, pushing the team members toward efficient cooperation. A bundle of rights enables the residual claimant-monitor in this role. Alchian and Demsetz list the right:

> 1) to be a residual claimant; 2) to observe input behavior; 3) to be the central party common to all contracts with inputs; 4) to alter the membership of the team; and 5) to sell these rights, that defines the ownership (or the employer) of the classical (capitalist, free-enterprise) firm.
>
> (ibid.: 783)

This bundle of rights defines the classical firm that is equipped to organize team production. In contrast to what Oliver Hart alleges, Alchian and Demsetz precisely consider whether the issues of team production and monitoring can 'be solved through the market' (Hart 1989: 1762).[17] In principle, could an outsider of team production offer to replace an excessively shirking, and so overpaid, team member? Competition between potential outsiders may generate a 'decentralized organizational control to work', revising a team in order to increase its productivity (Alchian, Demsetz 1972: 781). Incumbent members will experience the threat of replacement by outsiders. The idea is a spontaneous market ordering without a 'team leader, manager, organizer, owner, or employer' (ibid.). For that matter, the absence of such figures is reminiscent of the unsubstantial world of perfect competition that is contradictory to the positive transaction cost that bears the entire analysis. Therefore, further elaboration of the market option to address the team issue uncovers two serious problems. First, the outsider faces the cost of detection of the shirking. Second, the outsider as a newborn team member is as sensitive to shirking as he lacks the incentives of a residual claimant (ibid.). Hart opposes Alchian and Demsetz's position that the market cannot solve the team production issue. In this respect, he argues that 'auditing between independent constructors' provides evidence of the contrary (Hart 1989: 1762). The example is not very convincing. Apparently, there is a common interest that prompts them to audit one another. It is implausible that the apportion of such a common interest may be solved through the market. A firm-like device will be required. As noted in Section 6.2, there must be someone who initiates. Furthermore, basically, Hart misses the point that Alchian and Demsetz's residual claimant is an entrepreneur who deals with noncommunicable, idiosyncratic information.

Besides the classical firm, Alchian and Demsetz discuss other types of firms such as the profit-sharing firm and the corporation. The profit-sharing firm is appropriate for small teams of professionals whose individual productivity is difficult to monitor by a residual claimant. It enables the team to economize on the relatively substantial cost of managing their inputs by offering each member the incentive of a share in the residual value of the firm. The reduction in cost of monitoring inputs outweighs the loss in incentive to reduce shirking due to being a claimant for merely a part of the residual value. Clearly, 'incentives to shirk are positively related to the optimal size of the team under an equal profit-sharing scheme' (Alchian, Demsetz 1972: 786). An additional efficiency advantage is the economies of scale of sharing the common cost of, for example, the bureau that facilitates the professionals. Furthermore, the profit-sharing firm is a repository of common professional expertise. Apparently, the profit-sharing version seems to merely be a variation of the classical firm. Residual claims bear the rationality of the institutional device. However, team production is no longer essential in the profit-sharing firm; the example professionals may work independently of each other. Finally, the comparison with the agricultural share contract as discussed by Cheung forces itself. The difference is that mainly efficiency incentives plead the profit-sharing firm whereas the allocation of risk is the background of the agricultural share contract.

Clearly, profit sharing with a number of residual claimants weakens the incentives to maximize the residual value of the firm compared to the sole owner-residual claimant. *A fortiori*, it weakens the incentives of a residual claimant who shares his ownership with numerous other shareholders in a corporation as firm form. The corporation not only restricts the efficiency enhancing role of the separate residual claimants, but it furthermore also separates the roles of ownership and control. Unable to direct by themselves, the shareholders must delegate the control of the corporation to managers. This feature that is inherent to the corporation poses serious efficiency issues to the shareholders. Adam Smith denotes a manager's lack of motivation to watch over other people's money:

> The directors of such companies, however, being the managers rather of other people's money than of their own, it cannot well be expected that they should watch over it with the same anxious vigilance with which the partners in a private copartnery frequently watch over their own.
>
> (1776: 731)

Furthermore, the separation of ownership and control also breaks up the decision and its consequences, although they are basically inextricable, Knight emphasizes:

> The relation between management, which consists of making decisions, and taking the consequences of decisions, which is the most fundamental form of risk-taking in industry, will be found to be a very intricate as well as intimate one.
>
> (1921: 260)

Separating a decision from its consequences generates a moral hazard, Knight states, in advance of, for instance, Michael Jensen and William Meckling (1976), who interpret the management issues of corporate ownership in a principal–agent perspective.[18] The shareholder/owner is the principal against the manager as an agent. The agent has specific knowledge regarding his management tasks and develops his knowledge further while executing his management. Information asymmetry complicates the shareholders–manager relationship. It offers the agent opportunities within the legal margins of accountability to make decisions that generate a residual loss, that is, a 'divergence between the agent's decisions and those decisions which would maximize the welfare of the principal' (ibid.: 308). The information asymmetry together with the separation between decisions and their consequences enable the agent to honor his own preferences at the expense of his principal's. For instance, the manager may arrange perquisites as variables of his preference function that encompasses both pecuniary and nonpecuniary benefits. For that matter, the principal–agent perspective holds also for Alchian and Demsetz's shirking problem in joint production. In this aspect, the shirking issue in team production is but an instance of principal–agent relationships. They prevail in property rights contracts that afford opportunity for the attenuation of these rights. In this aspect, there is an imbalance in Alchian and Demsetz's paper. They interpret team production as the *raison d'être* of the classical capitalist firm. However, in the other types of firms, they do not discuss it as team production *per se* that needs to be addressed but the general issue of attenuation of property rights such as diverging interests of shareholders versus managers in the corporation to be interpreted as a principal–agent problem. At the same time, Alchian and Demsetz's view on the firm as a complex of contracts concurs with principal–agent theory as engaged in incomplete contracting. In this view, they discuss forms of market pressure to mitigate 'managerial shirking', for example, 'across-market competition from new groups of would-be managers' (Alchian, Demsetz 1972: 788). New opportunities discipline the existing contracts.

In this aspect, Jensen and Meckling (1976: 310) state in their paper on agency cost and the firm that firms like 'most organizations are simply *legal fictions which serve as a nexus for a set of contracting relationships among individuals*'. Accordingly,

> the private corporation or firm is simply one form of legal fiction which serves as a nexus for contracting relationships and which is also characterized by the existence of divisible residual claims on the assets and cash flows of the organization which can generally be sold without permission of the other contracting individuals.
>
> (ibid.: 311)

Jensen and Meckling analyze the principal–agent issue that arises when the owner sells part of his 100% equity. As a sole owner, he will operate decisions that maximize his utility generated by both pecuniary and nonpecuniary preferences. The nonpecuniary benefits, such as perks, offer the owner who sells a part of his equity advantageous opportunities. They are a source of externality. The newborn shareholder defrays the cost of the perquisites to the extent of his equity share-given profit proportional to equity share-against the owner/manager who benefits from the perquisites to the full extent. A manager/owner who owns 95% of the equity will expend resources until the marginal utility of a dollar's expenditure of the firm's resources is an additional 95 cents in residual value reduction and not one dollar (ibid.: 312). This practice evokes a response from prospective minority shareholders. They will take account of the managing owner's conduct that harms their interest and the monitoring cost it incurs. It lowers the share price. Jensen and Meckling conclude that the owner will continue concerting his claims on the firm into cash 'as long as the welfare increment he experiences ... is large enough to offset them', that is, the share-price reduction (ibid.: 313).

Jensen and Meckling immediately add to this overview of their analysis that it is likely that the most important agency issue arises from the managing owner's reduced incentive to initiate new, potentially risky, although also potentially profitable, ventures. Particularly when the managing owner's equity share is relatively limited compared to outsiders' shares may he tend to prefer a quiet life.

Since Knight, risky ventures, that is, of the entrepreneur, feature in the analysis of the firm. In the modern corporation, the shareholders specialize in risk bearing. They hold the residual claim and have the right to sell it. The management of the corporation is similar to a type of labor to be executed by figures who specialize in 'decision-making'. The manager coordinates the inputs according to the rental contracts that are negotiated before the production period with payoffs at the end of the period. The shareholders receive the residual, if any. This is the framework Eugene Fama (1980) presents when discussing the agency problems of the firm, that is, a clear 'division of labor' between risk bearers and managers.

The risk bearers finance 'the front money' to purchase the capital goods to guarantee the contractual payoff of the other input owners (ibid.: 290). Knight (1921: Ch. XI) identifies it as the *sine qua non* of a capitalist firm. The risk bearers face the agency problem of motivating the management team whose taking ventures and coordinating determine the outcome of their residual. At the same time, for the modern corporation owned by numerous shareholders, the separate risk bearer will hardly experience the incentive to monitor and motivate the management team. Moreover, as a shareholder, he will diversify his holdings in a portfolio, 'hedging against the failings of any given team' (Fama 1980: 291). It alters the idea of the efficiency enhancing role of the residual claimant as presented above by Alchian and Demsetz. Apparently, the modern corporation deepens the separation between (security) ownership and control.

Against positioning the solution of an agency problem within the organization, Fama poses that 'the signals provided by the managerial labor market and the capital market' discipline managers (ibid.: 292). On the managerial labor market, managers compete with each other. However, the corporation will lose its managers if the remuneration system is not responsive to their performance. Furthermore, Fama states, 'there is also much internal monitoring of managers by managers themselves' (ibid.: 293). This is another reminiscence of Knight (1921: 288), who points to 'the importance of indirect knowledge of fact through knowledge of others' knowledge'. The capital market disciplines the manager via the market price of shares. It is based on the premise that the share price indicates a corporation's quality of managerial efficiency. On this premise, Henry Manne (1965) founds his theory of a market for corporate control.

Manne's approach emphasizes the 'division of labor' between risk bearers and managers, as Fama denotes. Manne perceives corporate control as a specific asset that is transferable. Manne's main argument is as follows. The share price that reflects inadequate managerial efficiency at the same time indicates the potential capital gain of replacing the management team. Thus, Manne posits:

> The lower the stock price, relative to what it could be with more efficient management, the more attractive the take-over becomes to those who believe that they can manage the company more efficiently.
>
> (ibid.: 113)

In this perspective, a management team, that is, corporate control, becomes a valuable asset that determines a corporation's residual value. Apparently, the market for this asset curtails the shareholders' agency problem, disciplining managers' efficiency by threatening to be replaced in a takeover. Numerous instances of takeovers by private equity investors confirm the disciplining working of the capital market. Manne refers to it as 'one of the most important "get-rich-quick" opportunities in our economy today', offered by badly run corporations (ibid.).

The fiftieth anniversary of the publication of Adolf Berle and Gardiner Means's *The Modern Corporation and Private Property* occasioned *The Journal of Law and Economics* to devote a special issue to 'Corporations and Private Property' (Berle, Means 1932; Moore 1983). Berle and Means are engaged in the fundamental question that the modern corporation challenges economic theory as we have known it since Adam Smith. Its appearance amounts to 'the explosion of the atom of property'. Therefore, it

> destroys the basis of the old assumption that the quest for profits will spur the owner of industrial property to its effective use.
>
> (Berle, Means 1932: 9)

The corporation separates ownership and control. On one hand, ownership that spurs profit is subject to centrifugal power that tends to be subdivided among an ever-increasing number of shareholders. On the other hand, a centripetal force concentrates economic power in the hands of a few corporate management entities (ibid.). The diffusion of ownership weakens the 'traditional logic of profit' (ibid.: 340). It undermines the economists' idea that 'in seeking profits the individual would, perhaps unconsciously, satisfy the wants of others' (ibid.). No longer is there an invisible hand that is beneficent for all. In this perspective, the corporation announces a profoundly societal change as it dethrones private property rights as leading man's economic conduct, at least in a substantial part of the economy. Approvingly, Berle and Means quote Walther Rathenau:

> "The depersonalization of ownership, the objectification of enterprise, the detachment of property from the possessor, leads to a point where the enterprise becomes transformed into an institution which resembles the state in character"[19]
>
> (Rathenau, quoted in ibid.: 352)

This observation requires a broader analysis than just an economic one in terms of property rights. The elimination of the sole interests of the shareholder as a passive owner has 'cleared the way for the claims of a group far wider than either the owners or the control' (ibid.: 355). The corporation acquires a central position in society demanding that it serves all society, business practice as 'increasingly assuming the aspect of statesmanship' (ibid.: 357). It is of no surprise that Berle and Means' classic devotes a chapter to 'The Inadequacy of Traditional Theory'. Central concepts such as private property, wealth, and individual initiative that have figured in economic theory since Adam Smith are rendering obsolete, they argue. For instance, private property of a 'share of stock is only a token representing a bundle of ill-protected rights and expectations' (ibid.: 347). Comparably loses personal profit, its socially beneficent motivating force, as it does not reach the corporation controlling men whose actions are most important to the efficient conduct of the corporation (ibid.: 350). Thus, Berle and Means conclude that

> [n]ew concepts must be forged and a new picture of economic relationships created.
>
> (ibid.: 351)

In his introduction to the 'Corporation' issue of *The Journal of Law and Economics*, Thomas Moore mentions John Galbraith as someone who has taken up Berle and Means' intellectual challenge. Galbraith's *The New Industrial State* posits, for example, 'that managers are free to follow their own inclinations' (Moore 1983: 236).

Fama and Jensen (1983), in their contribution to the Berle and Means issue, do not follow the intellectual path as sketched in the conclusions of the celebrating anniversary classic. On the contrary, they adhere to the economic principles as stated in the law of demand. Stated otherwise, Fama and Jensen study 'the form of organization ... that delivers the product demanded by customers at the lowest price while covering costs' (ibid.: 301). In this context, they refer to Jensen's (1983) paper 'Organization Theory and Methodology'. The bearing of this *Accounting Review* paper is that, obviously, the financial reporting practices follow the type of organization. However, Jensen also states that a theory is required that explains the organizational variation. For instance, which variables determine the choice between 'the use of profit centers vs. cost centers' (ibid.: 324)? The explanation of such a choice takes account of the room that the frame allowed to referred to, that is, the lowest price while covering costs.

Berle and Means cover the emergence of the modern corporation while Alfred Chandler (1977) reports the managerial revolution in American business that supersedes Adam Smith's invisible hand. Berle and Means diagnose that organizational innovations challenge the economic theory of exchange and markets. 'The visible hand of management replaced the invisible hand of market forces', Chandler records (ibid.: 12). The modern business enterprise replaces the traditional 'single-unit business enterprise' (ibid.: 3). The former are 'monitored and coordinated by salaried employees rather than market mechanisms'.

> Modern business enterprise, therefore, employs a hierarchy of middle and top salaried managers to monitor and coordinate the work of the units under its control.
>
> (ibid.)

It creates an 'entirely new class of business men', that is, managerial experts. They formulate the objective function and command a panoply of managerial techniques for their managerial tasks. A prominent instrument is accountancy, indeed. Linear programing and statistical analyses of data may support business management. It regards policy prescriptions for management based on positive theories about how the world works. Obviously, the normative conduct of managers who are dedicated to an objective function presumes a positive approach to the world.

In this perspective, it is appropriate that Williamson (1975: 29) proposes the excellences of 'internal organization' as discussed in a preceding subsection. Referring to Berle and Means, Williamson submits

> that organizational innovations, which in the 1930's were just getting underway, have mitigated capital market failures by transferring functions traditionally imputed to the capital market to the firm instead.
>
> (ibid.: 136)

However, the danger looms that management renders a technical affair, for example, scientific management à la Frederick Taylor, while, at the same time, ignoring the positive theoretical insights of economics. Managers will pay for it, Jensen argues, if they do not incorporate in, for example, their operational research or linear programming,

> as constraints in their problems robust positive theories of the market, organizational and human behavioral phenomena that were important to the problems.
>
> (1983: 322)

It restores the primacy of the reality of the economic principles that are contrary to a declaration à la Berle and Means of its irrelevance and/or inappropriateness. Actually, Jensen states his trust in this quote that the tautological strength of economics warrants the explanation of organizational innovations, for example, of a choice between profit versus cost center. It is one thing to select the accounting arrangement that is appropriate to such a choice. It is equally important to recognize the economic rationality behind the organizational options. In the same way, an economic rationale hides behind the separation of ownership and control as discussed by Berle and Means. As far as it concerns the emergence of the modern corporation, this rationale is obvious and recognized as an efficient diversification of risks and a device for scale economies. The purported autonomy of the technocratically controlling manager who requires a search for the economic rationale behind it, rather than declaring the economic theory 'inappropriate' as done by Berle and Means, is correct. Basically, Berle and Means's approach is a token of methodological ignorance regarding the nature of economics. It disregards methodological individualism.

Economics is a 'positive' theory, as meant by Jensen, about the world as it regards the exchange of property rights between human beings who observe the law of demand. Therefore, when it happens that an organizational innovation changes the nature of property rights ownership, this, first, questions the origin of this change and, second, how to remedy the interests of the agents involved; both questions are addressed in terms of property rights. This methodological side road enunciates the significance of the perspective on the firm as 'a nexus of contracts' (Fama, Jensen 1983: 302).

Apparently, *prima facie*, the separation of ownership and control in the corporation amounts to an attenuation of shareholder's property rights. In this respect, Jensen refers to his colleague Bill Meckling with whom he interprets it as a principal-agent issue (Jensen, Meckling 1976: 308). In his methodological paper, Jensen further elaborates on it and provides a three-part taxonomy of organization. He and Meckling 'arrived at'

1. the performance measurement and evaluation system,
2. the reward and punishment system,
3. the system for partitioning and assigning decision rights among participants in the organization (Jensen 1983: 325).

The tripartite aspects dimension the firm as a nexus of contracts. Together, they determine the degree of completeness of a contractual relationship, that is, whether the attenuation of property rights occurs. The contractual relationships that constitute the firm as an organization specify

(1) the nature of residual claims and (2) the allocation of the steps of the decision process among agents.

(Fama, Jensen 1983: 302)

What is at issue is whether the risk bearing of the residual claimant is separated from the one who takes the decisions that eventually determine the residual payoff, that is, the choice between a closed versus an open corporation. Whenever risk bearing is separated from the decision rights, the attenuation of property rights renders opportune. So, the very question is this: Which circumstances unites the relative efficiency risk-bearing and decision rights versus that of separating them? In this aspect, Fama and Jensen distinguish four steps in the decision process.

1. *initiation* – generation of proposals for resource utilization and structuring of contracts;
2. *ratification* – choice of the decision initiatives to be implemented;
3. *implementation* – execution of ratified decisions; and
4. *monitoring* – measurement of the performance of decision agents and implementation of rewards (ibid.: 303).

On one hand, the initiation and implementation constitute the functions of *'decision management'*. On the other hand, *'decision control'* concerns ratification and monitoring (ibid.: 304). In the closed corporation with few residual claimants, risk bearing, decision management, and decision control are integrated. In an open corporation with unrestricted ownership, decision management will be separated from decision control.

Specific knowledge, that is, detailed information that is difficult to transfer among agents, makes it efficient to integrate decision management and management control in the hands of a few residual claimants. The closed corporation avoids the agency issue of diverging interests as occasioned by specific knowledge. An organization is *noncomplex* if the relevant decision information is concentrated in one or a few agents (ibid.: 305). The concept of specific knowledge refers to Knight's (1921: 212) commonsense knowledge based on estimating probability, which is therefore difficult to communicate and hard to use in contracting. It grants the Knightian (noncomplex) entrepreneur his economic significance. However, contrary to the advantage of interest alignment, the restricted ownership forgoes the opportunity of efficient risk diversification through the portfolio of the unrestricted ownership that features the open corporation. In this aspect, the residual claimant in a restricted ownership will be biased against the value of uncertain cash flows compared to the residual claimant in the unrestricted ownership. Fama and Jensen recap:

> The proprietorships, partnerships, and closed corporations observed in small scale production and service activities [that require specific knowledge] are the best examples of classical entrepreneurial firms.
>
> (ibid.: 307)

In the counterpart of the classical firm, the efficiency enhancing role of the residual claimants is limited due to the unrestricted nature of the ownership. A separation of decision management, decision control, and residual risk bearing features the modern alternative to the classical firm. The agency problems faced by the unrestricted owners who are specialized in risk bearing is symptomatic. At the same time, it is the strict division between initiation and implementation, on one hand, and ratification and monitoring, on the other hand, that may mitigate the agency problem. For instance, expert boards of internal managers and outsiders with complementary expertise exercise the decision control functions.

The tripartite separation concerns organizations that are complex,

> *complex* in the sense that specific knowledge relevant to different decisions –knowledge which is costly to transfer across agents – is diffused among agents at all levels of the organization.
>
> (ibid.: 308)

This complexity makes it efficient to unite initiation and implementation for agents who command the valuable knowledge at all the different levels within the organization. In a complex organization, specific knowledge, as defined, requests a diffusion of the decision functions. The decision managers may optimize their entrepreneurial capabilities by delegating the risk bearing to the shareholders. In the common complex organization, ownership is unrestricted with the residual claims diffused among a number of agents who efficiently diversify the risk bearing. Parallel diffusion of ratification and monitoring at all levels mitigate the agency issues.

Basically, the choice between integrating risk bearing and decision rights versus their separation amounts to a trade-off between the benefits of risk diversification and the cost of agency issues. The independent variable in it is 'specific knowledge'. In this respect, Fama and Jensen's analysis is reminiscent of Knight, who comparably deals with the relationship between risk bearing and management. Judgment and intuition complement the reasoned knowledge (Knight 1921: 211). Like Fama and Jensen, Knight perceives management as a matter of 'collection, digestion, and dissemination in usable form of economic information is one of the staggering problems connected with our modern large-scale social organization' (ibid.: 261). Furthermore, Fama and Jensen's concept of a complex organization finds its argument in Knight's concept of 'organized control of nature'. Knight:

> Organized control of nature in a real sense depends less on the possibility of knowing nature than it does on the possibility of knowing the accuracy of other men's knowledge of nature, and their powers of using this knowledge.
>
> (ibid.: 292–293)

The complex organization diffuses decisions regarding initiation and implementation, taking advance of the knowledge of others. The knowledge 'in the usable form of economic information' refers to the knowledge of Hayek's (1945: 524) "man on the spot", who knows 'of the particular circumstances of time and place'. The modern corporation as a repository of information takes advantage of 'the dispersed bits of incomplete and frequently contradictory knowledge which all the separate individuals possess' by diffused decision management and endures agency issues (ibid.: 519). Besides the expert board, there is a market for takeovers as well as a market for managers and the stock market that will mitigate the agency problems. Apparently, the efficiency-enhancing role of the residual claimant returns in a diffused form. For that matter, the concept of specific knowledge returns in the next section, reflecting the in this respect relative prominence of Knight compared to Coase.

Fama and Jensen accord to Jensen and Meckling (1976: 310) in perceiving the firm as a *'nexus for a set of contracting relationships among individuals'*. Before them, it is Alchian and Demsetz who emphasize the contractual nature of the firm. The firm is 'a *team* use of inputs' based on contractual arrangements with '*the centralized contractual agent in a team productive process*' (Alchian, Demsetz 1972: 778). As shown, the contractual nature of the firm is not in contrast with Coase's (1937: 391) firm concept of direction '*within certain limits*'. On the contrary, it is the inevitable outcome of applying Coasean economics as engaged in the exchange of property rights, however, that might not be costless. Time and again, the transaction-cost perspective invites passing over the existence question of the firm.

As yet, elaborating the thought experiment of the firm as a nexus of contracts, the perspective leaves open, following the continuum from just one contract to a number of them, from which number of contracts the firm appears. This is a question put forward by Hart (1989). It begs posing the question whether the classical firm or the modern corporation is 'a "standard form" contract' (ibid.: 1764). As discussed, Alchian and Demsetz identify team production as the *raison d'être* of the firm in which the residual claimant features. Hart champions the property rights approach to the firm, identifying it as follows:

> Finally, identify a firm with all the nonhuman assets that belong to it, assets that the firm's owners possess by virtue of being owners of the firm.
>
> (ibid.: 1766)

Actually, Hart elaborates on the residual claimant perspective as proposed by Alchian and Demsetz. In a world of positive transaction cost and incomplete contracting, the owner of property rights of a firm's assets has the incentives to affect the division of the ex post surplus in a relationship. For instance, in the event of a takeover changes the owner into a manager of his former firm, this agent's incentives to invest in the relationship will decrease (ibid.). The firm that acquires the ownership of another firm will presumably control the residual rights in the latter. Hart derives some propositions about the size of the firm based on the idea of the firm as an owner of nonhuman assets. 'First, ... , highly complementary assets should be owned in common' (ibid.: 1770). High complementarity blocks any increase in marginal productivity unless the complementary asset owner is prepared to contribute, that is, a potential holdup is present. It 'provides a minimum size for the firm', Hart adds (ibid.). Second, there is a limit to the size of the firm regarding the effect of the manager at the center on the marginal product at the periphery. Beyond this limit, a new firm should be created. At the same time, the argument is a bias against integration. Finally, the ownership of physical assets, in some respects, binds the human assets. For instance, a cost could be incurred when changing jobs. Additionally, physical asset specific knowledge or experience may be developed that is valueless outside the firm. In this aspect, the contractual employer–employee relationship is not equal to the exchange relationship between a grocer and his customer, as stated by Alchian and Demsetz (1972). This point alludes to the recurring question of this section: What defines the firm?

Finally, I discuss in this context Yoram Barzel's (1987) contribution to the theory of the firm. The concepts that are discussed earlier reemerge in his approach. First of all, there is a *prima facie* resemblance with Knight's notion of the entrepreneur. The entrepreneur is a residual claimant, Barzel contends, who pays a fixed remuneration to those with whom he collaborates. In Knight's (1921: 283) analysis, this arrangement reflects the difference in uncertainty preference in which the entrepreneur distinguishes himself with 'self-confidence combined with the power to make effective guarantees to employees'. However, the entrepreneur in Barzel's analysis is an agent who, as a residual claimant, particularly addresses the agency problem of moral hazard. This is reminiscent of Alchian and Demsetz's (1972: 778) residual clamant who addresses the metering problem *'in a team productive process'* that occasions shirking. Barzel concurs with Alchian and Demsetz in departing from the contractual nature of the firm as engaged in the exchange of property rights. However, Barzel's analysis proves to render Alchian and Demsetz's analysis as a secondary issue. The latter shows that joint production requires a residual claimant. Which team member is the obvious agent to acquire this role is of primary importance? Within a team, Barzel argues, differences in measurability exist of the separate contributions to the joint production. The one whose output is relatively difficult to meter has the best opportunities to exhibit moral hazard at the expense of the team. Therefore, as a residual claimant, he has the best opportunities to prompt team efficiency, guaranteeing a fixed wage for the other members whose output is relatively easy to meter. One of the team members subsequently turns out to be an entrepreneur. This analytical narrative, Barzel (1987: 103) emphasizes, is applicable to 'a narrow range of contracts'. The entrepreneur himself participates in the production and, meanwhile, spends part of his time in supervision, again, partly based on intuition and judgment. An example may substantiate Barzel's analysis.

It is commonly a small construction firm that is owned by an artisan with some personnel that refurbishes and makes alterations to a private house. The entrepreneur/artisan will take care of the details of the finishing touch of the project, which are difficult to communicate. It offers him a competitive advantage compared to a large construction company depending on staff carrying out the work. The entrepreneur as a residual claimant takes care of the non-contractable dimensions of the project. Barzel recaps:

> I hypothesize that among factors contributing to the value of common effort, the greater the difficulty in measuring one factor's contribution vis-á-vis that of others, the more likely is the owner of that factor to assume the position of the residual claimant.
>
> (ibid.: 105)

Furthermore, this hypothesis implies that the relative value of a factor vis-á-vis the other (input) resources affects who assumes the residual claimant role. The variability of the value of the joint outcome depends on both the variability in the physical inputs and the value of the input units. Therefore, 'change in relative wages are expected to lead to changes in organization' (ibid.). It is the relatively more valuable reduction of moral hazard instances that prompts leaving the residual claimant role to the one whose remuneration is relatively high. Hence, it is not uncommon that a reversal of the employer–employee relationship occurs. An increase in wages due to exogenous factors renders it increasingly beneficial to economize on the employer's supervision cost and moral hazard cost (agency loss) by becoming one's own boss.

As noted, Barzel presents an explanation of the appearance of the entrepreneur that is alternative to Knight, who puts forward entrepreneurs' preferences for uncertainty as the mainspring against the risk aversion of the fixed wage employee. Furthermore, Barzel argues, it is rather transaction cost than risk aversion that motivates the wage earner to opt for fixed remuneration. If it was solely risk aversion, it would be more expedient to accept a wage that would vary as a response to the market conditions of the industry. 'A risk averse person prefers lower-wage employment to unemployment' (ibid.: 111). Nevertheless, a fixed wage is preferable as information issues make it difficult for the employee to determine whether a potential wage reduction is justifiable within the terms of the contract. Apparently, transaction costs are prohibitively high for a wage that is responsive to market conditions.

Finally, the entrepreneur is not merely a monitor of fixed-salaried workers. The entrepreneur, in Knight's perspective, is someone who sees new opportunities in an open, though uncertain, reality. It is a Schumpeterian entrepreneur, that is, a businessman who sees profitable ventures. As a residual claimant, he is presumably the owner of the firm. Hence, usually the entrepreneur 'supplies capital of his own to the enterprise', Barzel (1987: 112) observes. In principle, the entrepreneur as a businessman can be a different person than the individual who brings in the capital, the businessman as the capitalist's employee. However, information issues again appear as a hindrance. The market will finance a businessman's actions if they are routine to which a predicable risk may be attached. However, that person's ventures exhibit a Knightian uncertainty for which the outcomes are, more or less, not formally related to the businessman's efforts. The information asymmetry manifests in substantive agency issues, as Jensen and Meckling's (1976) paper discusses. Moral hazard and adverse selection may obstruct a businessman's access to the capital market. Therefore, self-financing is required. Foreign capital might be lent against a rate that 'sufficiently exceeds the market rate of interest', compensating lenders' expectations of default (Barzel 1987: 113). The external financing changes the businessman's behavior as the lender takes the risk that the value of the loan falls to zero, but he does not share the gains. The loan value remains the same, indeed.

> The businessman, therefore, can be expected to search for riskier projects at the expense of a lower expected joint rate of return.
>
> (ibid.)

External financing generates an agency loss. It renders partial self-financing indispensable depending on the transparency of the businessman's efforts. Eventually, a fall in return must be borne by the businessman by paying the lender the market rate of return. This accords with Jensen and Meckling's (1976) analysis of an owner/manager who think he will take advantage of perks at the expense of his shareholders.

Self-financing is furthermore required to guarantee the owners of fixed salaried factors that they will be paid. It explains that capital usually hires labor. It is not merely an entrepreneur's wealth that serves as a warrant, Barzel puts forward. An owner's capital financing his investments amounts to being a commitment to the hired factors. When the hired factors are let go, the owner's factors are also idle. 'This may explain, Barzel adds, why in recessions both labor and capital are held idle' (ibid.: 114).

Summarizing the subsection, common in the elaborations on Coase's theory of the firm is the endeavor to articulate the economic rationality behind the various practices of the firm in its different manifestations and contractual relations. Cheung, for instance, frames the issue of incentive alignment in terms of externalities. It allows him to analyze the different contract structures as used in agriculture. Prominent in the theories discussed is the residual claimant as a safeguard to efficiency. He protects Alchian and Demsetz's team members against the negative externality of shirking. In this aspect, Barzel explains who the obvious agent is to be the residual claimant. Basically, the several insights discussed constitute applications of the null hypothesis that the normal economic system works itself. In this aspect, Berle and Means (1932: 9) are, in their dismissal of 'the old assumption that the quest for profit will spur', in sharp contrast with the discussed NIE approaches. Their approach to the issue of separation of management and control serves as a contrast to, for instance, Fama and Jensen's analysis of it who persist in the application of the rationality postulate. Actually, Berle and Means belong to preceding subsection as their approach demonstrates affinity with Williamson's heterodoxy as affirmed by Williamson himself.

6.4.4 A concluding summary

The two subsections that elaborate on Coase's 'Firm' paper represent two approaches that differ methodologically. The first discusses a fairly heterodox approach that juxtaposes market relations and hierarchy. Its main exponent is Williamson. The behavioral assumptions of bounded rationality and opportunism deprive Williamson of the microeconomic analytical tool to explain agents' behavior who cope with incomplete contracting and transaction costs. Opportunism and bounded rationality render an agent's behavior fundamentally erratic and thus unexplainable. Therefore, Williamson has recourse to the internal organization as a device to remedy the effects of opportunism and bounded rationality due to incomplete contracting. Furthermore, it is a heterodox approach as, within a certain, unspecified range of contract incompleteness, it adheres to the 'high-powered incentives' of market relations. Hence, *Markets and Hierarchies* is the title of Williamson's first book on the *Economics of Internal Organization* (Williamson 1975).

Against the economics of opportunism and bounded rationality, the second subsection discusses the contractual approach to the firm holding on to the postulate of economic rationality. It elaborates on the basic idea of Coase's 'Social Cost' paper, that is, how to redress the attenuated property rights, in this case, between the exchanging agents engaged in the firm. It is the character of the residual claimant who changes the transient and anonymous nexus of contracts into a firm organization of which the owner takes on the responsibility for efficient production. The firm aligns the performances of the resources' owners as promised in the contracts (Alchian, Woodward 1988: 66). The residual claimant may overcome the negative external effects of shirking occasioned by joint production, changing the prisoner's dilemma within the firm into an other-regarding game, as Alchian and Demsetz (1972) show. Furthermore, the contractual approach of Barzel (1987) explains who the appropriate figure is to assume the residual claimant role. It also addresses the economic rationale of the capitalist as a residual claimant, assuring other agents' fixed remuneration. In this respect, the theory shows, adhering to Knight, that the firm is a device for taking account of the allocation of uncertainty. Variation in contractual arrangements reflects a trade-off between the efficiency of uncertainty dispersion versus the incentive breach that such a dispersion entails. Briefly, the contractual approach to the firm is engaged in restoring incentive alignment and enhancing the efficiency of the production for others. In a broader perspective, however, the firm is a coalition of resource owners whose value joint production exceeds the market value that would be affordable separately. The entrepreneur, in a literal sense, who takes on the role as a residual clamant is not *per se* the capital owner. As Barzel (1987) identifies, the resource owner whose contribution is relatively difficult to monitor is the obvious candidate to be the residual claimant whether it is a capital or a labor owner. Apparently, economic rationality directs the analysis. Compared to the heterodox approach à la Williamson, the contractual approach is a search for an explanation of the institutional arrangements in accordance with an economics as we have known it since Adam Smith.

The contrast between the firm as a hierarchy and a residual claimant originates from the difference between nominalism and realism. On one hand, the former appears to be a realistic heterodox approach that aspires to arrive at refutable propositions, as yet found wanting. The latter, on the other hand, succeeds in explaining various market practices of residual claimants who conduct themselves as homunculi, substantiating economics as an exact science.

Finally, both distinguished approaches disregard management and production costs, even though their efficiency-enhancing proposals will affect production and management costs. NIE is only indirectly engaged in product cost issues, such as economies of scale and scope. An instance of connection between transaction cost issues and management offers Fama and Jensen's (1983:

304) distinction between '*decision management*' versus '*decision control*' to mitigate the agency loss potential of managers' decisions without hindering their potentially beneficial initiatives. In this aspect, they argue that the separation of ownership and control enables the corporation to reap the fruit of the 'specific information' of its agents, resulting in a layered organization of management decision and control (ibid.: 305). Furthermore, Fama and Jensen pay attention to decision managers' role of taking initiatives to be ratified by the controlling managers. For that matter, these notions feature in Knight's approach. As yet, however, NIE is predominantly engaged in the effects of incomplete contracting. Nonetheless, it strengthens the awareness that the firm is also a repository of knowledge as information is the very issue of the economics of property rights. The firm as an information repository might be interpreted as a human ecology that feeds the agents within the firm with information. In this aspect, the next section shows a movement from Coase as engaged in contracting to preserve property rights towards Knight as engaged in the entrepreneur who raises opportunities offered by uncertainty, a movement from statics to dynamics. It elaborates on the perception of the production theory of the firm as embodying 'specially appropriate experience and skill' (Richardson 1972: 888). A subsequent question is whether it complements the contractual theory of the firm or if it is its rival.

6.5 Production theory of the firm

Production theories of the firm shift the emphasis from property rights and contractual relationships of the firm as prominent in NIE toward analyzing the firm particularly as a production entity and a repository of knowledge and capabilities. This move from contracting and transaction toward production and, particularly, knowledge of production merely regards a shift in emphasis, indeed. Production theory elucidates the effects of the assumption of Knightian uncertainty rather than being engaged in the effects of a Coasean positive transaction cost. Central to the production theories is the notion that, by using knowledge and growing capabilities during production processes, the firm as a production entity becomes a repository of idiosyncratic information that has fundamental consequences for the working of the economic system. The idiosyncratic knowledge affords the firm to be able to distinguish itself in competitive markets. In this aspect, the production theory explicitly relates a firm's inside production with its outside relation to the market. The section is organized as follows.

The first subsection discusses some key concepts and critiques them. Production theories qualify production as a potential competitive advantage based on idiosyncratic knowledge. Together with this, the Knightian (1921: 211) concepts of "'judgment", "common sense," or "intuition'", enter into the analysis, complementing the reasoned knowledge. Both within the firm and in his market conduct, the entrepreneur/manager has to turn to such inaccurate notions. New situations, new personnel, and unknown variables generally force the production manager inevitably to venture as based on intuition and common sense. It is Knight, as was shown in Chapter 4, who knows how to cope with them using a scientific approach. Knight's analysis offers insights into dealing with the idiosyncratic knowledge that features the firm as an asset that reemerges in the production theory as discussed later. Notions such as 'an intuitive faculty of immediate judging personality' figures also into production theories (ibid.: 293). At the same time, for instance, Demsetz feels uncomfortable about the use of such vagueness to address uncertainty. He reinterprets uncertainty as reducible to risk and open to calculation. According to Alchian, the concept of evolution may replace the rationality postulate as uncertainty renders entrepreneurial purposiveness meaningless. As yet, contrary to Alchian's outside view on the firm, the methodological individualism account of competitive processes under the presence of uncertainty deepens the insight into competition and in the firm as a repository of knowledge, affording the Knightian entrepreneur to store a profit. The first subsection begins with Coase, who himself offers a nice bridge between NIE and a production theory of a Knightian make.

The second subsection, first, elaborates on Richardson's notion of a firm's idiosyncratic knowledge as a *sine qua non* of competition. It is an account of the firm as a production entity in its relation to its competitive outside. A discussion of its counterpart, that is, the inside of the firm, follows. On one hand, it considers Penrose, who focuses on a firm's growth as a matter of qualitative development based on (production) experience. On the other, it continues with Richardson, who elaborates on the firm as a repository of the knowledge and capabilities, identifying changes within industries. Basically, Richardson and Penrose present a development of Knight's analysis and of Hayek's Austrian notion of competition.

The third subsection discusses some instances of strategic management theory. It serves as a contrast vis-à-vis the realist approaches of Penrose and Richardson, who aim at explaining and understanding the working of a competitive economy with uncertainty present. Strategic management theories particularly investigate the relationships between competitive advantages and rent. Heterogeneity of capabilities and diversity of entrepreneurial versatility feature firms and found strategic management theories, denoting competitive advantages offering potentially superior and sustained profits. It raises the plausible empirical question of whether this correlate, which is promising for managers, might be confirmed or remains open to further investigation.

6.5.1 Production theory of the firm and some general notions

In a paper, 'Accounting and the Theory of the Firm', Coase (1990: 3) refers to his 1938 series of articles written for *The Accountant*. In this 1990 paper, he returns to his former plea for the concept of opportunity cost. Contrary to the idea that economists are engaged in how an individual should use his resources to maximize his utility, Coase poses that their economic problem is rather 'which individual should use them' (ibid.: 10). The entrepreneur brings together the resources for production that adds value. The relevant economic question is what to forfeit in order to obtain the resources needed for production; that is, what are the opportunity costs of these production resources? It concurs with the notion that economics is engaged in exchange rather than in scarcity. The market provides the entrepreneur with the price information to address this question. However, this line of thought is again interfered by the idea of zero-transaction cost. Coase repeats in this context that firms/entrepreneurs, first, emerge when arrangements of factors of production via market transactions are made relatively expensive because of their cost (ibid.: 10–11). If the market works without cost, the entrepreneur is superfluous. The neoclassical idea reemerges here that the selection of the profit-maximizing quantities of outputs and inputs occurs automatically. As Demsetz (1988a: 143) notes: 'The *cost of maximizing* is ignored or implicitly assumed to be zero'. However, the zero-cost idea is inconsistent with the concept of opportunity cost that is, as stated, indispensable to any production decision. The opportunity cost concept presumes a comparison by an outside agency; a resource cannot make it itself. That is, who makes the opportunity cost comparison? It again appears that Coase apparently adheres to the neoclassical idea that disregards a firm's own rationale of its existence, that is, an agent who produces for others. It renders his plea for opportunity cost incongruous.

Awareness of a related incongruency may be read when Coase continues his *Accounting* paper. The 'Firm' paper states that the expansion of a firm will halt when the cost of organizing a transaction within the firm becomes equal to the cost of carrying out the same transaction on the market or within another firm. In the *Accounting* paper, he adds this question to the 'Firm' paper proposition: 'But what determines where this point will be?' (Coase 1990: 11). The question alludes to a comparable meta question as posed earlier, or rather, *who* determines where this point will be? The comparison market versus within-firm transaction presumes an outside agency. Coase continues to address his question as follows:

> My present feeling is that, ... , once most production is carried out within firms and most transactions are firm-firm transactions and not factor-factor transactions, the level of transaction costs will be greatly reduced.
>
> (ibid.)

Transaction cost explains the existence of the firm, Coase repeats. At the same time, he recognizes the relative costs of different firms in organizing particular activities as the dominant factor in determining the institutional structure of production instead of merely transaction cost. This does not eliminate the relevance of transaction cost but, all the same, it removes the attention to the firm. It means to explain the *institutional structure of production* in the system as a whole it is necessary to uncover the reasons why the cost of organizing particular activities differs among firms.

(ibid.; emphasis added)

Clearly, this upgrades the significance of Coase's concept of the firm. It is no longer merely an economizer of transaction cost. The firm as such acquires autonomy. It appears to become an explaining variable in Coase's central theme: *The Institutional Structure of Production* (Coase 1992), as also the title of his Nobel Prize Lecture reads. Obviously, this shift in attention toward the firm as an entity is closely related to the accounting subject of his 1990 paper. By definition, the accounting system concerns the firm as an entity. As noted, the concept of opportunity cost observes that 'using a resource denies its use to others'. Thus, cost 'represents what it would yield elsewhere in the business' (Coase 1990: 11). '*In this planned society, the firm*', the internal accounting system computes and provides the opportunity cost information, mimicking the pricing system of the market (ibid.; emphasis added). Obviously, such an accounting system serves the firm as an authority with the knowledge required to bear responsibility. Implicitly, Coase recognizes that the firm is not a mere addition, that is, more than a mere nexus of contracts.

It is Knight who anticipates the super-additional value of the firm, that is, the entrepreneur. It likewise refers to the significance of knowledge in economics. At the same time, Knight adds a new dimension to it. In a world where uncertainty is present, some people have knowledge about potentially beneficial production that cannot be codified or transmitted unambiguously. It is the Knightian entrepreneur who, as a firm entity, epitomizes this idiosyncratic knowledge. As noted earlier, it regards entrepreneurial knowledge that cannot be traded in the marketplace as it cannot be contracted in an univocal tit-for-tat exchange relationship. Entrepreneurial knowledge refers to 'an intuitive faculty of judging personality' and 'an immediate perception of relations', the foundation that decisions may err (Knight 1921: 293). It changes the economics of certain, mechanic relationships of automata into an economics of conscious human beings who more or less intuitively judge '"new situations"' (ibid.: 294). Actually, as noted previously, from here starts (institutional) economics, presupposing human beings who are related to one another in their natural propensity to exchange, meanwhile establishing firms, becoming entrepreneurial 'merchants' (Smith 1776: 14). It renders economics as engaged by entrepreneurs who question, 'what to do and how to do it', economics as investigating 'a process of "cephalization"' (Knight 1921: 268). Uncertainty brings in human consciousness and, at the same time, it raises a tendency to economize on it, 'to make all possible adaptations by unconscious reflex response' (ibid.: 294). Within the organization, the uncertainty and the inherent responsibility may be reduced as it is possible to judge with a high degree of accuracy the capacity of a human individual to deal with the sort irregularities to be met with in the occupation.

(ibid.: 295)

It renders the firm, that is, the enterprise, a manifold of specialization of functions, resulting in the inseparability of two elements: '*responsibility* and *control*' (ibid.: 271). Therefore, the very nature of large-scale organizations is a matter of replacement of knowledge of things by knowledge of men who are able to deal with their exercise of judgment as routines. Knight's perspective is reminiscent of Hayek's (central) planner whose problem is

> to find some way or other in which the decisions depending on them can be left to the "man on the spot."

(1945: 524)

Knight denotes that the entrepreneurial initiative commences as a matter of judgment and intuition via 'cephalization' changes into a rationally organized order, à la Max Weber. In a comparable manner, Schumpeter discusses the tension between the intuition of the entrepreneur versus the indispensable rational organization of the daily pursuits of production. The success of the projected enterprise, Schumpeter (1934: 85) argues, 'depends upon intuition, the capacity of seeing things in a way which afterwards proves to be true'. He sketches the mundane pursuit of production as a pendant of entrepreneur's impalpably creative activity as follows:

> All people get to know, and are able to do, their daily tasks in the customary way and ordinarily perform them by themselves; the "director" has his routine as they have theirs; and his directive function serves merely to correct individual aberrations.

(ibid.: 84)

Basically, Knight's picture of the organization as a 'diffusion of entrepreneurship' and Schumpeter's sketch, for a large part reduced to routine, trace back to Adam Smith's (1776: 7) idea of the improvement of labor productivity, of 'skill, dexterity, and judgment with which it is anywhere directed' as the effects of the division of labor. Better judgment or superior knowledge feature the entrepreneur, prompting him to take a chance on profit. In contrast to what Coase suggests (1937: 401), this cognitive asset cannot be purchased as advice 'by making contracts with people who are producing'. The very nature of the knowledge of the firm/entrepreneur is that it is noncommunicable and so non-contractable. Knight's entrepreneur's judgment refers to such a vague thing as human competence immediately backed up by a rational organization. For instance, the entrepreneur knows people who know how to fix a problem, redressing rational conduct. Aside, as noted in Chapter 4, the entrepreneur judges and structures the uncertain situation he faces, making it eligible for homunculi.

Uncertainty evokes humans' creativity, generating the competence of judging and organizing unknown, new situations. The Knightian entrepreneur represents this attitude. It is instructive that Knight (1921: 268) explicitly distinguishes 'the two most important characteristics of social organization brought about' by uncertainty.

'In the first place, Knight notes, goods are produced for a market, on the basis of an entirely impersonal prediction of wants'. 'The producer takes the responsibility of forecasting consumers' wants' (ibid.). It refers to the supply dimension of the price-making process that basically cannot be deduced from objectively stated determinants. In this aspect, Richardson mentions Walras's process of tâtonnement in which provisional prices figure as '"*cries au hazard*"'. 'No doubt, Richardson notes, that the solution offered (by Walras) is exceedingly fanciful' (Richardson 1990: 13). Apparently, it is an act of imagination that, for instance, 'opens up an opportunity for particular entrepreneurs to increase the production of the commodity and sell it at a profit' (ibid.: 13–14). Thus, belief and postulated expectation found entrepreneurs' competence regarding market intelligence.

Second, Knight diagnoses that uncertainty evokes the social organization of

> the work of forecasting and at the same time a large part the technological direction and control of production are still further concentrated upon a very narrow class of the producers, and we meet with a new economic functionary, the entrepreneur.
>
> (1921: 268)

As noted, it is particularly an entrepreneur's ascendancy in terms of 'deciding what to do and how to do it' that renders that execution, and the organization of the productive groups, is no longer 'a matter of mechanical detail' (ibid.). Human consciousness is engaged in the entanglements of Knightian uncertainty that beset the production processes. The human strategy to cope with it is, for instance, to classify 'occupations [that] differ in respect to kind and amount of knowledge and judgment required for their successful direction' (ibid.: 269). At issue is placing each producer in the location where his combination of managerial capacity and skill 'seems to be most effective' (ibid.). In this respect, Knight identifies an organizational stratification that economizes on this combination of managerial capacity and skill. Managerial control amounts to appointing employees for whom the noncommunicable managerial capacity and skill concern merely routine. Knight:

> [T]he organization of industry depends on the fundamental fact that the intelligence of one person can be made to direct in a general way the routine manual and mental operations of others.
>
> (ibid.)

Knight's perspective renders the firm a repository of capabilities, that is, knowledge, skills, and routines. Competence is a feature of the Knightian entrepreneur, first, externally, as market intelligence, and, second, internally, as industrious competence. It is competence that generates an entrepreneur's profit as a residual income contrary to contractual income as a fixed remuneration (ibid.: 273). For that matter, it shows the difference in theoretical significance between uncertainty and positive transaction cost. The transaction cost theory adds a variable to the situational logic. The bearing of the uncertainty assumption is broader than the positive transaction-cost assumption. The former refers to the economic agent himself in his situation and, as such, encompasses the latter. Consequently, its theoretical impact is more profound as it seems to erode the economic logic of the situation, whereas transaction cost regards an added variable. Economics enters a domain in which an actor, such as the entrepreneur, '*thinks* of the *future*' (Knight 1921: 273). It makes economics an impalpable affair.

The seemingly vague domain that Knight enters occasions Demsetz (1988d: 239) to conclude: 'Knight seems to have worked his thoughts into a bind'. Knight's concept of people who 'may make "judgments" or form "opinions" about how likely an event is' is based 'on the *psychology* of a person', ... 'not on statistical or theoretical calculation' (ibid.: 238). The behavioral implications that Knight associates with uncertainty 'may, according to Demsetz, be considered (perhaps dismissed) as armchair psychology' (ibid.: 239). Demsetz disputes Knight's sharp distinction between risk and uncertainty. In Demsetz's perception, it is all about risks, albeit in varying degrees. For something to be imaginable, he contends, it must be that 'something "similar" has occurred already' (ibid.: 240). The "entirely new" to which Knightian uncertainty may refer would mean the defeat of purposive pursuit as

> uncertain events cannot be expected, contemplated, or even intuited; they are the purest of all windfall profits or surprises, *announced to unknowing minds only by actual occurrence*.
>
> (ibid.)

Demsetz's difficulties with purposiveness and uncertainty may be associated with Alchian's (1950) famous paper, 'Uncertainty, Evolution, and Economic Theory'. Like Demsetz, Alchian struggles with the 'precise role and nature of purposive behavior in the presence of uncertainty and incomplete information' (ibid.: 221). The clear statement that occasions Alchian's paper is

> where foresight is uncertain, "profit maximization" is *meaningless* as a guide to specifiable action'.
>
> (ibid.: 211)

Alchian finds the way out in evolutionary economics that renders the purposiveness of subjects unnecessary. The crux of Alchian's evolutionary economics is this: under the vigor of uncertainty, motivated purposeful action amounts to random behavior. The environment, the market system, selects the actors who perform relatively superior, that is, earn a positive profit. Concerning these actors, it is merely the variety in their adaptive behavior that matters, for example, imitation and trial and error. Conscious purposiveness, that is, intentionality, is unnecessary, although, *nota bene*, not excluded. The environment, as a system in all its objectivity, selects, that is, makes choices. The aggregate description becomes the appropriate level to which the economist may apply his analytical tools, predicting the survival-probability effects of environmental changes in, for instance, 'wage rates, taxes, government policy, etc.' (Alchian 1950: 220). In this context, the economist may experience the fruitfulness of his marginal analysis. However, from the evolutionary perspective, it would be irrelevant to distribute such a thing as Richard Lester's (1946) questionnaire about managers' use of marginal analysis. The uncertainty in a dynamic context renders the individual decision maker's course of action irrelevant. Alchian:

> Success is discovered by the economic system through a blanketing shot-gun process, not by the individual through a converging search.
>
> (1950: 219)

At the same time, he clearly states that

> this paper does not argue that purposive objective-seeking behavior is absent from reality, nor, on the other hand, does it endorse the familiar thesis that action of economic units cannot be expressed within the marginal analysis.
>
> (ibid.: 221)

However, it is the presence of uncertainty and incomplete information that forces the economist to refrain from studying the individual and addressing the adoptive system in which the individual participates. It enables Alchian to draw an analogy between the physicist's atoms and electrons as well as the economist's human beings who have sense and ambitions. As little as the physicist imparts a willful scheme to each atom, the evolutionary economist needs to impart foresight and motivation to his humans (ibid.: 216, n. 12). The upshot is an economic analysis that bans human subjectivity in a view from outside. Furthermore, Alchian's account evidently takes the economy as an extremely decentralized system, implicitly disregarding '*the cost of maximizing*' as this cost is senseless (Demsetz 1988a: 143).

Alchian's evolutionary approach is one of the 'Biological Analogies in the Theory of the Firm' as criticized by Edith Penrose (1952). Alchian avails himself of the *viability analysis* as one of the three biological analogies that Penrose criticizes (ibid.: 804). The two other concern the *life cycle* and the *homeostasis* analogy. The very danger of using analogies is that it produces a frame that may easily obscure significant aspects, Penrose warns.

In biology, natural selection replaces purposive creation; likewise, in economics, natural selection substitutes purposive (profit-maximizing) behavior. Darwin bases his theory on the postulate that a struggle for existence prevails as derived from two empirical propositions:

> all organisms tend to increase in a geometrical ratio, and the numbers of any species remain more or less constant.
>
> (ibid.: 812)

The struggle for existence explains the eventual number constancy of the species. By analogy, the rate of entry would explain competition in economics. However, there is no evidence that the rate of market entry is of 'a geometric type' (ibid.). Furthermore, if, as assumed, man acts randomly, competition cannot be explained for random behavior does not ensure that the number of firms that are created exceeds the number that can survive. As noted, Alchian (1950: 221) 'does not argue that purposive objective-seeking behavior is absent from reality'. This questions why firms' purposiveness would be restricted to adapting themselves to the environment, as Alchian's reasoning puts forward (ibid.: 214). 'There is no *a priori* justification', Penrose argues (1952: 813), that purposive firms 'will not attempt to adapt the environment to their own purposes'.

In his comment on Penrose's critique, Alchian poses his position against Penrose's by summarizing his 1950 paper as follows. Alchian:

> Economics predicts the observable effects of change in exogenous and endogenous factors impinging on the operation of the economic system.
>
> (1953: 600)

From this, it is natural that Alchian claims that it is 'fatal' to regard economics as a theory of individual behavior (ibid.: 601). At the same time, he must presume competition to make the analogy with the biological struggle for life, which is inconsistent with presumed random behavior. Moreover, all the same, Alchian (1950: 218) recognizes a firm's pursuit of profits, although 'this proximate objective is too high'. Apparently, he neglects the marginal approach of analyzing situations, for example, of entrepreneurs who 'tend to try to make, if they think they can, a bit more profit than they are making' (Penrose 1953: 606). The assumption of maximizing behavior is not meant to predict the actual conduct of a specific firm with certainty but to use it 'as an analytical technique to assist him in understanding the effect of change on prices, production, employment' (ibid.). Apparently, Alchian disregards that an individual's economic decisions are 'marginal, that is, they conform to "the little more, the little less"', as Howard Ellis (1950: 2) words it. It refers to one of 'the real virtues to the system', Kenneth Arrow (1974: 20) notes, that 'it requires of the participants in the economy relatively little knowledge'.

Basically, Penrose proposes, Alchian dismisses the individual as a methodological point of departure for *logical* reasons. Uncertainty renders the maximizing behavior meaningless, and so it is no guide for a firm's conduct. Uncertainty brings the mechanics of Hayek's (1937: 35) 'Pure Logic of Choice' in disarray. It refers to the logic of choices of people who are omniscient. Hayek:

> If people know everything, they are in equilibrium is true simply because that is how we define equilibrium'.
>
> (ibid.: 45)

However, if people are not omniscient, surrendering the perspective of the individual is not wanted as Alchian evidently does. Under discussion is rather to substantiate the pure logic of choice 'tautologies, of which formal equilibrium analysis in economics essentially consists' (ibid. 33). Central to this issue is the definition of statements about how knowledge is acquired and communicated. It is 'the *Division of Knowledge*', that is, Hayek's marvel of the market, that enables to the economic actors who are each armed with bits of knowledge and in spontaneous interaction to tend to a situation in which prices correspond to costs (ibid.: 49). Therefore, Knight's judgment of new situations is not a token of armchair psychology, as Demsetz claims, but a fundamental point of departure to acquire insight in the fundamental difference, as discussed previously, between economics as 'logical causality' versus economics as 'generative causality' (Jaffé 1976: 521). In this aspect, neither sophisticated psychology would be of relevance.

6.5.2 The competitive firm as a repository of capabilities and competence

Richardson's (1959) *Economic Journal* paper, 'Equilibrium, Expectations and Information', may be interpreted as an elaboration on Hayek's idea on the *Division of Knowledge*. It practices generative causality. Richardson's central proposition is that 'a hypothetical perfectly competitive economy' neither gravitates towards the familiar "general equilibrium production and exchange" nor would remain at rest in it (ibid.: 223). His analysis demonstrates that perfect and equally distributed information as usually assumed in the perfect competition model is incompatible with the (Hayekian) tendency toward general equilibrium. It is a minimum of idiosyncrasy that prompts the agents, that is, the entrepreneurs, to participate in the competitive process that tends towards an equilibrium that unwittingly furthers general interest.

Richardson's reasoning reads as follows. Naturally, purposive agents people the economic domain. Purposiveness presumes

> an immediate relationship between *beliefs* about the relevant conditions and *planned* activities which it may or may not prove possible to implement.
>
> (ibid.: 224)

The quote alludes to a domain outside the world of certain knowledge, a domain in which purposive men have recourse to *beliefs* and *plans* that might be complemented. They constitute the opposite of objective conditions and actions, respectively. The latter two are the building blocks of the neoclassical model of perfect competition as 'the incarnation of the logic of choice' (ibid.). The real question remains, as posed by Hayek, about which information requirements prompt the agents to substantiate their planned activities. In this respect, Richardson distinguishes information regarding primary and secondary conditions. Primary conditions concern the information about preferences, resources, and techniques that is possessed by the individual agent himself. The secondary conditions regard the conduct of others, that is, customers, suppliers, and other producers (ibid.: 225). Clearly, it is the latter type of information that the agents face with difficulties as the activities of the participants in the economic system are interrelated, aware of their intersubjectivity. This interrelatedness and mutual interaction are well recognized and analyzed in monopolistic and oligopolistic theories, inferring that one's strategy is basically indeterminate. Perfect competition with many suppliers would imply that the strategy issue is nonexistent. Certainly, it is irrelevant to know what another individual supplier is planning to do as it does not affect market conditions. At the same time, the prospective supplier requires some information about what the total supply of the competitors will be (ibid.: 231). Stated differently, the idea that perfect competition renders the price for an individual supplier as given disregards that the expected future price, which is relevant to him, is unknown. The mutual dependence is valid for both the oligopolistic and the perfectly competitive market. It clearly is a 'barrier to obtaining the necessary secondary information' before deciding to join the market (ibid: 230). How can this barrier be overcome? 'Business may proceed in an informational twilight, but not in utter darkness' (ibid.: 230–231; n. 2).[20]

'Suppose, Richardson continues, that there arises a demand for a particular commodity' (ibid.: 233). If such a potential profit opportunity 'is available to everybody, it is available to nobody in particular' (ibid.). Therefore, restraint is required against the availability of advantageous knowledge in order to prompt a single entrepreneur to initiate production, that is, 'some limitation upon the competitive supply to be expected from other producers' (ibid.: 234). The counterpart of the negative condition regarding substitutes is the positive condition that is appropriate for complementary production. Restraints on competition such as information advantages, for example, generated by Marshallian '"economies of experience" … by virtue of goodwill or other ties' found the tendency toward a competitive equilibrium. Therefore, in contrast to the long-standing tradition, it appears that some restriction on competition is not, by definition, injurious to the general interest. In this aspect, Richardson distinguishes natural versus artificial restraints. The latter originate, for instance, from government regulation.

It is entrepreneurial knowledge and intuition that prompt the entrepreneur to assume an uncertain remuneration, and fueled by his self-interest, he may unwittingly further the common good. An entrepreneur's self-interest over-comes the barrier of secondary knowledge by taking advantage of the imper-fectly distributed market information. It is the economic system of the market that spreads bits of knowledge about the intentions of others, enticing the self-interested agent to seize his advantage and producing a socially desirable result without deliberate coordination. In this aspect, Richardson arrives at notions that are reminiscent of Austrian economists such as Hayek and Israel Kirzner, the unintended outcome of individual conduct (Kirzner 1960). As a counterpart of the market economy, Richardson (1959: 232) mentions explicit collusion between producers as a method 'to obtain information about the prospective activities of those to whom they are interrelated'. It rephrases cen-tral planning, as engaged in primary conditions.

Richardson concurs with Hayek in explicating and substantiating how com-petition works. The tendency toward competition cannot proceed without the inherently restraining flaws in terms of unbridgeable differences in knowledge between market players. Richardson's analysis may be recapped in terms of the ring of the four data of economics.

The primary conditions refer to the data regarding resources, preferences, and technological state of the art as the first three, respectively. The secondary conditions, Richardson distinguishes, 'will refer to the relevant projected activ-ities of other people in the system, of customers, competitors and supplier' (ibid.: 225). They find their solution in the *institutional* environment of the economic system, for example, the competitive economy based on private property.

The data picture is instructive as it may be associated with Coase's (1990) perception of the economic problem as discussed in his *Accounting* paper. The economic problem of a Robinson Crusoe refers to optimizing the primary con-ditions. However, the genuine problem economics is engaged in, Coase puts forward, is this: 'which individual should use them'; economics as an institu-tional problem (ibid.: 10). Coase refers in this respect to the concept of oppor-tunity cost that is basically provided by market prices. Hayek and Richardson further analyze that the competitive tendency toward equilibrium prices rightly requires unequally dispersed information about the secondary conditions.

The comparison of Coase versus Hayek and Richardson may be expanded somewhat further. Coase's concept of transaction cost is an indicator of whether opportunity costs appropriately reflect secondary conditions. Trans-action costs impede the optimal solution of the competitive market. The Knightian uncertainty, on one hand, and inherently Richardson's idiosyncratic knowledge, on the other, basically coerce the competitive market to begin mov-ing. Both Coase and Hayek and Richardson identify the market as the institu-tion that solves economic problems. At the same time, vis-à-vis Coase, Hayek and Richardson further deepen the economist's insight into the genuine eco-nomic problem: 'which individual should use them' (the resources)? (Coase 1990: 10). The latter unravel the paradox of information restraint. Competitive advantages stemming from market intelligence and industrious competence both limit and generate the tendency toward competitive equilibrium. Hayek and Richardson show the 'causation in the real world', enabling 'to fill those formal propositions with definite statements about how knowledge is acquired and communicated' (Hayek 1937: 33). It renders the firm a repository of competence and capabilities in lieu of a mere nexus of contracts that economizes on transaction cost. It shifts the analytical emphasis toward production and away from exchange and contracts, hence the production theory of the firm.

Originally, it is Knight's concept of uncertainty and the inherent entrepreneurial initiative that expand into a perspective on the competitive system in which the firm/entrepreneur acquires its/his authoritative position. The firm as an entity producing for others exists and will be engaged in competitive activity as soon as uncertainty offers advantageous opportunities. Richardson shows that it is the very nature of 'producing for others' that originates the market for which the firm has to distinguish itself. The next theme to discuss is the inside of the firm.

Richardson's concept of the firm accords with the definition of the firm as formulated in Section 6.2: a universal in economics that is anterior to economic thought. At the same time, the contractual perspective on the firm as advanced in NIE maintains its validity. It is not in conflict with the substantive definition of the firm to take it also as an expression of contractual exchange of values resulting in a cohesive cooperation of resources fueled by incentive alignment, that is, a nexus of contracts. On the contrary, its legal identity creates the firm, as Hodgson (2002) argues.

Vis-à-vis the contractual theory of the firm offers the production theory insight into the unmistakably synergetic effects of such a nexus of contracts. From here, the production theory may accomplish the perspective of the firm. It defeats the assumption regarding the production of the contractual theory as stated by Demsetz:

> What one firm can produce, another can produce equally well, so the make-or-buy decision is not allowed to turn on differences in production cost.
>
> (1988a: 148)

The quote denotes the neoclassical perception of the firm as a production function. However, production rather concerns the opposite of the process that can be written out with mathematical exactness. A firm's production, for the most part, is a social business with its own dynamics such as employees engaged in learning-by-doing processes and organizational learning during the production process. Growth and thus the historicity profile of the unicity of firms, Penrose (1959) emphasizes in her classic *The Theory of the Growth of the Firm*. Therefore, it is heterogeneity rather than fungibility that features firms.

More specifically, it is heterogeneity between firms regarding knowledge that generates the competitive tendency toward an efficient equilibrium. Next, the firm/entrepreneur develops organizational competencies. In these things, the entrepreneur distinguishes himself from his competitors, potentially giving him a sustainable competitive advantage, that is, a durable rent. Therefore, Richardson (1959: 237) concludes: 'The existence of certain restraints (or "imperfections") in appropriate form and strength would make available the information required for economic adjustment'. It grants the analysis an explicitly dynamic dimension. A lack of transparency and unequally distributed knowledge caused by uncertainty restrain some suppliers and challenge others who venture toward a profitable entrepreneurial opportunity. Furthermore, Richardson notes, it offers the incumbent firms

> "economies of experience," they also, as Marshall indicated, have "particular markets," in which, by virtue of goodwill or other ties, they have a significant advantage.
>
> (ibid.: 234)

Such concepts shift the intellectual interest from a firm's efficient allocation of specific resources to a theory engaged in the dynamics of growth of the firm, witnesses Penrose's classic. In the foreword to the 1995 issue of her 1959 book, Penrose notices that, in the second half of the past century, a change occurred in the economic function of the (industrial) firms as operated by owner-managers. They transitioned from simply acquiring and organizing resources in order to supply goods and services for the market into corporations run by managers who '*qua* managers were primarily interested in the profitable expansion of the firms' (Penrose 1959 [Foreword 1995]: xii). From this managerial point of view, profits become a necessary condition for growth and merely secondary 'to keep the capital market happy' (ibid.). For that matter, it is a tendency that Knight already observed in his 1921 classic as progressive change by '*diversion* of productive resources from the creation of consumption goods to ... producers' goods' (Knight 1921: 323).

Like Richardson, Penrose (1959 [Foreword 1995]: x) notes a discontent with the role of the firm in the 'traditional theory of the firm' as 'an organization it is thought to be irrelevant'. Furthermore, the neoclassical concept of the firm is a source of theoretical trouble because, at the theory's profit-maximizing equilibrium, the firm will, under constant returns to scale – whereas, furthermore, the firm's organization is irrelevant, acquire a size that destroys 'the very foundations of the theoretical model of a perfectly competitive economy' (ibid.). Apparently, 'traditional theory has always had trouble with the limits to the size of firms' (Penrose 1959: 2).[21]

Size in neoclassical economics is a quantitative variable, and so, on one hand, 'growth' refers to an increase in amount, for example, in output. On the other hand, 'growth' in a biological sense refers to qualitative change and an unfolding process. In the latter sense, it concerns 'an *internal* process of *development* leading to cumulative movements in any one direction' (ibid.: 1). At the same time, Penrose (1952) guards against carrying the biological comparison too far as her critique on Alchian shows. Against the firm in the biological analogy as an organism without purpose, Penrose holds on to human motivation and conscious human decision:

> All the evidence we have indicates that the growth of the firm is connected with attempts of a particular group of human beings to do something.
>
> (1959: 2)

More specifically, Penrose takes the analytical apparatus of economics as the 'bricks and mortar' of her method (ibid.). She poses

> that the growth of firms can best be explained if we can assume that investment decisions are guided by opportunities to make money; in other words that firms are in search of profits.
>
> (ibid.: 27)

It distinguishes Penrose's theory from approaches to business firms that avoid such an analytical point of view, as Penrose notes herself in the 1995 foreword. In this respect, she refers to 'biological analogies ... treating firms as organizations' (Penrose 1959 [Foreword 1995: x]). In her *Theory of the Growth of the Firm*, 'human motivation and conscious human decision' do have a place in the process of growth (ibid.: 2).

As a Knightian point of departure, some human beings venture into investment and production, creating an industrial firm. The primary economic function of the firm is to make use of productive resources to supply goods to the economy according to plans developed within the firm. The inside nature of economic production distinguishes the firm from the market. Therefore, in contrast to the market, the firm is delimited. In the firm as a *'planned society'*, the economic activities are carried on with an 'administrative organization' (Coase 1990: 11; Penrose 1959: 25). A central management is the highest authority within the administrative framework, establishing a bureaucracy and limiting the further intervention by the central management.

Considering the definition of the industrial firm as an administrative organization within which the industrial activities are coordinated, Penrose's (1959: 20) concern regards the growth of the firm as 'area of co-ordination'. Basically, the problem is attempting to discover, in practice, the '"area of administrative co-ordination"' to determine 'the size of any given firm at any given time' (ibid.). This coordination area limits the pace of growth of the firm, particularly that aspired after by the salaried managers of corporations.

> The capacities of the *existing* managerial personnel of the firm necessarily set a limit to the expansion of that firm in any given period of time, for it is self-evident that such management cannot be hired in the market-place.
>
> (ibid.: 45–46)

Administrative coordination is teamwork, that is, 'something more than a collection of individuals' that can only 'be developed by individuals who have had experience in working together' (ibid.). Apparently, Penrose develops the temporal dimension of the inside of the firm that is inextricably bound up with growth in a biological sense. Plainly, first, as time passes, the organization may acquire the experience that is indispensable for the growth of the firm. However, as time passes, employees who are open to ideal-typical interpretation, that is, as homunculi, may evolve. It is as elementary as it is central to Penrose's theory of the firm. Penrose observes two managerial limits on the firm's rate of expansion. First, existing management limits the expansion of the organization as new personnel appeal to management to instruct and install them. Second, individuals in the expanding organization require opportunities to obtain experience with each other and with the firm for developing effective operation of the group. So, 'the plans put into effect by past management limit the rate at which newly hired personnel can gain the requisite experience' (ibid.: 47). For that matter, experience as limiting the management factor at the same time promises that the managerial limit will recede. It underlines the dynamic nature of what happens within the firm.

Penrose's theory reflects elements of the production theory that make it a significant counterpart of the new institutional economics theory of the firm. The encompassing feature is its perspective on the concept of knowledge. Penrose:

> Knowledge comes to the people in two different ways. ... The first form is what might be called 'objective' knowledge ... the second form in which knowledge appears – the form I have called experience.
>
> (ibid.: 53)

The latter regards knowledge that cannot be separated from the individual on whose experience it is based. It refers to Polanyi's (1966) concept of tacit knowledge and to Knight's (Knight 1921: 293) 'intuitive faculty of judging personality' and 'an immediate perception of relations'. Like Knight, Penrose extends the analysis beyond the pure logic of choice, analyzing entrepreneur's economic rationality under uncertainty. Apparently, rationality does not mean that the economic agent is omniscient. So, she refers to Knight, who notes that

> we assume human motives ...; but they are supposed to "know what they want" and to seek it "intelligently".
>
> (ibid.: 77)

The fruit of Penrose's theory is this. Experience and practiced cooperation both as limits on and conditions for growth render the firm an administrative organization that may exhibit 'entrepreneurial, technical and managerial versatility' (Penrose 1959: 36). These aspects of versatility correspond with Richardson's notion of capabilities. It substantiates that the firms feature heterogeneity. In the light of Richardson's (1959: 233) analysis, this is one of the "'restraints'" required to generate the tendency toward competitive equilibrium. As noted, it prompts the entrepreneur to venture into investing and producing for a potentially sustained rent. The firm is, in contrast to the market, a delimited entity that represents authority. Penrose (1959: 134) is engaged in the dynamics of a firm's market environment, for example, by diversification, 'often virtually forced on a firm as it tries to maintain its position in a given field'.

In this aspect, Richardson's (1972) 'The Organisation of Industry' studies the dynamics of the market as it occurs industry-wide. Richardson (1972: 888) thinks of 'the industry as carrying out an indefinitely large number of *activities*'. Within an industry, firms are engaged in the research and development of technology and products, manufacturing them, and marketing their goods. The activities are performed by organizations with the 'appropriate *capabilities*', that is, 'knowledge, experience and skills' (ibid.). In this context, he refers to Penrose's *The Theory of the Growth of the Firm*. As denoted earlier, in Richardson's (1959) *Economic Journal* paper, distinctive capabilities offer the entrepreneur competitive advantage opportunities while putting competition in motion. Firms equipped with their particular capabilities will expand into areas of activity that lend them comparative advantages (Richardson 1972: 889). Therefore, how can those countless different activities in which such distinctive firms are engaged be coordinated?

At the very end of his paper, Richardson adds a footnote that contains following:

> The explanation that I have provided is not inconsistent with his (Coase's) but might be taken as giving content to the notion of this relative cost by specifying the factors that affect it.
>
> (ibid.: 896, n. 1)

Furthermore, like Coase, Richardson begins his analysis by presenting what is happening in the reality of the economic world, for example, cases of business organizations in different industries, such as the tobacco industry.

> Cigarette Components Ltd. made filter tips for Imperial Tobacco and Gallaher using machines hired from these companies. It has foreign subsidiaries, some wholly and some partially owned.
>
> (ibid.: 894, n. 1)

From the industry information that he gathers, he infers that the dichotomy of the market and the firm is unsatisfactory in explaining what happens in reality. In this, Richardson practices an economics that is the opposite of what Coase (1992: 714) would call "'blackboard economics'". The industry cases he studies induce him to add interfirm cooperation to market and firm coordination. In Uskali Mäki's (1998) vocabulary, Richardson follows vertical de-isolation and applies horizontal de-isolation by including interfirm cooperation.

Another point in the comparison with Coase is this. As Richardson (1972: 896, n. 1) notices, his 'explanation of the boundary between firm and market in terms of relative cost ... of the kinds of coordination' 'is not inconsistent with' Coase's. Rather, Coase's explanation is incomplete. Coase's concept of transaction cost directs attention to the contractual dimension of the firm. However, the production theory of the firm as discussed previously expands the information issue of transaction cost in the quest for appropriate *capabilities*, that is, appropriate knowledge, experience, and skills regarding the chain of *activities* in which the firms are engaged. This perspective has immediate significance for the explanation of the boundary between market and firm but not much in terms of relative transaction cost at the margin of the market against the firm but rather in terms of production cost as featured by the respective capabilities of firms. It is firms engaged in various activities, and the prevalence of capabilities they entail that apparently result in a third coordination option, that is, interfirm cooperation.

Interfirm cooperation, in its simplest form, Richardson denotes,

> is that of a trading relationship between two or more parties which is stable enough to make demand expectations more reliable and thereby to facilitate production planning.
>
> (ibid.: 884)

The degree of stability of cooperation differs depending on the nature of the relationship that varies from mutual trust and goodwill via formal agreements, for example, about product innovation, to ownership of shares in the business of the concerned partner. It is reminiscent of Williamson's (1985) 'relational contracting' in the subtitle of his *The Economic Institutions of Capitalism*. At the same time, a basic difference distinguishes Richardson's from Williamson's perception of it. Williamson (1975: 108), however, concurs with Richardson that 'reputation of a firm for fairness is also a business asset not to be dissipated'. Furthermore, he continues, Richardson illustrates in his 1972 *Economic Journal* paper, 'numerous examples of intermediate forms of cooperative interfirm behavior' (ibid.: 108–109). Nevertheless, Williamson holds on to the dichotomy 'between normal sales and hierarchical relations' (ibid.: 109). This position stems from his transaction cost theme: markets and hierarchies. Williamson states: 'The "relevant" contracts, ... , are those which cluster around these modes' (ibid.). This notion originates in what Hodgson (2002: 48) calls 'the myth of the firm-market hybrid'. It is shared with Coase and many other new institutional economists. However, it is a myth that markets exist within the firm there. Hodgson states:

> Just as true markets could not exist in an economy that was entirely owned by and planned from the centre, similarly true markets cannot exist within firms.
>
> (ibid.: 47)

Firms and markets are one another's complement with distinguishing definitions. The firm is a legal entity that acts authoritatively to initiate production for others. The market, whether or not deliberately instituted, generates prices *"without the possibility of central interference"* (ibid.: 46, quoting Hayek). In contrast to Williamson, Richardson (1972: 890) distinguishes 'cooperation' as a separate coordination device besides consolidation and market. Several examples of coordination substantiate it as an autonomous concept. Richardson lists:

> a joint subsidiary of firms B and C, has technical agreements with D and E, sub-contracts work to F, is in marketing association with G – and so on.
> (ibid.: 884)

The examples observe a firm as a legal entity that seeks coordination with another firm. In principle, the examples presume an exchange of property rights. At the same time, 'relationship may acquire its stability merely from goodwill or from more formal arrangements' (ibid.). The added clause features the cooperation as a rather inexact affair, reflecting the problem to address by cooperation, that is, coordination of activities that require capabilities delineated by knowledge, experience, and skills.

The tripartite coordination device constitutes a choice out of tit-for-tat-market relations, a variety of interfirm forms of cooperation, and consolidation in a firm, which are effected in three ways: through *market transaction*, by *cooperation*, or by *direction*, respectively (Richardson 1972: 890). The coordination regards the 'activities' in which the industry is engaged, varying from research and development of products and markets, manufacturing, distribution, and sales. For that matter, Richardson's 'activities' is reminiscent of Stigler's 'distinct operations' as used in his 1951 paper. A firm specializes in activities that require certain capabilities which offer a competitive advantage. The larger the organization, the more capabilities it will be endowed with for executing an expanding 'number of complementary activities that can, *in principle*, be made subject coordination through direction' (ibid.: 891; emphasis added). If, furthermore, it might be assumed that scale does not affect efficiency, then there would be no limit to the extent to which coordination by direction could be extended. Under those conditions, it would have been possible 'that the economic system in Russia would be run as one big factory', as Lenin had stated (Coase 1992: 715). Yet, there are separate firms. It is the concept of transaction costs, Coase (1988a: 4–5) puts forward, that brings in 'the comparison of the cost of organizing a transaction within the firm and by means of a market transactions', explaining that there cannot be just one big factory and why there are market transactions. Coase's transaction cost concept renders the coordination system a matter of economic choice. Likewise, for Richardson, the manner of coordination is an economic choice. However, in Richardson's analysis, it is the nature of the activities and their attendant capabilities that serve as the critical variables, rendering it prohibitively inefficient to rely on coordination through direction if the 'factory' would expand unlimitedly. As denoted, this does not neglect the relevance of transaction cost, witness the market transaction as one of Richardson's alternatives to direction. Obviously, this difference between Richardson and Coase is due to the different dimensions of the firms in which they are theoretically interested: contractual relations versus productive processes. Furthermore, Coase's 'Firm' paper is about a firm's relationships with its resources. Richardson studies business relationships at an industry level.

Central to Richardson's elaboration on the tripartite coordination device is the distinction between *similar* activities that require the same capability for their undertaking and *complementary* that represents phases of a production process and require coordination (ibid.: 888–889). It is the latter type together with economies of scale that generate the coordination issue, actually, scope and scale. The ensuing question is,

> What is the appropriate division of labor, ... , between consolidation, co-operation and market transaction?
>
> (ibid.: 890)

It is the introduction of the two concepts, that is, 'cooperation' as a distinctive coordination device and 'activities' replacing production as a concept, that enables Richardson to present a theoretically innovative perspective on the boundaries of firms and their interrelationships, that is, the organization of industry. The tripartite coordination device matched with similar/complementary activities produce the following broad categories of industrial organization:

1. Activities, both similar and complementary: coordination by direction within a (consolidated) individual firm;
2. Dissimilar and complementary activities that require the responsibility of different firms may be divided into two subcategories:
   a. Market transactions generating coordination;
   b. Cooperation to match firms' *ex ante* plans.

Clearly, it is the second category that profiles an industry's organization. It is the complementary activities that require coordination, potentially both qualitative and quantitative. In subcategory 2.a., the market transactions offer appropriate coordination if the qualitative match is not specific, and furthermore, the complementary activities may easily find one another on the market. The law of large numbers that stabilizes the aggregates of demand and supply guarantees the complementary match between individual firms. For instance, the building constructor and the brickmaking entrepreneur rely in their reciprocal dependency on the market (ibid.: 891). In the same way, a firm may rely on the market for marketing activities.

Subcategory 2.b., however, entails consolidation or a broad range of inter-firm cooperation cases. They vary from issuing a license for producing a patent product to a joint venture in developing an innovation and *ex ante* engagement of a principal customer in the development of a new production part by the supplier. Intensive interfirm cooperation is required to match *closely comple-mentary* activities. The primary reason for the involvement of different firms is the dissimilarity of the activities of which the matching, both qualitative and quantitative, cannot be coordinated by market forces. Coordination by consol-idation within a firm of dissimilar activities remains versus interfirm arrange-ments such as equity participation, a formal institutional arrangement, or an informal gentlemen's agreement between a principal and subcontractors.

Interfirm cooperation, Richardson emphasizes, by no means excludes com-petition between business relations (ibid.: 895). Business experience, lasting relationships, and built-up trust generate a reciprocity that offers mutual bene-fits. This may also be valid for relationships between business partners that are unequal in size and economic power. Richardson:

> Firms form partners for the dance but, when the music stops, they can change them.
>
> (ibid:. 896)

Finally, Richardson notes, putting into perspective, 'theories of industrial or-ganization, ... , should not try to do too much' (ibid.: 896). National legislation and cultural differences cause an internationally varying picture of industrial organization. Moreover, the borders between coordination devices are more or less indistinguishable. For instance, market transactions may require some di-rection, and interfirm cooperation may, in fact, turn out to be the direction taken by the predominant partner. In these considerations, Richardson demon-strates his theoretical unpretentiousness. It is reminiscent of the theoretical modesty that Stigler (1951: 191) exhibits regarding classifying 'the variegated details of production, one finds how artificial and arbitrary "vertical" relation-ships are', as quoted earlier. At the same time, the diversity and ambiguity of the instance of interfirm cooperation make it a counterpart of the Knightian entrepreneur. Both have recourse to judgment and intuition due to the non-communicable and thus the non-contractable nature of the problem that has to be addressed. Therefore, all the arrangements of cooperation require that the parties 'accept some degree of obligation – and therefore give some degree of assurance – with respect to their future conduct' (Richardson 1972: 886). As noted, goodwill supports the stability of interfirm cooperation (ibid.: 884). It is 'goodwill', Ronald Dore (1983: 460) specifies, not in the sense of benevolence granted by a superior but as a 'principle of mutuality' between equals. It makes it an expression of reciprocity that is commensurable to the tit-for-tat relation-ships of the market. Frequency, Marshallian market experiences, 'linkages of traditional connection and goodwill', and reputation feature industrial rela-tions as a social world (Richardson 1972: 887). It regards notions that grant the social world stability, or better, express human *meaning* eligible to Schutz's (1932) analysis of *Der sinnhafte Aufbau der Sozialen Welt*. Apparently, the parties in a cooperation use the constructs of their social world that afford them in coming to terms with one another. Rephrased in Schutz's vocabulary as developed in Chapter 2, the interfirm cooperating parties are contemporaries like trading parties on a spot market, although to a lower degree of anonymity. Both are amenable to phenomenological operation and to figure as homunculi in an account of judging and sensing entrepreneurs that holds on the postulate of economic rationality.

This phenomenological interpretation expresses the bearing of Richardson's (1990: xxiv) analysis in that, in order to decide about economic adaptation and coordination in any particular situation, 'one needs to have a theoretical framework that accepts the uncertainty and dispersal of knowledge'. It is the restraints of competition that generate the economic agents' interest to participate in competitive processes. At the same time, this analysis holds on to the principle of economic rationality. Richardson and Penrose provide, in the tradition of Knight and Hayek, a theoretical account of how competition works practically. In this account, opportunity arises for paying attention to such things as cultural differences, noncommunicable heterogeneity, and the working of our mundane social reality.

The question that remains is whether the production theory is complementary to or rivalrous with NIE theories of the firm. It is complementary in the context that the former encompasses the latter. The firm is indeed a nexus of contracts in its coming into existence. However, the initiating idea of bringing together resources to make products for strangers creates the firm and its capabilities and logically precedes the property rights and transaction questions of the firm as dealt with in NIE. Therefore, it is the production theory of the firm that not only merely complements the new institutional perspective on the firm but enables also the NIE theorist to *denote* the nature of the firm, its boundary, and its interrelatedness with other firms, that is, the organization of the industry. The concept of capabilities explains that similar activities cause diversification within firms. However, complementary activities require capabilities that differ from one another, generating relationships between firms that need to be coordinated in one way or another. This is concisely Richardson's supplement to the new institutional economic perspective of the firm as a nexus of contracts.

Nonetheless, the production theory is rivalrous with the new institutional perspective on the firm as it depicts production activities as a materialization of exchanges of which the acting participants are aware of the very reciprocal nature of these activities. It is again the notion of capabilities, that is, knowledge, skills, and experience that highlights production as a social affair in which people acquire shared values. For instance, Penrose identifies the process of learning new personnel as a constraint on a firm's growth. Personnel require experience to become acquainted with the noncommunicable capabilities of the firm. It creates new ideal types, homunculi. This social dimension also matters in the cooperation between firms as far as it regards interfirm cooperation to match complementary activities. The exchange of idiosyncratic information requires the appropriate social environment, that is, of mutual trust and shared values and a sense of reciprocity to substantiate stable cooperation. It enables mutually beneficial exchange outside the mechanic model of perfect competition. Information asymmetry rightly originates cooperation rather than causing moral hazard and adverse selection. This contrasts with the NIE analysis that is engaged in incentive alignment and the cost of writing out contracts between people. Articulated in Schutzian vocabulary, in the NIE social world, contemporaries are more anonymous to one another than in the social world that affords (interfirm) cooperation as presented by Penrose and Richardson. Basically, the theoretical origin of Coase's firm is the model of perfect competition. For that matter, trust and shared values are not inconsistent with new institutional economics. In this aspect, Williamson's approach leaning on opportunism and bounded rationality deviates from new institutional economics as originated from Coase. It renders Williamson, in emphasizing the import of opportunism, the very rival of production theory of the firm à la Penrose and Richardson.

6.5.3 *Strategic management theory and empirical evidence*

The heterogeneity of firms, as elaborated on by Richardson and Penrose, potentially offers a competitive advantage with a sustained superior profit performance, that is, a lasting rent in expectation. Plausibly, the prospect of sustained rent constitutes a firm base for strategic management theories, aiming at evidence-based consultancy. For instance, David Teece and Gary Pisano (1994) study the dynamic capabilities of the firm. The dynamic capabilities as a source of competitive advantage refer, first, 'to shifting the character of the environment' and, second, to strategic management, 'adapting ... internal and external organizational skills, resources, and functional competences toward changing environment' (ibid.: 537). An extensive stream of theories proposes firms' heterogeneity, for example, referring to the evolution of 'routines as genes' (Nelson, Winter 1982: 134). Margaret Peteraf, for example, notes that the concept of firms' heterogeneity,

> in terms of their resources and internal capabilities, has long been at the heart of the field of strategic management.
>
> (1993: 179)

As far as these resources and capabilities are superior they may occasion competitive advantage with sustained rent in sight, the resource-based view argues (ibid.). Jay Barney, as another exponent of the resource-based view, recommends looking inside the firm for a competitive advantage. Barney:

> managers must look inside their firm for valuable, rare and costly-to-imitate resources, and then exploit these resources through their organization.
>
> (1995: 60)

Apparently, strategic management theorists discuss closely related topics. The focus on heterogeneity in terms of competence, skills, and routines that safeguards a sustained rent via competitive advantage is common among them. Peteraf (1993: 180) notes 'a considerable overlap of ideas. To the uninitiated this may be confusing'. In her paper, she aims 'to build some consensus for a parsimonious model' of the resource-based view. She distinguishes four conditions to guarantee a superior performance stemming from competitive advantage.

> The first of these is resource heterogeneity, from which come Ricardian or monopoly rents. Ex post limits to competition are necessary to sustain the rents. Imperfect resource mobility ensures that the rents are bound to the firm and shared by it. Ex ante limits to competition prevent costs from offsetting the rent.
>
> (ibid.)

The core hypothesis of the resource-based view and strategic management theories, in general, is this proposition: *competitive advantage produces sustained superior performance*, as Thomas Powell (2001: 875) formulates it. Central to it is that heterogeneity generates competitive advantage. The other three conditions that Peteraf puts forward guarantee that the competitive advantage persists and preserve a sustained superior performance.

Powell embroiders on the implicit conditions of the strategic management proposition. In logical form, the proposition reads:

> $q \supset p$ (*if q then p; if firm i had one or more sustainable competitive advantages, then firm i achieved sustained superior performance*).
>
> (ibid.: 876)

However, the assumption of strategic management theory and the basis for the hypothesis is its inverse. As Powell notes, 'Most empirical studies infer the existence of competitive advantages from ex post performance observations', that is, in logical form:

> $p \supset q$ (if p then q; *if firm i achieved sustained superior performance, then firm i had one or more sustainable competitive advantages*).
>
> (ibid.)

Yet, it is a logical fallacy to infer $q \supset p$ from $p \supset q$. In different terminology, one may observe sustained superior performance without the presence of sustainable competitive advantages. Furthermore, strategic management reasoning seemingly assumes that the absence of competitive advantages is the opposite of their presence. However, their very opposite is the presence of competitive disadvantages. Even if competitive advantages or a strategic policy oriented toward them exist, competitive disadvantages may obstruct the attainment of sustained superior performance. From this results a weak hypothesis that superior performance of firm i, suggests that it had one or more sustainable competitive advantages or did not have competitive disadvantages (ibid.: 879). The hypothesis based on Bayesian analysis finally remains using hypothetically estimated parameters that '*the probability of firm i having sustainable competitive advantages is greater in the presence of sustained superior performance than in its absence*' (ibid.). In general terms, Powell concludes 'that our expectations of sustainable competitive advantage improve under the empirical observation of sustained superior performance' (ibid.).

Powell further weighs the epistemological value of the resource-based view of the strategic management theory, which infers the sustainable competitive advantage from the assumption of a firm's heterogeneity, that is, 'no two firms i and j possess identical resource/capability portfolios' (ibid.: 881). A number of candidates responsible for a firm's heterogeneity announces itself in resource-based view theories. In this aspect, for the most part, it concerns variables that are inimitable, idiosyncratic, and not to be codified. Moreover, by definition, it is logically sound to posit that two firms are identical: 'two identical firms would be one firm, not two' (ibid.). Apparently, the heterogeneity assumption is analytical, that is, true by definition. Therefore, a firm, by definition, disposes of competitive advantages generating heterogeneity that may explain a firm's superior performance that is observed. If not found, this is no refutation of the resource-based view because, as noted, most of the heterogeneity variables are difficult to identify. A firm's heterogeneity as founding its competitive advantages renders the major proposition of the resource-based theory a tautology, and thus, this theory is irrefutable. Finally, Powell discusses a pragmatist epistemology as a methodological way out to rescue the impressive body of strategic management theories. Apparently, it regards that 'competitive advantage itself has survived competition among rival performance theories', Powell proposes (ibid.: 885). In this respect, he juxtaposes researchers versus managers.

> Researchers design their work to explain known performance outcomes, but managers do the reverse, identifying and mobilizing factors to create superior performance in periods to come.
>
> (ibid.: 886)

Managers assess and predict risks, judge their situation, and venture into an enterprise as noted at the beginning of this subsection. The strategic management researcher is like a historian who applies a quote from Carr:

> we (historians) do not render a photographic copy of the real world, but instead select, out of the infinite ocean of facts, the minute fraction that best supports our purpose.
>
> (Carr 1986: 98–99; quoted in Powell 2001: 886)

This comment on a strategy of researchers' methods illustrates the methodological *Werdegang* from economic analysis that aims to explain and understand a firm's conduct from inside towards instrumentalist strategic management theories that aim to predict sustained superior performances.

6.6 Conclusion: a phenomenological point of view

Knight and Coase denote the route away from an economics à la mechanics toward an economics of conscious human beings. Therefore, Knight's entrepreneur and Coase's firm render, by definition, the causality of the 'Pure Logic of Choice' insufficient. Their theoretical ambition and apparent necessity to introduce an entrepreneur or a firm as an agent who bears responsibility and who may experience a sense of '"new situations"' evoke a twofold theoretical response (Knight 1921: 294). The responses differ methodologically, tracing back to the philosophical position toward nominalism versus realism as discussed in Chapter 1.

Instead of applying the logic of choice, the nominalist economist observes self-interested actors who cannot be anything but boundedly rational and who act opportunistically as the same bounded rationality of their fellow men offers room for their self-interest at the expense of those others. It reflects a portrayal of man as a selfish atom, acting without any sense of humanity. Methodologically, nominalism produces an instrumentalist/positivist approach that formulates propositions to be tested empirically. I refer to four instances as discussed in the preceding information.

It is, first of all, Williamson who is a nominalist and an exponent of the instrumentalist approach. His main proposition regarding a causal relationship between asset specificity and vertical integration would have 'refutable implications' (Williamson 1984: 196). His nominalist stance entices Williamson to advance instruments such as relational contracting. In this aspect, he particularly weighs 'internal organization' on which he expands in his *Markets and Hierarchies* (Williamson 1975: 29). Observation might offer instruments to assist the boundedly rational economic actor who lives in a Machiavellian world (Williamson, Masten 1999: xiii).

Second, Berle and Means are comparable to Williamson in their approach (Williamson 1985: 8, n. 7). It is no surprise that Williamson refers to Berle and Means's (1932) classic *The Modern Corporation and Private Property*. Berle and Means observe that the modern corporation renders private property as the very foundation of the 'traditional logic of profits' obsolete (ibid.: 340). Like Williamson, they basically observe that the economic reality deviates from the pure logic of choice. Therefore, the traditional theory has become inadequate. Hence, Berle and Means conclude that

> [n]ew concepts must be forged and a new picture of economic relationships created.
>
> (ibid.: 351)

New concepts are required to develop an 'economic statesmanship', 'balancing a variety of claims by various groups ... assigning to each a portion of the income stream on the basis of public policy rather than private cupidity'. The '"control" of the great corporations should develop into a purely neutral technocracy' (ibid.: 356–357). Like Williamson, Berle and Means introduce concepts that reflect a view from outside. The nature of concepts, such as a 'purely neutral technocracy' or Williamson's relational contracting, is conjectural. They do not stem from an analytical framework.

The third instance of nominalism regards Alchian, who has recourse to positivism as uncertainty renders man's purposiveness meaningless. An observation from outside of what happens within the population is the aspiration level of the evolutionary economist. Conditions external to the individual actor determine one's success or failure. Therefore, Alchian's view on economics is this:

> Economics predicts the observable effects of change in exogenous and endogenous factors impinging on the operation of the economic system.
>
> (1953: 600)

The fourth manifestation of nominalism concerns the instrumentalist view of strategic management theories. The strategic management theorist seeks causal relationships to assist management in its pursuit of sustained superior performance. For instance, the resource-based view infers a sustainable competitive advantage from the assumption of a firm's heterogeneity. Regarding such a correlation, Powell proposes several methodological issues that basically originate from the lack of a sound analytical framework. Outside the domain of certainty, the economic actor as a strategic manager has recourse to positivist theories that develop a 'purely neutral technocracy', à la Berle and Means. However, such a technocratic solution is basically unaffordable as a human initiative is at stake simultaneously with uncertainty that cannot be technologically encapsulated. Banished from the pure logic of choice, the instrumentalist aims to restore a logical causality. Powell offers the strategic management theorist pragmatism as an appropriate alternative stance to positivism. Unable to meet the epistemological demands of positivism, the strategic theorist may be justified if, for example, the competitive advantage hypothesis helps the manager to create sustained superior performance 'as evidenced by, say, a vigorous stream of research, increased rate of adoption by managers' (Powell 2001: 884–885).

The denial of human invention as a theoretical problem is common in these nominalist instances. They neglect human intentionality. Alchian's evolutionary economics explicitly denies the relevance of man's initiative. Berle and Means's technocracy restores the mechanic perspective, assigning rewards from outside 'public policy'. Williamson counterbalances human (opportunistic) invention by reliance on internal organization. Against the bounded rationality and the opportunism of the actors on the market, that is, of interfirm relations, the intrafirm offers 'a wider variety and greater sensitivity of control instruments' (Williamson 1971: 113). The nominalist stance in economics is reminiscent of a Hobbesian atomistic psychology of the economic actors who are unable to attain a common wealth without outside power imposed on them. It reflects the postulate that merely particulars exist that we categorize as *nomina*. Reality is perceptible in language and human thought. In our language, we create concepts that *have* meaning, that is, that are attached to concepts (Kaufmann 1944: 17). Empirical observation founds our knowledge of the world, aiming at prediction. Empiricism is the fruit of nominalism.

Against the nominalist meta-view of the world stands realism that postulates reality as existing independent of human perception. At the same time, the reality is intelligible in universals that as *a priori* categories logically precede particulars. It induces the scientist to search for essences. For instance, Adam Smith (1776: 16) finds the origin of economics in human's propensity to exchange. As noted in the preceding information, this identifies the firm as a universal for which its essence is production for others. Another universal that, besides the law of demand, figures in economics is the law of diminishing returns as referred to by Demsetz (2008: 1). As posed in Chapter 1, the universals afford us to apply a deductive analysis; the particular is deduced from the universal. Realism enables rationalism.

The realist view encompasses a phenomenology that substantiates the exactness that realism recognizes pre-reflectively. The very phenomenological foundation is human consciousness, experiencing our fellow man as a somebody with whom we experience society and share intentionality in the *Lebenswelt*. Consequently, this perspective invites further reflection on what happens between these fellow men. Instead of mere observation, the phenomenologist perceives human experience as a thought object, a highly complicated construct of, for example, 'space relations in order to constitute it as a sense-object of several senses, say of sight and touch' (Schutz 1953: 1). Again referring to Chapter 1, these constructs constitute our knowledge as a set of abstractions and formalizations 'specific to the level of thought organization' (ibid.: 2). In daily pursuit, we use common sense constructs in our deliberation, conduct, and communication. In science, however, we formulate second-order constructs, removing the vagueness of commonsense constructs. Here enters Weber's ideal type that as used in the analysis of meaning. However, in the realist stance of phenomenology, the ideal type is an exact type as defined by Menger. Contrary to Menger, Weber's ideal type is an instance of what we find in reality. Menger's exact (ideal) type represents the inverse, that is, the fruit of pre-reflective discovery. This contrast may be interpreted as a duplicate of the contrast between logical versus generative causality.[22] In Schulz's vocabulary, it is the 'homunculus', a fictitious being gifted with consciousness and acting as a *Homo economicus*.

The use of the homunculus is an instrument of the analysis of meaning, that is, a *Verstehen* of the human phenomena to grasp the intentionality that bears human conduct. A second dimension of the analysis of meaning refers to the deductive removal of inconsistencies. The analysis of meaning of the synthetic proposition as a '*restriction of the frame of possibilities*' does not refer to the empirical test of its truth or falsity but to its logical soundness (Kaufmann 1944: 20). The fruit of this analysis is, for instance, the inconsistency detected hidden behind market and firm as one another's alternative. As in a novel, it is not an issue of whether something has actually happened but that it is logically sound, as Schutz denotes.

An explanation instead of a prediction of the firm/entrepreneur as related to market exchange is the very aim of contributions to the theory of the firm that may be interpreted in the phenomenological perspective. Chapter 5, 'On Coase', provides an elaborate phenomenological discussion of the 'Firm' paper. Here, I recap how the new institutional economic theories of Alchian and Demsetz, Barzel, Jensen and Meckling, and Cheung may be interpreted from the phenomenological perspective. Comparably validates this interpretation for Penrose's and Richardson's production theories of the firm. In brief, they *explain* how reciprocal purposiveness manifests in market practices, substantiating 'economics as an exact science' (Knight 1921: 3).

Alchian and Demsetz consider team production as the very feature of the firm. Team production renders remuneration in correspondence with the partial marginal productivity of the productive resources unaffordable due to their metering problem. This blocks the logical causality. Alchian and Demsetz introduce the residual claimant as an *ideal type* who restores the reciprocal purposiveness. This figure brings in generative causality as he generates incentive alignment that is guaranteed as far as the benefit of shirking reduction exceeds the cost of monitoring. Furthermore, the residual claimant will pay attention to the qualitative dimensions of production that cannot be communicated or contracted.

Barzel elaborates on the metering problem between the residual claimant and the employee(s) who receive(s) a fixed remuneration. The obvious residual claimant in a joint production is, Barzel argues, the one whose contribution is relatively difficult to measure. Clearly, fixed remuneration is relatively more appropriate for contributions that are relatively easy to measure. However, most important is that the one whose activities are most difficult to measure is the one who commands the best opportunities to monitor the noncontractual dimensions of production. A twist in the role of who becomes the residual claimant may occur, Barzel notes, when there is a substantial increase in the value of the contribution of the one with the fixed remuneration. The increased payment may cause the latter to become the residual claimant as the benefits of the drive for efficiency of the newborn residual claimant earlier surpasses the cost of monitoring that may further prompt efficiency. The argument shows the harmonic going together of homunculus's economic calculation and a sense of non-contractable dimensions as united in reciprocal purposiveness.

Jensen and Meckling expand on the incentive alignment issue as proposed by Alchian and Demsetz. The problem actually concerns a matter of information asymmetry as analyzed in principal–agent theories, Jensen and Meckling put forward. Their analysis also pairs a calculation and sense of intangible dimensions. For instance, the private corporation is a nexus for contracting relations regarding divisible residual claims on the assets and cash flows of the corporation. The owner-manager who has sold a part of his shares in the corporation finds himself in a situation that offers his enjoying the perquisites of which the cost is partly defrayed by the newborn shareholders. This practice evokes a response from prospective minority shareholders. They will take account of the managing owner's conduct that harms their interest and the monitoring cost it incurs. It reduces the share value. This interaction continues 'as long as the welfare increment he [owner-manager] experiences ... is large enough to offset them', that is, the share price reduction (Jensen, Meckling 1976: 313). Jensen and Meckling immediately add that a more relevant conflict between owner-manager and minority shareholders concerns the lessened incentive of the former to venture undertaking potentially profitable, although relatively risky, investments. In the remainder of the paper, they model the agency issues between the owner and shareholders generating a sophistication of contracts. The Jensen and Meckling paper features reasoning from inside the principal and agents as homunculi.

Cheung perceives the firm as combining owners of resources who exchange their property rights. Contrary to resource owners who transfer their property rights partially, for example, by a lease, stands the residual claimant who governs the acquired, contractually stipulated rights regarding the distribution of income among the parties and the conditions of the resource use. Cheung analyses it in terms of attenuating property rights occasioned by the partial nature of the transfer of them. It amounts to a strict analysis in terms of reciprocal purposiveness. At the same time, Cheung recognizes that uncertainty and prohibitively high transaction costs obstruct the route to complete contracting. In an example borrowed from French agricultural history, he demonstrates how a *fermier* acts as a middleman between the tenant farmer and the proprietor. The *fermier* assures the latter a fixed yield of the crop and contracts sharecropping with the tenant farmer. This *fermier* is an ideal type, a man on the spot, who epitomizes the required specific knowledge to economize on the transaction cost of a share contract. This *fermier* prompts the efficiency of risk reduction. As noted, the example is reminiscent of Knight's entrepreneur. Apparently, there is room that cannot be defined in tit-for-tat terms, rendering property rights susceptible to attenuation. Within that room appears Knight's entrepreneur and Cheung's *fermier* as ideal types coping with tacit, noncommunicable, local knowledge as it is presently indispensable under the assumption of uncertainty and/or positive transaction cost.

Richardson denotes that the flawless information of the perfect competition model cannot generate competition. It is rightly the unequally distributed knowledge regarding commercial opportunities that may entice entrepreneurs to venture undertaking production. Consequently, it is the ventured production process that causes a learning-by-doing growth of the firm, underlines Penrose. Heterogeneity is the fruit of competitive processes, generating capabilities that may give a sustained superior performance. At the same time, it is this growth in a qualitative context that sets limits to the growth of the firm, Penrose puts forward. First, the existing management is a limit for recruiting new personnel. Second, new personnel require experience in their new jobs in order to acquire the capabilities, that is, idiosyncratic knowledge. A process of experience and socialization is required to become acquainted with the competitive capabilities of the firm. It is reminiscent of Knight's (1921: 292) procedure in which management takes advantage of 'the knowledge of other men's knowledge of these things'. In phenomenological terms, it takes time and experience to develop employees as ideal types who command the capabilities that a firm features. It is to acquire reciprocity in purposiveness within the organization that sets limits to the growth of the firm. In a comparable manner, Richardson uses the concept of activities to explain a firm's boundary. Similar activities need certain capabilities. It alludes to reciprocal cooperation within an organization rather than atomistic behavior generating issues of incentive alignment. It reflects the idea of the firm as a repository of knowledge epitomized by the distinguished actors within the organization. It may readily be interpreted from the phenomenological perspective.

Both Richardson and Penrose adhere to the principle of economic rationality. For instance, Penrose (1959: 27) perceives the analytical apparatus of economics as the 'bricks and mortar' of her method. At the same time, they allow uncertainty and tacit knowledge as well as vague concepts such as capabilities and versatilities in their analyses. In a similar manner, NIE approaches to the firm may couple economic rationality with uncertainty and noncommunicable knowledge. It is the fruit of a methodological individualism that reasons from within, postulating human beings who are aware of their fellow man, be it as an associate, a consociate, or a contemporary. An explanation of the economic phenomena is the very aim. These theories represent realism in economics.

Contrary to this stand theories of the firm that reflect the nominalist stance. The patently complexity of the economic reality makes the theorist dismiss the analytical instrument of economic rationality. Observation and *nomina* guide the theorist in his search for refutable propositions. Nominalism results in positivism from without, that is, instrumentalism aiming at prediction, that is doomed to fail.

Notes

1 In contrast to Knight, Coase (1937: 401) sees opportunities to address uncertainty by contracting and rewarding people for 'better knowledge or judgment [although] not by actively taking part in production'. In this aspect, Coase ignores the very significance of Knight's entrepreneur, that is, to judge what is non-contractable, heading for a profitable venture. At the same, Coase accords with Knight in other instances, such as open-end contracts that afford flexibility.
2 The question refers to Plato's contradiction as pointed out in the *Meno*. Polanyi:

> He (Plato) says that to search for the solution of a problem is an absurdity; for either you know what you are looking for, and then there is no problem; or you do not know what you are looking for, and then you cannot expect to find anything.
>
> (1966: 22)

In Chapter 5 I refer to D.M. Armstrong (1983: 5), who, regarding Plato's contradiction, 'recalls Socrates' and G.E. Moore's "Paradox of Analysis"'.
3 The Coase Theorem states '*that the initial allocation of legal entitlement does not matter from an efficiency perspective as long as they can be exchanged in a perfectly competitive market*' (Cooter 1987: 457).
4 In explaining the importance of the personnel dimension in market relations, Menger (1976: 254) faces the reader with an affronting token of discrimination, apparently *bon ton* in his Vienna of the 1880s.
5 Coase (1988c: 36) refers to 'Wallis and North [who] have estimated that transaction costs are about 50 percent of the gross national product'. The cost distinction that is discussed raises serious doubts about the calculated figure. It presupposes disentanglement of the different cost types. Furthermore, it is highly probable that the high percentage contains double counts: once as a transaction cost and once as a production cost.
6 Here, I refer to Williamson who, in the prologue of his *The Institutions of Capitalism*, announces the book as follows.

> Contrary to earlier conceptions – in which the economic institutions of capitalism are explained by reference to class interests, technology, and/or monopoly power – the transaction cost approach maintains that these institutions have the main purpose and effect of economizing on transaction costs.
>
> (1985: 1)

7 This is a complicated proposition. It is correct as far as the irrelevance refers to the *mode* of organization. However, as far as the irrelevance refers to the organization of an economic activity *itself*, the proposition is untenable as the cost structures of the various production activities affect the organization of economic activity via the (de)composition pattern; witness Figure 6.1.
8 Referring to the preceding note, Williamson persists in his position as follows:

> In more numerous respects than are commonly appreciated, the substitution of internal organization for market exchange is attractive less on account of technological economies associated with production but because of what may be referred to broadly as "transactional failures" in the operation of markets for intermediate goods.
>
> (1971: 112)

9 In a 1996 reader, Williamson once again keeps silent about the relevant Coase–Fowler correspondence concerned:

> [T]ransaction cost economics attributes many of the problems of complex contracting to an hitherto little remarked but, in fact, widespread condition of "asset specificity".
>
> (1996: 13, n. 8)

10 The figure returns also in Williamson's (1996: 69) *The Mechanisms of Governance*.
11 Stigler's (1951) concept 'operations' within a production process is comparable to Richardson's (1972) concept of 'activities'.
12 The 'small numbers' condition refers to asset specificity that condemns parties to deal with each other.
13 Coase (2006) refers to them underpinning his critique. It concerns Casadesus-Masanell and Spulber (2000), Freeland (2000), and Miwa and Ramseyer (2000).

14 The context of this quote suggests that it is Coase's view that integration (within the firm) resolves opportunism. In Coase's 'Firm' paper, however, the firm is rather a device for flexibility to address contingencies. Conversely, Grossman and Hart's quote is properly applicable to Williamson's view regarding integration.

15 Williamson's organizational imperative reads as an incantation: '*Organize transactions so as to economize on bounded rationality while simultaneously safeguarding them against the hazards of opportunism*' (1985: 32).

16 *Metayage* is share cropping. A *censitaire* is someone who pays a quitrent to his feudal lord.

17 Hart's comment on Alchian and Demsetz is reminiscent of Coase's (1937: 401) critique on Knight, putting forward that contracted people may fulfil the tasks of the Knightian entrepreneur.

18 Jensen (1983) distinguishes principal–agent theory and agency theory. It is common in the engagement of both in issues of information asymmetry that offers the agent opportunities to give undue preferences to his own interest at the expense of his principal's interest. They differ in methodology. The principal–agent theory is normative and formal in its elaboration. It models:

> (1) the structure of the preferences of the parties to the contract, (2) the nature of uncertainty, and (3) the informational structure in environment.
>
> (ibid.: 334)

Given parties' risk preferences and information cost, the modelling concentrates on optimizing the contractual relationship (e.g., Spence, Zeckhauser 1971). The agency theory is positive and concentrates on contract and organization forms and the technology of monitoring (Jensen 1983: 334). Actually, Alchian and Demsetz (1972) present an instance of positive agency theory.

19 Walther Rathenau, industrialist and minister of foreign affairs during the Weimar Republic, assassinated June 24, 1922, at the age of 54.

20 This concept of Richardson is reminiscent of a quote by Armstrong (1983: 5) that is referred to in Chapter 5: 'We do not go from black night to daylight, but from twilight to daylight'.

21 It refers to the incompatibility as discussed by Stigler:

> Either the division of labor is limited by the extent of the market, and, characteristically, industries are monopolized; or industries are characteristically competitive, and the theorem is false or of little significance. Neither alternative is inviting.
>
> (1951: 185)

22 This interpretation is based on following quote from Menger, also referred to in Chapter 1. Menger:

> Die theoretische Wirtschaftslehre hat das generelle Wesen und den generellen Zusammenhang der volkswirtschaftlichen Erscheinungen zu erforschen, nicht etwa die volkswirtschaftlichen Begriffe zu analyseren und die aus dieser Analyse sich ergebenden Consequenzen zu ziehen.
>
> (1883: 6, n. 2)

References

Alchian, A.A., 1950, Uncertainty, Evolution, and Economic Theory, *The Journal of Political Economy, Vol. 58, No. 3*, 211–221.

Alchian, A.A., 1953, Biological Analogies in the Theory of the Firm: Comment, *The American Economic Review, Vol. 43, No. 4, Part 1*, 600–603.

Alchian, A.A., H. Demsetz, 1972, Production, Information Costs, and Economic Organization, *The American Economic Review*, December, *1972, Vol. 62, No. 5*, 777–795.

Alchian, A.A., S. Woodward, 1988, Review: The Firm Is Dead; Long Live The Firm; A Review of Oliver E. Williamson's The Economic Institutions of Capitalism, *Journal of Economic Literature, Vol. 26, No. 1*, 65–79.

Allen, G.C., 1929, *The Industrial Development of Birmingham and the Black Country, 1860-1927*, London: Allen & Unwin.

Arena, R., 1999, Austrians and Marshallians on Markets: Historical Origins and Compatible Views. In: S.C. Dow, P.E. Earl, eds., 1999, *Economic Organization and Economic Knowledge*, 14–35, Cheltenham: Edward Elgar.

Armstrong, D.M., 1983, *What Is a Law of Nature?*, Cambridge: Cambridge University Press.

Arrow, K.J., 1974, *The Limits of Organization*, New York: W.W. Norton & Company.

Barney, J.B., 1995, Looking inside for Competitive Advantage, *The Academy of Management Executive, Vol. 9, No. 4*, 49–61,

Barzel, Y., 1987, Entrepreneurial Reward for Self-Policing, *Economic Inquiry, January, XXV*, 103–116.

Berle, A.A., G.C. Means, 1932, [1982], *The Modern Corporation and Private Property*, New York: Macmillan; Reprint Edition, Buffalo, NY: William S. Hein & Co., Inc.

Carr, E.H., 1986, *What is History?*, 2nd ed., London: MacMillan.

Casadesus-Masanell, R., D.F. Spulber, 2000, The Fable of Fisher Body, *The Journal of Law & Economics, Vol. 43, No. 1*, 67–104.

Chandler, A.D., Jr., 1977, *The Visible Hand*, Cambridge, MA: The Belknap Press of Harvard University Press.

Chandler, A.D., Jr., S. Salsbury, 1971, *Pierre S. DuPont and the Making of the Modern Corporation*, New York: Harper & Row.

Cheung, S.N.S., 1969, Transaction Costs, Risk Aversion, and the Choice of Contractual Arrangements, *The Journal of Law & Economics, Vol. 12, No. 1*, 23–42.

Cheung, S.N.S., 1970, The Structure of a Contract and the Theory of a Non-Exclusive Resource, *The Journal of Law & Economics, Vol. 13, No. 1*, 49–70.

Cheung, S.N.S., 1983, The Contractual Nature of the Firm, *The Journal of Law & Economics*, April, *Vol. 26, No. 1*, 1–21.

Clark, J.B., 1891, Distribution as Determined by a Law of Rent, *The Quarterly Journal of Economics, Vol. 5, No. 3*, 289–318.

Coase, R.H., 1937, The Nature of the Firm, *Economica, Vol. 4 (n.s.)*, 386–405.

Coase, R.H., 1960, The Problem of Social Cost, *The Journal of Law and Economics, Vol. 3*, 1–44.

Coase, R.H., 1966, The Theory of Public Utility Pricing, *Papers presented at a Conference Held at Northwestern University June 19-24, 1966*, 96–106.

Coase, R.H., 1988a, The Nature of the Firm: Origin, *The Journal of Law, Economics, & Organization, Vol. 4, No. 1*, 3–17.

Coase, R.H., 1988b, The Nature of the Firm: Meaning, *The Journal of Law, Economics, & Organization, Vol. 4, No. 1*, 19–32.

Coase, R.H., 1988c, The Nature of the Firm: Influence, *The Journal of Law, Economics, & Organization, Vol. 4, No. 1*, 33–47.

Coase, R.H., 1990, Accounting and the Theory of the Firm, *Journal of Accounting and Economics, Vol. 12*, 3–13.

Coase, R.H., 1992, The Institutional Structure of Production, *The American Economic Review, Vol. 82, No. 4*, 713–719.

Coase, R.H., 2000, The Acquisition of Fisher Body by General Motors, *The Journal of Law & Economics, Vol. 43, No. 1*, 15–32.

Coase, R.H., 2006, The Conduct of Economics: The Example of Fisher Body and General Motors, *Journal of Economics & Management Strategy, Vol. 15, No. 2*, 255–278.

Cooter, R.D., 1987, [1991], Coase Theorem. In: J. Eatwell, M. Milgate, P. Newman, eds., 1987, [1991], *The New Palgrave, A Dictionary of Economics, Vol. 1*, 457–459, London: The Macmillan Press Limited.

Demsetz, H., 1988a, The Theory of the Firm Revisited, *The Journal of Law, Economics, & Organization, Spring, Vol. 4*, 141–161.

Demsetz, H., 1988b, [1990], *Ownership, Control, and the Firm, the Organization of Economic Activity*, Vol. I, Oxford: Basil Blackwell Ltd.

Demsetz, H., 1988c, Vertical Integration: Theories and Evidence. In: H. Demsetz, ed., 1988a, [1990], *Ownership, Control, and the Firm, the Organization of Economic Activity*, Vol. I, 166–186, Oxford: Basil Blackwell Ltd.

Demsetz, H., 1988d, Profit as a Functional Return: Reconsidering Knight's Views. In: H. Demsetz, ed., 1988b, [1990], *Ownership, Control, and the Firm, the Organization of Economic Activity*, Vol. I, 236–247, Oxford: Basil Blackwell Ltd.

Demsetz, H., 1995, [1997], *The Economics of the Business Firm*, Cambridge: Cambridge University Press.

Demsetz, H., 2008, *From Economic Man to Economic System*, Cambridge: Cambridge University Press.

Dore, R., 1983, Goodwill and the Spirit of Market Capitalism, *The British Journal of Sociology, Vol. 34, No. 4*, 459–482.

Dow, G.K., 1987, The Function of Authority in Transaction Cost Economics, *Journal of Economic Behavior and Organization, Vol. 8*, 13–38.

Dow, S.C., P.E. Earl, eds., 1999, *Economic Organization and Economic Knowledge*, Cheltenham: Edward Elgar.

Eatwell, J., M. Milgate, P. Newman, eds., 1987, [1991], *The New Palgrave, a Dictionary of Economics*, Vol. 1, London: The Macmillan Press Limited.

Ellis, H.S., 1950, The Economic Way of Thinking, *The American Economic Review, Vol. 40*, 1–12.

Fama, E.F., 1980, Agency Problems and the Theory of the Firm, *Journal of Political Economy, Vol. 88, No. 2*, 288–307.

Fama, E.F., M.C. Jensen, 1983, Separation of Ownership and Control, *The Journal of Law & Economics, Jun., 1983, Vol. 26, No. 2*, Corporations and Private Property: A Conference Sponsored by the Hoover Institution, 301–325.

Fourie, F.C.V.N., 1993, In the Beginning There Where Markets? In: C. Pitelis, 1993, *Transaction Costs, Markets and Hierarchies*, 41–64, Oxford: Basil Blackwell Ltd.

Freeland, R.F., 2000, Creating Holdup through Vertical Integration: Fisher Body, *The Journal of Law & Economics, Vol. 43, No. 1*, 33–66.

Grossman, S.J., O.D. Hart, 1986, The Costs and Benefits of Ownership: A Theory of Vertical and Lateral Integration, *The Journal of Political Economy, Vol. 94, No. 4*, 691–719.

Hart, O., 1989, An Economist's Perspective on the Theory of the Firm, *Columbia Law Review, Vol. 89, No. 7, Contractual Freedom in Corporate Law*, 1757–1774.

Hayek, F.A. von, ed., 1935, *Collectivist Economic Planning*, London: Routledge & Kegan Paul Ltd.

Hayek, F.A. von, 1937, Economics and Knowledge, *Economica, New Series, Vol. 4, No. 13*, 33–54.

Hayek, F.A., 1945, The Use of Knowledge in Society, *The American Economic Review,* *Vol. 35, No. 4*, 519–530.

Hodgson, G.M., 2002, The Legal Nature of the Firm and the Myth of the Firm-Market Hybrid, *International Journal of the Economics of Business, Vol. 9, No. 1*, 37–60.

Holmström, B., J. Roberts, 1998, The Boundaries of the Firm Revisited, *The Journal of Economic Perspectives, Autumn, 1998, Vol. 12, No. 4*, 73–94.

Jaffé, W., 1976, Menger, Jevons and Walras De-homogenized, *Economic Inquiry, Vol. XIV*, 511–524.

Jensen, M.C., 1983, Organization Theory and Methodology, *The Accounting Review, Vol. 58, No. 2*, 319–339.

Jensen, M.C., W.H. Meckling, 1976, Theory of the Firm: Managerial Behavior, Agency Costs and Ownership Structure, *Journal of Financial Economics, Vol. 3*, 305–360.

Joskow, P.L., 1988, Asset Specificity and the Structure of Vertical Relationships: Empirical Evidence, *The Journal of Law, Economics, & Organization, Vol. 4, No. 1*, 95–117.

Kaufmann, F., 1931, Was kann die mathematische Methode in der Nationalökonomie leisten? *Zeitschrift für Nationalökonomie, Vol. 2, nr. 5*, 754–779.

Kaufmann, F., 1933, On the Subject-Matter and Method of Economic Science, *Economica, No. 42*, 381–401.

Kaufmann, F., 1944, *Methodology of the Social Sciences*, Atlantic Highlands, New Jersey: Humanities Press.

Kitch, E.W., 1983, The Fire of Truth: A Remembrance of Law and Economics at Chicago, 1932-1970, *The Journal of Law and Economics, Vol. 26, No. 1*, 163–234.

Kirzner, I.M., 1960, *The Economic Point of View*, Kansas City, MO: Sheed and Ward, Inc.

Kirzner, I.M., 1999, Rationality, Entrepreneurship, and Economic 'Imperialism'. In: S.C. Dow, P.E. Earl, eds., 1999, *Economic Organization and Economic Knowledge*, 1–13, Cheltenham: Edward Elgar.

Klein, B., 1988, Vertical Integration as Organizational Ownership: The Fisher Body-General Motors Relationship Revisited, *The Journal of Law, Economics, & Organization, Vol. 4, No. 1*, 199–213.

Klein, B., 1998, The Hold-Up Problem. In: P.K. Newman, M. Milgate, P. Newman, eds., 1998, *The New Palgrave Dictionary of Economics and Law 2*, 241–242, New York: Stockton Press.

Klein, B., 2000, Fisher—General Motors and the Nature of the Firm, *The Journal of Law & Economics, Vol. 43, No. 1*, 105–142.

Klein, B., R.G. Crawford, A.A. Alchian, 1978, Vertical Integration, Appropriable Rents, and the Competitive Contracting Process, *The Journal of Law & Economics, Vol. 21, No. 2*, 297–326.

Knight, F.H., 1921, [1971], *Risk, Uncertainty and Profit*, Chicago, IL: Chicago University Press.

Lester, R.A., 1946, Shortcomings of Marginal Analysis for Wage-Employment Problems, *The American Economic Review, Vol. 36*, 63–82.

Machlup, F., 1967, Theories of the Firm: Marginalist, Behavioral, Managerial, *The American Economic Review, March, Vol. 57, No. 1*, 1–33.

Mäki, U., 1998, Is Coase a Realist?, *Philosophy of the Social Sciences, Vol. 28, No. 1*, 5–31.

Manne, H.G., 1965, Mergers and the Market for Corporate Control, *The Journal of Political Economy, Vol. 73, No. 2*, 110–120.

Marshall, A., 1890, [1920], *Principles of Economics*, 8th ed., London: Macmillan and Co., Limited

McNulty, P.J., 1967, Allocative Efficiency vs. "X-Efficiency": Comment, *The American Economic Review*, December, *Vol. 57, No. 5*, 1249–1252.

Menger, C., 1883, [2005], *Untersuchungen über die Methode der Socialwissenschaften und der Politischen Oekonomie insbesondere*, Leipzig: Verlag von Duncker & Humblot; [Elibron Classics].

Menger, C., 1892, On the Origin of Money, *The Economic Journal, Vol. 2, No. 6*, 239–255.

Menger, C., 1976, [2007], *Principles of Economics*, translated by J. Dingwall, B.F. Hoselitz, Auburn, AL: Ludwig von Mises Institute; original title: *Grundsätze der Volkswirtschaftslehre*, 1871.

Miwa, Y., J.M. Ramseyer, 2000, Rethinking Relationship-Specific Investments: Subcontracting in the Japanese Automobile Industry, *Michigan Law Review, 98*, 2636–2667.

Moore, T.G., 1983, Introduction, *The Journal of Law & Economics, Vol. 26, No. 2, Corporations and Private Property: A Conference Sponsored by the Hoover Institution*, 235–236.

Nelson, P., 1970, Information and Consumer Behavior, *The Journal of Political Economy, Vol. 78, No. 2*, 311–329.

Nelson, R.R., S.G. Winter, 1982, [1996], *An Evolutionary Theory of Economic Change*, Cambridge, MA: The Belknap Press of the Harvard University Press.

Newman, P.K., M. Milgate, P. Newman, eds., 1998, *The New Palgrave Dictionary of Economics and Law 2*, New York: Stockton Press.

Penrose, E.T., 1952, Biological Analogies in the Theory of the Firm, *The American Economic Review, Vol. 42, No. 5*, 804–819.

Penrose, E.T., 1953, Biological Analogies in the Theory of the Firm: Rejoinder, *The American Economic Review, Vol. 43, No. 4, Part 1*, 603–609.

Penrose, E.T., 1959, [1997], *The Theory of the Growth of the Firm*, Oxford: Oxford University Press.

Peteraf, M.A., 1993, The Cornerstones of Competitive Advantage: A Resource-Based View, *Strategic Management Journal, Vol. 14*, 179–191.

Pitelis, C., 1993, *Transaction Costs, Markets and Hierarchies*, Oxford: Basil Blackwell Ltd.

Polanyi, M., 1966, [2009], *The Tacit Dimension*, Chicago, IL: Chicago University Press.

Powell, T.C., 2001, Competitive Advantage: Logical and Philosophical Considerations, *Strategic Management Journal, Vol. 22, No. 9*, 875–888.

Richardson, G.B., 1959, Equilibrium, Expectations and Information, *The Economic Journal, Vol. 69, No. 274*, 223–237.

Richardson, G.B., 1972, The Organisation of Industry, *The Economic Journal, Vol. 82, No. 327*, 883–896.

Richardson, G.B., 1990, *Information and Investment*, Oxford: Clarendon Press.

Robertson, D.H., 1923, [1947], *The Control of Industry*, London: Nisbet & Co. Ltd.

Robinson, A., 1934, The Problem of Management and the Size of Firms, *The Economic Journal*, June, *Vol. 44, No. 174*, 242–257.

Schumpeter, J.A., 1934, [1993], *The Theory of Economic Development*, New Brunswick: Transaction Publishers.

Schutz, A., 1932, [1967], *The Phenomenology of the Social World*, New York: Northwestern University Press; [*Der sinnhafte Aufbau der sozialen Welt*, Wien: Julius Springer].

Schutz, A., 1953, Common-Sense and Scientific Interpretation of Human Action, *Philosophy and Phenomenological Research, Vol. 14*, 1–38.

Smith, A., 1776, [2005], *The Inquiry into the Nature and Causes of the Wealth of Nations*, London: W. Strahan and T. Cadell; The Electronic Classics Series, Penn State: Pennsylvania State University.

Spence, M., R. Zeckhauser, 1971, Insurance, Information and Individual Action, *The American Economic Review, Vol. LXI, No. 2*, 380–387.

Stigler, G.J., 1951, The Division of Labor Is Limited by the Extent of the Market, *The Journal of Political Economy, Vol. 59, No. 3*, 185–193.

Teece, D., G. Pisano, 1994, The Dynamic Capabilities of Firms: An Introduction, *Industrial and Corporate Change, Vol. 3, No. 3*, 537–556.

Williamson, O.E., 1971, The Vertical Integration of Production: Market Failure Considerations, *The American Economic Review, Vol. 61, No. 2, Papers and Proceedings*, 112–123.

Williamson, O.E., 1975, *Markets and Hierarchies*, New York: The Free Press.

Williamson, O.E., 1979, Transaction-Cost Economics: The Governance of Contractual Relations, *The Journal of Law & Economics, Oct., Vol. 22, No. 2*, 233–261.

Williamson, O.E., 1981, The Modern Corporation: Origins, Evolution, Attributes, *Journal of Economic Literature, Vol. 19*, 1537–1568.

Williamson, O.E., 1983, Credible Commitments: Using Hostages to Support Exchange, *The American Economic Review, Vol. 73, No. 4*, 519–540.

Williamson, O.E., 1984, The Economics of Governance: Framework and Implications, *Zeitschrift für die gesamte Staatswissenschaft / Journal of Institutional and Theoretical Economics, Bd. 140, H. 1., The New Institutional Economics: A Symposium (März 1984)*, 195–223.

Williamson, O.E., 1985, *The Economic Institutions of Capitalism*, New York: The Free Press.

Williamson, O.E., 1994, *Comparative Economic Organisation, The Analysis of Discrete Structural Alternatives*, San Francisco, CA: Institute for Contemporary Studies.

Williamson, O.E., 1996, *The Mechanisms of Governance*, New York: Oxford University Press.

Williamson, O.E., S.E. Masten, eds., 1999, *The Economics of Transaction Costs*, Cheltenham: Edward Elgar Publishing Ltd.

7 Market and government

7.1 Introduction

Adam Smith's *The Wealth of Nations* 'is a book that still lives and from which we continue to learn', commented Ronald Coase in March 1976 when commemorating the two hundredth anniversary of its publication (Coase 1994: 75). The comment seemingly confirms Richard Posner's (1993) view on Coase's methodological position. According to Posner, it is the anecdote and the narrative of 'historical and even journalistic methods of empirical research' rather than 'random sampling and statistical inference' that feature Coase's 'Adam Smithian approach' (ibid.: 203). Coase represents the opposite of what Posner (1993: 199) contends: 'A science tends to forget its founders: physicists don't read Newton, or for that matter Einstein'. Apparently, Posner alludes that Coase missed the boat of modern economics. Posner:

> Coase's influence in economics has been diminished by the fact that his articles do not speak the language of modern economics, which is mathematics, and by the fact that he has not attempted to develop a *theory* of transaction costs.
>
> (ibid.: 207)

For a definition of this modern economics, Coase himself refers to Posner who denotes it as follows:

> Economics is the science of human choice in a world in which resources are limited in relation to human wants. It explores and tests the implications of the assumption that man is a maximizer of his ends in life, in his satisfactions -what we shall call his '"self-interest"'.
>
> (Posner, quoted in Coase 1994: 42)

It is modern economists' employment of quantitative methods that enables them 'to move into neighbouring disciplines', rendering economics a general science of human choice (Coase 1994: 40). It refers to the application of the rational choice model axiomatically explaining the behavior of actors who aim

DOI: 10.4324/9781315764221-7

to maximize their utility in whatever action they undertake. It broadens the scope of economics to previously unknown domains such as politics, crime, and marital choice. At the same time, it is 'a narrowing of professional interest to more formal, technical, commonly mathematical, analysis' (ibid.: 42).

This modern economics is in sharp contrast with Coase's concept of economics. It is Adam Smith, Coase notes, who succeeded 'in creating ... our system of analysis' (ibid.: 79). Smith addresses 'the extremely difficult question' as posed by the division of labor:

> How is the cooperation of these vast numbers of people in countries all over the world, which is necessary for even a modest standard of living, to be brought about?
>
> (ibid.: 80)

A complement of Coase's Adam Smithian approach is an economics in which the axiom is evidenced that men will purchase less when the price of the commodity increases. The theorist may refrain from referring to the awkward axiom of maximizing utility to be substantiated in domains not acquainted with the '"measuring rod of money"' (Coase 1994: 44).

An additional methodological point in Posner's modern economics definition, as quoted by Coase, regards the adherence to positivism, that is, testing the implications of maximizing '"self-interest"'.[1] Coase minimizes the relevance of testing and refers to insights of John M. Keynes's *General Theory* and Edward Chamberlin's *Theory of Monopolistic Competition*. During the 1930s and 1940s, their intuitions were adopted on all sides with 'nothing remotely resembling' an empirical testing procedure (Coase 1994: 23). It concurs with Coase's search for insight into the working of the economic system rather than accurate predictions. The fruit of theory is the explanation (ibid.: 16–18).

Furthermore, Coase finds important grounds for his objections against math and theoretical rigor in economics in the so-called high theory as studied by, for example, James Meade, Abba Lerner, and Paul Samuelson. It is omniscience that makes them high-powered economists. Omniscient about demand and cost functions enables, for instance, Meade to propose government production in those cases in which monopoly is inevitable, for example, 'where a community needs only one gas-works, or electricity station'. Meade states:

> In these cases, socialisation in one form or another, of the industries concerned, is the only radical cure to ensure that they are run in such a way as to equate marginal costs to prices of the product produced (or the prices of the factors of production to the value of their marginal products) rather than to make a profit.
>
> (1944: 322)

The marginal cost pricing, as Meade prescribes in the quote, is a paragon of what Coase (1992: 714) repeatedly labels as 'blackboard economics'. Coase

(1945: 113) comments that Meade's 'price and output policy of state enterprises' ... 'would tend to move it away from the optimum'. It initiates what he titled in 1946 as 'The Marginal Cost Controversy' (Coase 1946). In this *Economica* paper, he further elaborates the objections against government interference in realizing marginal cost pricing as presented in Harold Hotelling's (1938) paper. At that time, Hotelling had been appreciated as an 'abstract theorist' who, according to James Bonbright (1941: 385), formulated 'one of the most distinguished contributions to rate-making theory in the entire literature of economics'. It is justifiably this type of abstract, that is, theoretical building, that Coase debunks as it is based on the patently untenable assumption that government has sufficient data to imitate efficient allocation as if Knightian uncertainty would be nonexistent. For instance, 'the indifference loci, unlike measures of pleasure, are objective and capable of empirical determination', that is, 'by means of questionnaires ... mapping out in a tentative manner the indifference loci', Hotelling (1938: 245) argues. Coase vehemently dismisses such an approach.

However, in the manner that Posner (2011: S39) considers it, Coase is chiefly prejudice-ridden: 'Coase's extreme hostility to government regulation, reflected everywhere in his work'. Intriguing is what Posner adds to this claim. He argues, *nota bene* in his 2011 paper:

> His (Coase's) hostility to government regulation does not have the analytical basis that one finds in the works of Friedrich Hayek and other members of the Austrian school of economics or in those of Milton Friedman, Mancur Olson, or George Stigler.
>
> (ibid.)

Apparently, Posner maintains the opinion that Coase is basically anti-theoretical, picking 'his case studies with an eye to probable government failure' (ibid.). He attributes Coase's 'stubborn adherence to ... commonsense economics' to the 'confidence with which he [Coase] rejects formal theory and formal empirical methods' (ibid.).

Obviously, Posner fancies a caricature of Coase's position regarding government in economics and the alleged lack of a theoretical foundation for it. Quite the contrary, Coase's position toward government interference and regulation stems straightforwardly from his theoretical frame. As little as, in the 'Firm' paper, Coase's questioning the reason for the firm in a market economy would be a sign of an ideological preoccupation, does his questioning government's role in the economy stem from such a bias, let alone hostility.

Again, the fundamentally theoretical stance is how to advance a comparatively efficient institutional arrangement beginning from the notion that the economic system works itself? Therefore, the first Section, 7.2, elaborates on the null hypothesis that is theoretically specified as the Coase Theorem. Section 7.3 discusses the government and a third sector that are allocation alternatives to the market. Finally, the allocation of scarce recourses regards a sophisticated play of market and nonmarket solutions. It refers to the theoretical legacy of economics from Knight and Coase, who emphasize the fundamental role of property rights; that is, economics originates from someone who takes care of scarce resources. Section 7.4 elaborates on the origin and nature of property. Attention is required toward the specific interpretation of property in the new institutional economics (NIE) as a bundle of rights.

These sections prelude the elaboration of the institutional arrangements that begins with Section 7.5 discussing how Coase deals with government interference in the market. One by one, the cases decrease the intensity of the argument for the interference of established economic theory. It is the fruit of Coase's case study methodology that is so condescended by Posner. Section 7.6 extends on the comparative institutional approach. Section 7.7 applies it to classic cases of market failure. Section 7.8 provides a summary of the chapter.

7.2 The zero hypothesis of the market mechanism

Since Adam Smith, economics has fostered its null hypothesis, that is, the normal economic system works itself. Smith:

> by directing that industry in such a manner as its produce may be of the greatest value, he intends only his own gain, and he is in this, as in many other cases, led by an invisible hand to promote an end which was no part of his intention.

> (1776: 434)

The Marginal Revolution stipulates the conditions to arrive at 'the greatest value'. George Stigler recaps them as follows:

1. The marginal rates of substitution between commodities must be equal for all individuals. If this is not so, an exchange of goods will help one person without injuring the other.
2. Marginal costs must equal prices. If this condition is not met it is possible to reallocate resources in such a way as to increase outputs of some goods without decreasing outputs of any.

> (1943: 356)

The efficiency conditions formalize the concept of the invisible hand that has occupied economists since the publication of *The Wealth of Nations*, Coase (1992: 713) notes in his Nobel Prize lecture. It has led to an economics of extreme decentralization in which 'information remains full and free' (Demsetz 1988: 148). The efficiency conditions concern prices and outputs, disregarding what occurs within the black boxes of production. It constitutes the background of Coase's (1992) 'Firm' paper. Hence, *The Institutional Structure of Production* is the title of his Nobel Prize lecture. In this aspect, even more striking is the neglect of 'the institutional arrangements which govern the process of exchange'; the *sine qua non* of the system of prices (ibid.: 714).

Making these institutional dimensions explicit substantiates why and in which manner 'the normal economic system works itself'. When studying the economic system, the economist questions in imitation of Adam Smith, 'How is the cooperation of these vast numbers of people ... to be brought about?' (Coase 1994: 80). The objective of the economic system is to reconcile the preferences of people competing for available resources. It must solve the relative value problem of allocation, that is, the cost of employing resources as excluding their use in another opportunity.

Harold Demsetz identifies two tasks that 'any acceptable allocation mechanism' must manage:

- firstly, that information must be generated about all of the benefits of employing resources in alternative uses, and
- secondly, that persons be motivated to take account of this information.

(1964: 16)

Market exchange generates information regarding the relative value problem that is reflected in opportunity costs. The prerequisite for ensuing that 'persons be motivated' regards the assignment of property rights. As noted in Chapter 5, Frank Knight words the fundamental significance of property rights as follows:

> If an agency is limited relatively to the need for its use, it must be appropriated by some one, to be administrated, to decide who is to have the use of it and who is to do without.
>
> (1921: 188–189, n. 2)

Coase (1959, 1960) elaborates on this idea of Knight in his 'Federal Communication Commission' ('FCC') and 'Social Cost' papers. Coase: 'the delimitation of rights is an essential prelude to market transactions', enabling the market to work (1959: 27). The highest bidder may have the use of the agency. However, as Coase (1960: 6) proposes, the very assumption behind this outcome is that the property rights are well defined, and the 'pricing system is assumed to work smoothly (that is, costlessly)'. The bearing of this zero-transaction-cost assumption induces George Stigler to formulate the Coase Theorem. Given a zero-transaction cost,

> the manner in which legal rights were assigned would have no effect whatever upon the methods of production.
>
> (Stigler 1972: 11)

The resources will be used in the production that offers the greatest value. The Coase Theorem is the analytical elaboration of the null hypothesis regarding the working of the market. In his *Notes on the Problem of Social Cost*, Coase refers to Francis Edgeworth's contract curve as an expedient device to exemplify the Coase Theorem. Obviously, if nothing hinders the individuals engaged in exchanging goods, they will 'end on the "contract curve"', making 'both of them better off' (Coase 1988: 160). In this context, he further refers to Paul Samuelson, who proffers that a bilateral or multilateral monopoly may lead to indeterminate situations hindering the negotiators' arrival at the contract curve and unable to profit from mutual benefit in spite of the zero-transaction cost (ibid.: 159). A comparable comment makes Robert Cooter (1987) in his *New Palgrave* entry on the Coase Theorem. Apparently, Coase neglects strategic behavior that may hinder a beneficial trade. 'The Coase Theorem errs in the direction of optimism', Cooter diagnoses (ibid.: 459). Cooter continues:

Although accurate as a rule of thumb, the transaction cost interpretation is not strictly true.

(ibid.)

From a methodological perspective, this is a significant supplementary comment. For that matter, Coase occupies the same line of defense in his reply to Samuelson. 'Normally, Coase concludes, we would expect them to end up there' (on the contract curve; Coase 1988: 162). Cooter, and so Coase, disregard that the Coase Theorem is the fruit of analysis of meaning à la Felix Kaufmann (1944). They fall prey to confounding the analysis meaning with the causal explanation of facts.

The Coase Theorem is a theoretical proposition, like the law of demand. It describes the conduct of homunculi who observe the *postulate of rationality*, and *of subjective interpretation*, as explicated in Chapter 2. The former postulate forbids that the homunculus declines a Paretian efficiency improvement. The latter observes homunculi's common sense as 'typical thoughts must be attributed to it (homunculus' conduct) to explain the fact in question' (Schutz 1943: 147). Benefit from mutual gain substantiates what is assumed to be typical for human beings who recognize themselves in their fellow man. The phenomenological point of view warrants economics as a non-atomistic social science through maintaining methodological individualism.

Thus, the market mechanism as a zero hypothesis finds its analytical elaboration in the Coase Theorem as a theoretical law. In contrast to the theoretical law as the fruit of the analysis of meaning stands the causal explanation of facts as the empirical counterpart of the former. Regarding the Coase Theorem, at issue is its empirical significance. If the theoretical law or proposition does not agree with the facts,

the divergence is referred to disturbing factors, without anything positive being said about the latter.

(Kaufmann 1933: 388)

The *ceteris paribus* condition is a shorthand of 'disturbing factors'. In the Coase Theorem, the *ceteris paribus* condition regards the zero-transaction-cost assumption that renders the proposition non-falsifiable. At the same time, the obvious empirical nonconformity of such a theoretical law demands further analysis (of meaning). The concept of transaction cost is a theoretical trouvaille that exhorts the analyst to formulate a new deductive logic, that is, a new situational logic, that explains the empirical nonconformity. Whether the new answer is correct 'brings the procedural rules into play' (Kaufmann 1944: 232). The theoretical laws determine the direction of the economic analysis. This is definitely valid for the Coase Theorem.

The concept of transaction is inextricably related to property rights and legal systems. If there is then empirical evidence of a positive transaction cost, the Coase Theorem does not hold and guides the economic analysis in the direction of 'knowing how legal systems work' (Stigler 1972: 12). This is the Kaufmannian methodological procedure: renew the theoretical proposition. The new theoretical proposition addresses the *ceteris paribus* conditions that feature a homunculus's situational logic in which the assignment of rights does have an effect 'upon the methods of production' or, more generally, on the outcome of the economic process (ibid.: 11). A rephrased Coase Theorem of Stigler reads: '"under perfect competition private and social costs will be equal"' (Stigler 1966: 113; quoted in Coase 1988: 158). If perfect competition does not hold, the theoretical question arises of which legal, institutional design may near, for example, equalizing prices and marginal cost to maximize the value of production.

The Coase Theorem has no empirical pendant. The exchange of property rights as concluded without cost renders that the normal economic system works itself. Under this condition, the allocation mechanism seemingly reduces the situational logic to arithmetic. Its analysis is engaged in explicating, as Lionel Robbins sees it, '"the governing factor of all productive organization -the relationship of prices and cost"' (1932: 70; quoted in Coase 1992: 714).

In the 'Firm' paper, Coase demonstrates that the mere relationship of prices and cost does not apparently suffice in the normal economic system of markets. 'Professor Knight introduces managers who co-ordinate. ... Why are there these "islands of conscious power"?' Coase (1937: 388) asks. However, Coase shows in the 'Marginal Cost Controversy' paper that, when Robbins's governing factor of the relationship between prices and cost fails, interference in this relationship does not *per se* remedy it. Thereafter, the 'Social Cost' paper introduces, as Benjamin Klein advances, the issue of the failing governing of prices and cost under one heading: transaction cost as 'a missing element in our models' (Kitch 1983: 202). It identifies transaction costs as the analytical point to examine 'the constraints on the trading process in trying to explain real world institutions, including the nature of the firm' (ibid.).

The marvel of the price mechanism has unjustly diverted theorists' attention from the internal arrangements within organizations and the institutional arrangements that govern the process of exchange (ibid.: 714). These institutional arrangements establish, assign, protect, and enforce property rights, accompanying the exchanges. It establishes the NIE research agenda: 'a *comparative institutional approach*' (Demsetz 1969: 1). In mundane economic reality, the economic agent has recourse to a trade-off between positive transaction costs and institutional arrangements to substantiate his situational logic. It is the refutation of the null hypothesis of the market mechanism that directs theorists' attention to comparative institutional arrangements. Market failures abound: externalities, natural monopoly, public goods, a failing market for innovation arguing for patents, and failing health insurance solidarity. They constitute just as much the reason for the search for alternative institutional arrangements. The *comparative* analysis of institutional arrangements regards, first of all, a comparison of the relative efficiency of markets versus government as their alternative in solving the allocation question though not excluding other nonmarket options. It regards interference or noninterference in the normal economic system.

7.3 Market, government, and allocation

Since the rise of socialism as a political-economic alternative to capitalism, economists have been engaged in the debate about governmental central planning versus voluntary market exchange as alternative allocation options; witness, for example, Hayek's (1935) *Collectivist Economic Planning*. In discussing government interference in the market economy, Coase (1946: 171) takes up this debate. He begins with a 'turn to a consideration of fundamentals'. How can goods and services be allocated? It is either the individual consumers commanding various sums of money in order to obtain goods and services by paying for them 'in accordance with a system of prices', or 'it would be possible for the Government to decide what to produce and to allocate goods and services directly to consumers' (ibid.: 171–172). It is reminiscent of Léon Walras's (1954: 67) duo, individualism versus communism, granting primacy to allocation as the preceding economic question.

As noted in Chapter 3, Walras disconnects the tie between economics and appropriation, implicitly ignoring the market. It is an ideal-type competition that generates equilibrium between ratios of marginal utilities and prices (ibid.: 71). He disregards whether state ownership or private property markets prime the economy. A comparable scenario, for instance, is Guido Calabresi's (1991: 1214), who proposes 'that neither market nor nonmarket forms of organization are primary'. He continues that people are primarily engaged in finding 'the most efficient (least costly) way of structuring their relationships' (ibid.). They use power, either by wealth in a market regime or by power in a command structure. Calabresi takes them as alternative agents. Additionally, Kenneth Boulding (1969) takes 'the universal problem' of allocating scarce resources as fundamental and preceding the market-versus-command issue. In an elegant elaboration, he distinguishes 'three groups of social organizers', that is, 'the threat system, the exchange system, and the integrative system' (ibid.: 4). The threat system refers to the state in which political decisions and structures allocate via coercion. The integrative system represents the very opposite of threat, allocating based on community spirit, for example, via eleemosynary institutions and public benefactors. Economics allocates via exchange and occupies the middle position of the three systems. At the same time, 'it edges over towards the integrative system insofar' as economics has some jurisdiction over the study of the '"grants economy"', that is, 'one-way transfers of exchangeables' (ibid.). On the other side, economics interfaces with the threat system, for example, in studying strategic bargaining options. Clearly, exchange, coercion, and integrative benevolence show several interrelationships that may be recognized in the elaboration of the market-versus-state issue. Boulding's perspective shows that a moral moment precedes the allocation system choice. Hence, the title of Boulding's paper reads: 'Economics as a Moral Science'.

Obviously, the economic reality is embedded in humans' social life, and economics merely studies an aspect of it. At the same time, in presenting state command as an alternate allocation option, Boulding, and Walras and Calabresi with him, gloss over a basic nature of the allocation question, that is, that, in economics, it regards the allocation of scarce means to satisfy the ends of idiosyncratic human beings, of *individuals*. It is as Ellis emphasizes in his presidential address to the American Economic Association:

> economic analysis rests fundamentally upon individual choice; and where the individual cannot choose, economics does not exist.
>
> (1950: 1)

Economics regards an individual's '"the little more and the little less"' as being engaged in making his (own) ends meet with his scarce means (ibid.: 2). Economics is profoundly individualistic, both regarding the means and the ends; not engaged in "given ends" as Lionel Robbins (Robbins) asserts it would be. An individual's free choice is basic, that is, stipulating his own ends in a weighing of costs against utilities in the economic process of the market. At the same time, the primacy of an individual's free choice does not result in an apology for the *laissez-faire* economy but is the very leitmotif in designing interference to remedy market failures such as monopoly and side effects. Not counting the macroeconomic distress of mass unemployment and hyperinflation, the free-choice economy collects an immeasurable number of market failures. Apparently, there is *prima facie* a good case for intervention by the government. However, as far as government intervention curtails free individual choice, it rules out economics, at least in Ellis's view. In Boulding's vocabulary, it edges over to another allocation system. In the delicate assessment of market regime versus command structure, the very criterion is this: How can free individual choice be restored? (Ellis 1950: 11). This is a fundamental question that an economist is compelled to pose and not, as Posner alleges, a token of hostility toward government regulation. The individualistic nature of property rights and exchange of them to address scarcity demands a basic reservation against the role of the state.

In Richard Musgrave's (1959) *The Theory of Public Finance*, allocation represents one of the three branches of government activity in the economy. Fundamentally, however, the idea of state allocation of scarce means is opposite to the economics of 'the man on the spot' who commands the relevant information regarding his means and ends to determine the logic of an exchange situation. State allocation of scarce means, by definition, rules out the primacy of the free individual choice of ends. Moreover, the government lacks information regarding individual preferences and faces unpredictable effects of its allocative action. Thus, arbitrariness enters into a state's role in the economy that goes diametrically against the rule of law as the standard for a state's taking action. Hayek describes the rule of law as follows. 'Stripped of all its technicalities',

> this means that government in all its actions is bound by rules fixed and announced beforehand.
>
> (Hayek 1944: 75)

It offers the individual certainty and security about authority's conduct and use of its coercive power in given situations that enables the individual to plan his affairs by providing him with the rules of the game to experience his situational logic. The absence of arbitrariness in an authority's conduct is the essence of the rule of law. Interference or not is not the question in a *laissez-faire* economy. The important question is, as Hayek puts forward,

> whether the individual can foresee the action of the state and make use of this knowledge as a datum in forming his own plans, with the result that the state cannot control the use made of its machinery, and that the individual knows precisely how far he will be protected against interference from others, or whether the state is in a position to frustrate individual efforts.
>
> (ibid.: 84)

The rule of law creates the same objective opportunities for different people, enabling the individual to oversee his situation. At the same time, the subjective chances will differ and consequently cause inequality. However, it is not an inequality that stems from arbitrary decisions about societal status that affect particular people in a certain way. Referring to Sir Henry Maine, Hayek interprets the rule of law as the true opposite of the rule of status handing out privileges (ibid.: 82).

Therefore, contrary to Walras, Boulding, and Calabresi, market regime versus state command are no *ex aequo* alternate allocation systems. From an individual's perspective, state allocation needs to be applied prudentially as it inevitably causes an arbitrary incidence on the citizens both in terms of taxation and revenue. The inherent arbitrariness endangers the rule of law that continues to exist even when a democratically authorized process of legislation precedes the allocative actions of the state. Legislation does not guarantee the rule of law, that is, 'whether the law prescribes unequivocally how' somebody who has full legal authority has to act (ibid.: 85). The rule of law is primary and limits the scope of legislation (ibid.: 87).

When markets fail to honor individual preferences, the rule of law prescribes (the economist) searching for an allocation alternative to the markets that restores or takes account of the free individual choice as much as possible.

Therefore, in his book, *Law, Legislation, and Liberty, Vol. 3*, Hayek is

> mainly concerned with the limits that a free society must place upon the coercive powers of government.
>
> (1979: 41)

In this aspect, Hayek hastens to add that he is 'far from advocating ... a "minimal state"' (ibid.). Advanced economies should levy taxes to provide a number of services that markets fail to supply. However, in the elaboration of the state's task in the economy, Hayek has an underlying projection of individual freedom. In this perspective, he distinguishes a double task of government. On one hand, it requires coercive power to raise funds, that is, taxation. On the other hand, however, it is expedient in organizing or supplying publicly funded services for seeking opportunities that render coercive power superfluous. As an example, Hayek refers to Milton Friedman's (1962) concept of vouchers for education funded by the government, enabling children's parents to express their preference sovereignty. The basic idea is that market failures such as positive externalities and public goods do not automatically imply an integral government provision. Rightly in civil society, there exists what Hayek (1979: 49–50) calls, 'an independent sector' stemming from community-inspired individuals or groups of people who provide the means to fund public services in which markets fail, such as health care, hospitals, museums, and theaters. This 'third, *independent sector*' occupies the middle position 'between the commercial and the governmental' with the appealing advantage that it originates from free individual choices that also affect its organization and operation (ibid.: 50). Clearly, Hayek's independent sector corresponds to Boulding's integrative allocation system. An advanced economy of a civil society is a fertile seedbed for integrative initiatives to support services for which the market works poorly. Furthermore, both Boulding and Hayek note interfaces between their respective systems and sectors.

The market exchange is central and merely viable based on self-interest. If the motive of self-interest is inadequate in allocating the scarce resources via exchange, (state) authority coercion as a second best may remedy the market's failure. Advanced economies require a nonminimal involvement of the state, Hayek admits. At the same time, market elements are preferred that edge over the governmental sector, generating an extensive interface in which the self-interest of markets goes together with a state's coercion. Aside, this interface is reminiscent of the market-versus-hierarchy dilemma of firms. Opposite coercion as a remedy to failing market exchange, announces the integrative, indirect sector itself; benevolence replaces self-interest. Instead of coercion, benevolence takes care of funding services that the market neglects. Like the interface between a state and a market, an interface between an integrative system and a market will concern the organization of the (charity) services.

From this taxonomy of sectors, it may be inferred that there is no strict distinction between a state and a market. Apparently, a mixture of coercion, self-interest, and benevolence founds our economic reality. The economy bears the integrative tendencies in advanced economies of civil societies that constitute a clear token of a sliding scale from self-interest to benevolence. It closely accords with the phenomenological view of the *Lebenswelt* in which people experience intersubjectivity and recognize themselves in their fellow man. Contrary to the economics of atoms, it refers to economics as a moral science. Furthermore, the interfaces in the taxonomy adumbrates the theme of the NIE, that is, the relative efficiency of institutional arrangements. Apparently, there is no allocative Nirvana.

7.4 On property

An economically relevant allocation mechanism motivates people to generate information to make choices about the benefits of resources in alternative uses (Demsetz 1964: 16). It is, as Knight (1924: 586–587) contends, 'private appropriation and exploitation' that will bring about the ideal situation (of efficient use) 'through the operation of ordinary economic motives'. Scarce resources need to be administrated and taken care of, that is, they 'must be appropriated by some one', as he worded it earlier (Knight 1921: 188–189, n. 2). This insight nearly becomes a platitude, indeed. As yet, it founds Coase's 'FCC' and 'Social Cost' paper. The Federal Communication Commission (FCC) is engaged in addressing the etheric bedlam by assigning frequency licenses; however, it is not very successful in doing so. In the two papers, Coase further elaborates on the following diagnosis of the problem:

> But the real cause of the trouble was that no property rights were created in these scarce frequencies.
>
> (1959: 14)

A property right is the building block of an economist's reasoning. Economics stems from man's propensity to exchange property rights of one thing for those of another, as Adam Smith argues. This 'something that goes without saying' acquires new significance with Coase's concept of transaction cost. Exchange of property rights goes, to a great extent, with cost, that is, the very subject of the NIE. Therefore, I expand on the origin and nature of property. Furthermore, it turns out that the concept of property rights as interpreted in the NIE deviates from the usual interpretation of it by students of law. In this aspect, it is particularly Coase's approach to property as a bundle of rights that raises questions from a legal perspective. Therefore, three subsections are distinguished. The first discusses the origin of property. Is property a prey grasped from the state of nature, or is it the fruit of self-conscious human beings recognizing that 'this is mine and not yours'? (Schlatter 1951: 14–15). The second subsection questions the nature of property. Is property a matter of convention or a thing of natural law? Subsection three concerns the alleged improper use of the property concept in the NIE. The phenomenological perspective reemerges particularly in the first sections and considers a nominalist versus realist concept of property.

7.4.1 The origin of property

In a kind of NIE approach, John Umbeck wonders why economists engaged in market forces 'completely ignore the question of how (property) rights emerge and are initially allocated' (Umbeck 1981: 38). Umbeck finds the 1848 California gold rush illustrative to show how property emerges. Referring to the gold rush as happening in a state of nature, Umbeck argues that

> potential force is the relevant constraint underlying any initial agreements (and subsequent agreements) which allocate wealth among competitors.
>
> (1981: 40)

It is a challenging view of a situation that even precedes Thomas Hobbes's state of nature. Hobbes opines that a social contract of all authorizes the Leviathan as a political authority to enforce private property. The invariable ingredients of these types of private property rights theories are the state of nature, initially common property, and the idea of first possession.

David Hume offers a variation on Hobbes's view and interprets private property as the *sine qua non* 'upon which human social life depends' (Panichas 1983: 396). The indispensability of private property originates from man's basic selfishness and relentless avidity that only can be mitigated by private ownership as the impediment to the potentially disrupting force of these human traits. George Panichas paraphrases Hume as follows:

> The intense desire for immediate gain (which will be insecure) is forestalled by a system of property allowing for eventual, secure gains in a context where, as Hume eventually argues, all property is owned by some individual.
>
> (ibid.: 400)

What is common in these accounts of the rise of property is the pre-social nature of acting agents who are assumingly insatiable, pathologically avaricious, and omni-desirous of infinite wants. Panichas introduces two points against Hume that *mutatis mutandis* are also valid for Hobbes. First, it is false to assume that people are cursed with infinite wants and necessities of which some are infinite in the context of being perpetual and insatiable (ibid.: 401). Not all people want and need all things or states of affairs. Apparently, Hume has in mind an abstract man who is gifted with a 'plethora of wants ... for most anything'. In a pre-social state of nature, man has unqualified, nonspecific basic needs for food, clothing, and shelter. However, given a *moderate* scarcity, there is 'no likelihood (let alone inevitability) of a conflict between individuals' (ibid.: 402). Conflict may arise in a social context that occasions specific needs, for example, the desire for quiche, of which the desire presupposes its existence and, foremost, is recognized as a specific type of food in a social context of meaning. In the pre-social world, there is no meaning.

Second, it is inconsistent to presume that avidity is perpetual and insatiable as a desire may be overridden by other inclinations. When Hume presupposes that avidity is perpetual and insatiable, he must maintain that avidity itself is a unique desire '*not* to be overridden by some desire *other* than itself'. However, Panichas infers, if avidity can be overridden by other desires and interests, this takes away the necessity of a system of private property. For instance, a system of trusteeship may secure possession instead of private property to live a decent social life (ibid.: 404). Without the challenging hypothesis, 'Hume's argument for a system of private property collapses' (ibid.: 403). Thus, so does Hobbes's account, which assumes that, in the state of nature, 'each man has a valid claim, not merely to his equal share, but to the whole stock' (Schlatter 1951: 139).

Hobbes's and Hume's property rights theories maintain an inapt psychological makeup of man. Furthermore, in their theories, man figures as an atom who lacks any social dimension. For that matter, this holds also for, for example, Jeremy Bentham's (1843: Ch. viii) utilitarian approach, which refers to 'the savage, who has hidden his prey, may hope to keep it for himself so long as his cave is not discovered'. Likewise, Jeremy Bentham's savage lacks a socially endurable context without which such a concept as property right is unthinkable in a literal sense. In Bentham's world, it is not the Leviathan that rescues man from his predicate state of nature but civil law that creates property rights, the outcome of a social contract. Bentham states: 'The legislator ... does all that is essential to the happiness of society' (ibid.). This legislator is a *deus ex machina* who apparently senses the societal longing for property rights that enhances happiness. Bentham, and likewise Hobbes and Hume, avail themselves of the assumption of the existence of a social reality that they aim to erect with at least law and order as an indispensable dimension of it.

It is common to them that they fall prey to 'the fallacy of misplaced concreteness' (Schutz 1953: 1). They avail themselves of 'rationality on the common-sense level' that, according to Alfred Schutz,

> is always action within an unquestioned and undetermined frame of constructs of typicalities of the setting, the motives, the means and ends, the course of action and personalities involved and taken for granted.
>
> (ibid.: 25–26)

As noted in Chapter 2, this phenomenological perspective directs the attention to human beings' *Lebenswelt* as the pre-reflective world in which we find ourselves in our consciousness. It is the logical necessity of human intersubjectivity that founds this position. It regards the dimensions of a common consciousness that, as Edmund Husserl argues,

> "offers us more than a reduplication of what we find in our self-consciousness, for it establishes the difference between 'own' and 'other' which we experience, and presents us with the characteristics of the 'social life.'"

> (quoted in Wagner 1970: 7)

This intersubjectivity between 'own' and 'other' reemerges in an immediate manner in what defines private property: mine versus thine. In this aspect, the distinction is a constitutive formula of society by which human beings combine themselves 'into the synthesis "society"' (Simmel 1910: 376). It conveys Aristotle's argument as paraphrased by Schlatter:

> that in the nature of things the particular individual really exists; where there are no individuals – no persons who can say 'this is mine and not yours' – there can be no true community.

> (1951: 14–15)

It distinguishes man from the animal, as Adam Smith puts forward:

> Nobody ever saw one animal by its gestures and natural cries signify to another, this is mine, that yours; I am willing to give this for that.

> (1776: 16)

It is the fundamental concept of the particular individual who experiences his *ego* as something independent of any representation and therefore believes that the *thou* is likewise something that is 'just as really for itself' that constitutes a synthesis that we call society (Simmel 1910: 375). It concerns a feeling of solidarity with the *thou* denoting the moral dimension that carries our society. By its grace, the particular individual has the faculty to rely on concepts such as property rights to get on terms with his fellow man.

Therefore, the appropriate point of departure in the search for property rights is not Bentham's (1843: Ch. viii) savage who may keep the prey for himself 'so long as he is awake to defend it' but the account of the origin of human consciousness and intersubjectivity as the pre-reflective foundation of our social reality. This regards a material difference that enables the theorist to overcome the indeterminate state of nature and obtain access to a reality of meaningful artifacts such as ownership that structure the situation in which man finds himself. It safeguards the analysis from what Karl Popper (1945: 345) denotes as 'psychologism', that is, 'that all laws of social life must be ultimately reducible to the psychological laws of "human nature"', ultimately, to the psyche of the savage. On the contrary, in our social life, we avail ourselves of concepts that *are* meaning (Kaufmann 1944). As abstract and ideal-type situational elements, they animate the postulate of rationality without which there is no scientific discourse of social action, as Popper (1967: 359) claims, emphasizing that this animation does not refer to the human *anima* but correctly *replacing* 'concrete psychological elements'. The only one animating law involved, he proceeds, regards 'the principle of acting appropriately to the situation' (ibid.).

In brief, the concept of private property finds its origin in the pre-reflective *intersubjectivity* descrying mine versus thine. Clearly, private property primes self-interest and incentives as has been recognized since Aristotle (Schlatter 1951: 15). They are the alpha and the omega of economics and the immediate cause to reflect on private property. Self-interest founds the utilitarian account of property such as Bentham's. However, Bentham disregards the fundamental origin as identified that renders ownership inextricably related to someone's individuality and existence. It is the close observation of human nature that founds the notion of private property, that is, the fruit of natural law. As an aspect of human nature, the concept of ownership renders a universal and, as such, obtaining a moral dimension.

7.4.2 The nature of property

Morality is adumbrated, for instance, in John Locke's property right theory claiming that the labor to acquire a good justifies its possession. Locke:

> for this labour being the unquestionable property of the labourer, no man but he can have a right to what that is once joined to, at least where there is enough, and as good, left in common for others.
>
> (1690: 11–12)

In this quote, Locke proves himself to be a practitioner of natural law. It is the nature of man, for example, his unquestionable property of labor, that comprises rights. The natural law approach searches for the essentials of law that give rights their universal nature. Accordingly, a right acquires the moral quality that holds toward anyone. Against this *ius naturale* stands *ius gentium*, that is, the product of governments that enact laws. The latter regards conventions, for example, 'slavery, an institution contrary to the natural law, was based on the law of nations' (Schlatter 1951: 27). As noted, Hobbes and Bentham have recourse to an authority from outside to establish property rights, albeit enforced as a social contract. They are exponents of positive law established by government, differing from natural law as it may vary with time and place and accordingly nonuniversal, lacking the moral dimension of natural law. Furthermore, natural law grants, by definition, the individual primacy, emphasizing an individual's justice. Apparently, the differences in the account of the origin results in differences in the nature of property.

In a mature civil society as we know it, these contrasts diminish over time; positive law complements, if not prevails, vis-à-vis natural law. At the same time, natural law is preconditional for positive lawmaking as, for instance, William Blackstone argues: "'no human laws are of any validity, if contrary to this (law of nature)'" (quoted in Epstein 1989: 714, n. 6). It opposes the positive law position that law is a matter of power rather than moral sense. Richard Epstein qualifies the difference between natural versus positive law by substantiating that the utilitarian foundations of positive law are also valid for natural law. Basically, the difference amounts to a supposedly dissimilar epistemological stance, Epstein (1989) contends. He recaps their mutual relationship as follows. 'The basic rules of natural law operate as a first round of presumptions.' It is positive law that, in a process of refinement, may 'exhaust all the possibilities for gain in the structuring of social institutions' (ibid.: 750). Casuistry complements universal concepts such as individual autonomy, property, and contract in order to converge on a set of utilitarian rules.

7.4.3 Property as a bundle of rights in NIE

It is precisely the positive, utilitarian interpretation of law that finds its application in economics. It constitutes the very foundation of law and economics as a branch of the NIE as it originates from the Coase Theorem. Without transaction cost, the theorem dictates, the establishment of property rights renders a matter of trade about the costs and benefits of the rights assignment between parties to conclude a Pareto-efficient exchange. Apparently, Coase understands property as a bundle of exchangeable rights in which 'property has no content on its own', Henry Smith (2009: 128) comments.

In this perspective, there is no initial position as a normative commencement when there is interference with one's property right. It is this view that justifiably worries Stigler (1943: 355) in discussing the consequences of new welfare economics that claims to be able to show the merits of many policies 'without entering a dangerous quagmire of value judgments'. The value-free potential finds its origin in the application of the marginal Paretian welfare conditions as quoted earlier. It corresponds to the value-free nature of the Coase Theorem. In this perspective, there is nothing that argues against the idea that any Paretian-relevant efficiency improvement that is affordable is desirable.

> By compensating successful thieves for the amounts they would otherwise steal, we save these resources and hence secure a net gain.
>
> (ibid.: 356)

Government net gain concerns expenditures for policemen, courts, jails, and so on. In his defense of Arthur Pigou against Coase, A.W. Brian Simpson embroiders on Coase's idea that the reciprocal nature of property rights renders them eligible for exchange. Brian Simpson states:

as when women object to the idea that the way to stop sexual assaults on the streets at night is for them to stay at home.

(1996: 60)

If one interprets a harmful effect as reciprocal, Brian Simpson argues, one cannot withstand such immoral reasoning. Furthermore, an unlimited range of alternative courses of action to solve the harming interaction present themselves. Running railways versus growing crops is just one combination of possibilities (ibid.). The very problem is the atomistic view of man behind the idea of reciprocity. In the purely utilitarian interpretation of property rights à la Bentham, ownership is a device to maintain one's autonomy against others. In the immoral elaboration of the Coase Theorem makes itself felt that the utilitarian interpretation of private property lacks the notion of 'a working social system (as) a consensus on ends', as Stigler (1943: 357) diagnoses. Referring to Stigler's bribing-thieves idea, James Buchanan further accentuates the significance of consensus. First, he argues that 'presumably, those individuals who are thieves at any moment have supported laws which are designed to prevent theft'. Therefore, Buchanan (1959: 132) further presumes, 'no consensus could be expected on a proposed change in the law that would involve bribing all future thieves'. Clearly, the idea of consensus dovetails with the phenomenological interpretation of property rights as universal and originating from human consciousness and intersubjectivity as the pre-reflective foundation of our social reality.

This phenomenological view denotes the very essence of private property, again substantiating a philosophically realist position as defended in preceding chapters. In these chapters, it is argued that Coase (1975: 28) is a realist theorist who aspires to 'understand the working of the real economic system'. However, as Henry Smith proposes, in his 'FCC' and 'Social Cost' papers, Coase shows himself to be the very opposite of a realist in a philosophical sense, specifically, a *legal* realist, that is, a nominalist who adopts the bundle of rights conception in which

property has no content on its own but instead emerges from policy-driven decisions about the actions that people might take.

(Smith 2009: 128)

In this perspective, a bundle of rights is assigned to an individual who has the '"authority" to select, for specific goods, any use from a nonprohibited class of uses' (Alchian 1977: 130). It denotes that a person may expect 'that his decision about the uses of certain resources will be effective' (Alchian, Allen 1969: 158). Alchian adds a legal restriction apparently to safeguard his approach against immoral outcomes such as noted. In this respect, lawyers' conceptual frameworks are more effective. They call the concept of a bundle of rights *in personam* rights that is the opposite of *in rem* rights (Merrill, Smith 2001: 371). This difference is significant.

In personam rights delimitate an individual's bundle of use rights (*usus, usus fructus, abusus*). For instance, 'what the land-owner in fact possesses is the right to carry out a circumscribed list of actions', Coase (1960: 44) notes. In this aspect, Coase interprets the *Sturges v. Bridgman* case as a dispute regarding the use of their respective premises (ibid.: 8). In a zero-transaction-cost world, Sturges and Bridgman come to (contract) terms about the most profitable use without going before a court. If the transaction cost is positive, the court should delimitate a Pareto efficiency, enhancing the assignment of use rights between the disputants. In the 'Social Cost' paper, an administrative decision replaces the rearrangement of rights with a contract (ibid.: 16).[2] For that matter, it is comparable to the replacement of market transactions by an organization in the 'Firm' paper. Both under the zero-transaction-cost assumption and under positive transaction cost, Coase applies the analysis to two-party conflicts. However, the analysis in terms of (use) rights *in personam* encounters difficulties when '"indefinite and numerous"' parties are involved, for example, in nuisance cases (Merrill, Smith 2001: 371). For that matter, such a trade-off between rights proves to obstruct the Paretian welfare criterion, that is, interpersonal comparisons of utility, which is discussed later.

In rem rights regard things, 'good against the world', 'excluding intrusions by strangers from a delimited space' (ibid.: 384; 373). The *in rem* conception of property is particularly appropriate to the issue of Coase's 'FCC' paper regarding the allocation of frequencies. It assigns a frequency property against all others who would interfere. Assignment by regulation affords the opportunity for a secondary market.[3] The assignment of frequency property as *in rem* rights is preferable to Coase's initial idea of the assignment of use right regarding broadcasting equipment. Against the advantage of a customized assignment of *in personam* rights stands the disadvantage of legal fragmentation that raises legal uncertainty. What is more is that parceling out the use rights of a thing raises a logical issue as it presupposes an authority who is apparently the owner in an absolute sense. Furthermore, clearly stated *in rem* rights with minimal legal refinement, good against the world, economizes on information cost toward duty holders. In addition to this, the legal security of the *in rem* right enhances owners' incentives to conserve and invest in his resource. Finally, in contrast to *in personam* rights, the *in rem* right is crystal clear about the causality regarding intrusion or nuisance. It is inherent in the *in personam* rights that they occasion to compete for alternative uses of the resource concerned. Therefore, Coase identifies harmful effects as reciprocal, that is, cases of competing uses. An *in rem* right is unilaterally causal, safeguarding the right effectively against the world. In this reemerges the moral dimension of property. As demonstrated, private property as an *in rem* right belongs to a human's individuality that cannot be suspended at one's own discretion. For instance, Stigler's thought experiment that was referred to exemplifies that disregarding the *in rem* nature of property by considering it as a bundle of (*in personam*) use rights may generate morally abject proposals.

The relationship *in rem* versus *in personam* right can be equated with an elaboration of the relationship between natural versus positive law. Natural law constitutes the framework within which positive law may proceed. Likewise, *in rem* rights mark the moral domain within which the *in personam* bundle of use rights may be customized in order to prompt Paretian efficiency improvements. In this aspect, Coase's conception of property 'favored by the *Legal* Realists' remains representing a form of nominalism in law that is compatible with his philosophically realist position (ibid.: 383; emphasis added). For that matter, it is social cost issues such as harmful effects to which the concept of the bundle of use rights is particularly applicable. The *in rem* property remains basic, for example, as in a money payment for a commodity.

Finally, Coase's pioneering in the elaboration of property rights as a bundle of use rights accommodates advanced economies that have surmounted the violation of basic ownership rights and are becoming increasingly complicated. Highly industrialized economies face a myriad of side effects, market interferences, complicated organizational structures, and managerial challenges. They report a twentieth-century tendency that more or less coincides with the theoretical development of the NIE. It accompanies Coase's quest: How does the institutional structure (of production) in general and the assignment of property rights in particular determine the working of the economic system of market exchanges? The starting point of the analysis is the market in which people are engaged in the reciprocally beneficial exchange of – inherently – *in personam* use rights. Therefore, Coase disregards the *in rem* ownership and its unilateral nature that is allowable as far as this does not go against its moral dimension.

Summing up, it has significance for the nature of the homunculi of the economic analysis that property originates from a society in which self-conscious human beings experience mine and thine. Respect for others' property is a feature of their logic of the situation. Basically, property is an aspect of human nature regarding a relationship between man and a thing, that is, an *in rem* right. As Locke argues, labor and its product are unquestionable property of the laborer and not a matter of convention. In the NIE analysis as condensed in the Coase Theorem, the *in personam* right supersedes the *in rem* right of property. The inherently reciprocal nature of the transaction perspective of the Coase Theorem articulates property as a bundle of use rights, generating the potential of a mutually beneficial exchange of a bundle's parts. The NIE analysis searches for the efficiency opportunities of legal rearrangements of property rights, that is, comparative institutional arrangements. At the same time, it remains preconditional that it regards an analysis in which figure homunculi who respect mine and thine as a vital feature of society in experiencing the rationality of their situational logic.

7.5 Coase on cases of interference

It is a constant in Coase's work: criticizing cases of government interference that find their foundation in established economic theory. As early as 1935, Coase published together with Ronald Fowler an *Economica* paper on the government's interference with the pig industry. It is an interference that has its theoretical pendant in the cobweb theorem as coined by Nicholas Kaldor (1934), who predicts a perpetual market price disequilibrium. A patent case of critique is Meade's, and Hotelling's theoretical plea for interference in the case of decreasing-cost industries (Coase 1946). Another case regards the development of a lighthouse service. Coase (1974: 358–359) refers to John Stuart Mill, Henry Sidgwick, and Paul Samuelson, who unanimously perceive it as an instance of indispensable government interference in spite of antipodal evidence. Similarly, Coase (1955: 37) shows that it has been unnecessarily argued that nationwide uniform postage requires a governmentally protected postal monopoly to enforce cross-subsidization. Apparently, in the course of his career, Coase (1960) collects a number of instances that gainsay tenets that theoretically regard more or less conventional wisdom regarding government interference. It finds its theoretical grand finale in 'The Problem of Social Cost' that generalizes the case of government interference with broadcasting frequencies. It opposes Pigou's government interference to iron out externalities.

Another case of government involvement Coase (1947, 1948) discusses in two *Economica* papers about the British government's stake in broadcasting during the early decades of the twentieth century. Private companies and persons become aware of the unprecedented opportunities of the innovation of wireless broadcasting. In spite of promising private initiatives, it resulted in the establishment of the British Broadcasting Corporation (BBC) in 1923. It was argued by the authorities that "'if the chaos in the United States was to be avoided one broadcasting authority was essential'" (Coase 1947: 208, n. 2). It may be interpreted as a *testimonium paupertatis* of the British authorities who fail to organize an efficient wavelength allocation (ibid.: 208). The created monopoly is a permit for inefficiency. It lacks incentives to economize, particularly as there is no relation between BBC's funding and its performance. It contains all the detrimental features of a monopoly. Furthermore, the authorities face substantial regulation costs; for instance, to enforce the advertising ban (ibid.: 204).

Common in all the cases as discussed by Coase is that textbook-instances of market failure such as lighthouses, decreasing-cost industries, and uniform postal service might nevertheless be resolved without the direct involvement of a government authority. The government's assignment of a spectrum of different property rights may prove to be a more effective efficiency-enhancing procedure than direct interference, for example, licenses to broadcast, invest, and levy an allowance. In this aspect, Coase emphasizes the difference between the assignment of property rights versus the allocation of the resources concerned. Thomas Hazlett et al. (2011: s126) refer to it as Coase's 'allocation/ownership dichotomy', explaining the creation of secondary markets. It supplements governments and markets as alternative forms of resource coordination; 'determining the socially efficient mix requires symmetric appraisals' (ibid.) Briefly, as a mixture of market versus nonmarket allocation, the cases discussed announce a polymorphic spectrum of institutional arrangements, as noted earlier.

Collectively, these papers illustrate Coase's methodological route from specimens to abstraction by formulating a theoretical framework to address interference in the market economy stemming from how economics works in mundane reality. Illustrative in this respect is his discussion of a private initiative regarding broadcasting in the 1948 *Economica* paper on this subject. Coase thoroughly reports about someone's broadcasting adventures.

Mr. A.W. Maton, owner of an electrical shop and a local cinema, devised a rather simple innovation in 1924 that challenged the BBC monopoly:

> To enable his wife to hear the programmes when she was in another part
> of the house, Mr. Maton, as an experiment, connected the set by wire
> with a loudspeaker in another room.
>
> (Coase 1948: 194)

The success of this device inspired Mr. Maton to experiment with reproducing the broadcasts over longer distances. Thus it happened that he consequently invented an opportunity to serve (wired) broadcasts to people who did not possess a radio receiving set. Mr. Maton extended his wire system and began to charge 1s. 6d. per week for his services. 'In this way, the first relay exchange in Great Britain was started in January, 1925' with permission from the Southampton Post Office (ibid.: 194–195). Through the 1920s, a new industry of wire broadcasting came into existence with several relay exchanges and a number of subscribers. The system offered evident advantages. It saved the cost of purchasing a radio as loudspeakers were sufficient. It avoided the difficulties caused by the limitation of wavelengths. It improved the reception quality. 'The master set of the relay exchange was able to pick up programmes from foreign stations' (ibid.: 200). Moreover, as Mr. P.P. Eckersley, then chief engineer of the BBC, proposed 'the primary advantage that [wires] would enable more programmes to be broadcast' (ibid.: 196). However, the BBC rejected the idea of the wire broadcast.

Referring to Posner (1993: 203) as quoted earlier, he justifiably notes that anecdotes and narratives constitute elements of Coase's methodology. They match with Coase's orientation at *understanding* 'the behavior of *individuals and institutions*' rather than prediction. They belong to the British tradition of '*inductive methodology* in building a theory', Richard Zerbe and Steven Medema (1998: 210) note. The instances that reinforce Coase's interference critique exemplify his methodological disposition. The instances represent his safeguard against the 'blackboard economics' departing point on the methodological route from details as they occur in mundane economic reality toward abstract theoretical inferences.

7.6 Comparative institutional arrangements

The comparative institutional approach features the difference between Pigou and Coase. Instead of an endeavor to recover an unattainable optimum, the objective of the comparative approach is to restrict inefficiencies whether by government and/or otherwise. It is reminiscent of welfare economics. This is discussed in the following subsections. The first discusses Pigou versus Coase as a prelude. The second subsection presents a legal case illustrating an institutional arrangement as a welfare trade-off. The third subsection introduces the concept of presumptive efficiency to sidestep a normative welfare judgment regarding an institutional (re)arrangement. Against the contrast between Pigou and Coase in the first subsection, the fourth discusses a consensus between them. Both maintain the premise of the measuring rod of money as a forceful analytical instrument. The final subsection considers the measuring rod of money compared to the concept of presumptive efficiency. It assists the theorist/political economist in his comparative institutional approach.

7.6.1 Pigou versus Coase

The marginal efficiency conditions as referred to by Stigler (1943: 356) form a part of the seven marginal conditions regarding production and consumption that – given resources, technology, preferences, and institutional setting – together constitute a general equilibrium as written out by Léon Walras. Boulding (1969: 5) subtitles them as "'Snow White (the fairest of all) and the Seven Marginal Conditions'". Fulfillment of these conditions implies that no one can better his position without harming the position of someone else, that is, expresses a Pareto optimum. This is the analytical edifice that also founds the welfare economics of Pigou.[4] In several methods, he formulates the welfare optimum or movement toward it. For instance, as follows:

> When complete equality among the values of marginal social net products is wanting, a diminution in the degree of inequality that exists among them is likely to benefit the national dividend.
>
> (Pigou 1920: 137)

In a style that is reminiscent of Adam Smith and Alfred Marshall, he observes, in several countries, the

> adjustment of institutions to the end of directing self-interest into beneficial channels. ... But even in the most advanced States there are failures and imperfections.
>
> (ibid.: 129)

It is wanting equalities of marginal conditions that set Pigou's research agenda. Pigou continues:

> The study of these (inequalities) constitutes our present problem ... its purpose is essentially practical. It seeks to bring into clearer light some of the ways in which it now is, or eventually may become feasible for

governments to control the play of economic forces in such wise as to promote the economic welfare, and, through that, the total welfare, of their citizens as a whole.

(ibid.: 129–130)

This quote precisely compresses what Demsetz (1969) calls the Nirvana fallacy. It regards how to restore the Pareto optimum, which is an optimum that never existed and will never come through. At the same time, Pigou shows some qualification in his thought. The three preceding quotes represent Pigou's basic line of reasoning. First is the general equilibrium conditions as *summun bonum*, constituting the point of reference. Second, he observes deviations from the optimum. Monopolistic tendencies, indivisibilities, and externalities thwart the channels toward the *ex hypothesi* maximum national dividend (ibid.: 136). In this aspect, Carl Dahlman (1979: 154) maintains that Pigou plainly assumes 'deviations from an attainable optimum'. What is normally done in the welfare literature, Dahlman argues, is this:

the divergence between private and social cost is never proved to exist, but always *initially assumed* to exist.

(ibid.)

Apparently, Dahlman disregards that Pigou (Pigou 1920: 183–184) discusses a number of instances regarding the divergence that stems from the circumstance that 'incidental services are performed to third parties from whom it is *technically difficult to exact payment*' (emphasis added). Obviously, such a difficulty may be interpreted as transaction cost. Pigou further discusses, for instance, a number of incentive difficulties between a landlord and tenants that might be addressed by contract terms (ibid.: 179–183). Such digressions not only qualify the view on Pigou. They may also put the third element into perspective in Pigou's reasoning, that is, 'governments to control the play of economic forces', as the very remedy to repair market failures. Apparently, he considers alternative remedies. At the same time, Pigou's research agenda, as quoted, occasions his focus on government as a solution. Moreover, his straightforward application of bounties and taxes to obtain the ideal output of 'simple competition' additionally supports the interpretation. For instance,

for every industry in which the value of the marginal social net product is less than that of the marginal private net product, there will be certain rates of tax, the imposition of which by the State would increase the size of the national dividend and increase economic welfare.

(ibid.: 224)

To calculate the divergence, Pigou stages a type of panoptic authority who '*so to speak, from outside*' records the marginal social net product in order to compare it with the marginal private net product that is initiated, so to speak, *from the inside* of the individual actor (ibid.: 131–132; emphasis added). In Pigou's calculation, the initial distribution of property rights is leading. The distinction of 'outside versus inside' enables Pigou to identify the differences between marginal-social versus marginal-private net products. An increase in the use of resources by a firm in one industry may cause external economies that are internal to the industry or increase the production costs of a firm in another industry. 'Everything of this kind must be counted in', Pigou emphasizes, to arrive at a calculation from outside (ibid.: 134).

Such proposals constitute a major element of Coase's critique of Pigou. Pigou intends to reestablish the ideal output situation by equalizing the marginal conditions. Coase comments as follows:

> The Pigovian analysis shows us that it is possible to conceive of better worlds than the one in which we live.
>
> (1960: 34)

Here, the general equilibrium as a point of reference makes itself felt. It is a *summun bonum* that does not exist, which results in an analysis that is diminished with the Nirvana fallacy. First, in his recovery proposals, Pigou (1920: 183–184) disregards the origin of the nonoptimal situations in spite of observing transaction issues such as 'technically difficult to exact payment' as a cause of nonoptimality. Second, he does not take into account the implementation issues that tax and bounty entail as general remedies.

Basically, Pigou labors under the Walrasian general equilibrium analysis, which hinders him to take account of positive transaction cost, and thus of institutions, in an *analytical* sense. It might explain the ambiguity that, at the same time, he observes in several countries' 'adjustment of institutions to the end of directing self-interest into beneficial channels' (ibid.: 129). Apparently, such an empirical concept does not induce Pigou to take the *analytical* inference that theoretical engagement in the institutional framework of the economy is more appropriate for prompting the marginal equalities that are intended than formulating proposals regarding the distribution of bounties or imposition of taxes that are, by definition, inept for restoring the equalities that are concerned. In this aspect, Pigou confounds the analysis of meaning with a causal explanation of facts or, rather, omits applying Kaufmann's methodological procedure.

This account of Pigou's economics of welfare serves as a contrasting picture to profile the NIE as a comparative search for institutional arrangements. The latter concerns a partial equilibrium analysis à la Alfred Marshall, comparing marginal variables to determine the relative efficiency of an allocation of resources in a trade-off between transaction cost and institutional arrangement. Instead of being engaged in a nonexistent world, 'the problem is', Coase argues,

> to devise practical arrangements which will correct defects in one part of the system without causing more serious harm in other parts.
>
> (1960: 34)

This phrasing of the question stems from Coase's recognition of the reciprocal nature of the problem. A recur to suppress an activity of A that harms B has inevitable repercussions on A. This is the very question Coase already poses in the 'FCC' paper:

The problem is to avoid the more serious harm.

(1959: 26)

As noted in the preceding, reciprocity is adherent to economics as it features the concept of transaction. In this aspect, the reciprocal nature of (harmful) side effects alludes to an opportunity to transact. However, as Coase argues:

[s]uch transactions are not costless, with a result that the initial delimitation of rights may be maintained even though some other would be more efficient.

(ibid.: 27, n. 54)

This reflects the very contrast between Coase and Pigou. For Coase, the 'initial legal delimitation of rights merely provides the starting point for the rearrangement of rights through market transactions' (ibid.). For Pigou, on the contrary, the initial delimitation of rights is given or, rather, *must* be given as it constitutes the basis for the welfare optimum of marginal equality conditions as a point of reference. Rephrased, the delimitation of rights is irrelevant as the cost of transaction is presumed to be zero, as the Coase Theorem reads. In this contrast between Coase and Pigou reemerges the difference between *in personam* versus *in rem* property. For Pigou, a side effect as an infringement on the initial delimitation is a unilateral matter that requires being restored. As denoted in Chapter 5, a state of nature directs Pigou's thought. Coase's *in personam* property interpretation invites comparing the value of the different person's use or interest regarding resources and avoiding the more serious harm.

However, a positive transaction cost obstructs the opportunity to trade the value differences in the marketplace; that is, it obstructs the idea of reciprocity as a natural cause of mutually beneficial transactions. It changes the reciprocity concept as recognized in side effects. Rather, it is reciprocity as the fruit of a welfare economist who, from the outside, perceives efficiency opportunities; that is, how to avoid more serious harm? In this aspect, correspondence occurs between Coase and Pigou. Both seem to be engaged in the trade-off between individuals' welfare from their theoretical vantage points. It concerns a methodological issue that returns later. Furthermore, it introduces conceptual issues regarding welfare, issues for which welfare economics is famous.

7.6.2 *A case of welfare trade-off*

Warren Samuels (1971) discusses a very instructive case of welfare trade-offs in a paper on the interrelations between law and economics. An example that contains all the constituent elements of these interrelations is the *Miller et al. v. Schoene* case. The case involves the owners of red cedars versus apple tree orchard owners. Cedar rust is a plant disease of the red cedar 'whose first phase is spent while the fungus resides upon its host' (ibid.: 436). The fungus does not harm the hosting red cedar; however, during a second phase, it severely harms the apple tree. The result is that ornamental red cedars may have devastating impacts on apple tree orchards in their neighborhood. Therefore, the Virginia state legislature of 1914 empowered

> the state entomologist to investigate and, if necessary, condemn and destroy without compensation certain red cedar trees within a two-mile radius of an apple orchard.
>
> (ibid.)

Plausibly, this Cedar Rust statute makes the cedar owners (plaintiffs) in error who finally initiate legal proceedings to reverse the decision. They argue as follows:

> "The statute is invalid in that it provides for the taking of for public use, but for the benefit of other private persons".
> (Miller et al. v. Schoene, 276 U.S. (1928), quoted in ibid.: 437)

However, the Supreme Court affirms the judgment of the lower state court. The central point in its argument addresses Coase's (1959: 26) question of how 'to avoid the more serious harm'. Justice Stone argues as follows:

> "On the evidence we may accept the conclusion of the Supreme Court of Appeals that the state was under the necessity of making a choice between the preservation of one class of property and that of the other wherever both existed in dangerous proximity. It would have been none the less a choice if, instead of enacting the present statute, the state, by doing nothing, had permitted serious injury to the apple orchards within its borders to go on unchecked. When forced to such a choice the state does not exceed its constitutional powers by deciding upon the destruction of one class of property in order to save another which, in the judgment legislature, is of greater value to the public".
> (Miller et al. v. Schoene, 276 U.S. (1928), quoted in Samuels 1971:
> 437–438)

Basically, Justice Stone substantiates the NIE perspective. He demonstrates that institutions matter, that is, that the Coase Theorem is not valid. The justice faces a choice between two institutional settings that impose their respective economic consequences on the conflicting interests of the parties. The greater public value compared to 'doing nothing' argues for legislative action. All the same, the 'doing-nothing' option regards anything but legislative inactivity.

Notably, it preserves the property rights of the cedar tree owners. However, Justice Stone opines that the former option avoids the more serious harm. First, it seems plausible that the 'public value' of the apple tree orchards will exceed the value of the ornamental cedar trees. Clearly, the Cedar Rust statute favors the orchard owners at the expense of the cedar tree owners. Second, if the doing-nothing option prevails, this may afford the cedar tree owners strategic opportunities to exploit their position. It would have a reverse distributional effect by generating payment from the orchard owners to the cedar tree owners. Apparently, the distribution of economic benefit and the allocation of risk are 'a partial function of law' (ibid.: 440). For that matter, in both options, the government is involved. At the same time, there is a difference in the degree of governmental involvement compared to market forces. In this aspect, the government and the market operate as communicating vessels. Obviously, in the doing-nothing option and maintaining the preexisting right configuration, the market forces prevail. This reflects the economy as a system of power, mutual coercion or reciprocity, and partially determined by law.

In brief, Samuels records:

> the courts recognized the ineluctable choice of determining the marginal public welfare.
>
> (ibid.: 443)

Apparently, welfare regards a choice based on the comparative analysis of institutional arrangements addressing how to avoid more serious harm. At the same time, this choice entails crucial methodological issues as recognized in welfare economics. How can this patently normative question within the economic discipline be addressed?

7.6.3 Presumptive efficiency and benefit

Without the possibility of an interpersonal comparison of utility, economists are actually restricted to judging cases that meet the Paretian conditions of welfare improvement, at least from a positive economics perspective. Seemingly, the comparative institutional approach as adhering to methodological individualism has a severely limited scope. The answer may be found in Buchanan's (1959) perspective on political economy, which is reminiscent of Schutz's phenomenological approach to subjectivity.

Buchanan aspires to formulate propositions in political economy or welfare economics that are '"positivistic"', that is, eligible for confirmation or refutation 'in the observable behavior of the individuals *in their capacities as collective decision-makers*' – in other words, in politics (ibid.: 127–128). This concurs with Kaufmann's distinction between theoretical versus empirical propositions. In the comparative institutional analysis, the theoretical propositions concern the relative efficiency of an institutional arrangement. To be interpreted as an analysis of meaning à la Kaufmann, Buchanan develops an "'efficiency criterion'" for the political economist as an independent observer who aims to avoid the pitfalls of omniscience and normativity. Buchanan states:

> The observer may introduce an efficiency criterion only through *his own estimate of his subjects' value scales.*
>
> (1959: 126)

He refers to it as *'presumptive efficiency*, based on an economist's *'own* estimate of individual preferences' (ibid.: 126–127). In his definition of the concept, Buchanan remains within the Paretian domain as the observer is presumed to accept the individual preferences *'as he thinks they exist'* (ibid.: 127). Schutz's *postulate of subjective interpretation* is prominent in the meaning analysis that requires understanding

> the social phenomena ... within the scheme of human motives, human means and ends, human planning – in short – within the categories of human action.
>
> (1943: 146)

Closely related to this postulate is the *postulate of adequacy*, conditioning the political economist as a diagnostician that his interpretation would be 'understandable for the actor himself, as well as for his fellow men' (ibid.). Buchanan further accords with Schutz regarding the *postulate of rationality*. 'We proceed on an *as if* assumption' about an individual's reasonability, he suggests (Buchanan 1959: 134). Finally, the *postulate of relevances* determines the domain to which the presumptive efficiency refers. It derives its relevance from the statement: *'There exist mutual gains from trade'* (ibid.: 137). For that matter, the scope of the mutual gains refers to "'changes in law," that is, changes in the structural rules under which individuals makes choices', such as the enactment of the Virginia Cedar Rust statute (ibid.: 131).

Apparently, Buchanan's *presumptive efficiency* may be interpreted as an ideal type in a Schutzian context, that is, a second-order construct, as discussed in the preceding chapters. It enables the social theorist to grasp the subjective meaning of an individuals' efficiency in an objective meaning context. Observation of the postulates safeguards political economists' 'non-normative role in discovering "what is the structure of individual values"' (ibid.: 137). The political economist takes account of the individual preferences involved in a structural change in law as the choices *'appear to the observer'*, Buchanan adds again (ibid.: 133).

The idea of presumptive efficiency as an ideal-typical concept basically stems from the philosophical view of society as a synthesis of human beings who recognize one another in their irreducible identity. A literal common sense enables people to get on terms with one another. This fundamental notion features the search for mutual gains stemming from structural political-economic measures. For instance, Stigler (1943: 358) refers to this concept and substantiates that it would be bizarre to approve recompensing 'manufacturers for not degrading the quality of their product' as a mutual gain from trade. Apparently, there exists what Talcott Parsons calls, '"a moral consensus of its (society's) members"' that founds such a concept as efficiency (ibid.). This notion also goes with substantiating the presumptive efficiency of a specific political-economic change. It is sufficient that the political economist shows that a potentially mutual gain exists, that is, that 'there is more "welfare" to go around than before the change' (Buchanan 1959: 129). Whether or not potential compensation actually occurs surpasses the scope of the presumptive efficiency concept as it does not function to suggest anything about the distributional dimension of bargaining about the gain. It would surpass the scope of common sense on which presumptive efficiency is based. At the same time, the concept of welfare does not *per se* exclusively refer to an increase in income but to satisfying individuals' preferences in a general sense. Therefore, benevolence as an expression of an independent sector à la Hayek may generate mutual gain by, for example, reducing one's own income in favor of an increase of others' income, that is, a Paretian-relevant income redistribution (Hochman, Rodgers 1969). In this aspect, government action, safeguarding the contribution of others makes this type of presumptive efficiency more likely. Finally, the major problem of side effects of consumption or production requires taking account of the costs involved. By reference to the classic smoking-chimney externality, Buchanan words the search for the presumptive efficiency as follows:

> The problem for the political economist is that of searching out and locating from among the whole set of possible combinations one which will prove acceptable to all parties.
>
> (ibid.: 131)

This search of the observer/political economist is based on what he *thinks* in which manner the welfare of the parties concerned are affected by a government measure, a change in law or a 'possible combination' such as a 'tax-compensation-smoke-abatement' (ibid.).[5] The formulation 'which will prove acceptable to all parties' underlines the theoretical nature of the presumptive-efficiency proposition.

As noted, the scope of the (political) economist to which Buchanan applies the presumptive efficiency concept is '"changes in law"' (ibid.: 131). The focus on change concurs with the economist's preoccupation with gradual changes of an individual's economic position of 'little more, little less'. These 'changes in law' concern changes in the structure of legitimate property rights that inherently possess a political-economic dimension. The political economist searches out which change in property rights offers a potential Pareto-relevant efficiency improvement for the social group concerned. The Paretian nature of the formulated presumptive efficiency proposition first requires unanimous consent. Second, such common consent with a structural change in property rights accords with the rule of law as discussed previously.

Against changes in the structure of property rights stand changes that stem from the remaining exogenous variables of the ring of economic data, that is, preferences, technological state of the art, and quality and/or quantity of resources. Obviously, the latter three types of data are not 'deliberately imposed through collective action' (ibid.: 132); neither do they obstruct the rule of law. Therefore, they are not a subject under discussion for the political economist. Such exogenous changes may definitely affect the economic position of owners of property rights and consequently cause winners and losers. However, it would be against the nature of the working of markets if there was political-economic engagement in compensating the losers by the winners, let alone if possible. Shifts in these variables generate Knightian uncertainty addressed by 'entrepreneurial rewards and punishments', as Buchanan notes (ibid. 133). The inequalities are justified regarding preferences, technological knowledge, and resources that generate an economic outcome of not *per se* mutual benefits. Furthermore, compensation for losses would annihilate any incentive.

Thus, the political economist's analysis of meaning makes a theoretical proposition based on *estimating* the individual preferences regarding the law change, stating that it produces an efficiency that will achieve universal consent. This is a refutable proposition, indeed.

The counterpart of the analysis of meaning is the causal explanation of facts (Kaufmann 1944). Will the presumptive efficiency proposition pass the empirical test, or will the proposed change in law be approved unanimously? It is plausible that reasonable people assent to measures that improve the welfare of all. The efficiency proposition postulates *as if* reasonableness exists, that is, that society consists of reasonable men who comply with collectively imposed rules; reasonableness warrants unanimity. In this aspect, Buchanan (1959: 134) refers to the 'contract theory of the state'. From a phenomenological perspective, this consensus vitalizes society. However, outside of the ideal-type society, some individuals may make unanimity unattainable. Some may be '"antisocial"' and others uninformed. (ibid.: 135). It forces the political economist to lower his expectations regarding the presumptive efficiency criterion. Clearly, a nonunanimous consent refutes the proposition. At the same time, a majority that approves the proposal places responsibility upon the economist. In this aspect, Buchanan turns to implementation issues which a majority rule entails. For instance, the 'consensus that all collective decisions are temporary and subject to reversal and modification' gives the majority rule its practical value (ibid.: 136).

The empirical failure of the presumptive efficiency proposition corroborates that economics is not famous for its empirically confirmed hypotheses. Paraphrasing Benedetto Croce, the presumptive efficiency proposition is a theoretical one that 'expresses rationality, not madness' and not "antisocial" behavior. Croce (1913: 370) continues: 'Those propositions, like all the others of economic science, are therefore certainly not descriptions, but *theorems*'.

For that matter, Buchanan's efficiency concept is a reference to Knut Wicksell's (1958) fiscal theory, 'A New Principle of Just Taxation'. As with a change in legitimate property rights, taxation may also obstruct the sovereignty of an individual's property rights. Both instances question how to remain within the domain of Paretian efficiency while observing individuals' sovereignty. Like Buchanan, Wicksell takes subjects' value scales as a point of departure in his search for a just tax principle. Wicksell refers to it as the 'benefit principle, the well-known principle of equality between Value and Countervalue'. (ibid.: 72). He continues:

> I apply the modern concept of marginal utility and subjective value to public services and to the individuals' contributions for these services.
>
> (ibid.)

Basically, it is a *presumptive benefit principle*. It amounts to *estimating* citizens' marginal utility and subjective value attributed to public services against the marginal value of their contributions to these services. In the Kaufmann perspective, Wicksell is engaged in the analysis of meaning, resulting in a tax principle of a society peopled by homunculi who endeavor after presumptive efficient public services. *Sine qua non* of a just tax principle is a simultaneous decision regarding public service and the expenses for it, simulating the *quid pro quo* of the market exchange. At the same time, Wicksell recognizes that it is difficult to 'express numerically' the individual benefits of a public service as 'each person can ultimately speak only for himself' (ibid.: 90). However, this is not a prohibitive objection as long as, *in an observer's estimate*, everyone gains, and no one can feel exploited from this very elementary point of view. Wicksell significantly adds that a perchance difference in gains does not *per se* hinder voluntary consent, as

> give and take is a firm foundation of lasting friendship and even if one cannot count on the taking, there are few men who are completely indifferent to the welfare of their fellows.
>
> (ibid.)

The notion of consensus that features society as a synthesis of human beings who recognize themselves in their fellow men reemerges in this quote. However, Wicksell realizes that the opportunities to apply the benefit principle are limited. For instance, 'cases of clear necessity' such as the national army require coercion, although private initiatives may be found alongside state organizations (ibid.). For instance, Wicksell puts forward, churches support schools and institutions for higher education with their own financing. It alludes to a justified optimism regarding the applicability of the presumptive benefit principle in financing public services. Demarcated interests prompt the vitality of the principle.

The empirical test of a proposal based on the benefit principle questions whether it acquires unanimous consent. The possibility of unanimous approval depends on the choice between many alternative possibilities regarding the incidence of the combination of the expenditure concerned and the tax revenue to cover the cost. As Buchanan (1959: 131) notes regarding *presumptive efficiency*: 'a whole set of possible combinations one which will prove acceptable to all parties'. It is rather unlikely that the presumptive benefit principle will successfully pass the empirical test given the demanding condition of unanimity. Again, economics is not famous for its empirical laws. Buchanan's presumptive efficiency criterion and Wicksell's benefit principle regard theorems.

7.6.4 Coase in accord with Pigou

The objective of the comparative institutional approach is, as quoted earlier,

> to devise practical arrangements which will correct defects in one part of the system without causing more serious harm in other parts.
>
> (Coase 1960: 34)

The 'Social Cost' paper discusses several sample calculations about the classic example of trains causing fire damage to crops. The calculations show the reciprocal nature of the problem and thus its dependence on liability law. They substantiate that

> "uncompensated damage done to surrounding woods by sparks from railway engines" is not necessarily undesirable. Whether it is desirable or not depends on the particular circumstances.
>
> (ibid.)

Taking account of particular circumstances may express Coase's aversion to 'blackboard economics'. It depends on actual legislation and transaction cost issues. At the same time, this poses a challenging task for the economist. It is one thing to elaborate sample calculations. However, the very issue is to determine the variety of data that will address the question of 'how to avoid the more serious harm' (Coase 1959: 26).

In the various examples and the legal cases regarding side effects discussed by Coase, transfers of a 'sum of money' or 'a bargain', that is, financial calculations prevail. (ibid.: 27). It concurs with Coase's lecture on *Economics and Contiguous Disciplines* in which he points at the great advantage that economists possess compared to other social scientists. They 'are able to use the "measuring rod of money"' (Coase 1994: 44). Apparently, Coase is not concerned with the possibility of an interpersonal comparison of utility, disregards the perspective of new welfare economics, and joins Pigou in his view on welfare as a cardinal thing. In this aspect, Coase assents to Pigou's research agenda. Pigou recaps:

> Hence, the range of our inquiry becomes restricted to that part of social welfare that can be brought directly or indirectly into relation with the measuring-rod of money. This part of welfare may be called economic welfare.
>
> (1920: 11)

It corresponds with this Pigovian idea on welfare that, according to Coase (1994: 45), economists study the economy as a 'unified interdependent system' in which people purchase less at higher prices 'and to a large extent, people choose their occupations on the basis of money incomes'. It reflects an unassuming substantiation of an individual's self-interest and his economic rationality in financial terms. Self-interest measured in money appears to feature the homunculus's rationality in Coase's economic system.

Clearly, this interpretation does not accord with new welfare economics, which denies the possibility of the interpersonal comparison of utility restricting its welfare judgment to Paretian-relevant changes. New welfare economists subscribe to Wicksell's (1958: 90) principle: 'each person can ultimately speak only for himself'. Wicksell endorses William Jevons (1871: 21), who had already declared earlier that 'every mind is ... inscrutable to every other mind, and no common denominator of feeling seems possible'. Therefore, welfare is merely a matter of an individual's preferences that are eligible for ranking, that is, an ordinal thing. From a positive perspective of economics, it renders revealed preferences as the very foundation of welfare and efficiency judgments of value.

New welfare economics poses to the analysist of comparative institutions the question of how to calculate the harm to be avoided without a common denominator. Alternatively, how can the greater public value of an apple orchard compared to some ornamental red cedars be determined? Obviously, Coase neglects the question, or rather, he has reason to continue grasping the Pigovian concept of welfare. First of all, it accords with Coase's (1994: 38) idea of the subject matter of economics that constitutes the 'kind of question' and 'the cohesive force that makes a group of scholars a recognisable profession'. Coase specifies the subject matter as follows:

> What economists study is the working of the social institutions which bind together the economic system: firms, markets for goods and services, labour markets, capital markets, the banking system, international trade and so on.
>
> (ibid.: 41)

In brief, the economist studies exchange on markets. It regards a reorientation from production and distribution towards exchange as the subject matter which, as John Hicks (1976: 212) proposes, stems from the Marginal Revolution. Marginalists or 'catallactists', as Hicks proposes to rename them, 'construct a "vision" of economic life out of the theory of exchange' (ibid.). They study 'economics from within', wondering how independently acting agents unintendedly entail some order. In this aspect, the catallactics of the market determine value in exchange, which corresponds to marginal utility. In marginalist tradition, use value as counterpart of value in exchange merely figures as a prerequisite for a good to be exchanged. Therefore, the Marginal Revolution renders it plausible to treat utility as a basically cardinal quantity. It is prices that direct consumers' conduct and profit opportunities that entice entrepreneurs. The role of the concept of utility 'has been largely sterile', Coase contends. Referring to Stigler, he stresses that what is of relevance is the implication of utility theory, that is, that consumers '"will surely buy less when the price of a commodity rises"' (Stigler, quoted in Coase 1994: 43).

These concepts express the intellectual habitat of Coase. At the outset of his 'Firm' paper, he mentions the powerful instrument of 'substitution at the margin' (Coase 1937: 386–387). He practices economics from within and the catallactics of the normal economic system, generating prices and exchange ratios that beacon our economic conduct. It renders it plausible that the 'Firm' paper, besides providing a marginal analysis, aspires '"formal relations which are capable of being *conceived* exactly"' (ibid.: 387). This frame makes it understandable that Coase (1994: 45), in contrast with prevailing new welfare economics, takes 'full advantage of those opportunities which occur when the "measuring rod of money" can be used'. Coase continues:

> what are measured by money are important determinants of human behavior in the economic system.
>
> (ibid.: 44)

Obviously, money prices allocate resources and determine the outcome of the economic system. The new thing in Coase's (1937: 391) institutional economics is that he offers a 'conceived exactly' redefinition of market relations, that is, subjected to 'costs … of using the price mechanism'. Nevertheless, the difficulty remains for stating exactly these costs. Basically, the monetary measuring rod represents the theoretical stance to apply 'realism in assumptions (which) forces us to analyse the world that exists, not some imaginary world' (Coase 1994: 18). It is the realism of the assumptions on which the logical constructions of economic theory are founded, that is, 'assumptions such as that, faced with a choice between $100 and $10, very few people will choose $10.' (ibid.: 24–25). It reflects the methodological ambition of the theorist to confine himself. From a theoretical perspective, it is a confinement to exchange relations, to transactions via the market, or, otherwise, addressing Adam Smith's question: 'How is the cooperation of these vast numbers of people?' (ibid.: 80).

Obviously, demand and cost conditions determine what happens with prices. However, the actual problem is discovering the relevant data, Coase adds. *A fortiori* the data problem is relevant for 'determinants of human behavior' that are not originally in currency units. Prices and costs

> may appear in various guises, but an economist is likely to see through them. Punishment, for example, can be regarded as the price of crime.
>
> (ibid.: 45)

Like Pigou, Coase keeps the opportunity open to bring the determinants 'indirectly into relation with the measuring-rod of money' (Pigou 1920: 11). In this aspect, Pigou distinguishes a sliding scale of opportunities to do that, varying from '"can easily" to "can with violent straining"' (ibid.). The challenge is to translate instances of unpriced scarcity into money terms.

7.6.5 Presumptive efficiency in terms of money

In the *Miller et al. v. Schoene* case that was discussed, apple trees and red cedar trees compete with one another for a certain geographical area. One another's vicinity causes scarcity. To what extent this will remain *unpriced* scarcity depends on whether the parties engaged succeed in concluding a positive outcome. In particular, manifestations of strategic behavior may thwart an agreement. For instance, one may deliberately plant red cedars to exact money from the neighboring apple orchard owner. Apparently, prevailing property-rights structures do not warrant an efficient outcome. The Virginia Cedar Rust statute argues to prompt the efficiency compared to doing nothing. In the further appeal against the statute, the Supreme Court proposes that '"the judgment legislature, is of greater value to the public"' (Miller et al. v. Schoene, 276 U.S. (1928), quoted in Samuels 1971: 438). It is a different question whether it also illustrates *presumptive efficiency*. In this respect, Coase (1960: 34) adds that whether a certain institutional arrangement 'is desirable or not depends on the particular circumstances'. In the apple versus cedar case, the justice estimates that the value of protecting apple tree orchards exceeds the value lost due to destroying the ornamental red cedars. At the same time, it is improbable that this decision nears the presumptive efficiency criterion. The cedar tree owners do not receive compensation other than that 'they could retain possession and make use of the cut trees' (Samuels 1971: 436). The protection of the orchard owner at the expense of the cedar owner without compensation for the latter will clearly not receive unanimous approval. The case exhibits an obvious difference in protecting the interests between the parties. The safeguarded value of the orchard will exceed the value loss of the cedars. It offers opportunities for estimating the presumptive efficiency. The estimated sizable financial loss from which the statute indemnifies the orchard owners determines the financial room within which compensation to the cedar owners is affordable. The next issue is attempting to estimate the financial compensation that might receive unanimous approval. It is a *prima facie* good case for a Pareto-relevant improvement. It assumes the as-if reasonability of the parties involved and renders their individual preferences in money terms. It is an analysis of meaning to formulate a theoretical proposition, for example, the refutable proposition that money amount x paid by orchard owners to compensate red cedar owners achieves consensus. It reflects a (political) economist's endeavor, like Adam Smith, to organize cooperation between people to bring about more welfare. The refutability of the presumptive efficiency proposition safeguards a theorist's methodological individualism.

7.7 Comparative institutional analysis applied

Basically, the presumptive efficiency concept, and so Wicksell's benefit principle, stretches the tit-for-tat principle as far as possible. How to safeguard individuals' sovereignty founds the comparative-institutional analysis. It is the constant in all those cases in which markets threaten to fail. I discuss three of them.

7.7.1 British lighthouse history as a specimen

The case of market failure in the British history of lighthouses is exemplary. Economists of renown, John Stuart Mill, Henry Sidgwick, Kenneth Arrow, and Paul Samuelson, concur that the non-excludability of lighthouse services renders them unsuitable for market procurement. Their non-excludability imposes an absolute limit on "'the Laissez-Faire or Non-Interference Principle'", Mill concludes (quoted in Coase 1974: 357). However, Coase's detailed historical information regarding the British lighthouses shows that the organization and procurement of the lighthouse services radically differ from the expected immediate government involvement. Apparently, the institutional arrangement depends on the particular circumstances, as Coase (1960: 34) emphasizes. In contrast to theoretical expectations, Coase examines privately built and operated lighthouses. During the seventeenth century, private initiatives of shippers and shipowners were honored with a patent from the Crown empowering private entrepreneurs to build lighthouses and levy tolls on ships benefitting from the service (Coase 1974: 364). It was a response to the reluctance of Trinity House, the principal lighthouse authority in England and Wales, that evolved out of a sailors' guild that was responsible for a number of maritime affairs. Later, Trinity House adopted the policy to apply for patents to operate lighthouses and to subsequently grant a lease for a rental to private individuals who would then build and finance the investment (ibid.: 365). The British lighthouse history reveals the engagement of stakeholders such as shippers, fishermen, and shipowners taking advantage of the built-in incentives of granting leases to private investors who adopt the commercial risk of cost recovery. The token of reasonability of the maritime stakeholders and investing entrepreneurs who apparently recognize their mutual gain in a venture potentially fraught with free rider issues is remarkable. It is merely the institutional arrangement of a lighthouse patent and a license to collect toll that suffices to bring together individuals' contributions to the cost of a public service. Actually, it amounts to a variation on Wicksell's (1958: 72) benefit principle, that is, linking 'marginal utility and subjective value to public services and to the individuals' contributions for these services'.

7.7.2 *The creation of property rights of emission*

Climate Change: The Ultimate Challenge for Economics, reads the title of William Nordhaus's (2019) Nobel Prize lecture in a revised version held in 2018. The anthropogenic nature of climate change renders it an economic problem *par excellence*, if not the all-dominating economic question of the twenty-first century. Referring to Paul Samuelson, Nordhaus identifies the problem of climate change as basically an externality or public good, or rather, it is a '"public bad" in the form of greenhouse-gas (GHG) emissions' (ibid.: 1992).[6] It regards activities 'whose costs or benefits spill outside the market and are not captured in market prices' (ibid). In Pigovian terms, private marginal cost (price) does not equate the social marginal cost. This may be repaired by imposing a price on the source of this inequality, that is, the combustion of carbon.[7] Pricing may take place either with a carbon tax or by placing a limit on the amount of allowable emissions that may be transferred, that is, the cap-and-trade mechanism. Nordhaus contends that the global nature of the problem renders an internationally uniform carbon price preferable to the latter. A single carbon price (tax) will facilitate international negotiations and ease the supervision of compliance and the possibility of sanctions (ibid.: 2011). Its simplicity and transparency facilitate the constitution of a 'climate club' of countries to overcome free riding. Nordhaus defines such a club as follows:

> A club is a voluntary group deriving mutual benefits from sharing the costs of producing a shared good or service.
>
> (ibid.: 2010)

The primary feature of a climate club is that its members 'would be penalized if they did not meet their obligations', which regard 'an "international target carbon price" that is the focal provision of the agreement' (ibid.: 2011). Vis-à-vis the inevitably multiple quantity caps, the single harmonized carbon price, for example, $40 a ton, offers a focal point in the international negotiations that is additional to its simplicity.

> With penalty tariffs on nonparticipants, the climate club creates a strategic situation in which countries acting in their self-interest will choose to enter the club and undertake ambitious emissions reductions because of the structure of the incentives.
>
> (ibid.)

The penalty tariffs change the payoffs of the strategies of the club members that otherwise unrelentingly would result in the equilibrium of the prisoner's dilemma. Furthermore, it is rather easy to produce evidence of noncompliance with the carbon price as a basis for a change in a member's payoff. Contrariwise, the evidence of noncompliance with a multiple of national quantity caps presents itself as 'an updated version of Kenneth Arrow's voting paradox' (ibid.). Briefly, it may be argued that pricing carbon affords opportunities that are more advantageous for addressing free riding than a set of national quantity caps. In his plea for pricing, Nordhaus refers to Martin Weitzman's (2017) paper in *Research in Economics*. The immediate cause for it is 'the COP21 Paris Agreement' of 2015 in which the participating countries promised to comply with the mitigation of GHG emissions (ibid.: 199). Article 4.4 of the Paris Agreement reads as follows:

> Developed country Parties should continue taking the lead by undertaking economy-wide absolute emission reduction targets. Developing country Parties should continue enhancing their mitigation efforts, and are encouraged to move over time towards economy-wide emission reduction or limitation targets in the light of different national circumstances.
>
> (United Nations 2015: 4)

These targets result from 'so-called "Intended Nationally Determined Contributions" or INDC's' (Weitzman 2017: 200). It reflects the strictly voluntary nature of the agreement and, as such, a license for free riding. Therefore, Weitzman argues for

> a "top down" solution in prices *vs.* quantities, using the fiction of a "World Climate Assembly"(WCA) voting on emissions via majority rule.
>
> (ibid.)

Such a WCA may constitute binding agreements and penalize noncompliance provided that nations are prepared to forego part of their sovereignty. Voluntarism dooms the Paris Agreement to fail, Weitzman fears.

The simplicity and transparency of a harmonized carbon price offer relatively more chances of successful negotiations for concluding a binding agreement. Moreover, a price agreement is easier to enforce than multiple national quantity caps. The latter entails a second round of negotiations, that is, a 'fractional subdivision formula for disaggregating the majority-voted aggregate worldwide quantity cap' into national targets; another occasion to free riding (ibid.: 201).

Nordhaus's Climate Club and Weitzman's WCA express the endeavor to overcome the free-riding problem that features the collective good of mitigating climate change. They intend to change the payoffs of the strategies, which reduces the probability that the agreement will be crippled by a prisoner's dilemma equilibrium.

The idea of organizing a club or an agency as a mutual dependence is reminiscent of both Buchanan's presumptive efficiency concept and Wicksell's benefit principle. For instance, Weitzman's comment that his paper regarding 'his' WCA 'has been laced with subjective judgments' reminds of Buchanan's political economist who *presumes* knowledge about the manner in which a government measure affects people's welfare (ibid.: 209). It is a political economist's search for presumptive efficiency, that is, taking account of individual efficiency to nearly obtain a Paretian-efficient solution. As Buchanan words it,

> searching out and locating from among the whole set of possible combinations one which will prove acceptable to all parties.
>
> (1959: 131)

In this aspect, Weitzman proposes reasons that argue in favor of a negotiated carbon price over negotiated quantities. First, it argues in support of pricing that the 'revenues from a carbon price are nationally collected, so that the contentious distributional side is somewhat hidden and there is at least the appearance of fairness as measured by equality of marginal effort' (Weitzman 2017: 209). Second, as discussed, it is its negotiations facilitating simplicity and transparency that favors pricing. Third, it is

> the built-in countervailing force of an imposed uniform price of carbon, which tends to internalize the externality and gives national negotiators an incentive to offset their natural impulse to otherwise bargain for low tax rates for themselves.
>
> (ibid.)

In the context of an international treaty that covers all major emitters of carbon, the model in Weitzman's paper (although 'so abstract, so over-simplified, and so removed from reality') confirms that a binding price comes closer to a social optimum than a multiple of binding quantities (ibid.). Therefore, Weitzman argues for a 'futuristic "World Climate Assembly"' that votes 'on a universal price (or tax) that is internationally harmonized, but the proceeds from which are domestically retained' (ibid.: 199). Weitzman's reasoning may be interpreted as Wicksell's (1958: 72) endeavor, as expressed in his benefit principle quoted earlier, to link 'marginal utility and subjective value to public services and to the individuals' contributions for these services'. The artificial creation of reciprocity that features markets is common.

As yet, it is not without reason that the Paris Agreement, in spite of a substantiated preference for pricing carbon, opts for the mitigation of emission quantities, that is, the INDCs. The international dimension gives preference to the pricing of carbon. Vis-à-vis the international dimension, however, climate change is, first of all, a microeconomic problem. Almost all economic activities of consumers, producers, and governments affect GHG emissions. The very economic question is to investigate 'the decision calculus for these activities', that is, the situational logic of the agents involved (Aldy, Stavins 2012: 45). Besides mandatory measures to change the emission performances and subsidizing emission-reducing measures, it is pricing the emissions that directly changes the logic of the situation. Which of them is preferable from an allocative efficiency perspective?

A command-and-control regulation may be appropriate when the regulator is well informed about the performance of the regulated standards such as a zero tolerance of a certain pollutant or about a local case of pollution. At the same time, it hardly affords opportunities for incentives for developing innovative technologies that may surpass a prescribed emission standard.

The inherent disadvantage of subsidies is that they disturb the decision calculations of others due to the taxes they entail. Furthermore, subsidies may generate adverse effects, stimulating subsidized technology undermining 'incentives for efficiency and conservation' (ibid.: 46).

In contrast to these options, the preferable regulation regards the market parameters of prices and quantities as they are directly connected to the very condition of allocative efficiency, that is, equilibrium of supply and demand, trading a quantity that equates marginal cost to market price. The next question regards the choice between price versus quantity regulation. Price regulation concerns a tax on carbon (GHG) emissions that incorporates the cost of the emission's damage. It reflects the Pigovian approach to externality, that is, pricing (taxing) the unpriced cost of carbon to equate social marginal costs to prices. Basically, pricing the emission grants the emitter the *right to emit*.

The counterpart of pricing is the quantity regulation of emission. It finds its analytical basis in Coase's interpretation of externality, that is, that the allocative inefficiency of externality labors under the nonexistence or poor definition of property rights. It is the transferability of the *right to emit* that is the featuring difference between price and quantity regulation, that is, as a cap-and-trade regulation. Property rights are attached to whatever finds its way to the highest bidder, equating price to its marginal cost.

The matter at issue remains the relative allocative efficiency of pricing carbon versus quantity cap-and-trade. If the regulator would be well-informed about the cost and benefit functions of the emission reduction, the choice between price and quantity would be indifferent; the efficiency quantity may be inferred from the price and vice versa. In this aspect, reemerges the difference between Pigou and Coase. Apparently, Pigou assumes that the gap between the private marginal versus the social marginal cost of a GHG emission is knowable. The Coase approach basically leaves the determination to the market.

Therefore, in mundane reality the market may assist the regulator who is ill informed about the agents to be regulated. The regulator is behind the firm that has, as a version of 'the man-on-the-spot', knowledge about its situation in order to respond appropriately to the regulated price or quantity. A carbon price (tax) induces seeking alternative production methods. At the same time, the opportunities to reduce emissions will strongly differ between industries and within industries and between firms both nationally and internationally. They generate significant differences between firms in the costs of emission reduction, offering opportunities for mutual gains under a regime of cap-and-trade regulation. It prompts a relatively cost-effective emission reduction. Rephrased, it is not a Pigovian regulator who values the right to emit, but it is the market that grants it to the one who values it most as further commented on in the following.

Therefore, the price-versus-quantity comparison must be specified as pricing versus a quantity-cap-and-trade mechanism. It is essential that the quantity approach enables trading such as, for instance, Article 6.2 of the Paris Agreement alludes to the transferability of quantity caps:

> Parties shall, where engaging on a voluntary basis in cooperative approaches that involve the use of *internationally transferred mitigation outcomes* towards nationally determined contributions, promote sustainable development.
>
> (United Nations 2015: 7; emphasis added)

Since Knight (1921) and Coase (1959, 1960), economists are well aware that the very *sine qua non* of transferability and trade is the existence of well-defined property rights. The application of this seminal concept in auctioning frequencies has created billions of dollars of efficiency gains (via reductions in tax distortions) as Thomas Hazlett et al. (2011: S156) establish. Billions of dollars of social net value may also be documented as the fruit of auctioning pollution property rights.

J.H. Dales was an early exponent in 1968 of economists who recognize the pollution of natural resources as a property rights question (1968a). In his paper, 'Land, Water, and Ownership', Dales (1968b: 791) criticizes the artificial pricing for water, that is, shadow pricing, that expressed the 'increasing public concern about the pollution of natural water systems' during the early 1960s. Shadow pricing reemerges in the Pigovian remedy to augment the private marginal cost with the cost of the externality until they equal their social marginal benefit. However, this academic exercise disregards the very cause of the unpriced scarcity that the pollution apparently generates, which is a property right; that is, ownership of water will bring about trade between competing users granting the ownership to the highest bidder. Real prices that reflect the reality of the scarcity of water shove aside the awkward shadow price issue. This has been economists' narrative of markets since Adam Smith and David Ricardo. Ricardo applies it to the use of land, substantiating that each piece of land will generate a rent in accordance with its fertility. Obviously, what is required is ownership, that is, '*transferable* property rights (which) stand in a one-to-one relationship to prices' (ibid.: 796). Under the heroic assumptions of efficient markets, prices command an optimal efficient degree of pollution in its competition with other uses. The market price determines the quantity of polluting discharges, that is, the quantity cap. Apparently, price versus quantity is a nonissue. 'The normal economic system works itself' reemerges as a null hypothesis.

Unfortunately, however, waters are not suitable to be subdivided into pieces to which ownership may be assigned. How can property rights be organized for hardly tangible natural resources such as waters and atmosphere that, to an ever-lesser degree, we may command as ubiquities? It might be possible to assign rights regarding uses that are suitable for zoning. It enables conflicting local activities to compete for a right of settlement. However, the primary polluting activities of waters and atmosphere concern the very opposite of local externality conflicts. They are dispersed and frequently globally dispersed in a literal sense. Therefore, indivisible natural resources such as water and atmosphere harmed by dispersed pollutants need *one* owner who takes care of them as a steward. As Dales contends:

> The only sensible alternative is the one actually adopted, namely, monopoly ownership by government.
>
> (ibid.: 797)

Prima facie, this is opposite to what 'economics from within' instructs as based on methodological individualism. The basic economic problem is to determine the efficient use of a resource, that is, of efficient pollution, equating 'the value of a marginal increment in the one good ... to the value of a marginal decrement in the other' (ibid.: 798). However, the increment of a pollutant that serves the production of one good may decrease the value of a myriad of amenities provided by the natural resource. The multidimensional amenity of natural resources makes them ineligible for calculating the economic equation concerned. '*Faute de mieux*', Dales infers, making a political decision about pollution control is required. It is ecologists and other scientists who have influence in decisions at the aspiration level constituting the trade-off between pollution versus a resource's multidimensional amenity (ibid.). Economists may rather be silent.

Economists' silence is contrary to the Pigovian remedy to tax the putative cause of the externality, that is, the pollutant. The Pigovian economist does not merely assume to know about the cost of the damage caused, but he also suggests knowing that the damage occurs in one direction. The latter occurs, for example, by the upstream river polluter who harms the downstream swimmer. The Pigovian tax-subsidy scheme assumes 'that it is possible to make the distinction between emitters and recipients', Dahlman (1979: 157) notes. Aside, this refers to Pigou's perception of property right as an instance of *ius naturale*, as discussed in the preceding section. Consequently, this neglects the reciprocity of the harmful effect, as underlined by Coase (1959). It is not just reciprocal in the context that the swimmer 'harms' polluter's right to pollute. Additionally, the polluter himself harms his own right and opportunity to swim downstream in the river. Clearly, the Pigovian blackboard economics runs into serious conceptual and calculation issues. Neither a broad social welfare function encompassing all types of dimensions and showing the social-decision problem may solve them (Dales 1968b: 799). It is the noneconomic arbitrary act of fixing the aspiration level of a government as an ownership monopoly that is required to decide on the competing uses of the natural resource asset.

The arbitrary act of imposing a carbon tax or fixing a quantity cap of polluting discharges, of GHG emissions, creates anew a setting in which the economist regains an active role. A quantity cap amounts to an artificial and, foremost, arbitrary allocation that might generate exchange if allowed and facilitated by property rights. The earnestness of a quantity cap to pollute will differ between the polluting agents, which offers trade opportunities. The counterpart of the quantity of allowances or emission rights is the price they entail. As noted, hypothetically, the fixed quantity may result in a price that equals the marginal cost of the emission reduction. Apparently, the regulator is then well informed about the cost function of emission abatement. Armed with this information, it is indifferent whether the emission quantity is fixed or the price (tax) is based on per emission unit. The regulator produces equilibrium coordinates T, $Q_{trading}$ in Figure 7.1, both left and right. Obviously, in reality, the regulator can merely make conjectures about the cap quantity or the price of emission. Uncertainty abounds, for instance, causing a difference between the expected and the actual marginal cost of emission abatement. It once again renders the choice significant between quantity versus price. Figure 7.1 illustrates the different efficiency effects of quantity versus price regulation. The picture on the left refers to the short term and the right to the long term.

In the context of a climate-change policy, the MB curve represents the marginal benefit of carbon-emission reduction. The MC curve refers to the

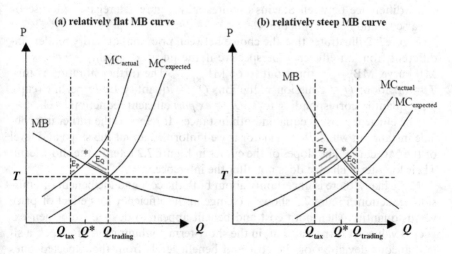

Figure 7.1 Price versus quantity cap.

(*Source:* Hepburn 2006: 232.)

marginal cost of emission reduction. Q = carbon emission reduction; T = carbon tax; at Q^* holds MB = MC_{actual}, that is, the *ex post* efficient reduction level; $Q_{trading}$ = quantity emission cap; Q_{tax} = emission reduction, given T; $(Q_{tax} < Q^*)$ = E_P, that is, efficiency loss of price instrument; $(Q_{trading} > Q^*) = E_Q$, that is, efficiency loss of quantity instrument.

The slope of the curves is crucial in the efficiency comparison of price versus quantity regulation. In the left-hand image, the MB curve is relatively flat against rather steep MC curves. They reflect the short-term situation in which the rather flat MB curve represents the limited benefits of emission reduction. However, the steep shape of the MC curve indicates the limited opportunities to reduce emissions in the short term. As a consequence, the latter causes relatively substantial inefficiency of a quantity cap vis-à-vis a carbon tax (price), that is, $E_Q > E_P$. The quantity cap presses the emitter to defray expenses that substantially exceed the MB of the emission reduction.

The right-hand picture regarding the relative inefficiency results in the opposite, $E_P > E_Q$. Compared to the short term, the damage of the carbon emission is substantial in the long run, if not devastating due to its cumulative effect.[8] Therefore, the relatively steep MB curve indicates the long-term effect of emission reduction. At the same time, the rather flat shape of the MC curves reflects the increased adaptability of the emitters in the long run. It is the configuration of the slope of MB and MC curves that determines the relative efficiency of price versus quantity as alternative instruments.

Figure 7.1 depicts the impact of uncertainty about the $MC_{expected}$, which turns out to be lower than the MC_{actual}. Robert Stavins (1996) graphically elaborates on the efficiency effect of price versus quantity regulation when other uncertainty profiles occur. In the following figures, Stavins substantiates Weitzman's formal analysis of *Prices vs. Quantities* (Weitzman 1974). The (irrelevant) difference between Stavins's figures and Figure 7.1 regards the use of linear cost and benefit functions.

Figure 7.2 illustrates that the choice between price and quantity renders indifferent from an efficiency perspective if the uncertainty only concerns the MB curve. $MB_{(E)xpected}$ turns out to be $MB_{(R)ealized}$. The further notation is this: T = taxation: Q = emission reduction; Q_{TP} = quantity trade permit (cap); Q_T = quantity corresponding to T; Q^*_2 = *ex post* efficient reduction level.

The efficiency loss is equal in both instances. It refers to the rather improbable instance in which the regulator is well informed about the slope and level of the MC curve. The slopes of the curves in Figure 7.2 refer to the short term. Their long-term change does not alter the inference.

More likely, there is uncertainty about both the cost and the benefit of emission reduction. Figure 7.3 shows a change in the efficiency loss effect of price versus quantity when both cost and benefit appear to deviate from their expected values. It turns out that, in the short-term configuration of slopes, a simultaneous deviation of the cost and benefit levels from the expected ones produces a relatively large efficiency loss of price (tax) regulation vis-à-vis the efficiency loss of a quantity cap, triangle $ABC > CDE$.

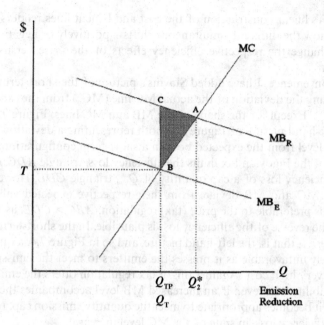

Figure 7.2 Price versus quantity cap.
(*Source:* Stavins 1996: 221.)

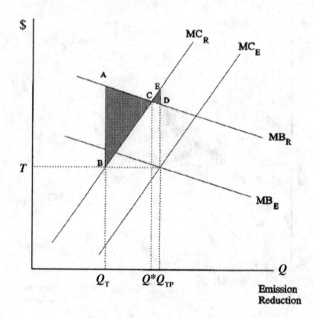

Figure 7.3 Price versus quantity cap.
(*Source:* Stavins 1996: 222.)

Stavins's linear construction of the cost and benefit lines renders it easy to imagine how the different simultaneous shifts – positively or negatively correlated – change the respective efficiency effects of the price versus quantity regulation.

For convenience, I have added Stavins's picture of the short-term situation representing the deviation of the actual MC line (MC_R) from the expected MC line (MC_E). Except for the shape of the MB and MC lines, Figure 7.4 is equal to the left-hand picture of Figure 7.1, both representing a deviation of the actual MC level from the expected both in a short-term configuration. Again, it shows that the Pigovian tax limits the efficiency loss, triangle *ADC*, compared to the efficiency loss of a cap quantity of Q_{TP}, triangle *CDE*. However, when both the MC and MB deviate from their respective expected values, a cap quantity is preferable to the price (tax) regulation; *ABC* > *CDE*, as Figure 7.3 shows. The reverse of the efficiency loss is plausible. In the short-term situation of Figure 7.1, that is, the left-hand picture, and so in Figure 7.4, a quantity cap is relatively unfavorable as it presses the emitters to meet the emission reduction at a very high cost. Against this, a tax regulation offers the emitter short-term flexibility. However, if an increased MB level accompanies the MC level increase, it becomes appropriate to meet the quantity emission cap, resulting in limited efficiency loss, in spite of the MC level increase.

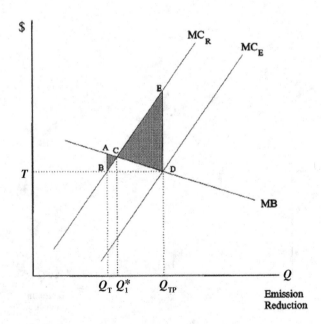

Figure 7.4 Price versus quantity cap.

(*Source:* Stavins 1996: 220.)

The issue behind the differences in the inevitable efficiency losses is a regulator's uncertainty about the benefits and the costs of emission abatement. In due course, the configuration of the slopes of the MB and MC curves evolves, which changes the relative efficiency loss of the price versus quantity regulation. The depicted curves of MB and MC concern a reformulation of the basic efficiency principle of emission abatement. This principle regards, first, as Nicholas Stern (2007: 352) notes: 'the point where the costs of going any further (with GHG emission reduction) would outweigh the extra benefits'. In this aspect, the benefits of emission reduction amount to a recovery or no further deterioration of the amenity and functionality value of the atmosphere. The puzzle of the calculation of these benefits can only be solved by an arbitrary act as discussed, that is, postulating MB curves as depicted in the figures earlier, and an environmental/atmospheric benefit as a function of emission reduction. The second overarching efficiency principle, as Stern refers to it, is the adoption of a price signal or a quantity cap. Given the international dimension of GHG emission, Stern proposes,

> a common price signal is needed across countries and sectors to ensure that emission reductions are delivered in the most cost-effective way.
>
> (ibid.)

Basically, the price signal pinpoints the marginal benefit of emission reduction by adopting a GHG/carbon tax or its equivalent, that is, the inherent quantity cap. Given the postulated MB curve, the well-informed regulator arrives at $Q_{trading}$ as depicted in Figure 7.1.

Obviously, an international harmonization of the price signal is required to forestall international competition that would harm the emission reduction targets. Besides the issue of achieving an international agreement, the regulators face the question that they 'must implement a climate policy (prices versus quantity) before uncertainty about the cost of emission mitigation can be resolved' (Aldy, Stavins 2012: 52). Figure 7.1 substantiates the effects of a higher-than-expected mitigation cost: less emission reduction in the case of a tax and a higher cost of cap quantity regulation (ibid.).

As a general principle, a price such as a carbon tax is a simple instrument for reducing emissions. For instance, a carbon tax '"upstream"' based on carbon fuels would cover a major part of carbon dioxide emissions 'through a relatively small number of firms' (ibid.: 47). Furthermore, it offers short-term flexibility as a relatively limited efficiency loss due to a regulator's underestimated abatement costs. However, the very problem of GHG emissions is that their devastating effects present themselves in the long run and that they do that exponentially. This argues for cap-and-trade regulation. First, the emission quantity is an absolute standard that directly correlates with global warming. Second, the allocation of the permits/allowances to emit generates a (second) market that trades the permits to the highest bidder. The selling partner finds cheaper methods to reduce emissions. The cap-and-trade generates incentives for innovation and creative alternatives, which flattens the long-term MC curve of emission reduction.

Thus, against Nordhaus's and Weitzman's plea for a harmonized price (tax) motivated by the international dimension of the problem stand reasons that argue for the cap-and-trade mechanism. Both options generate incentives to economize emissions, and both wrestle with adopting the appropriate regulation of price and quantity, respectively. A potential disadvantage of emission trading is the cost uncertainty of the permit market that may discourage investments. Joseph Aldy and Robert Stavins discuss some measures to mitigate this cost uncertainty. It concerns 'offsets, allowance banking and borrowing, safety valves, and price collars' in the cap-and-trade system (ibid.: 49). The offset allows compensation of emissions with a reduction of others outside the mechanism, that is, in an industry outside the regulated cap, the safety value puts an upper bound on the firms' costs, offering additional allowances at a fixed price. The price collar concerns an upper safety value plus a price floor. In this aspect, an emission–reduction–credit system works as a complementary tradable allowance system. It may 'bring about emission reductions by awarding tradable credits to unregulated entities for certified emission reductions' (Jaffe et al. 2009: 794). Basically, these measures, particularly banking and borrowing opportunities, indicate the degree of maturity of a secondary market based on the created property rights.

Linkages between tradable allowance systems may further prompt market maturity. For instance, the European Union Emission Trading System (EU ETS) is actually a multinational linkage among the ETSs of the EU member states that is harmonized and enforced by the European Commission (ibid.: 798). Linkages between tradable allowance (permit) systems offer the opportunity to lower the costs of emission reduction, particularly if systems face 'very different marginal abatement costs', Jaffe et al. add, for the sake of completeness (ibid.: 799).

The cap-and-trade mechanism basically stems from the idea that the normal economic system works itself. The departing point is the Coase Theorem. However, prohibitively high transaction costs stultify the agents engaged in climate change to procure the immense, potentially mutual, gains of GHG emission reduction. The cap-and-trade mechanism accentuates that government is the indispensable producer behind it. First, it decides the emission cap that limits the emission rights. Second, it must decide which industries and firms are covered by the cap. In this respect, the effectiveness of the trade-and-cap mechanism greatly depends on the possibility of the definition of emission rights and thus on their enforceability. Third, it must decide whether to auction or to grandfather the emission rights. Fourth, the regulating government must decide about complementary arrangements such as offset facilities, banking, and borrowing as discussed earlier. Fifth, it must take account of the dynamic aspects of the problem and fine-tune the GHG's short-term standards with the long-term effects. Apparently, institutional arrangements constitute an inextricable combination of market versus (governmental) hierarchy.

The enforcement faculty of government may help to overcome the free-riding problem that plagues the collective bad of climate change. In this aspect, government engagement is just an option as an alternative when other civil society devices fail to overcome free riding.

Price and quantity are the natural ingredients of the economics of climate change abatement, for example, as parameters of GHG emission reduction, assuming it is the all-dominating variable. An arbitrary and imaginary price–quantity relationship constitutes an economist's analytical commencement to rescue him from his overwhelming ignorance about the costs and benefits of emission reduction. Obviously, the cap-and-trade mechanism is a paragon of an NIE institutional arrangement à la Coase and Demsetz. The assignment of property rights to the emission of GHG generates a market for ideal types, homunculi who use their knowledge as men on the spot to conclude mutually beneficial trades in scarce emission rights. As noted, it reflects the null hypothesis of the comparative institutional approach. The very analytical question is to ascertain the hidden assumptions behind the concept that the market works itself. This is valid for both the cap-and-trade and the price regulation. Therefore, the imposition of a price (tax) on GHG emissions is no less an institutional arrangement than the installment of a cap-and-trade mechanism. As in the case of the latter, the imposition of a GHG price presupposes a number of requisites. Clearly, the price regulation presupposes a property right definition of the GHG emission that is not different from the transferable quantity cap. Furthermore, an unambiguous definition of, for example, carbon emissions, is one thing. The very issue is to design accounting methods that enable appropriate carbon calculation. For instance, the Environmental Development Fund (EDF) shows its endeavor to prompt the working of the ETS. It has developed

> a carbon market simulation tool, *CarbonSim*, based on artificial intelligence-enhanced, multi-lingual, multi-user, software application that teaches the principles of emissions trading and brings markets to life.
>
> (EDF 2022a)

In this aspect, the EDF emphasizes that an ETS regards a joint effort of 'policymakers, regulated companies, NGOs [nongovernmental organizations], and the public' (ibid.). The EDF documents a number of ETSs varying from the multinational EU system, state or national systems of, for example, California and Brazil, to a local ETS of Tokyo (EDF 2022b). As a nonprofit organization, an EDF basically substantiates Coase's methodological stance as discussed in Chapter 5. The ETS as an elaboration of the trade-and-cap mechanism stems from the Coase Theorem as a null hypothesis. A theorist's next challenge is to proceed to the route of vertical de-isolation as substantiated by, for example, EDF and other NGOs such as Carbon Tracker and Global Climate Insights (GCI). It regards NGOs that document the track record of major carbon emitters. For instance, the GCI (2022) reports about Shell, BP, and Sasol, addressing questions about their mid- and long-term alignment with the 2015 Paris

Agreement regarding carbon emission reduction. In this aspect, Carbon Tracker (2022) concludes in its blog, *CA100+ A Long Way from Destination*, as follows:

> A disappointing 158 out of 164 (Climate Action, CA100+ focus companies) did not appear to incorporate material climate-related matters and assumptions into their 2020 financial statements.

Another NGO, Follow This (2022), particularly targets Shell in its nonalignment with the 2015 Paris Agreement. The relevance of these NGO initiatives manifests itself in fueling financers with information about the GHG emission reduction performance of the CA100+. Particularly, pension funds in civil societies prove to be sensitive to negative track records in this respect, threatening to withdraw their investments.

The GHG emission cap constitutes a criterion to assess the major GHG emitters, offering societal forces that are communicated by NGO research institutes to exercise pressure to improve their performance. The latter alert the former to their responsibility for the inconsistencies in their emission reduction policy, showing their situational logic in the event that they do not avoid the emission cap to which they are subordinated. On one hand, a government's authority is prominent in the cap-and-trade mechanism. At the same time, private initiatives such as research institutes, environmentalist pressure groups, consumers' associations, and, last but not least, financiers find a forceful instrument in the emission cap to support the government's policy. They refer to Boulding's and Hayek's integrative, independent sector that features civil society.

7.7.3 *Patents and the creation of property rights of invention*

As it may happen that the benefits of a well-placed lighthouse will not be remunerated by the ships that enjoyed its service, so it happens that the inventor of a discovery or a design of highly practical utility will not be paid by those who benefit from such inventions. Following Arnold Plant (1934: 33), an invention may be defined 'as the devising of new ways of attaining given ends', representing valuable information that is potentially subject to an exchange. Like lighthouses, inventions constitute another example of failing markets, Pigou (1920) notes in his *The Economics of Welfare*. The marginal private net product of the investment in it does not satisfy the expectations of the marginal social net product. Patent lawmaking intends to bring them 'more closely together' (ibid.: 185). It offers a reward prospect for certain types of invention which is to direct the inventive activity 'into channels of general usefulness', Pigou adds (ibid.). Patents may repair the market failure of the positive externality of inventive activity.

A comparable diagnosis is made by Kenneth Arrow. 'To sum up, we expect a free enterprise economy to underinvest in invention and research' (Arrow

1962: 619). Arrow subsumes them under collective goods as information is the product of invention and research exhibits indivisibility (i.e., increasing returns in use) and non-appropriability. Furthermore, the information production of an invention regards a risky investment, another cause of the market economy's suboptimality, Arrow puts forward. Therefore, optimal inventive activity requires a government or 'some other agency not governed by profit-and-loss criteria to finance research and invention', he concludes (ibid.: 623). Apart from the peculiar condition that an agency should not be hindered by profit-and-loss criteria, this conclusion occasions Demsetz (1969) to present Arrow as someone who is vulnerable to the *Nirvana* fallacy.

Obviously, the features of information production impede market partners from contriving a Paretian optimum. However, this does not imply that the optimality of a government alternative is self-evident. As noted, what is required is a comparison of actual institutional arrangements or, as Demsetz coins it, in this context, 'a *comparative institution* approach' (ibid.: 1). First, regarding the uncertainty that an investment in information entails, government allocation does not *per se* remove the potential nonoptimality of the market. Both options must cope with uncertainty generating unpredictable outcomes. At the same time, both the market and the government may possess opportunities to address it more or less successfully. In fact, it is particularly the Knightian entrepreneur who, probing the market, is the proper agency to deal with such a risky investment. He is gifted with the profit incentive that the government does not have. Although both the market and the government may pool and diversify the investment risks, it is rightly the entrepreneur as a market agency whose incentives as a residual claimant direct the attention to the profit-and-loss criteria regarding a risky investment. Moral hazard may complicate the insurance device of an investment and limit the preparedness to invest. However, this does not mean 'an underinvestment in risky activities', as Arrow (1962: 614) claims. Rather, the investment level results from calculating the cost and benefit of addressing the moral hazard. People happen to be sensitive to moral hazard and, for that matter, both in markets and in government. Proper economic calculation takes account of this human trait. In this aspect, Arrow proves to be susceptible to 'the logical fallacy', Demsetz (1969: 2) proposes, that '*the people could be different*'.

Second, indivisibility as an attribute of information makes it unruly to apply a marginal analysis to calculate its optimal production. Information and inventions appear to be collective goods that are closely related to the well-placed lighthouse that conveys information to nearing vessels. Their marginal cost is zero. From a welfare perspective, Arrow (1962: 616) argues, such a good should 'be available free of charge'. Stated differently, apply the marginal cost pricing rule as advocated by Harold Hotelling (1938). It is 'an ideal socialist economy', Arrow continues, that may offer information free of charge. In this aspect reemerges the idea of Hotelling that government should procure such amenities and finance them from taxation. It separates production from distribution; more precisely, the decisions regarding production (level) are not privy to the relevant information about consumers' preferences. It renders the suggestion of potential underinvestment or '"underutilization"' to be inapt concepts by definition. Production and consumption 'simply cannot be judged independently' (Demsetz 1969: 11). A la Hotelling, surveys of statisticians and engineers may procure a 'certain amount of large-scale experimentation for the sake of gaining information about [cost and demand] functions' (Hotelling 1938: 269). Economics renders a matter of statistics and experiments, raising the marginal cost controversy, an instance of blackboard economics from outside, calculating the *Nirvana* solution based on marginal cost pricing. Contrary to this, the objective of the comparative institutional approach is searching for the relative allocative efficiency of institutional arrangements, *in casu* a market economy versus an ideal socialist economy. Rephrased in the basically methodological individualist comparative institution approach: How may the individual with his preferences be involved in the procurement of information production, for example, inventive activity, as a relative efficient alternative to a socialist economy procurement based on statistics? In this aspect, the third feature of information production emerges, that is, its lack of appropriability.

Third, the counterpart of indivisibility is the lack of appropriability of information. Information as a collective good labors under its investor's inability to establish and maintain its property rights. Basically, the property rights issue that hinders market exchange varies from nonexistence to instances of more or less attenuated property rights, that is, from a prohibitively high cost to exchange them to a relatively low cost of safeguarding these rights in an exchange. In this aspect appears the NIE perspective: the institutional arrangement defined as a trade-off between the robustness of property rights and the cost of exchanging them. The question is to create property rights that safeguard both the interests of the producer of valuable information and of those who are prepared to pay for it.

The patent system attaches property rights to an invention enabling the inventor to sell it. However, the patent system is inherently a source of controversy. On one hand, it rewards the efforts of the inventor with the exclusive property rights of his invention. On the other hand, the patent system turns out to be a practice of granting monopoly privileges to the inventor. For instance, Fritz Machlup and Edith Penrose (1950) record this controversy as it happened during the nineteenth century. Opponents of the patent system are 'linked to the free-trade movement' (ibid.: 5). Against this position, Machlup and Penrose summarize the main arguments of the supporters of the patent system: (1) 'man has a natural property in his own ideas'; (2) 'justice requires that a man receive ... reward for his services in proportion as these services are useful to society'; (3) 'to grant exclusive patent rights in inventions' is the most effective way to establish incentives for inventions and exploitation of inventions; and (4) the patent system secures that 'new inventions become generally known as part of the technology of society' (ibid.: 10). It is a combination of ethical considerations and social desirability of industrial progress that unites the proponents of the patent system.

The matter at issue is the merits of the patent system considered from a comparative institutional economic point of view. Patent lawmaking creates property rights of an intellectual asset such as an invention. In this aspect, Plant (1934: 30) refers to David Hume who argues that property rights are worth protecting 'solely on account of their utility' to secure the productivity of 'scarce "means"'. However, Plant continues, '[t]hey (property rights in patents (and copyrights)) are not a *consequence* of scarcity' (ibid.: 31). Lawmaking of patents and copyrights makes

> possible the *creation* of a scarcity of the products appropriated which could not otherwise be maintained.
>
> (ibid.)

Plant emphasizes that this deliberate creation of statute law amounts to conferring the 'power of raising prices' (ibid.). He comments as follows:

> Whereas we might expect that public action concerning private property would normally be directed at the prevention of the raising of prices, in these cases the object of the legislation is to confer the power of raising prices by enabling the creation of scarcity.
>
> (ibid.)

Apparently, Plant disregards that 'the products appropriated' themselves result from the allocation of scarce means.[9] An intellectual product such as an invention represents a combination of scarce means that deserves property rights protection.

In this aspect, it is expedient to refer to Knight's (1924) paper 'Some Fallacies in the Interpretation of Social Cost', which was also discussed in Chapter 4. From a general welfare perspective, the effect of taking account of the property rights of (a combination of) scarce means that turn(s) out to be so valuable to others is that it enables their owner, for example, an inventor, to *set* a (high) price cannot be harmful as it merely regards a transfer of purchasing power and rendering a surplus to the fortunate owner/inventor. In this context, Knight notes that 'these activities (of appropriation) are indeed subject to a large "aleatory element"; they are much affected by luck' (ibid.: 592). Furthermore, inventive activity fuels the Schumpeterian dynamics of the capitalist market offering opportunities to the Knightian entrepreneur.

However, as Plant (1934: 31) argues, the very question that bothers the economist is that the patent system generates monopoly conditions that tend to divert 'the scarce means of production from a more to a less generally preferred utilisation'. Stated differently, having the patent as a remedy to take account of scarce means turns out to have an adverse effect. The monopolist sets a price that exceeds the marginal cost. In this aspect, the very question is whether the alleged '"general usefulness"' of patentable inventions outweighs 'the usefulness that would result from the other inventions or other output foregone' (ibid.: 43).

Plant proposes that economics is unable to 'provide any criteria for the approval of this method of special encouragement' (ibid.). For instance, the stimulating effect of patents is uncertain as a part of the inventing activity stems from spontaneous contrivance. At the same time, the patent system may divert the inventive activity and hazarding of scarce means. Furthermore, a fear of missing priority rights may induce premature patenting and applications of discoveries (Barzel 1968: 348). Against the patent, it is price changes and development of cost that particularly support and/or divert inventive activities (Plant 1934: 41). The next question is whether a patent system is required to secure the investment in and exploitation of an invention. According to Michael Polanvyi (1944: 64), speculative capital would 'no longer be forthcoming for the backing of inventions if these could not be protected by patents'. However, Plant considers it doubtful that the patentable inventions would require such a large investment 'that fears of duplication will provide a frequent deterrent to entrepreneurs'. Additionally, frequently, there is market room for more than 'a single specialized productive unit' (Plant 1934: 43). Basically, the patent system as engaged in safeguarding the market position of firms does not merely protect monopoly profits but may also impoverish the entrepreneurial ambitions of firms to keep ahead and 'to be first in the market with new improvements in its products and new reductions in their prices' (ibid.: 44). Strong patents may deter others to invest in research and development to improve patented technology (Boldrin, Levine 2013: 3). Furthermore, poorly defined patents place a competitive entrepreneur 'at risk of ruinous litigation' (Moser 2013: 23). Moreover, scientific breakthroughs since the beginning of the twentieth century have weakened the effectiveness of secrecy and increased the relevance of patents as an instrument. This both safeguards inventor's property rights and diffuses innovative knowledge, generating wider exploitation of an invention (Moser 2013: 30–31). Therefore, knowledge will be patented if the inventor expects that the period it can be kept secret is shorter than the term of the patent. Therefore, this deprives the patent system of its relevance to diffuse knowledge (Boldrin, Levine 2013: 9). At the same time, as Michele Boldrin and David Levine put forward, inventors 'hope to corner the market for a functioning device by patenting it' (ibid.: 10). For instance, flight technology patents enabled the Wright Brothers 'both to monopolize the US market and to prevent further innovation for nearly 20 years' (ibid.). An intriguing case that further puts the significance of patenting into perspective concerns the 'contemporary FLOSS (Free/Libre and Open Source Software) community' that exhibits

> how collaboration and exchange of ideas can thrive without the monopoly power granted by patents.
>
> (ibid.)

It confirms G.B. Richardson's (1972: 896) observation of 'co-operative arrangements specially contrived to pool or transfer technology'. In Richardson's vocabulary, it concerns dissimilar and complementary activities that require the responsibility of different firms. Inventive activities need cooperative arrangements to correspond with firms' *ex ante* plans rather than coordination by market transactions. Therefore, parties engaged in inventive activities and technology transfers

> are often associated with the acceptance by the parties to them of a variety of restrictions on their commercial freedom – that is to say with price agreements, market sharing and the like
>
> (ibid.)

For instance, an *ex ante* engagement of a principal customer in the development of a new production part by the supplier requires intensive interfirm cooperation according with *closely complementary* activities. It puts into perspective the relevance of patents as a prerequisite to transact innovative activity. Apparently, the qualitative nature of inventive activity renders it expedient to avoid the tit-for-tat device of the market transaction as facilitated by a patent system.

The patent system alludes to the Schumpeterian concept that inventive activity requires a monopolistic situation (Schumpeter 1950). Boldrin and Levine identify three conditions that render patents 'socially valuable'; that is,

> the fixed costs of innovation were truly very high, the costs of imitation were truly very low, and demand for the product was really highly inelastic.
>
> (Boldrin, Levine 2013: 14)

The patent safeguards an inventor's incentive to invest with the prospect of a monopoly profit. The strict conditions hold for a limited category of inventions, for example, in the pharmaceutical industry. Nevertheless, as a limited category, it is inconsistent with, for instance, the exploding number of patents in the United States over the period from 59,715 patents issued in 1983 to 2010 when 244,341 new patents were approved. This quadrupled flow of patents was accompanied by neither innovation nor research and development nor factor productivity of 'any particular upward trend' during this period, Boldrin and Levine note (ibid.: 4).

Considering the insights of the political economy of patents, Boldrin and Levine further condition that a patent system should be designed 'by impartial and disinterested economists and administered by wise and incorruptible civil servants (who) could serve to encourage innovation' (ibid.: 14). However, the US patent figures above suggest that the system may easily be victimized by regulatory capture, that is, patent authorities acting in the interests of the regulated. The system creates a habitat of mutual interests of potential patentees, on one hand, versus the patent office and the patent lawyers who file and litigate patents, on the other. Patenting generates substantial administrative costs.

Moreover, patentability criteria such as 'substantial novelty' or "'non-obvious-ness'" contain non-objectifiable elements that offer opportunities to honor private interests at the expense of a general welfare perspective (Kitch 1977: 281, 284). In this aspect, Mancur Olson's collective action issue reveals itself in two versions. On one hand, the incentives stemming from the concentrated benefits of potential patentees outweigh those of consumers who experience the minor diffused disadvantages of monopoly prices (Olson 1965). On the other hand, in a patent infringement lawsuit, the interests of the patentee/plaintiff will outweigh a defendant's potential benefits of winning the lawsuit as the latter are diffused over the industry and dispersed over all of the consumers concerned; 'many patent lawsuits have a public goods aspect' (Boldrin, Levine 2013: 16).

Against the Schumpeterian idea of monopolistic power as a requisite to innovate stands the concept of competitive markets which themselves generate innovation. For instance, Knight and Richardson, as discussed before, contend that it is rightly the competitive market that raises the surmise of advantageous knowledge, for example, regarding an invention to prompt a single entrepreneur to initiate innovative production. Stated differently, there must be 'some limitation upon the competitive supply to be expected from other producers', for instance, generated by an invention (Knight 1921; Richardson 1959: 234). Knight (1921: 286) presents competition as a product of intersubjectivity between conscious human beings who surmise profitable opportunities, arranging methods to come to terms with the world of which their 'knowledge is (as it is in fact) very imperfectly or not at all communicable'.

Inventive activity and innovation constitute a major inducement to entrepreneurs to invest with the prospect of the first-mover advantage and a rent. As Plant argues:

> A very great deal of invention goes on outside its range, without any inducement beyond that provided by the operations of the open market.
>
> (1934: 45)

Frequently, the first-mover advantage may be substantial as imitation takes time. Marketing research, product imitation design, development of production capacity, and distribution facilities precede entry into a market. In this aspect, Rajshree Agarwal and Michael Gort (2001) ascertain that the imitation time tends to decline, at least for the data they investigated. Following Joe Bain's classification, they summarize the barriers to entry as follows.

> (a) economies of scale and sunk costs, (b) absolute cost advantages, and (c) product differentiation advantages.
>
> (ibid.: 162)

The research concerns data for 46 major product innovations covering a mix of consumer, producer, and military goods during the period from 1887 to 1986. They find a remarkable decline in the average time between the commercial introduction of a new product and the entry by later competitors. It declined from 33 years at the end of the nineteenth century to 3.4 years for innovations between 1967 and 1986 (ibid.: 161). They distill two variables that explain this change. First, the growth of markets due to globalization and population growth renders economies of scale no longer a barrier to new, imitating entrants. Second, the accelerating rate of diffusion of information diminishes the relevance of the absolute cost advantage, for example, of innovation, as a barrier to entry. Their analysis further reveals that neither product differentiation nor sunk cost plays a role in the explanation of the declined imitation time. All product characteristics, consumer/nonconsumer, technical/nontechnical, and high/low capital intensity perform the same mean duration of interval prior to competitive entry (see Table 4 in ibid.: 171).

These results, however, do not imply that the first-mover advantage as an incentive to innovate would also have been declining over the course of time. The simultaneous globalization of the economy commensurably enhances 'the rewards per unit of time for a monopoly position' (ibid.: 173). A first-mover advantage remains, and competitive markets do not block a sustainable innovation climate. The entrepreneur finds himself in contestable markets that induce all types of refinements and improvements of industrial products whether or not hindered by patent litigation.

For that matter, Boldrin and Levine recognize a kind of life-cycle pattern in an industry's use of patents. In this aspect, the competitive market induces an eclectic use of a patent system. Initially, innovative firms profiting from their first-mover advantage are not engaged in patenting. It rather happens in an industry with mature technology when innovative activity is low that 'patents are widely used to inhibit innovation, prevent entry, and encourage exit' (Boldrin, Levine 2013: 11). In this respect, the discontinuous cyclical pace of an industry's technological development is a relevant variable of the first-mover advantage; hence, the cyclical pattern reflects an industry's patent use (Short, Payne 2008: 267). Another dynamic element that follows the first-mover advantage phase concerns the second-mover advantage. It might be more advantageous to imitate than to innovate. Imitation might benefit from the disclosed information of an innovation to improve the product. Such a market interdependence generates strategic incentives as analyzed by Eric Rasmusen and Young-Ro Yoon (2012):

> Knowing more surely what is the best choice, the better-informed player wants to delay to keep his information private and the less-informed player wants to delay to learn.
>
> (ibid.: 374)

The delay that follows the strategic behavior regards a delay in applying an innovation with an expected added value from a general welfare point of view. Thus, Rasmusen and Young-Ro Yoon infer: 'More accurate information can actually lead to inefficiency by increasing the incentive to delay' (ibid.). In this respect, Edmund Kitch offers a helpful interpretation of the patent system (Kitch 1977). The opportunity to imitate also denotes that an innovation exhibits a scope that may reach well beyond the initial idea. Therefore, Kitch interprets

> a process of technological innovation as one in which resources are brought to bear upon an array of prospects, each with its own associated sets of probabilities of costs and returns.
>
> (ibid.: 266)

In this perspective, the patent system may be viewed as a claim system regarding a prospect, that is, 'a particular opportunity to develop a known technological possibility' (ibid.: 266). It is relevant to distinguish between the invention as a concept and 'the physical embodiment of the invention' (ibid.: 268). Kitch lists a number of inventions (51) showing a varying time span between the year of first patentability and the year in which it appears as a commercial product. It varies from three years for Bakelite and Freon refrigerants to several decades for a large number of the list. For instance, silicone was invented in 1904 and first applied in 1944 (Table 1 in ibid.: 272). Such time spans render the prospect function of the patent system relevant. A patentable invention does not mean that it is commercially relevant. 'It only requires something that works', Kitch notes (ibid.: 271). For instance, 'Carlson, the inventor of xerography' merely requires to claim effectively that he is able to practice the process of making copies, although it makes only 'poor copies of no use' (ibid.: 268–269). Apparently, a patented innovation predominantly affords opportunities to subsequent commercial applications authorized by the patentee as a licensee. The prospect function of the patent 'increases the efficiency with which investment in innovation can be managed' (ibid.: 276). It puts the

> patent owner in a position to coordinate the search for technological and market enhancement of the patent's value so that duplicative investments are not made and so that information is exchanged among the searchers.
>
> (ibid.: 276)

Kitch's prospect approach to patenting emphasizes that an innovation rather regards a scope of technological opportunities than the invention of a new product or technologically improved production process. In the perspective of an innovation as 'an array of prospects', Kitch recognizes 'the institutional analogy' between the patent and the mineral claim (ibid.: 271). Like the mineral claim system makes it possible for private firms to efficiently find and extract minerals from public lands, the patent applicant acquires the opportunity to exploit his invention. Neither the candidate mineral claimant nor the patent applicant needs to prove that their right is commercially significant. Another analogy is that like a mineral claim; a patent right is transferable as the licensing opportunity shows. The overtone of Kitch's paper is that the safeguarding of property rights of inventive activity enhances efficiency. For instance, it incentivizes the patent owner to invest in order to maximize the value of the patent; the patent signals others, reducing the 'amount of duplicative investment in innovation'; and, 'a patent system improves the structure of the returns to innovations' (ibid.: 278, 279). Kitch's prospect approach to the patent system extends the creation of property rights to the potentially broader scope of an invention.

Finally, how can the patent system be assessed from the perspective of the comparative institutional approach? In this aspect, a qualification precedes. The comparative approach here does not cover the government procurement alternative as proposed by Arrow as it concerns economics from outside and disregards the sovereignty of the individual. The question at issue is the institutional-economic merits of patenting. As Plant (1934: 43) poses whether the '"general usefulness"' of patentable inventions outweighs 'the usefulness that would result from the other inventions or other output foregone'? From the preceding, it may be inferred that an unequivocal verdict would not reflect the contrasting aspects of a patent system.

On one hand, the patent system as a property rights item refers to the fundament of new institutional economics; without property rights, there are no markets to carry on beneficial trade. On the other hand, the marginal cost of innovative information would prohibit pricing it. The patent system itself embodies this contrast, entailing a lasting controversy between the protection of property rights versus limiting production to an inefficient monopolistic level, albeit the latter is under the assumption of a downward-sloping demand curve. These considerations stem from textbook economics that is based on the marginal analysis of economic efficiency. However, the application of the findings of this analysis generates a type of second-order effect.

The patent system, as creating new property rights, affects the situational logic of the individual. It may be interpreted as a reward system to incite inventive activity. At the same time, there are inventions that are not dependent on any reward or merely affected in their direction by patenting. 'Induced inventions', Plant (1934: 34) notes, owe their nature, 'if not their volume, to the circumstances of time and place'. It renders the assessment of the patent system a rather disappointing affair and a challenge to social science researchers. Against this, from an economic point of view, that is, assessing the 'general usefulness' of the patent system following three points may be inferred from the earlier discussion.

- The patent system exhibits general usefulness in the case of pressing inventions, for example, in the pharmaceutical industry that demands a substantial amount of fixed costs of investment and development, very low imitation costs, and a genuine, high price-inelastic demand (Boldrin, Levine 2013: 14).
- The patent system generates administrative costs and must cope with information asymmetries as a fertile medium for a habitat in which strategic economic conduct flourishes. Inherently, qualitative criteria constitute a source

of claims and ruinous litigation. Furthermore, collective action issues cause biases in awarding patents and infringement litigation.

- Basically, the patent system is a no-confidence motion against the entrepreneurial resilience of the market economy. It protects the entrepreneur against competition. At the same time, it undermines the uncertainty of the market as the very source of profits that fuel the market. It renders the entrepreneur an applicant for a privileged position, replacing his role as an agent who senses the market searching for new opportunities. For that matter, it is inherent to the system to expand and offer protection to a number of minor innovations. The outgrowth of the patent system infringes on the very nature of the market economy. It changes the 'aleatory element' of the entrepreneurial system into an effect of successful patenting. Against the patent system stands the system of entrepreneurs who, as conscious human beings, address uncertainty, sensing market opportunities. It renders economics a matter of thought; 'a process of "cephalization"' follows, as Knight (1921: 268) refers to it. It is the prospect of a first-mover advantage as a profit that incites investing. In this aspect, the rent of the first-mover advantage is reminiscent of two-tariff pricing to reimburse the fixed cost of a natural monopoly. Apparently, the market may generate alternatives to marginal cost pricing as an efficiency rule.

The information as a product of inventive activity exhibits, if revealed, all the features of a collective good. It is an indivisibility, and it is not appropriable, useless in a market trade, and arguing for an institutional remedy, that is, a patent system. At the same time, however, this remedy is an interference that, in a fundamental manner, changes the situational logic of the entrepreneur and undermines his dynamic market force. Therefore, it is doubtful that the general usefulness of patentable inventions outweighs the practicability that would result from the other inventions or other foregone outputs.

Conclusion

The comparative-institutional approach stems from discontent with the dichotomy of market or government. The normal economic system that works itself is, at the same time, a type of diffusion of market and government marks. Economics studies the logic of the situation of an individual, properly, his situation in a potential exchange of property rights. In civil society, the concept of property rights is unthinkable without a government's authority. All the same, the picture is diffused. Our social reality results from 'processes of consciousness and their intended objects', as Alfred Schutz (1932) asserts. Government is such an object, and property is basically the fruit of man's recognizing 'this is mine and not yours' (Schlatter 1951).

Self-interest has the primacy in studying the institutional arrangements that serve the exchange. It founds the automatic working of the market as the NIE's null hypothesis. However, man experiences his fellow man as the fact of the *thou*. It presents itself in, for example, Boulding's integrative sector, instances of promoting common interests, and mutual trust. Authority and coercion complement the picture, aiding man's self-interest in his daily pursuit. The three instances discussed of institutional arrangement substantiate this scenario.

The lighthouse refutes the null hypothesis. However, limited involvement of the government, that is, a license to collect a toll as a transfer of authority, and the recognition of common interests and mutual trust enable private parties to trade the basically indivisible and not appropriable information of lighthouses.

Climate change policy begins with the creation of property rights attached to resources that no longer concern ubiquities. The null hypothesis inspires government to create new scarcity, that is, emission rights. Next follows the search for further assumptions to substantiate the efficiency of the emission rights market. It regards demanding issues such as a definition of equivalents of emission resources, strategic behavior, monitoring, and enforcement. At the same time, social processes such as pressure groups, NGOs, and stakeholders with 'integrative' motivation may support appliance to the efficiency of the emission rights market. In this aspect, Nordhaus puts forward that a focal point such as a single carbon price eases supervision of compliance may, in the context of an international club of countries, prevent the danger of the prisoner's dilemma and change it in a the other-regarding game (Nordhaus 2019).

Finally, the patent aims to restore the null hypothesis, safeguarding the invention information from indivisibility and lack of appropriability. The patent makes the invention information tradeable indeed, but at the same time, it kills competition. Furthermore, practical issues complicate the creation of patents. For instance, it is difficult to objectivate such a criterion as the non-obviousness of an invention, and political economy issues will bias the patent policy. The main idea behind patenting as an institutional arrangement seems to be that the market can only work in terms of tit-for-tat security. However, as Knight (1921) underlines, the normal economic system works based on conjectures and expectations and searching for new market opportunities. This idea places the need for patents into perspective, at best, appropriated to a limited category of inventive activity for which there is no chance of private initiative.

The comparative institutional approach dismisses the dichotomy of market or government. At the same time, as a fruit of the NIE analysis, it begins from the hypothesis that the normal economic system works, fostering individual's sovereignty. The phenomenological insights of notably Schutz broaden the perspective given room for integrative phenomena that accompany the exchange of institutionally protected property rights.

7.8 Summary

Economics is engaged in exchange relationships, wondering about the origin of their working without a coordinating authority. This has consequences for the market–government relationship. Economics departs from the null hypothesis that markets work and disregards the institutional setting. However, markets fail, and people have recourse to the government to remedy the allocative inefficiency of markets. In this aspect, the government is both an institutional prerequisite to the market and an anomaly as an allocative device. It is the latter feature that orients the economic thought on the government's allocative merits. This view constitutes the background of the comparative institutional approach, that is, that markets fail. At the same time, it is not self-evident that government is the obvious means to remedy markets' failures. Economics searches for allocative solutions that honor and safeguard an individual's sovereignty as much as possible. This basic attitude does not express a hostility toward government regulation and is not a type of anarchistic worldview but merely follows the tradition in economic thought since Adam Smith, claiming that economic analysis fundamentally rests on individual choice. In the allocative role of markets versus government, two tasks must be addressed:

- First, an allocative task regards the generation of information about the benefits of resources in alternative uses.
- Second, the allocative mechanism must motivate the economic agents to take account of this information.

Government is not famous for executing these tasks. It uses databases and statistics to acquire information. Additionally, coercion replaces motivation. However, markets use knowledge from men on the spot who are motivated by self-interest. This suggests a strict dichotomy of the market or the government. Actually, however, there is an interface between the government and the market; for example, the government may take advantage of market forms in executing its policy. Furthermore, a third 'independent sector' qualifies the concept of a dichotomy (Hayek 1979). It regards a domain in social life inspired by empathy and benevolence that may accomplish the self-interest of the market and constitute an alternative to the government's coercion. For that matter, this qualified picture basically stems from a view of man that accords with the phenomenological perspective.

At the same time, government constitutes a prerequisite to maturely working markets. A government that maintains the rule of law protects private property rights as the *sine qua non* to motivate market parties to take benefit from resources in alternative uses. Some further digression on property preludes the elaboration on the comparative institutional approach. Property is the fruit of self-conscious human beings who in their *Lebenswelt* recognize 'this is mine and not yours'. Such a concept of property protects economics against an atomistic and mechanistic perspective. In this returns the philosophical disposition that affords opportunities for theoretical propositions in which the economic agents figure as conscious human beings who represent meaning. In this respect, it is significant to distinguish two kinds of property rights. Basically, property regards the relationship between man and a thing. On one hand, it regards *in rem* rights, that is, 'good against the world', without exception excluding intrusions by strangers from a delimited space. On the other hand, there are *in personam* rights that connect a certain use of a resource to somebody (Merrill, Smith 2001). The former is unilaterally causal, safeguarding the good against the world. Contrariwise, the latter allows viewing a certain use of a resource as an alternative to another one's use. From this, it is a small step to conceive property rights as exchangeable as soon as they compete with one another. In this view, property rights are reciprocal but not unilateral as Coase (1960) identifies in his 'Social Cost' paper. It makes property a bundle of exchangeable rights in which it has no content of its own, that is, positive law. The very consequence is that everything that occurs may be mutually beneficial. For instance, it might be mutually beneficial if government seduces criminals to refrain from crime by compensating them (Stigler 1943). Therefore, natural law as a realist's search for the essentials of law is preconditional for positive lawmaking and preventing the latter from immoral outcomes. Coase's pioneering in the elaboration of property as a bundle of use rights (*in personam* rights) accommodates the advanced industrial economy that exhibits a myriad of side effects, market interferences, and managerial challenges. Exchange may solve them and disregard the unilateral nature of *in rem* property insofar as it does not conflict with the moral dimension of the latter; natural law is preconditional.

The application of property rights as *in personam* rights accords well with Coase's casuistic and inductive methodology in constructing a theory. Furthermore, this methodology accords with the ambition to understand the behavior of individuals and institutions rather than to predict. Coase's pioneering property rights theory studies a polymorphic spectrum of institutional arrangements such as the creation of secondary markets; licenses to levy an allowance, for example, for a lighthouse service; licenses to broadcast; and patents to reward inventive activity. Amended property rights change collective goods and side effects into exchangeable items. Obviously, newly created or amended property rights change the initially delimited rights. This features the difference between Pigou and Coase. For Pigou, the initial delimitation is given and should be restored in the event of side effects. Here, it appears that Pigou adheres the *in rem* version of property. An infringement is a unilateral matter. Contrariwise, Coase interprets property as *in personam* right and an instrument to avoid more serious harm. At the same time, both prove to be engaged in the trade-off between individuals' welfare and run into the conceptual issue of interpersonal welfare comparison. For instance, how can the more serious harm be valued in a case in which cedar tree rust damages apple tree orchards?

It is Buchanan's (1959) presumptive efficiency concept that offers *a* solution to the restriction on interpersonal comparison of welfare. Buchanan introduces an efficiency criterion based on an observer's/economist's 'own estimate of his subjects' value scale'. It is reminiscent of Schutz's postulate of subjective interpretation of the social phenomena 'within the categories of human action', as Schutz (1943) states it. It is a theoretical concept belonging to what Kaufmann (1944) refers to as 'the analysis of meaning'. Buchanan (1959) calls it a searching out of which of the entire set of possible combinations 'will prove acceptable to all parties'. The presumptive efficiency concept is an instrument of the political economist, and to the judge who considers the welfare effects of a law change, or a sentence regarding property rights. Comparable to Buchanan's concept is Wicksell's (1958) benefit principle to base taxation and preserving individuals' preferences as perceived in observer's estimate, that is, a presumptive benefit principle. Against this stands the causal explanation of facts, that is, the empirical test of the presumptive efficiency of the measure concerned. Given the demanding unanimity of the (Paretian) presumptive efficiency criterion, it is unlikely that it will successfully pass the empirical test. As yet, it figures as a theoretical proposition, a theoretical device to consider which change in property rights avoids the more serious harm.

The presumptive efficiency concept may serve Coase's ambition to devise practical arrangements to correct the side effects without causing more serious harm elsewhere in the economic system. It is Coase's 'Pigovian' adherence to the measuring rod of money as a direct or indirect criterion of welfare that facilitates his comparative institutional approach. The idea of presumptive efficiency finds its counterpart in practical rearrangements of property rights that presumptively generate a mutually beneficial exchange. As yet, the idea of presumptive efficiency and the benefit principle represents economists' ambition to safeguard individuals' sovereignty. Its practical application is particularly tailored to conflicts of interest between identifiable agents potentially having a lawsuit as a sequel. Obviously, it remains a theoretical exercise in all those cases in which competing interests and welfare effects fall down diffusely and dispersedly.

Three instances of institutional arrangements conclude this chapter. Common among them is the creation of property rights. It intends to prompt private initiative and beneficial trade. At the same, it shows the government as a producer of the economic system. The instances further exhibit the role of 'integrative' elements such as common interests between participants in seafaring, the role of reputation in climate change policy, and the concept of commercial sense for market opportunities in discussing the role of patents.

The comparative institutional approach makes that the market–government dichotomy needs to be qualified. The normal economic system works itself; that is, the null hypothesis essentially concerns a theoretical proposition referring to homunculi who, as rationally acting agents, find themselves supported by juridically enhanced property rights and as exponents of conscious human beings giving room to empathy and benevolence. Economics is not engaged in mechanistic atoms but in human beings who express meaning as man's irreducible essence. It exhibits itself in creating a domain accomplishing the tit-for-tat regime or replacing the government's coercion. In this social domain, man senses new opportunities for mutual benefit by venturing an innovation, appealing to one's reputation, or experiencing one another's trust. Its phenomenological perspective enables the social scientist to embrace man's meaning without repudiating his scientific standards.

Basically, the instances of a comparative institutional arrangement as discussed regard an exercise in an analysis of meaning à la Kaufmann, that is, a search for the *ceteris paribus* conditions that afford homunculi's efficiency. It practices economics as an exact science as far as it is engaged in theoretical propositions, that is, theorems for which it is famous.

Notes

1 Posner's definition in the fourth edition of his *Economic Analysis of Law* deviates somewhat from the definition in an earlier issue as apparently used by Coase. Omitting 'testing', Posner has clearly decreased his positivist ambition. In the 1992 edition, the wording reads as follows.

> As conceived in this book, economics is the science of rational choice in a world -our world- in which resources are limited in relation to human wants. The task of economics, so defined, is to explore the implications of assuming that man is a rational maximizer of his ends in life, his satisfactions- what we shall call his "self-interest."
>
> (Posner 1992: 3)

2 In this respect, Merrill and Smith denote a tension in Coase's analysis. On one hand, a low transaction cost requires clearly assigned property rights. On the other hand, the court's aim to design efficiency-enhancing rearrangements of the property (use) rights raises uncertainty about them (Merrill, Smith 2001: 370, n. 57).
3 In the 'FCC' paper, Coase (1959: 33), in fact, adheres to the assignment of frequency in terms of property (use) rights *in personam*, that is, 'the right to use a piece of equipment to transmit signals in a particular way'.
4 As long as Pigou remains silent about the possibility of interpersonal comparison of utility, the Pareto optimum applies to his analysis.
5 Apparently, Buchanan is not quite clear in defining the scope of the presumptive efficiency concept. On one hand, he explicitly restricts it to 'change in law'. On the other, he discusses political economists' engagement in side effects that are not *per se* brought about by a change in law.
6 Main GHGs concern carbon dioxide, methane, and nitrous oxide.
7 Carbon and carbon dioxide are linearly related; one ton of carbon equals 3.67 tons of carbon dioxide.
8 Figures 7.1 to 7.4 compare carbon tax versus carbon emission as a main GHG.
9 At the same time, hereafter, Plant (1934: 40) criticizes Jeremy Bentham and Jean Baptiste Say for ignoring the withdrawal of scarce resources from other operations in favor of inventive activity.

References

Agarwal, R., M. Gort, 2001, First-Mover Advantage and the Speed of Competitive Entry, 1887–1986, *The Journal of Law & Economics, Vol. 44, No. 1*, 161–177.

Alchian, A.A., 1977, *Economic Forces at Work*, Indianapolis, IN: Liberty Press.

Alchian, A.A., Allen, W.R., 1969, *Exchange and Production, Competition, Coordination, and Control*, Belmont, CA: Wadsworth Pub. Co.

Aldy, J.E., R.N. Stavins, 2012, Using the Market to Address Climate Change: Insights from Theory & Experience, *Daedalus, Vol. 141, No. 2, The Alternative Energy Future, Vol. 1*, 45–60.

Arrow, K.J., 1962, Economic Welfare and the Allocation of Resources for Invention. In: National Bureau of Economic Research, ed., 1962, *The Rate and Direction of Inventive Activity, Economic and Social Factors*, 609–625, Princeton, NJ: Princeton University Press.

Barzel, Y., 1968, Optimal Timing of Innovations, *The Review of Economics and Statistics, Vol. 50, No. 3*, 348–355.

Bentham, J. 1843, *Principles of the Code Civil*, (PCC Part 1, Chapter 8, Jeremy Bentham, Principles of the Civil Code (utexas.edu)), London: Dumont accessed 09/2021.

Boldrin, M., D.K. Levine, 2013, The Case against Patents, *The Journal of Economic Perspectives, Vol. 27, No. 1*, 3–22.

Bonbright, J.C., 1941, Major Controversies as to the Criteria of Reasonable Public Utility Rates, *The American Economic Review, Vol. 30, No. 5*, Papers and Proceedings of the Fifty-third Annual Meeting of American Economic Association, 379–389.

Boulding, K.E., 1969, Economics as a Moral Science, *The American Economic Review, Vol. 59, No. 1*, 1–12.

Brian Simpson, A.W., 1996, "Coase v. Pigou" Reexamined, *The Journal of Legal Studies, Vol. 25, No. 1*, 53–97.

Buchanan, J.M., 1959, Positive Economics, Welfare Economics, and Political Economy, *The Journal of Law & Economics, Vol. 2*, 124–138.

Calabresi, G., 1991, The Pointlessness of Pareto: Carrying Coase Further, *The Yale Law Journal, Vol. 100, No. 5, Centennial Issue*, 1211–1237.

Carbon Tracker, April 2022, CA100+ a Long Way from Destination - Carbon Tracker Initiative.

Coase, R.H., 1937, The Nature of the Firm, *Economica, Vol. 4 (n.s.)*, 386–405.

Coase, R.H., 1945, Price and Output Policy of State Enterprise: A Comment, *The Economic Journal, Vol. 55, No. 217*, 112–113.

Coase, R.H., 1946, Marginal Cost Controversy, *Economica, New Series, Vol. 13, No. 51*, 169–182.

Coase, R.H., 1947, The Origin of the Monopoly of Broadcasting in Great Britain, *Economica, New Series, Vol. 14, No. 55*, 189–210.

Coase, R.H., 1948, Wire Broadcasting in Great Britain, *Economica, New Series, Vol. 15, No. 59*, 194–220.

Coase, R.H., 1955, The Postal Monopoly in Great Britain: An Historical Survey. In: J.K. Eastham, W. Culross, eds., 1955, *Economic Essays in Commemoration of the Dundee School of Economics, 1931-1955*, 25–37, Dundee: The School of Economics.

Coase, R.H., 1959, The Federal Communications Commission, *The Journal of Law and Economics, Vol. 2*, 1–40.

Coase, R.H., 1960, The Problem of Social Cost, *The Journal of Law and Economics, Vol. 3*, 1–44.

Coase, R.H., 1974, The Lighthouse in Economics, *The Journal of Law & Economics, Vol. 17, No. 2*, 357–376.

Coase, R.H., 1975, Marshall on Method, *The Journal of Law & Economics, Vol. 18, No. 1*, 25–31.

Coase, R.H., 1988, *The Firm, the Market, and the Law*, Chicago, IL: The University of Chicago Press.

Coase, R.H., 1992, The Institutional Structure of Production, *The American Economic Review, Vol. 82, No. 4*, 713–719.

Coase, R.H., 1994, *Essays on Economics and Economists*, Chicago, IL: The University of Chicago Press.

Coase, R.H., R.F. Fowler, 1935, Bacon Production and the Pig-Cycle in Great Britain, *Economica, New Series, Vol. 2, No. 6*, 142–167.

Cooter, R. 1987, [1991], Coase Theorem. In: J. Eatwell, M. Milgate, P. Newman, eds., 1987, [1991], *The New Palgrave, A Dictionary of Economics*, Vol. I, 457–460, London: The Macmillan Press Limited.

Croce, B, 1913, *Philosophy of the Practical; Economic and Ethic*, translated from the Italian by D. Ainslie, London: Macmillan.

Dahlman, C.J., 1979, The Problem of Externality, *The Journal of Law & Economics, Vol. 22, No. 1*, 141–162.

Dales, J.H., 1968a, *Pollution, Property & Prices: An Essay in Policy-making and Economics*, Toronto: University of Toronto Press.

Dales, J.H., 1968b, Land, Water, and Ownership, *The Canadian Journal of Economics/ Revue canadienne d'Economique, Vol. 1, No. 4*, 791–804.

Demsetz, H., 1964, The Exchange and Enforcement of Property Rights, *The Journal of Law & Economics, Vol. 7*, 11–26.

Demsetz, H., 1969, Information and Efficiency: Another Viewpoint, *The Journal of Law & Economics, Vol. 12, No. 1*, 1–22.

Demsetz, H., 1988, The Theory of the Firm Revisited, *The Journal of Law, Economics, & Organization, Spring, 1988, Vol. 4*, 141–161.

Eastham, J.K., W. Culross, eds., 1955, *Economic Essays in Commemoration of the Dundee School of Economics, 1931-1955*, Dundee: The School of Economics.

Ellis, H.S., 1950, The Economic Way of Thinking, *The American Economic Review, Vol. 40*, 1–12.

Epstein, R.A., 1989, The Utilitarian Foundations of Natural Law, *Harvard Journal of Law and Public Policy, Vol. 12*, 711–751.

Environmental Defense Fund (EDF), April, 2022a, CarbonSim: EDF's Carbon Market Simulation Tool|Environmental Defense Fund.

Environmental Defense Fund (EDF), April, 2022b, The World's Carbon Markets|Environmental Defense Fund (edf.org).

Follow This, April 2022, Follow This|Green Shareholders Change the World (follow-this.org).

Friedman, M., 1962, *Capitalism and Freedom*, Chicago, IL: University of Chicago Press.

Global Climate Insight (GCI), April 2022, Global Climate Insights - Global Climate Insights (accr.org.au).

Hayek, F.A. von, ed., 1935, *Collectivist Economic Planning*, London: Routledge & Kegan Paul Ltd.

Hayek, F.A., 1944, *The Road to Serfdom*, London: George Routledge.

Hayek, F.A., 1979, *Law, Legislation, and Liberty*, Vol. 3, London: Routledge & Kegan Paul.

Hazlett, T.W., D. Porter, V. Smith, 2011, Radio Spectrum and the Disruptive Clarity of Ronald Coase, *The Journal of Law & Economics, Vol. 54, No. 4, Markets, Firms, and Property Rights: A Celebration of the Research of Ronald Coase*, S125–S165.

Hepburn, C., 2006, Regulation by Prices, Quantities, or Both: A Review of Instrument Choice, *Oxford Review of Economic Policy, Vol. 22, No. 2*, 226–247.

Hicks, J.R., 1976, 'Revolutions' in Economics. In: S. Latsis, ed., 1976, *Method and Appraisal in Economics*, 207–218, Cambridge: Cambridge University Press.

Hochman, H.M., J.D. Rodgers, 1969, Pareto Optimal Redistribution, *The American Economic Review, Vol. 59, No. 4, Part 1*, 542–557.

Hotelling, H., 1938, The General Welfare in Relation to Problems of Taxation and of Railway and Utility Rates, *Econometrica, Vol. 6, No. 3*, 242–269.

Jaffe, J., M. Ranson, R.N. Stavins, 2009, Linking Tradable Permit Systems: A Key Element of Emerging International Climate Policy Architecture, *Ecology Law Quarterly, Vol. 36, No. 4*, 789–808.

Jevons, W.S., 1871, *The Theory of Political Economy*, London: Macmillan and Co.

Kaldor, N., 1934, The Equilibrium of the Firm, *The Economic Journal, Vol. 44, No. 173*, 60–76.

Kaufmann, F., 1933, On the Subject-Matter and Method of Economic Science, *Economica, No. 42*, 381–401.

Kaufmann, F., 1944, *Methodology of the Social Sciences*, Atlantic Highlands, New Jersey: Humanities Press.

Kitch, E.W., 1977, The Nature and Function of the Patent System, *The Journal of Law & Economics, Vol. 20, No. 2*, 265–290.

Kitch, E.W., 1983, The Fire of Truth: A Remembrance of Law and Economics at Chicago, 1932-1970, *The Journal of Law and Economics, Vol. 26, No. 1*, 163–234.

Knight, F.H., 1921, [1971], *Risk, Uncertainty and Profit*, Chicago, IL: Chicago University Press.

Knight, F.H., 1924, Some Fallacies in the Interpretation of Social Cost, *The Quarterly Journal of Economics, Vol. 38, No. 4*, 582–606.

Latsis, S., ed., 1976, *Method and Appraisal in Economics*, Cambridge: Cambridge University Press.

Locke, J., 1690, *Second Treatise of Government*, London: published anonymously (The Project Gutenberg EBook, 2010).

Machlup, F., E.T. Penrose, 1950, The Patent Controversy in the Nineteenth Century, *The Journal of Economic History, Vol. 10, No. 1*, 1–29.

Meade, J.E., 1944, Price and Output Policy of State Enterprise, *The Economic Journal, Vol. 54, No. 215/216*, 321–339.

Medema, S.G., ed., 1998, *Coasean Economics: Law and Economics and the New Institutional Economics*, Boston, MA: Kluwer Academic Publishers.

Merrill, T.W., H.E. Smith, 2001, What Happened to Property in Law and Economics? *The Yale Law Journal, November, Vol. 111, No. 2*, 357–398.

Miller, D., ed., 1985, *Popper Selections*, Princeton, NJ: Princeton University Press.

Moser, P., 2013, Patents and Innovation: Evidence from Economic History, *The Journal of Economic Perspectives, Vol. 27, No. 1*, 23–44.

Musgrave, R.A., 1959, *The Theory of Public Finance*, New York: McGraw-Hill.

Musgrave, R.A., A.T. Peacock, eds., 1958, *Classics in the Theory of Public Finance*, London: Macmillan.

National Bureau of Economic Research, 1962, *The Rate and Direction of Inventive Activity, Economic and Social Factors*, Princeton, NJ: Princeton University Press.

Nordhaus, W., 2019, Climate Change, *The American Economic Review, Vol. 109, No. 6*, 1991–2014.

Olson, M., 1965, *The Logic of Collective Action*, Cambridge, MA: Harvard University Press.

Panichas, G.E., 1983, Hume's Theory of Property, *Archiv für Rechts- und Sozialphilosophie/Archives for Philosophy of Law and Social Philosophy, Vol. 69, No. 3*, 391–405.

Pigou, A.C., 1920, [1950], *The Economics of Welfare*, London: Macmillan and Co., Limited.

Plant, A., 1934, The Economic Theory Concerning Patents for Inventions, *Economica, New Series, Vol. 1, No. 1*, 30–51.

Polanvyi, M., 1944, Patent Reform, *The Review of Economic Studies, Vol. 11, No. 2*, 61–76.

Popper, K.R., 1945, The Autonomy of Sociology. In: D. Miller, ed., 1985, *Popper Selections*, 345–356, Princeton, NJ: Princeton University Press.

Popper, K.R., 1967, The Rationality Principle. In: D. Miller, ed., 1985, *Popper Selections*, 357–365, Princeton, NJ: Princeton University Press.

Posner, R.A., 1992, *Economic Analysis of Law*, 4th ed., Boston, MA: Little Brown and Company.

Posner, R.A., 1993, Nobel Laureate Ronald Coase and Methodology, *The Journal of Economic Perspectives, Vol. 7, No. 4*, 195–210.

Posner, R.A., 2011, Keynes and Coase, *The Journal of Law & Economics, Vol. 54, No. 4*, S31–S40.

Rasmusen, E., Y.-R. Yoon, 2012, First versus Second Mover Advantage with Information Asymmetry about the Profitability of New Markets, *The Journal of Industrial Economics, Vol. 60, No. 3*, 374–405.

Richardson, G.B., 1959, Equilibrium, Expectations and Information, *The Economic Journal, Vol. 69, No. 274*, 223–237.

Richardson, G.B., 1972, The Organisation of Industry, *The Economic Journal, Vol. 82, No. 327*, 883–896.

Robbins, L., 1932, [1962], *An Essay on the Nature and Significance of Economic Science*, 2nd ed., London: MacMillan & Co, Ltd.

Samuels, W.J., 1971, Some Fundamentals of the Economic Role of Government, *Journal of Economic Issues, Vol. 23, No. 2*, 427–433.

Schlatter, R., 1951, *Private Property*, London: George Allen & Unwin Ltd.

Schutz, A., 1932, [1967], *The Phenomenology of the Social World*, New York: Northwestern University Press; [*Der sinnhafte Aufbau der sozialen Welt*, Wien: Julius Springer].

Schutz, A., 1943, The Problem of Rationality in the Social World, *Economica, New Series, Vol. 10, No. 38*, 130–149.

Schutz, A., 1953, Common-Sense and Scientific Interpretation of Human Action, *Philosophy and Phenomenological Research, Vol. 14*, 1–38.

Schumpeter, J.A., 1950, *Capitalism, Socialism and Democracy*, New York: HarperCollins Publishers Inc.

Short, J.C., G.T. Payne, 2008, First Movers and Performance: Timing Is Everything, *The Academy of Management Review, Vol. 33, No. 1*, 267–269.

Simmel, G., 1910, How Is Society Possible? *American Journal of Sociology, Vol. 16, No. 3*, 372–391.

Smith, A., 1776, [2005], *The Inquiry into the Nature and Causes of the Wealth of Nations*, London: W. Strahan and T. Cadell; The Electronic Classics Series, Penn State: Pennsylvania State University.

Smith, H.E., 2009, Law and Economics: Realism Or Democracy?, *Harvard Journal of Law and Public Policy, January,32*, 127–145.

Stavins, R.N., 1996, Correlated Uncertainty and Policy Instrument Choice, *Journal of Environmental Economics and Management, 30*, 218–232.

Stern, N., 2007, *The Economics of Climate Change*, Cambridge: Cambridge University Press.

Stigler, G.J., 1943, The New Welfare Economics, *The American Economic Review, June, Vol. 33, No. 2,* 355–359.

Stigler, G.J., 1966, *The Theory of Price,* 3rd ed., New York: Macmillan Co.

Stigler, G.J., 1972, The Law and Economics of Public Policy: A Plea to the Scholars, *The Journal of Legal Studies, Vol. 1, No. 1,* 1–12.

Umbeck, J., 1981, Might Makes Rights: A Theory of the Formation and Initial Distribution of Property Rights, *Economic Inquiry, Vol. XIX,* 38–59.

United Nations, Paris Agreement, 2015, April 2022, The Paris Agreement|UNFCCC.

Wagner, H.R., ed., 1970, *Alfred Schutz, On Phenomenology and Social Relations,* Chicago, IL: The University of Chicago Press.

Walras, L., 1954, *Elements of Pure Economics,* translated by W. Jaffé (1977), Fairfield: Augustus M. Kelley Publishers.

Weitzman, M.L., 1974, Prices vs. Quantities, *The Review of Economic Studies, October, Vol. 41, No. 4,* 477–491.

Weitzman, M.L., 2017, Voting on Prices vs. Voting on Quantities in a World Climate Assembly, *Research in Economics, 71,* 199–211.

Wicksell, K., 1958, [1896], 'A New Principle of Just Taxation. In: R.A. Musgrave, A.T. Peacock, eds., 1958, *Classics in the Theory of Public Finance,* 72–118, London: Macmillan.

Zerbe, Jr., R.O., S.G. Medema, 1998, Ronald Coase, the British Tradition, and the Future of Economic Method. In: S.G. Medema, ed., 1998, *Coasean Economics: Law and Economics and the New Institutional Economics,* 209–238, Boston, MA: Kluwer Academic Publishers.

Index

Printed in the United States
by Baker & Taylor Publisher Services